HONKY TONK DEBUTANTE

HONKY TONK DEBUTANTE

The history of honky-tonk music as I care to tell it

CHRISTINE WARREN

BOTTLE SHOCK PUBLISHING

AUSTIN TEXAS

Honky Tonk Debutante: The history of honky-tonk music as I care to tell it

Bottle Shock Publishing, LLC
PO Box 41642
Austin, Texas 78704
www.bottleshockpublishing.com

First printing: January 2014

ISBN: 978-0-9911685-0-7

Edited by Christie Stratos, Proof Positive
Printed at Litho Press, Inc., San Antonio, Texas
Bound at Universal Bookbindery, Inc., San Antonio, Texas
Designed by Hornaday Design
Dust jacket images:
    Sunburst Background © nrws/Vectorstock.com;
    Armadillo © Yulia Avgust/Shutterstock.com;
    Author photo © Tosh Brown Photography

Images that appear without a detailed photo credit in the caption are personal family photographs belonging to Christine Warren, her husband, Tom Warren, and/or her parents, Nancy and Duck Johnston.

This book is dedicated to my parents for making certain I cut my teeth on good music right from the start, and to Tom and Sophie, who lovingly allow me to sing it around the house, sometimes badly, always loudly.

CONTENTS

A Fairly Useful Foreword

The word "fore", in the cautionary sense, has been used for well over a hundred years to warn allies and friends to "look ahead". Golfers yell out, "Fore!" to fellow players if an errant ball is flying recklessly, threatening to land squarely on someone's head. In 17th and 18th century warfare, artillery men would shout out, "Beware before!" so infantrymen would have a chance to hit the ground and avoid falling artillery shells. Similarly, I am using this foreword to shout out a warning and offer a look ahead at what this book holds, just in case you feel the need to run from its covers. In a nutshell, I am going to convey my lifelong love of honky-tonk music because I truly worship everything about it: the twang, the tears, the beers, the fringe. *The fringe*! I also hope to illustrate how I spent the better part of my early years yearning to be closer to its sound and storyline; that is, until I found myself in a midlife emotional nosedive, ironically leaning on the music itself to pull me out of a spiritual free fall and landing back on my feet…and in a much better place.

Fore!

Hardly falling from the sky and crashing down on me like a rogue golf ball or artillery shell, country and western music seeped into my life by osmosis. As a young girl in Texas in the 1970s, it was simply all around me, especially in our home, where my parents always had a record spinning on the turntable. I was blessed to have parents with excellent taste in music. We never thought about genres or the various types of music labels back then; we just played anything that sounded good to us. As a result, I tend to enjoy everything from Blues to Motown,

Soul, Southern Rock, Pop, Reggae, Disco, Sinatra, ABBA, Americana, Outlaw, and, yes...even Show Tunes. But the one sound that was with me from the start and remains closest to my heart is Honky-Tonk music.

Occasionally people are surprised to learn I am such a honky-tonk fan. I don't know what stereotype I may or may not be portraying to generate such confusion, but I am quick to assure anyone who is interested (and countless who aren't) that I am faithful and unwavering in my passion for this category of music, its artists, and its history. No other songs get me going like honky-tonk songs, no other music is as nostalgic to me, and no other genre makes it onto my shower set list. I sometimes feel the urge to cry out, "If you cut me, do I not bleed neon?" But I decided to write a book about it instead.

As I set forth to create my outline and research the history of country music, specifically honky-tonk, I became utterly confused. As it turns out, country music and its subgenres defy clean codification – this is not an assignment well suited for Type A personalities. The first thing that threw me was the fact that country music wasn't always called country music. In fact, it's had several labels. In the beginning, before there was really even much of a recording industry, it was loosely referred to as old-time. Then people started referring to it as hillbilly music. After that, it was called country and western, which was ultimately shortened to just country. So basically:

OLD-TIME = HILLBILLY = COUNTRY AND WESTERN = COUNTRY

Once I had a grip on this genre's many labels, I was ready to peel back the layers of its history. I devoured books, articles, and websites by fascinating experts who taught me volumes about country music, and I encourage you to explore these sources, which are cited at the end of this book. From them, I distilled the most potent storylines for you. For example, here are eight watershed dates that altered the course of country music:

1922 – Texas fiddler Eck Robertson records and releases the first country song, "Sallie Gooden".

1923 – WBAP, a radio station in Fort Worth, Texas, launches the first barn dance radio program, which ignited a nationwide craze for similar country-format radio shows.

1925 – An unnamed string band from Galax, Virginia records with producer Ralph Peer at Okeh Records. In the session the musicians flippantly refer to themselves as "hillbillies". Based on this comment, Peer names the band "The Hill Billies". But through grassroots evolution, the term "hillbilly" begins to define this entire genre of music that would ultimately be called country.

1925 – WSM radio station in Nashville, Tennessee launches a barn dance radio program. Two years later it is renamed the *"Grand Ole Opry"*.

1927 – Ralph Peer does a field recording in Bristol, Tennessee which is often hailed as the start of the modern country music industry. Mississippi born Jimmie Rodgers, a white blues singer, records at these sessions and almost immediately becomes the first solo country star. The Carter Family also records at the Bristol Sessions and launches a multi-generational family act that would span decades.

1930s – America becomes fascinated with the image of the Hollywood Cowboy, which shifts the country music themes and costumes from that of the mountain hillbilly to the western cowboy hero.

1941 – Texan Ernest Tubb has the first nationwide honky-tonk hit with "Walking the Floor Over You". This launches the golden era of honky-tonk music, which continues into the 1950s. Today, when people talk about "traditional country music", they are often referencing the sound made popular during the honky-tonk heyday of the 1940s and 1950s.

1949 – *Billboard Magazine* officially replaces the label "hillbilly" music with "country and western".

Don't be concerned if your head is starting to hurt. It's a lot to absorb, I know. I really became confused when I tried to organize the subgenres of country.

Subgenres!? Did I just get hit in the head with a golf ball?

The earliest form of American folk music, old-time, was from the Appalachian mountain region and used string-based instruments. But as adventurous souls traveled among other ethnicities, the music of these British Isle immigrants began to incorporate the sounds of Native American Indians, African American slaves, Creoles, and Mexican ranchera music. Subcategories of country music began to develop.

The two subgenres of bluegrass and western swing both emerged in the 1930s. Bluegrass started in Kentucky and became popular in southern states east of the Mississippi, while western swing originated in Texas and Oklahoma. Western swing never totally fit with old-time or hillbilly, in sound or image, and was sometimes referred to separately as western music.

Honky-tonk took hold as a subgenre in the early 1940s. It emerged in the same area where western swing was popular and shares more of a sonic foundation with this Texas/Oklahoma music than it does with bluegrass or Appalachian mountain music. While it didn't shape up formally until the early '40s, the term honky-tonk was used as early as the 1800s. The etymology of the term "honky-tonk" is officially tagged as "Origin Unknown", but that didn't keep me from stubbornly trying to find its roots.

Unfortunately, I failed. But the journey helped me sketch out these four (unofficial) phases of honky-tonk, which clarify its evolution.

Vaudeville-style theaters – In the 1800s, "honky-tonk" described the dancehalls or vaudeville-style theaters along the cattle drives, especially in Texas and Oklahoma.

Black piano music – Around the turn of the century, "honky-tonk" described a style of piano playing similar to ragtime that was played by many black musicians.

White country music in Texas – In the late 1930s and early 1940s, some white musicians in Texas mixed western swing with black piano and blues to create a sound of music called "honky-tonk". This is the genesis of a style of music that today is often referred to as "traditional country". The term "honky-tonk" also described the rough, low-class beer joints where such music was played.

Modern country – Now, "honky-tonk" is a sweeping term, practically synonymous with all country music as well as connoting the southern lifestyle.

I practiced explaining all of this to my family as I was working it out in my own mind. My feeble attempt at compartmentalizing and communicating the subgenres instead merely revealed the melting-pot nature of American country music. When you start to consider the deep impact of black blues music on the nascent stages of country, things become even less linear and infinitely more fascinating. Perhaps the fact that there are so many shared influences and overlapping sounds is, in fact, what makes this genre of music so enduring.

One thing that can be said of country music, and certainly honky-tonk, is that it is deeply rooted in *a sense of place*. I am lucky to have lived, or have had ties to, certain cities and states where honky-tonk's history unfolded. For that reason, I abandon a clear cut chronology in this book and instead offer a collection of stories that are linked to geographical regions where this powerful music was born and flourished. Here is a roadmap of where the following chapters will take us and why:

Willie Nelson – Now, I realize Willie Nelson isn't a geographical location, per se. But he *is* a state of mind. We simply have to start with Willie.

Fort Worth – It is the birthplace of western swing.

Oklahoma – A mind-boggling amount of good music has come out of this state. Not to mention the Dustbowl migration, which pushed a multitude of Oklahoma musicians to California, where they became an integral part of the famed Bakersfield music movement.

Dallas – There are a variety of musicians, venues, and promoters in Dallas who made lasting contributions to honky-tonk and blues music.

London – When my family lived in London we fell under a mysterious curse which, to this very day, precludes us from enjoying the best road trip song of all time. We simply can't play one of country music's greatest hits! (At least not while we are traveling.)

Louisiana – You won't believe how many country music superstars got their big break in Louisiana, specifically in Shreveport.

Nashville – It's called "Music City, USA", in large part thanks to WSM Radio and the *Grand Ole Opry*.

Chapel Hill, NC – It's better known for basketball than honky-tonk, but that didn't stop me from looking for it everywhere when I went to college there. I'm going to tell you what I found instead.

Texas Hill Country – This is where I learned to two-step, skinny-dip, and monopolize the jukebox.

Dallas – We'll take another pass at Dallas to look at the prolific live music scene it experienced during the early

1990s, particularly with bands that were part of the emerging alt-country subgenre.

Boston – A Texas music fan heads north only to find that no one in Boston shares her taste in music.

Austin – In the 1970s a supernova of bands, fans, and music venues created a one-of-a-kind musical landscape.

Alabama – It's the home of Hank Williams – need we say more? Actually, we do. Alabama has a rich music heritage, especially in honky-tonk.

Austin – I know, I know, I already said Austin. But we are going to circle back and take a look at the current Austin music scene, spotlighting the new wave of artists who are keeping its legacy of live music very much alive.

And that, my friends, is the last time this book will lay out anything quite so cleanly. I have relinquished the notion that I will be the first person in the world to determine the true etymology of the term "honky-tonk". Instead, I will outline for you, flavored with my own personal editorial, the various theories that are floating around out there. I am loosening the grip on precise stratification of country music as a genre and embracing it at its messy core: a sound and a history that is colorful, complex, and constantly evolving.

I will mix in stories from my life, in which honky-tonk is inextricably linked, as well as spotlight the artists and songs that have sparked my soul for a variety of reasons. It's going to be part history, part memoir, and all heart (flavored with some laughs!). Hopefully at the end of this rollicking tale you can, at the very least, say you had a fun ride. Whether you're a honky-tonk novice or a lifelong music historian, I aim to meet you exactly where you are with the simple goal of igniting, or perhaps rekindling, a warm feeling for this music.

While I do feel called to evangelize the spirit of honky-tonk to anyone and everyone who will listen, I should make it clear that I am no musician. Everyone in my family seems to have been blessed merely with the gift of music *appreciation*. I am a passionate music fan, but I am not a singer, not a songwriter, and I've never been in a band outside of my own daydreams. I received my musical education leaning over jukeboxes in beer joints, two-stepping on the hardwood floors of Texas dancehalls, and pouring over the liner notes of various albums. I imitated singers with my hairbrush microphone, soaked up any trivia that radio DJs would allow, and watched TV documentaries about musicians as often as I could. Despite a few fleeting piano and saxophone lessons in elementary school, I have zero skills with any instrument. I can't read sheet music, and I've never taken a music theory class. My (non)working comprehension of composition, chords, range, and arrangement is rudimentary at best. Basically, it's safe to say that what I don't know about music can fill a book.

And here it is.

Consider yourself forewarned.

CHAPTER 1

The Best Raccoon Penis
Story I Have Ever Heard

My love for Willie Nelson cannot be overstated. I was at a Willie concert in Alabama not long ago, after not having seen him live in many years, and the moment he took the stage, a powerful feeling washed over me. Nostalgia, awe, butterflies, and goose bumps all worked together as a perfectly choreographed team to create a physical and emotional sensation within. Lest I had forgotten, or merely let the notion slide a bit, I instantly remembered that any poetry I had in my heart was all thanks to Willie Nelson. True, I lived in London for a short time as a girl, and at a young age I had seen incredible works of art at some of the best museums in the world. I fell in love with Shakespeare in high school, largely due to a dynamic teacher who rivaled Robin Williams in *Dead Poets Society*. I was an English major in college and devoured classics such as "The Rime of the Ancient Mariner", Paradise Lost, and Dante's Inferno. I've even experienced the wonder of motherhood. All of these are easily dense and rich enough to be labeled poetry superfood, and each one has certainly added to the nutrition of my soul. But the fact remains, Willie was there first. I was listening to his rhymes as a baby, through every phase and stage that followed, and I still tune in to his words and melodies to this very day. No artist was there sooner or stayed with me stronger throughout my ever-changing geography, age, tastes, and moods.

If you've ever been to a Willie Nelson concert, you know I'm not the only one who keeps Willie up on a pedestal. I've seen him at Billy Bob's in Fort Worth, the Wind Creek Casino in Atmore, Alabama, Cattle Baron's Ball in Dallas, and even the South Shore Music Circus in Cohasset, Massachusetts. He draws fans of all ages and from all walks of life. The rednecks, hippies, bikers, snowbirds, fraternity boys, sorority girls, socialites, stoners, and buttoned-ups all love the man in the red bandana. Governors and glamazons are just as giddy in his presence as the RV fans decked out in jean shorts and black "Willie" t-shirts. A Willie crowd is very democratic. Once he strums his guitar a few times and launches into "Whiskey River", it doesn't matter who you are, where you come from, or where you're headed – you just start singing along.

My husband and I have a friend named Jeff Glass who is a true music aficionado. One time we were bantering about music and Texas and Austin, which of course led us right into a conversation about Willie. Jeff saw Willie back in the '70s up close and personal, right at the front of the stage. He noticed women were throwing offerings at Willie's feet such as flowers and various underpinnings. Jeff was so inspired by the Red Headed Stranger, he too was compelled to throw something up on stage but didn't have anything with him. He gave himself a quick pat-down, reached into his pocket and pulled out an Abraham.

At this point in his story Jeff recognized a blank look on my face and stopped to explain the term "Abraham". Apparently, unlike most mammals, raccoons have an *actual* bone in their penis, and hunters maintain an age-old tradition of cutting out the penis bone and saving it after they shoot a raccoon. They call this good luck charm an Abraham. I suppose it's not any more grisly than the overly dyed purple and orange rabbits' feet we used to collect as school girls. (Were those real rabbits' feet, by the way?) But the penile aspect does make this custom a tad more sensational, nay...*fabulous*.

Jeff, an avid raccoon hunter himself, explained that Abrahams were a coveted souvenir back in the day as ladies of the genteel class even used them as drink stirrers. Jerry Hall once told her quasi-husband Mick Jagger that growing up in Texas, when a boy liked a girl he would give her an Abraham as a love token. You can do a quick search on eBay to see these are still highly prized treasures.

I was agog. I couldn't believe I had never even heard of this Abraham culture. As the new knowledge of raccoon penis traditions barely started to sink in with me, Jeff continued with his story, "I reached into my pocket and found an old Abraham. So I threw it up on stage to Willie. Willie reached down, immediately recognized what it was, smiled, and put the Abraham right in his pocket!"

Whoa! Willie Nelson was performing on stage with my friend Jeff's raccoon penis bone right in his pocket. Too, too cool.

As if that wasn't enough, what good Willie story doesn't involve Waylon? A decade or so later, Jeff was going to see Willie and Waylon in concert in Albany, Georgia. A friend who worked for the local radio station was able to secure a backstage pass so Jeff could meet them before the show. Unfortunately Willie got sick and had to cancel, so Waylon had to carry the show on his own. Jeff was backstage enjoying his meet-and-greet with Waylon and decided to tell him his old story about throwing the Abraham on stage to Willie. Jeff told Waylon how Willie smiled, knew precisely what it was, and pocketed it right there on stage. Waylon's face lit up in a flash. Because Willie Nelson had given that very Abraham to Waylon!

I could hardly contain myself. What are the odds? Jeff throws a penis bone on stage to Willie Nelson, who stops strumming his guitar to pick it up and put it in his pocket. As if that weren't a good enough story to get you through every cocktail party for the rest of your life, Willie later gives it to his epic outlaw partner-in-crime, Waylon Jennings. And in some serendipitous fold of fate, Jeff has the opportunity to learn about it. After making him retell the tale over and over I exclaimed, "That is the best raccoon penis story I have ever heard!"

Certainly there is a song title in there somewhere.

Jeff was so tickled that I was so tickled that he made yet one more generous offering. He gave me my very own Abraham. I must admit I feel a little more connected to Willie keeping a raccoon penis bone in my jewelry box, sitting immodestly among the diamond stud earrings my grandmother gave me for my sixteenth birthday and the watch my dad gave me for high school graduation.

Just a few weeks after Jeff shared all this with me, I found myself in a car with three other PTA moms driving down to the beach, volunteering on our children's fifth grade field trip. I recounted Jeff's entire story bit by bit and bragged shamelessly about the raccoon penis bone I had in my possession. Imagine my surprise when the driver, Ashley, totally and utterly topped me.

"Oh yeah, Willie loves those things! He is in a club with my dad here in Austin. I call it the raccoon wiener club; I can't remember the real name. They get together and talk about Texas history and Texas culture, that sort of thing."

Um...yeah, I am going to have to get to one of those meetings as soon as possible.

Long after we completed our assignment of grilling hot dogs on that fifth grade beach trip, I stalked both Ashley *and* her sister, Natalie, to confirm whether their dad's club was real or if I had conjured it up in a fanciful dream. Oh, it is 100% real. There is a group of people in Austin, mostly men and some women, who hold regular meetings and occasional ceremonies to celebrate Texas Independence Day as well as Armadillo Day in lieu of Ground Hog Day. Instead of Punxsutawney Phil they have an armadillo named Bee Cave Bob. Their group is called The Benevolent Knights of the Raccoon, and they each receive an Abraham upon initiation. And Willie Nelson is, in fact, a member.

Willie Nelson is Texas culture. If his birth certificate didn't read 1933 I'd be inclined to say he himself shaped Texas from scratch, although he would likely claim it was the other way around. Born in Abbott, Texas, he learned gospel music in the church where he first performed as a young boy with his musical grandparents who raised him. But his influences didn't stop there. He lived across the street from a few Mexican families, picked cotton with African Americans, and played music halls for Czechoslovakian immigrants, so he was schooled early on in "south of the border" music, black blues, polkas, and waltzes. Like so many, Willie listened regularly to Roy Acuff and Minnie Pearl on *Opry* radio.

Willie's hero, however, wasn't in Nashville, he was Texas' own Bob Wills. At age fourteen Willie Nelson booked Bob Wills to play a gig in Whitney, Texas. With help from his brother-in-law, the young teen hired, promoted, and paid the king of western swing. Willie was captivated by Wills and his ability to lead a big band so effortlessly with his fiddle bow, not to mention his unique blend of jazz and blues. Willie recognized the blues element from the black cotton pickers he knew in the fields of Abbott and claims this is what made Bob Wills' western swing so danceable. Anything Bob Wills was playing, Willie started out covering. I listened to so much Willie as a child that I didn't know until years later some of his songs like "Faded Love" and "Bubbles in My Beer" are actually Bob Wills covers.

The songs that were played on the radio and in the Texas dancehalls dictated Willie's early set list as much as anything. Willie covered Ernest Tubb, Lefty Frizzell, Hank Williams, anyone who was popular on the jukebox at the moment. Back when no one knew the name Willie Nelson, he knew he had to play foolproof songs that always kept the crowd revved up, and he maintained, "Hank Williams was my savior every night."

Between Bob Wills and Ernest Tubb – two of the first to incorporate the electric guitar into country and western music – Willie heard amped up sounds in country early on. Ernest Tubb famously claimed he had to go electric because the honky-tonks he played were so rowdy it was the only way the band could be heard. Later in his career Willie Nelson was on an airplane and by chance was seated next to Nashville country star Whispering Bill Anderson. Whispering Bill said, "You do pretty good in those clubs in Texas. I just can't seem to catch on down there. Can you give me any pointers?"

Willie replied, "Well I think they drink beer louder than you sing."

After bouncing around the beer joint circuit of Waco, Fort Worth, Dallas, Houston, and other Texas towns, Willie Nelson made his way to Nashville. This was a prolific period for Willie Nelson, the Songwriter. Pictures of him from this era portray a clean-shaven All-American boy wearing suits and ties. He looked like he could be the fifth Beatle on *The Ed Sullivan Show*. One of the first people he befriended in Nashville was Charlie Dick, Patsy Cline's husband. They met at Tootsie's Orchid

Lounge, a dive bar across the alley from the Ryman Auditorium where the *Opry* was performed in those days. Country stars and their spouses would slip out the back of the Ryman, across the alley to Tootsie's, which developed its own satellite music culture in the shadows of the *Opry*. Charlie Dick enjoyed one of Willie's songs on the jukebox, so Willie played him a tape of a song he'd written called "Crazy". Charlie Dick liked it so much, he dragged Willie over to his house in the middle of the night and woke up the great Patsy Cline to hear it. She recorded it the very next week. In his book, <u>Roll Me Up and Smoke Me When I Die</u>, Willie shares that Patsy Cline's version of his song "Crazy" would go on to become "the biggest jukebox song of all time".

Willie also met Hank Cochran at Tootsie's. Cochran, who wrote hit songs for Patsy Cline, Merle Haggard, George Strait, and countless others, spotted immediate songwriting talent in a young Willie Nelson and mentored him, even sharing part of his salary with him at one point to keep him afloat in Nashville. Another singer whom Willie met at Tootsie's Orchid Lounge was Faron Young, who had a hit with Willie's song "Hello Walls". It seemed things were clipping right along for the Texas songwriter. In 1965 Willie Nelson became a member of the *Grand Ole Opry*.

Unfortunately, his Nashville momentum stalled out almost as quickly as it started. Willie still wanted to perform as much as he wanted to write songs but he struggled to find bars and clubs in Nashville that booked live music. Concurrently, the "Nashville Sound" was taking shape as music producers like Owen Bradley arranged songs with lush orchestral backgrounds and ornamental accompaniment. Willie's music label relentlessly tried to push him toward this hyper-produced sound which felt unnatural to him. He became so frustrated that he semi-retired from music and became a pig farmer. His daughter, Susie, writes about this seemingly normal period with her dad in overalls, milking cows, feeding pigs, and handing her a Coke while he'd scribble out the words to a song. As told in Kinky Friedman's introduction to <u>Roll Me Up and Smoke Me When I Die</u>, Willie Nelson and Hank Cochran wrote a song around Christmastime in 1969 called "What Can You Do to Me Now" in which Willie vented about the Nashville music scene. A few days later his farmhouse burned to the ground. It was all pretty much a collective sign for Willie to head home, or as he describes it, "I got back to Texas, I got back in my element."

I was born in Nashville while my parents were young, married college students wrapping up at Vanderbilt University. I was less than a year old when they graduated and moved us to Dallas in 1971. So basically Willie and I both left Nashville about the same time, landing in Texas, where we each came into our own. Unfortunately, the similarities end there. I was a toddler, still transfixed by an episode of *Sesame Street*, while Willie was jamming the night away making music with his friends. I've always said, "I wish I could have been twenty-two in Austin, Texas in 1972." I wish I could have been in Austin when Willie hit the scene, forever altering the genome of country music. He returned to find a younger audience, and hippies listening to country right along with the rednecks. With the help of Austin's unique vibe, Willie had the ability to bring seemingly different constituencies together under one roof, as he still does, all in the name of good live music. In doing so, Willie cut out the Nashville music executive middle man and took his songs directly to the fans – fans who literally couldn't get enough. This was the era when Willie would stake a claim on his rights to creative freedom in the face of artistic suppression.

In the 1970s and 1980s, Willie Nelson's keen instincts as a performer propelled him into a unique sonic realm and charted the way for a new subgenre of country: outlaw music. Willie Nelson's music wasn't crafted with perfection in mind, it was well suited for live audiences and was prone to long jams which mirrored the southern rock movement that was happening in parallel. Outlaw music was blues, rock, and honky-tonk all rolled up together. It incorporated a bluesy tonality, rock and roll jams, and honky-tonk lyrics about cheating, drinking, and the low-down bad luck of the working man. The artists were scruffy, western, long-haired hippies in cowboy boots and hats. Compared to the tailored suits, ties, and Nudie suits in Nashville, the outlaw musicians in their blue jeans and western snap shirts ironically looked more working-man country than the Nashville establishment. They *looked* like people who *listened* to country music.

So many talented musicians are compelled to chase after the industry, grappling to get a break and maintain momentum if, in fact, the door cracks. (The same can be said about writers, actors, and a number of other creative types.) I can understand why so many musicians and artists are purely thankful for a deal and don't feel like they are in any position to negotiate and push for control. Which is why, as a person with creative tendencies myself, Willie Nelson is my hero. Once he returned to Texas, plugged back in with his live audiences, and veered his music more in line with his natural instincts, he cut a new type of record deal with Columbia Records – one in which he negotiated a clause that granted him total creative control. He had full artistic license on the upcoming album. So he cut a concept album called *The Red Headed Stranger*, based on a 1950s song by Arthur Smith bearing the same name. Back when Willie was a radio DJ in Fort Worth, he hosted an afternoon children's show and played the song regularly. He also sang it to his own children at bedtime. He liked its tale of a western drifter and wrote several other songs that expanded on the storyline of the "Red Headed Stranger". He recorded the album in Garland, Texas, and when he sent the tracks to Columbia, it was so bare that they assumed it was the demo tape. Compared to the complex symphonic sounds coming out of Nashville, this unvarnished, simple album was completely unsettling to the record executives. In Willie's own words, "They thought I'd gone insane because there wasn't that much there. It was very sparse." Willie, however, had complete control and insisted that it be released as it was. The album went multi-platinum and gave Willie several significant things: his first number one hit with "Blue Eyes Crying in the Rain", a lifelong nickname as the Red Headed Stranger, and a role in the subsequent *Red Headed Stranger* movie. It is listed as #184 on *Rolling Stone's* list of the 500 Greatest Albums of All Time.

To hear how revolutionary it was back in 1975, it's important to listen to the album and compare it to the popular Nashville Sound of the '60s and early '70s. Go to Spotify or YouTube, and listen to Jim Reeves' "Welcome to My World" – a song I really like, for the record. Make sure to click on the version with the hearty orchestral intro. Or try Glen

Campbell's "Rhinestone Cowboy" – a song I've never really cared for. These were the popular and complex sounds of the day. Very intricate, hyper-produced. Then go to Willie's *Red Headed Stranger* and listen to, well, just about anything on it because all the songs illustrate this point, and they are all damn good. But for the sake of experiment, try "Can I Sleep in Your Arms". The contrast is palpable. The song is in no rush, it's not building to some Phil Collins "In the Air Tonight" drum crescendo…don't wait for it because it never comes.

Willie Nelson's "Can I Sleep in Your Arms" is one of the most hauntingly beautiful and poetic songs I've ever heard. The melody is borrowed from an age-old folk song called "Red River Valley". But the treatment and lyrics are classic Willie Nelson. Like any good poetry, less is more. As with famed architect Frank Lloyd Wright, who felt negative space was just as important as positive space, what you don't hear is as important as what you do. There are moments – mere nanoseconds perhaps – but points within the song that are silent. No vocals, no instruments. But the emotion continues to build exponentially in these brief moments *because* of these moments. It feels to me like that weightless pause at the top of a rollercoaster. Suspended animation.

Willie Nelson captures the ache of romance and the barest of all human emotion in his lyrics. He knows the basic building blocks of good song structure. His singing voice is incredibly unique and sounds beautiful harmonizing with others. He is a renowned guitarist, capable of long, impressive blues jams. He is one of the most original song-writers in American recording history, and yet, he is unafraid to do a cover of someone else's song…and he picks damn good ones. He sees no discriminatory boundaries and has been known to perform duets with artists from all genres – yes, even Julio Iglesias. When not playing music, he works to help the American farmer, is a peace-loving soul, and seems like he'd be a hell of a lot of fun to hang out with. If you read any interview, biography, or self-penned book, it's clear how much this man loves musicians as well as music. In <u>Roll Me Up and Smoke Me When I Die</u> he lists some of the great pickers who influenced him. I loved seeing this peek behind the curtain and will share just a few from his list, especially the ones I plan to discuss at some point in this book.

From Willie's List...

Bob Wills
Ray Price
Kitty Wells
Loretta Lynn
Ted Daffan
Ernest Tubb
The Louvin Brothers
Lulu Belle and Scotty
Waylon Jennings
Kris Kristofferson
Johnny Cash
Carl Smith
Jimmie Rodgers
Marty Robbins
Lefty Frizzell
George Jones
Floyd Tillman
Billy Joe Shaver

Their music is in his music. When you consider how many venerable greats he cites as his influences, then factor in all of his countless hits, it becomes clear Willie Nelson is like a living, breathing, one-man, honky-tonk jukebox. And yet, for someone who plays so well in the sandbox with others, Willie Nelson is without peer. He is on a special list, all on his own.

Again, I'm not the only one who is just a little bit nutty in their Willie-love. There are legions of fans that are, shall we say, over the top in their passion for the Red Headed Stranger. But that doesn't make my one-way relationship with Willie Nelson any less special. Throughout my beer-drinking youth, I never once smoked pot or touched an illegal substance, a fun fact about me that many find fascinating for some per-plexing reason. For years I simply shrugged off drugs and maintained, "The only person I will ever smoke pot with is Willie Nelson." Now that I am a mom in my forties, I think my window on *starting* to smoke pot is closed, even if an unlikely Willie encounter unfolded. But that's the least of what interests me about this artist – what moves me to the core is his music. I used to dream about singing with Willie in some Austin music venue. When I stayed at hotels I would belt out his songs in the shower just a little bit louder than usual in case a music producer or promoter was staying in the room next door and might connect us for a future gig.

As my family has been instructed repeatedly, I want Willie Nelson music playing at my funeral. First and foremost I want "Angel Flying Too Close to the Ground", an achingly appealing tune about love lost. Folklore claims the song is about a Hells Angel biker friend who died in a motorcycle crash. In his book, <u>The TAO of Willie</u>, he responds to this simply: "Now I'd be the last person to tell a big group of kick-ass bikers that they're wrong. As far as I'm concerned, whatever they feel the song means is just fine. Theirs is far from the only interpretation of the song, and I make it a point not to disagree with any of the inter-pretations (as long as you're not trying to sell your junk food or your god or your war with my songs). It's not up to me to tell you what my songs mean. The meaning is already in the song. And the song is in the meaning." For those who simply cannot leave well enough alone, or infuse their own meaning, it has also been hypothesized that the song is about his former wife, Connie. Regardless, Willie has plainly given me full permission to use it at my funeral. If you're not familiar with the tune, run don't walk, take a listen, and you'll understand what I've known for years: there won't be a dry eye at my funeral.

What can I say? I love Willie. His music permeates my soul and has found a natural place in all the meaningful moments in my life. And some that aren't even all that meaningful, like doing the laundry, for example. When my husband and I began dating and he visited my house for the first time, he couldn't believe I had a framed picture of Willie Nelson on my wall in the laundry room. I hung him there alongside a portrait of my beloved basset hound (RIP). I figured there might as well be some friendly faces hovering over the dryer while I pick out lint and fold the towels. I don't know if my now-husband was scared or impressed as he reacted, "Wow. Now you're a real fan there."

Recently my husband asked me a hypothetical question that left me stammering for a thoughtful reply. Knowing full well he was flipping a light switch that would trigger such anxiety he smiled, thoroughly entertained, as he asked me, "What would you say if you ever met Willie?"

I was stumped. My husband knows all too well I have a history of clamming up around musicians. As loquacious as I tend to be out in the wild on my own, I shut down like a shy school girl when face-to-face with an actual singer. And not just with big stars, even with cover bands that enjoy cult popularity only regionally. I simply choke. What in the world would I have to say to *Willie Nelson*? What hasn't he heard a million times before? What does one share with the man who embodies everything I love about honky-tonk – the bluesy sound, the storylines in the lyrics, the driving beat, the musical experimentation. He is a living, breathing, singing monument, not only to his own brilliant body of work, but also to Bob Wills, Ernest Tubb, Hank Williams, even the myth of the American Cowboy. He is a little bit western, a little bit Woodstock, and totally Texas. So what in the hell does one say to the Poet Laureate of Country and Western Music?

"I got it!" I spouted out as if I were on a game show. My husband peered over at me, surprised I had found a solution as quickly as I did. As if this conjured up scenario was suddenly a real possibility, I earnestly announced my game plan. "I'm just going to give him my Abraham as a token of love, and say, '*For all the music...*'."

Obviously I'm a reasonable person and recognize this is probably never going to happen. But I will admit to keeping a careful eye on his tour schedule. If I see a show in Austin, I grab that Abraham out of my jewelry box and keep it in my purse…just in case. You never know, I might just bump into him, so I need to have it handy. It's the only thing I've got, the only souvenir to show how grateful I am for all the poetry he's brought into my life. Not to mention it's also a part of the best raccoon penis story I've ever heard.

CHAPTER 1 SOUNDTRACK:

Bubbles in My Beer – Willie Nelson
(CINDY WALKER, TOMMY DUNCAN, BOB WILLS)

Crazy – Patsy Cline
(WILLIE NELSON)

Can I Sleep in Your Arms – Willie Nelson
(HANK COCHRAN)

Angel Flying Too Close to the Ground – Willie Nelson
(WILLIE NELSON)

Shall We Gather at the River – Willie Nelson
(ROBERT LOWRY)

Christine's very own Abraham, stored in a jewelry box

Willie Nelson in the laundry room

CHAPTER 2

The Balls of Cowtown

The only little person I've ever hung out with is Verne Troyer, the 2-foot 8-inch actor who famously played Mini-Me in the *Austin Powers* trilogy. It was the summer before my sophomore year in college, and I was visiting my grandparents in Fort Worth, Texas, which is where my mother grew up. I had made plans to step out on the town with one of my sorority pledge sisters, who was also from Fort Worth and home for summer break.

I don't remember my initial internal reaction when Verne Troyer walked into her parents' family room as the group we'd collected was gearing up for a night out. This was a few years before Verne took on Hollywood. At this point he had just moved to Fort Worth and was working for Sprint Telephone in their customer service department.

Somehow, a friend of a friend had connected Verne, who really didn't know anyone in town, with my friend's brother, and they had become buddies. I wish I could say that at age nineteen I instinctively knew exactly how to behave around a person born with cartilage-hair hypoplasia dwarfism, but I will be the first to admit I was a tinge nervous and praying like hell that it didn't show. I was nervous wondering how he would get around with us out in the world, nervous that I would say something accidentally offensive, nervous that a drunk stranger would say something purposely offensive. Luckily these cerebral acrobatics only lasted for a few seconds – any anxiety I felt was immediately quelled by Verne himself. From the outset he was charming, gregarious, and seemed grateful to meet the group. He was so self-assured and comfortable talking with anyone and everyone that it literally took no time at all to wash away any awkwardness from the situation.

I have no idea who thought to take one of the world's smallest men to a monumentally massive-sized bar. This oversized club was called The Cheyenne, and with its airbrushed cowboy murals it was practically drowning in its own western-ness – not all that unusual in a city nicknamed "Cowtown", but this place was more than just a little contrived. In the center of the rectangular nightclub that had most likely been a warehouse just a week before, there was an area my fifth grade peers in 1982 would have called a roller rink. I think it was supposed to be a kicker-style western dance floor, but when we arrived, a radio DJ was emceeing a wet t-shirt contest in the middle of it. Come to think of it, I don't know why I say he was a radio DJ, he was probably the only assistant manager at a nearby Hooter's with a booming voice.

Clearly Verne could have been trampled at The Cheyenne. Three intoxicated girls rushing to the bathroom would have been a virtual stampede to him – *if* he'd been walking on the ground. But when I think back on that night, I remember him being at eye level with us the entire time. We would take turns carrying him on our shoulders, then prop him along the edge of the roller rink dance floor so he could cheer for the wet t-shirt contest. At one point Verne asked if I would set him up on the high-top cocktail table where our group had congregated. He sat in the middle of that table top nestled among the ashtrays and the beer bottles, and I'm telling you he *held court*. I remember thinking, "Wow, with these people skills he really has a future in customer service!" Or he would stand on the bar, able to lean against the cash register while ordering a worldly-sized long neck. At one point a bartender snapped at Verne to get off the bar to which Verne snapped right back that he obviously couldn't reach it without standing up there. After more verbal sparring, the management got involved and by way of an apology, not to mention compensation for his pain and suffering, Verne was invited to be a judge in the tan line competition. And just like that, a star was born. Verne Troyer became a mini celebrity at The Cheyenne that night.

I don't know if Verne enjoyed his time in Fort Worth, as it wasn't too many years later he would head west for bigger and brighter ambitions than the customer service career I had mentally endorsed for him. But I will say we certainly enjoyed our time with him in Fort Worth. Verne Troyer, whose measureless bravado was juxtaposed against his abbreviated height, seemed to fit naturally with a town that boasts such a history of colorful characters and countless contradictions.

Fort Worth, which is now the sixteenth largest city in the United States, was originally just a small military fort, designed to protect Texans from the Indians that had already been living on this vast frontier land. Eventually a treaty was formed, and the Indians agreed to stay west of a line that would run through the future site of the city of Fort Worth. This delineation was described as "Where the West Begins", which remains a proud slogan for the city. I've also heard people refer to Fort Worth, in an unabashedly romantic tone, as "The Gateway to the West".

During the post-Civil War era of about 1860-1890, crime, corruption, and lawlessness were rampant along the frontier plains. Most cowtowns – places where drovers, people who were driving cattle to market, could refuel their food and supplies – had a red light district generically referred to as Hell's Half Acre. As a frequent stopover along the famed Chisholm Trail, Fort Worth had one of the most notorious Hell's Half Acres, somewhat lazily shortened to just "The Acre". There was a constant push-pull between The Acre and city leadership. Gunfights and murdered prostitutes nailed to the sides of outhouses were a definite blight. Attempts were made to clean things up in this rowdy area of town, but then again, legitimate businesses didn't mind relieving cowboys of their cash and knew The Acre was the place that drew them in. The saloons and gambling establishments in this part of town would attract cowboys, buffalo traders, gamblers, and even famous outlaws like Butch Cassidy and The Sundance Kid (hence the name of Sundance Square in present day downtown Fort Worth). In 1878 the *Fort Worth Democrat* newspaper described the range of patrons at the dancehalls as "lewd women of all ages 16 to 40...

the most respectable of citizens, the experienced thief…the ordinary murderer, the average cowboy and the ordinary young man of town."

A veritable western stew. Sounds like my night at The Cheyenne.

It's hard to cleanly define and compartmentalize the various types of drinking establishments of 19th century Texas and the frontier. Saloons and gambling rooms were for men only, while dancehalls, hurdy gurdy shows, and honky-tonks had both men and women. The women, of course, were not exactly upstanding would-be members of the future Junior League. These were the "soiled doves" or "lonesome doves", nicknames for the prostitutes along the cattle trails. Other non-pay-for-sex women were there, perhaps as singers or dancers, but they were still considered women of ill repute by association. This is why, from its earliest incarnation, the term "honky-tonk" invokes a bawdy connotation, evocative of the raucous underbelly of the night-life scene. If you read the newspaper articles from the 1800s that first mention honky-tonk in print, it would seem the term is associated with vaudeville-style variety acts that included some sort of singing and dancing, perhaps even comedy bits. It's unclear whether the term was always a noun that described the physical venue for these wild musical shows or whether it was originally synonymous with the musical show itself. Either way, the term was ultimately interpreted to mean an adult establishment, a place for drinking and entertainment.

As vague as the term's roots are, it seems music is at the core of its definition. Without some musical element, the establishment is merely a bar or saloon; a honky-tonk was associated with music from the beginning. (In my mind, music is the key element that continues to differentiate a honky-tonk from a bar to this very day.) In the late 1800s and early 1900s the term "honky-tonk" spread across the plains of Texas, Oklahoma, Kansas, all the way west into Montana, and even up into New York. Clearly the cattle drives moved more than just cows, also distributing terms and culture to areas otherwise too far to be so connected. The term "honky-tonk" had legs, most likely due to the vast reach of the cattle drives.

Given my family connection to Fort Worth, I feel a deep and genuine pride that the first mention of honky-tonk in print (in any derivative) that researchers have found so far appeared in the *Fort Worth Daily Gazette*. It was Thursday January 24, 1889, and it reads:

> "A petition to the council is being circulated for signatures, asking that the Honky Tonk theater on Main street be reopened."

At first, a modern eye would notice that it's used as a proper name since "Honky Tonk" is capitalized. But given the lowercase "theater" and lowercase "street", it appears the writer is not subscribing to our same capitalization standards. Since "Honky Tonk" is used in conjunction with the word "theater" as opposed to beer hall, dancehall, or saloon, it is some sort of musical variety show reference.

On the same page of the newspaper, a doctor's advertisement just a few inches above the honky-tonk petition truly illustrates just how wild and corrupt cowtown life was during frontier times. At first glance below I read the word "ligation" as "litigation", but on a second pass I realized they aren't talking about binding contracts, but a binding surgical procedure. Perhaps this doctor's office is strategically close to the previously mentioned honky-tonk on Main Street?

> "DR. M'COY. SPECIALIST. Cures piles, fistulas, and urethral strictures without cutting or ligation. Venereal diseases, etc. Over 2000 references. Office 502 Main street, Fort Worth, Tex."

But perhaps the most curious announcement in the January 24th 1889 edition of the *Fort Worth Daily Gazette* appears just before the historic honky-tonk mention:

> "The grand jury have indicted fifteen women for keeping disorderly houses."

Damn, sister! If the dangerous but inevitable allure I'm sure I would have felt from the honky-tonk theaters and saloons of The Acre didn't destroy me back in 1889, clearly the domestic tyranny would have been my downfall. That is, unless this is code for running a brothel? In which case I'd be perfectly innocent and free to let the dishes pile up in the sink and brush crumbs right off the couch onto the floor.

Just speaking hypothetically, of course.

Fort Worth almost met its downfall in the early 1870s. A railroad was being constructed that was due to pass through the city, but when the Wall Street firm bankrolling the project failed, they stopped laying track thirty miles shy of Fort Worth. A hard winter in 1873 decimated the cattle business and added to the city's burdens. People fled and the population dropped from 4,000 to under 1,000. One of the defectors, a lawyer named Robert E. Cowart, wrote a letter to a Dallas newspaper claiming that Fort Worth was so stark and desolate that a panther had been spotted sleeping in the middle of a downtown street. Demonstrating the unwavering confidence and fun-loving nature of its residents, Fort Worth not only brushed off the derogatory editorial, but somehow turned the slam into a positive by adopting it as a nickname for the city. It was often referred to as Pantherville or Panther City. Panther saloons began to open, a fire truck was named "The Panther", and other businesses were adopting the title. Two panther cubs were purchased and housed at the fire hall. Even today, the city police wear a badge with a panther on top of the shield.

Meanwhile, a gutsy group of citizens, who believed the town would only survive with a railroad, set about constructing the remaining tracks. They barely finished within a state-mandated deadline, and in 1876, just a year after the panther dig in the Dallas paper, the first train entered Fort Worth. This converted the city from a mere stopover point along the cattle drives to the actual end-game for the drovers bringing heads of cattle to market. Cattle pens were built and a shipping center established. No longer just a cowtown on the Chisholm Trail, Fort Worth had just become Cowtown with a capitol "C".

Fort Worth continued to thrive. By 1900 there were over 26,000 residents. It became clear that instead of just shipping cattle, the city could prosper from its own packing house industry. In 1902 three well known packing houses came to Fort Worth, building adjacent to the existing Stockyards and cultivating one of the greatest livestock and meatpacking industries in the country. The Livestock Exchange building was called "The Wall Street of the West".

Quite a contrast from the rough and tumble reputation of The Acre.

In 1917 the oil boom hit north Texas, and Fort Worth was positioned right in the middle of two successful oil fields. Refineries were built and the oil business took over the lobby of the Westbrook Hotel. The people of Fort Worth were never short on personality, but now they had the money to bring the city itself to life. Culture boomed along with oil through the years between the two world wars. Fort Worth had become a metropolis within the state and hosted glamorous festivities during the summer of 1936 to celebrate the Texas Centennial.

The music scene was developing in a more sophisticated manner. Blues came to Fort Worth around 1930, about the same time a fiddler from the Panhandle named Bob Wills arrived in town. Having debuted in blackface, Bob Wills was familiar with black music and effusive about his passion for the blues. Wills famously once rode a horse fifty miles just to hear blues singer Bessie Smith. He blended the black blues style with his traditional waltzes to create a thoroughly new sound. Teaming up with Milton Brown in Fort Worth, he formed the band that would become the Light Crust Doughboys. Together they are credited with creating the musical genre of western swing.

Western swing was made for dance parties. Wills and Brown blended hillbilly sounds with blues and jazz to create a technically sophisticated musical combination – all for the purpose of getting people on the dance floor. After just two years together, Bob Wills split with Milton Brown to form his own band, Bob Wills and his Texas Playboys, and moved his home base between Texas and Oklahoma through the years. Wills was a big band leader like Tommy Dorsey and Benny Goodman; in fact, Bob Wills' shows would often draw bigger crowds. The difference was that Bob Wills led with a fiddle instead of horns.

Wills was known for his visceral "ah-hahh!" callouts while The Texas Playboys rocked it and Tommy Duncan crooned as lead vocalist. I used to assume these vocal outbursts were phonetic derivatives of the cowboys shouting, "Caa! Caa!" while herding cattle. But I was wrong. This is called field hollering, and it stems from a black blues tradition that traces back to slaves working in the fields. Field hollering is also associated with the black spiritual church tradition of call and response between preacher and congregation. By all accounts it would seem Bob Wills was preaching the crowd into a musical frenzy, and dancing was the message. Wills was reportedly so passionate and enthusiastic during a show, he would field holler and fiddle and call out to the band and work the crowd with unparalleled charisma.

Sounds intoxicating! How could you *not* get up and dance? I'd be swinging around those hardwoods so fast I'd have vertigo without even a sip of liquor.

In 1949 a West Texas musician named Hoyle Nix, a devotee of Bob Wills, wrote and released a song called "Big Ball's in Cowtown". If you're unfamiliar with the tune, please note the placement of the apostrophe and realize it's not as crude or bodacious as it might initially seem. Even though honky-tonk and western music regularly utilize puns and comedic elements, I don't think in this instance Hoyle Nix was toying with a testicular double entendre. The big ball *is* in Cowtown… as in a big gala, a huge celebration, an epic party. It becomes even more clean when you learn that Hoyle Nix didn't write the song from scratch, but in fact merely tweaked the lyrics and melody of an existing song called "Big Ball in Brooklyn", performed by a popular Georgia band called The Skillet Lickers. "Big Ball in Brooklyn" went on to become a cultural gem of the old-time and bluegrass genres, while western swing took ownership of "Big Ball's in Cowtown". Long considered the unofficial anthem of Fort Worth, it has been covered by a cadre of who's who in country music, including the likes of Bob Wills, George Strait, Asleep at the Wheel, and Hoyle Nix's own son, Jody. The song fits Fort Worth like a glove; it's western, upbeat, and celebratory. Fort Worth continues to embrace its western heritage, the people are buoyant and good natured, and this town never shies away from a good time.

My grandparents were on the scene for many of those Fort Worth parties. My grandfather was a banker in South Texas, but moved the family to Fort Worth in 1962. Fort Worth had long enjoyed a strong and progressive banking scene, dating back to the 1870s and the cattle drive era. The banking community thrived hand-in-hand with the booming cattle and oil industries. My grandfather looked like actor Gregory Peck, had deep Christian morals, and was a respected leader in the Fort Worth business community, all of which I'm sure helped my grandparents ease into the Fort Worth social scene. By this point, Fort Worth was brimming with culture, including world-class art museums and proper social organizations. The early honky-tonks, illicit dancehalls, and murderous gun fights of The Acre were a dim memory as more proper, "upstanding" citizens became keepers of the scene. My mom always says, "Fort Worth is the only town I know with a hardbound Social Directory that is used more regularly than the phone book." It's true. My grandmother keeps her Social Directory by the phone, alongside her monogrammed notepad and pens. She references it any time she needs to ring someone. Next to an individual's name in the book is a complicated code that looks like hieroglyphics and indicates all of the person's pertinent social details: sorority, social organization, civic memberships. The more letters the better, of course, sort of like the bars on a military hero's chest.

My mother, the middle of three sisters, made her debut in Fort Worth in 1969 during her junior year of college. Most of her fellow debutantes attended Texas Christian University in Fort Worth, The University of Texas in Austin, or they dropped out for the entire fall semester in order to attend all of the parties and teas. My mother was at Vanderbilt University in Nashville, which kept her at a safe distance from having to commute home every single weekend for parties and bow practices. In her own words, the debutante scene "wasn't exactly her thing." That said, conflict was even less of her thing, so she went along with it. The actual deb ball was held the first weekend of November. Although she was already dating my father, also a junior at Vanderbilt, he was playing in the Vanderbilt-Tulane football game that weekend and couldn't join her at the presentation. Given the fact that she had a fixer-upper date from the preapproved deb party list and isn't really the sort to enjoy the spotlight on stage, my mother doesn't exactly wax poetic of her role as debutante. She speaks of it with an insouciant tone, if at all. That said, one month after the ball, my grandparents threw her obligatory deb party, and I will say, my mother *does* get excited describing that event. My dad was able to come as her date, the country club was overhauled to exude a Winter Wonderland theme, and she liked her bejeweled dress with an empire waist that, in her words, was evocative of Olivia Hussey in *Romeo and Juliet.*

"It was a very popular look back then, Christine."

I think my mother's overall lack of enthusiasm signaled what was to come for the deb scene. The balls would continue, of course, but their old-world significance began to wane. The notion that a young woman needed a coming out party to present her to society was beginning to feel irrelevant after a decade of impassioned feminist messaging. Four years later when her little sister was due to make her debut, she simply put her foot down and wouldn't have a thing to do with it. "A sign of the times," my mother says matter-of-factly.

The charm did not fade from my grandparents' life one bit. As a child in the 1970s I *loved* visiting them in Fort Worth. Completely naïve to the cattle drive heritage or honky-tonk culture of the town, I was simply playing in the equivalent of a six year old's resort. They had a pool in the backyard where I would swim for hours on end. Their country club had silver bowls filled with mints and no one said anything about how many I could take. The golf course was across the street from their house so my cousin and I would run from one sand trap to the next, pretending we were spies trying to capture the Ayatollah Khomeini and rescue the hostages in Iran. Then I would come inside and beg my grandmother to paint my nails coral, which was the color all the beautiful women in Texas seemed to have on their nails. Strangely, my nails never looked as good as hers did. (Of course now I know it's because my grandmother probably had her nails professionally manicured.) Her closet was fantasyland. Rows of evening gowns and shoes and purses. It wasn't the type of grandmother closet where you would go try things on. Nothing was ever stated outright, but it was pretty clear I was to keep my paws off the threads.

Their friends were glamorous, too. My grandmother and her girlfriends were, and still are, the most elegant women I'd ever seen up close. And they were so *Texas.* Done-up hair, bright nails, fabulous accessories. Their friends had big ranches and private airplanes and lots of stories. There were rumors of kidnappings all the time in Fort Worth when I was a kid, friends in the banking community were always being kidnapped and tied up and ransomed. I'm telling you, it was high times in Pantherville in the late '70s and early '80s.

It would seem the sophisticated, moneyed culture of Fort Worth would be at odds with its western heritage and cattle drive persona, but that's not the case. The tension between these on-the-surface polar opposites isn't at all fractious; in fact it yields a unique kinetic energy and civic pride. The upper crust is unapologetic in claiming cowboy roots. As a city Fort Worth has always exuded a certain self-confidence, hospitality, feisty ambition, and jubilant attitude. Not one to play Mini-Me, Fort Worth doesn't live in the shadow of Dallas, which is a mere thirty miles away. According to writer and Fort Worth historian Ann Arnold, when Dallas won the bid to host the 1936 Texas Centennial celebrations, Fort Worth civic leader, Amon Carter, proclaimed, "Let 'em go to Dallas for education, let 'em come to Fort Worth for entertainment." Fort Worth has a long tradition of gumption. Plus, the people there simply know how to have a damn good time. They may have cleaned up their act since the days of The Acre, but as my mom always says, "Fort Worth was a wild town to grow up in."

I was something of a drover myself the way I popped in and out of Fort Worth through the years, using it for my own personal pleasure. In high school I moved in with my grandparents for a month while I did an internship at the Amon Carter Museum. In college I drifted to Fort Worth occasionally and would balance my time between family and friends. One Christmas my dad took me to have custom cowboy boots made at historic Leddy's, which has been making boots and saddles in the Fort Worth Stockyards since 1941. Before you could blink, I went from western to well-bred as I switched into a navy taffeta ball gown and attended a Fort Worth deb party. Doug Clark and the Hot Nuts played.

A few years later, after college, I found myself back in Fort Worth. Once again it was Christmastime, and once again I was clad in an evening dress. But this wasn't another deb party, this time I was a bridesmaid in my pledge sister's wedding.

I had forgotten about our night out with Verne Troyer four years prior and wasn't expecting to see him at the wedding. But Verne was there, front and center for all three days of the festivities. I don't know if he was still living in Fort Worth or if he traveled in just for this affair, but I do know he *had* started his career as an actor and stuntman by this point. I remember him telling us about breaking into the movie business with roles as a stunt baby. *Wow, that's a far cry from being the judge of a tan line competition in a pseudo western bar!* Who could have predicted the success that was just around the corner with his Mini-Me role? But Hollywood had already made Verne more Verne as he soaked up attention and held everyone's focus for hours. As the Thursday night party rolled on downtown to a crowded bar, I didn't even blink an eye as I hoisted him right up onto a cocktail table. *Oh it's okay, y'all, I know what to do, we've hit the town together before*. At the Saturday night formal wedding reception, Verne ruled the dance floor and cut a rug with every lady in the country club. While the rest of the crowd was draped in full length gowns and tuxedos, Verne was sporting all denim, and he totally owned it. Now let's be honest, it takes pretty big cojones for an adult man to show up at a black tie wedding in Baby Gap blue jeans. But if I've learned anything about Fort Worth, it's that Cowtown brings the people out to the balls and brings the balls out in people.

CHAPTER 2 SOUNDTRACK:

Big Ball's in Cowtown – Asleep at the Wheel

(HOYLE NIX)

Faded Love – Bob Wills and his Texas Playboys

(BOB WILLS, JOHN WILLS)

Roly Poly – Bob Wills and his Texas Playboys

(FRED ROSE)

Bob Wills is Still the King – Waylon Jennings

(WAYLON JENNINGS)

Does Fort Worth Ever Cross Your Mind – George Strait

(DARLENE SHAFER, SANGER D. SHAFER)

Christine's mother, Nancy, at her deb ball with her parents and sister
Fort Worth TX, 1969
Photo credit and courtesy: Rhea-Engert Photography

Christine's parents, Nancy and Duck, at Nancy's deb party, Fort Worth TX, 1969

CHAPTER 3

First Guitar, Second String

I was away at college when I called home and begged my parents to buy me a guitar, throwing my upcoming birthday at them as leverage. The fact that I didn't know how to *play* a guitar was an inconsequential detail, because the gorgeous, shiny black Fender I had already picked out came with a workbook that would teach me everything I needed to know. Problem solved! The used guitar was in pristine condition except for one missing string which the seller assured me would be easy to replace. It took some cooing and cajoling, but before long, I was holding my first guitar.

I would sit on the couch singing songs and strumming along as if I were playing an actual melody. I wouldn't let my roommates, or anyone else for that matter, put their mitts on my beautiful Fender. I loved it with all my heart. Learning how to play it, however, proved to be a different matter entirely. I thumbed through the book and tried to learn a few basics, but it was too abstract. Plus there was the matter of the missing string. As it turned out, all strings were not equally interchangeable and I would have to determine which one was missing. I analyzed the schema in the workbook in great detail and finally figured it out. The G string. *Damn. Do I really have to walk into a music store and ask them for…a G string*? I felt inadequate. It sounded dirty. Inertia got its hooks in me.

Months went by and my parents would ask about the guitar. I assured them that I totally loved it and was working with the notebook to learn how to play. Not one to suffer a fool, my mother sniffed out the truth pretty quickly. I confessed that I hadn't gotten around to replacing the missing string because it was…well, the *G string*. I could practically feel her eyes rolling on the other end of the telephone. She managed to keep my secret from my dad for a few weeks but somehow it conveniently leaked out around the holidays. My father gave me unmitigated grief about it for days on end – he was relentless. It mushroomed into a widespread joke that involved friends and relatives; I was pretty much the constant target of ridicule, not to mention any and all thong jokes. By the time we were at my grandparents' house in Fort Worth for Christmas, I hoped we had reached a truce. I was excited Christmas morning when I reached into my stocking and pulled out a bag that had the name of a Fort Worth music store printed on it. I looked up, and my dad was smiling. *Finally! The string for my guitar…he got it for me*! I pulled out the somewhat excessive wrapping tissue and unfolded it to discover…scandalous drumroll…a miniscule pair of thong underwear. There's really nothing that screams Greek Tragedy quite like holding up a pair of sexy underwear that your dad bought you. In front of your entire family. On Christmas. The room fell into peals of laughter. People were rolling off of couches, falling flat on the floor. Just when I thought it couldn't get any more twisted, my grandfather handed me a Victoria's Secret bag. Inside it was a G string for my guitar.

Well played, fellas.

Delightfully, the spotlight shifted from me onto my dad and my super straight-laced, elegant, leader-of-the-community, always-on-the-vestry grandfather. I thought a few members of my family were going to have a hernia laughing as we listened to the tale of the two of them skulking into a bustling Victoria's Secret in the Fort Worth mall a few days before Christmas. Because two men wandering into a lingerie store together were unable to avoid detection, the sales associate approached my grandfather and asked if they needed help. He was ill-prepared for this scenario and stood in silence, blushing. Thinking he was suavely rushing in to save the situation, my dad replied, "Oh, we're just here to get a thong for my daughter."

And that is the story of my first guitar and the two G strings I got for Christmas.

I imagine the very first guitars to reach North America arrived without such inane hilarity. Then again, it was Spanish soldiers, explorers, and missionaries who introduced the guitar to America, and Spaniards are a pretty fun-loving lot. The first guitarist in America is cited in St. Augustine, Florida in the mid-1500s. I wonder if guitar players had the same mesmerizing effect on women as they do now. I bet he was a lady-killing virtuoso strumming away under the Spanish moss with nothing but the sound of the ocean to interrupt his long, self-indulgent jamming solos.

At any rate, tracking the imprint of Spanish exploration, one would have to assume the guitar was also prevalent back then throughout Mexico, Texas, and the entire Gulf Coast. The French were almost as enthusiastic as the Spanish about their guitars and were also traipsing around the same regions. The guitar would become a mainstay in Louisiana Creole music which would later influence the music of New Orleans. Back in Europe, around 1810, people had become so crazed in their guitar-love that the trend was labeled *guitaromanie*. The *guitaromanie* phenomenon reached America by the 1830s as the instrument was exploding in popularity here as well.

It was around this time, the 1830s, that rural black musicians in Texas and the Deep South first began playing the guitar. A few decades later, with the 1863 Emancipation Act, southern black slaves were freed. Eventually they began to travel throughout the South and Texas finding work as migrant farmers. They carried their music with them from place to place, and by the 1880s the guitar experienced a steep rise in favor with black musicians. Unlike other instruments, the guitar did not invoke imagery of slavery, minstrel music, or other pre-Civil War stereotypes. At the time, the guitar wasn't even associated with the South. In addition, more sophisticated transportation channels were being developed that could get affordable, mass-produced instruments into the hands of more people more quickly than ever before.

While blues music evolved from the black oral traditions of the South, by the early 1900s its sound was far-reaching. Blues singers were typically migrant workers who chased a crop harvest, a boomtown, or a successful lumber camp. While some settled down to farm in one place, others continued to drift from one job to the next, spreading their musical styling around the South as well as Texas, even Chicago and New York. Unlike Appalachian ensembles and other music of the period, blues music highlighted the individual experience. It involved a solo performance which held deeply personal messages. In blues music, the focus on a lone, drifting soul is evocative of the spirit of the West. While the music itself displays no western influence, the blues singer's lyrics are often akin to the real-world ache and poetic longing of the roving American Cowboy. Through this lens, it's easy to see how emerging western swing and honky-tonk music would share thematic and sonic elements with the blues.

Pursuant to birthright, the Mississippi Delta justly claims the throne of the blues. Louisiana, St. Louis, Chicago, and Texas all bow to the history of Mississippi blues and stand behind its well-deserved glory. That being said, Texas has its own rich blues heritage, espe-cially during the genre's nascent recording era. In the 1920s Blind Lemon Jefferson was a popular blues singer living in the Deep Ellum area of Dallas, Texas. He was the first to commercially record blues songs that garnered phenomenal success. His lyrics were typically about the topics of everyday life, picnics, and honky-tonks. So it's curious that his first recordings were spiritual songs under the name Deacon L.J. Bates. In 1926 he followed up with recordings under his own name that were commercial victories. In 1927 he recorded "See That My Grave is Kept Clean", which would be one of his biggest hits. Once again, it was spiritual and recorded under the pseudonym Deacon L.J. Bates, but it was an immediate score with fans, so he quickly re-recorded it in 1928 under his own name. The song has been covered by musical juggernauts from a multitude of genres including Bob Dylan, The Grateful Dead (re-titled as "One Kind Favor"), and B.B. King, just to name a few.

I did not even know about Blind Lemon Jefferson in the early 1990s when I was just out of college and racing around the then-hip

Deep Ellum scene in Dallas. One of our favorite places to socialize was a bar called The Blind Lemon, nothing more than a curious name to me at the time. I was obviously the blind one.

But no one could turn a blind eye to Blind Lemon's success back in the 1920s. Blues singers from all over Texas and beyond flocked to Dallas to record their own music and try to replicate his success. Blind Lemon Jefferson had an immeasurable influence on the development of blues in Texas as well as on many musicians. T-Bone Walker, Bessie Smith, and Louis Armstrong are just a few who noted his significance. It didn't take long for the blues to drift westward on down the road to Fort Worth, initially popping up in a neighborhood called Como. The area was established by upper class white families who wanted their black housekeepers to have nearby housing. In the 1930s a music venue called The Bluebird opened in Como. Two railroad cars were affixed together, and it offered a modest setting for the blues that poured out of The Bluebird on and off for the next 60 years.

In 1931, right around when blues and The Bluebird hit Como, the electric guitar was invented. Based on the number of patents from the early 1900s, all sorts of people had experimented with ways to amplify sound in stringed instruments such as the violin, banjo, and guitar. The first electronically amplified guitar on record was built in 1931 by the National Guitar Corporation, although several others claim to have pulled it off earlier. Late musician Stephen Bruton discovered that someone near Fort Worth (in a town called Weatherford) had, in fact, invented the very first electric guitar. In an interview with National Public Radio, Stephen's good friend, T. Bone Burnett, replays Bruton's theory. "Stephen dug up that the first electric guitar was made in Weatherford. One of the guys stuck a needle from a phonograph into the top of the guitar to act as the microphone and ran it through the phonograph to make it louder with the Texas swing band."

While music historians may or may not bless the notion that the first electric guitar was invented near Fort Worth, the city does have another undisputed impact on the early history of the electric guitar. Hawaiian musicians had been the first to record with an electric guitar in 1933. For two years, that was the only style of music heard on records with the newly amplified sound. But a Fort Worth musician named

Bob Dunn changed that in 1935. Dunn was a member of Milton Brown's Musical Brownies, the western swing band Brown formed after he and Bob Wills split. Dunn was the first to break from the Hawaiian sound when he recorded jazz and blues with the electric guitar. Perhaps Bob Dunn was, in fact, the western swing musician Stephen Bruton claimed developed the earliest electric guitar. Regardless, after his recordings many musicians from a variety of mainstream stylings incorporated the amped up guitar into their records; henceforth girls across the country would forever lose their minds (and let's face it, sometimes even their panties) when an otherwise gangly and scraggly looking guy would slip that guitar strap over one shoulder and barely start to strum down on those metallic strings. Game set match. The boys with electric guitars are still winning this one.

Now personally, I love an unproven theory because it means I can hang my hat on it all day long. They may not be able to prove that Stephen Bruton was right, but they can't prove he was wrong either. My Fort Worth loyalty and Texas pride *wholeheartedly* back up his claim that the first electric guitar was invented around Fort Worth for a western swing band.

Besides, Stephen Bruton knew more than just a thing or two about guitars. He was a longtime picker for both Kris Kristofferson and Bonnie Raitt, he was an avid guitar collector, and he had his own solo career that spanned decades. While it may seem Fort Worth played second string to other, more notable music cities like Austin, New Orleans, Chicago, or Nashville, there is much more than meets the eye with Cowtown.

Toward the end of his life Stephen Bruton would team up with his old Fort Worth friend, T. Bone Burnett, to direct all the music for the 2009 movie *Crazy Heart*, including co-authoring several songs on the soundtrack. The film tells the story of the once glorious, outlaw-style honky-tonk singer, Bad Blake. Stephen Bruton was crucial in providing the director and lead actor, Jeff Bridges, with subtle details that would bring the character to life in an authentic way. All of the input certainly came together because it's a great movie.

Right when it came out my mother called and asked if I'd seen it. At that point, I still hadn't. "Not yet," I replied. "But I can't wait, it looks good."

"Me neither. You know my old boyfriend did all the music?"

"What? What old boyfriend?"

"An old boyfriend from Fort Worth. He just died, it's so sad."

"Mother, what boyfriend are you talking about?"

"Oh, his name is Stephen Bruton, you probably haven't heard of him," she offered nonchalantly.

"Uh, *yes*. Yes I have. I've heard of Stephen Bruton. I just had never heard that you *dated* him!"

"Well, dating is such a strong word, Christine. I wouldn't say we dated. It was the 8th grade, Lord knows I wasn't allowed to go anywhere. I just remember him showing up at my front door a few times and giving me gifts. I guess you would say we were going steady. I think his dad owned the only record store in town."

And just like that I learned about my mother's brief teenage brush with a rock and roll life. When I press my mom for more information about the Fort Worth music scene back in the day, her memories bounce back and forth between totally blank and utterly fabulous. For example, she has no recollection of the Bluebird in Como, neither the original venue nor its reincarnation in the '70s as The New Bluebird Nite Club. But she definitely remembers sneaking into the Skyliner Ballroom. And when she and my dad were dating they saw Tammy Wynette at Panther Hall. She doesn't remember much about the show except she thinks Tammy sang "D-I-V-O-R-C-E". I am dizzy and in complete awe just to be tossed a few nostalgic crumbs straight from the frontline of this musical era.

Back when blues was taking hold in Como, Fort Worth was still The Gateway to the West. Instead of cattle the money was in oil, and instead of the Chisholm Trail, the beaten path was the Jacksboro Highway just north of town. Thunder Road was a three and a half mile stretch of Jacksboro Highway packed with entertainment venues catering to the fat-cat ranchers traveling on their way out to their West Texas ranches – which were in dry counties. Bootleggers would buy liquor on Jacksboro Highway then travel out to West Texas to peddle it. In the 1940s and 50s, the big band sound was in, and well known acts were booked all up and down Thunder Road. And serious mobster activity followed the burgeoning entertainment scene to Fort Worth.

One of the nightclub strippers even had ties to a Las Vegas gangster. Ann Arnold, author of the book <u>Gamblers & Gangsters: Fort Worth's Jacksboro Highway in the 1940s & 1950s</u>, explains that there were car bombings and at least sixteen gang-related murders on Jacksboro Highway between 1940 and 1960, not one of which was ever solved.

The Skyliner Ballroom was a fixture on Thunder Road. At 2,500 square feet it was the largest dance hall in town when it opened in the late '30s. Despite the racial segregation that persisted well into the 1960s, the Skyliner Ballroom catered to a diverse clientele by booking a variety of big name acts. Louis Armstrong, Ike and Tina, Delbert McClinton. T. Bone Burnett says the Skyliner was the first gig he ever played. I asked my mom if she remembers who she saw when she snuck into the Skyliner. "Oh! Little Richard…" she said in a whispered tone as if she were still eligible to be grounded by her parents. "And Melvin was always so excited when Ray Charles played there." (Melvin was my grandmother's housekeeper.) "She was going to the Skyliner to see Ray Charles, and we had these dates that were taking us there, and I was so nervous I would run into her and get in trouble! I was way too young to be in there. Or was it Melvin who got us the tickets? I can't remember. I just know she was the one who got me all excited about seeing Ray Charles at the Skyliner."

The Skyliner survived until 1966, overlapping just three years with another Fort Worth institution, Panther Hall. If I could go back in time and visit only one of these two joints, I'd have to pick Panther Hall. It opened in 1963 as a bowling alley that started booking rock and roll bands. But they couldn't pack the place with rock and roll, so they quickly converted to a country format. Every Saturday evening they would broadcast a local TV show called *Cowtown Jamboree*, which hyped that night's upcoming live performance. Everyone who was anyone on the honky-tonk circuit played Panther Hall. Bob Wills, Ernest Tubb, Waylon Jennings, Johnny Cash, Hank Thompson, Faron Young, Merle Haggard, Loretta Lynn…the list goes on and on. Of course I think it's just too damn cool that my parents saw Tammy Wynette there. We'll just assume my mother's foggy memory is instead dead-eye accurate and that Tammy did in fact sing her mega hit "D-I-V-O-R-C-E" that night. This was the song her producer, Billy

Sherrill, initially predicted would be her all time biggest hit, until of course "Stand by Your Man" came along.

The other country powerhouse to grace the Panther Hall stage quite regularly was Willie Nelson. He lived in Fort Worth off and on during his early career and was a staple on *Cowtown Jamboree*. In 1966 he was a brand new pledge-like member of the *Grand Ole Opry* in Nashville, but traveled down to Panther Hall in Fort Worth to record his first live album. Longtime friend and Texas musician, Johnny Bush, backed Willie during the live show and recording. (Years later Willie would have a monumental hit with the song "Whiskey River", which Johnny Bush wrote. To show loyalty to his friend, Willie opens every single one of his concerts with "Whiskey River".) The album at Panther Hall was plainly called *Live Country Music Concert*, which hardly captures the creativity of such a romantic songwriter and storyteller. Similarly, the album cover shows a clean-shaven, tailored Willie, which was the exact opposite of the musical renegade and redneck hippie icon he would ultimately become. Regardless, the music on the album spoke for itself. A mix of covers and self-penned tracks, *Live Country Music Concert* revealed a soulful, distinct musician and offered plenty of hints to anyone paying attention that this guy was going to blaze a new trail for country music.

The only other Fort Worth musical moment I have been able to lure out of my mother took place at the annual Fat Stock Show and Rodeo circa 1972. Texas-born Tanya Tucker was only thirteen years old and had just released her first song. Billy Sherrill (the same producer who fueled Tammy's meteoric rise to fame) signed the teenaged Tanya to Columbia Records and decided her first release would be "Delta Dawn". My parents were at the Fort Worth rodeo when Tanya Tucker came barreling out on horseback, galloping around the arena and belting out "Delta Dawn". (*Could you die?* I myself have indulged in countless daydreams about performing that song on stage with a fifty-person gospel choir in full-length robes. Granted, probably not what Billy Sherrill had in mind, but if you listen to the song and really soak up every repeat of the chorus and soulful key change, I think you will see the genius of my fantasy arrangement.) I suppose the Cowtown rodeo was a fitting place for my parents to see Tanya's debut song because the Texas teen was no stranger to being on a horse. In a 1988 interview Tanya talked about the song "Delta Dawn" and said, "I was fortunate to have latched onto that one, and that was all Sherrill's doing. If it hadn't been for Sherrill, I probably would have been a rodeo queen or something." That said, I still have a hard time picturing Tanya as a simple western girl since I had her *TNT* album in 1978, released around the time she decided to rebrand herself as a sex symbol. I was eight years old and was both shocked and intrigued by the image of her on the album, twisting in her sassy black leather pants and pulling that microphone cord through her legs while singing "Texas (When I Die)".

While the rodeo lives on in Fort Worth, long gone are the days of The Bluebird, Thunder Road, The Skyliner Ballroom, and Panther Hall. Stephen Bruton is no longer with us, but his brother, Sumter, still runs Record Town, the family music store. Dial him up or just wander in and he will gladly share stories about the history of music in Cowtown. Not long ago a popular western swing joint called Big Balls of Cowtown changed ownership and its name. Now it's Pearl's Dancehall and Saloon, and if you're lucky, you can catch Johnny Bush playing there. And of course, there's always Billy Bob's, the world's largest honky-tonk. A quick Google search of the phrase "Live at Billy Bob's" produces so many different albums, it's instantly clear that musicians with guitars are still rocking in Cowtown.

Sadly my Fender and I were never among them. My beautiful black guitar slipped away from me before I ever learned to play it. Some shady character in college borrowed it and the trail pretty much drops off from there. I would own one other guitar in my thirties, but again, I never found the time to learn how to do anything with it other than strut around in front of my bathroom mirror looking cool as all hell. Times got tough when I quit my real job in favor of writing, so I sold it to a pawn shop for tens of dollars. I know in the early days Willie used to pawn his guitar on a weekly basis. He'd borrow money from a friend to get it out for the weekend, and then each Monday he'd pawn the guitar to repay his debt with his buddy. I just don't think I ever got bit by the same sort of *guitaromanie*.

While I have a soulful appreciation for the guitar, I clearly don't have the true heart of a picker. The only reason I ever wanted one was because the person with the guitar always controlled the songs during any late night sing-along, and I always wanted to sing more songs than Whoever-Was-On-The-Guitar knew how to play. Conversely, they always resorted to playing something like "Brown Eyed Girl", which was my cue to yawn and fix another drink. Quite simply, I wanted a guitar because I wanted to create the set list for these impromptu sessions. In my overly imaginative mind, fueled by the brashness of my youth, the guitar played second string to my would-be vocals. Because if there was ever going to be a musical career I dreamed of having but never actually attaining, it wasn't picking, it was singing.

CHAPTER 3 SOUNDTRACK:

Half a Man – Willie Nelson

(WILLIE NELSON)

Undo the Right – Johnny Bush

(HANK COCHRAN, WILLIE NELSON)

D-I-V-O-R-C-E – Tammy Wynette

(BOBBY BRADDOCK, CURLY PUTMAN)

Delta Dawn – Tanya Tucker

(LARRY COLLINS, ALEXANDER HARVEY)

I Don't Know – Ryan Bingham

(STEPHEN BRUTON, T. BONE BURNETT)

Ernest Tubb at Panther Hall, Fort Worth TX
Photo credit: Wayne Beckham
Courtesy: The Panther Hall Photograph Collection, The Wittliff Collections,
Texas State University

CHAPTER 4

Don't Mess With Oklahoma Either

When specialty retailer Neiman Marcus first opened its doors in September 1907, Oklahoma wasn't even a state yet. From the flagship Neiman's store in downtown Dallas, you could drive roughly two hours north and be in The Territory, or Indian land. When Oklahoma finally became the 46th state on November 16, 1907, it hardly traded in its tough, proud, independent spirit. Given their bold personalities, it's not a stretch that Oklahoma and Texas have had a complex next-door-neighbor relationship since the beginning. From the early days these two states have quarreled and loved like siblings. The Red River is the border between the two and serves as both the referee – keeping them safely in their corners – as well as the glue that seams them together. They compete and cajole until someone from the outside criticizes them, and then they have each other's back like blood. My dad, who was born and raised in Ardmore, Oklahoma, paints the picture, "Texas is the rich cousin and Oklahoma is the poor cousin."

I remember clearly in the 1980s when the Texas Department of Transportation launched their "Don't Mess With Texas" campaign aimed at stopping litter along Texas highways. Even though the stodgy "Keep America Beautiful" types at the TX-DOT were hesitant to approve the brash slogan, they ultimately did bless it, and this legendary creative concept by Austin-based ad agency GSD&M struck a chord with the public instantaneously. The saying was everywhere in the late 1980s, evolving into a near rallying cry from proud Texans. I imagine it became quite a bore for neighboring states. The most hilarious spin-off was a bumper sticker I once saw that coolly stated, "Don't Mess With Oklahoma Either."

Which, on many levels, is brilliantly funny.

In the mid-1800s bumper stickers should have warned, "Don't Mess With The Chickasaw Either" as these Indians ran the show in the territory area around my dad's hometown of Ardmore. When the Chickasaw Indian tribe was removed from Mississippi and placed in Indian Territory, it was originally part of the Choctaw Nation. But they became frustrated with their lack of self-government, so in 1855 the Chickasaw separated to create their own Nation in which Ardmore would become the largest town.

After the Civil War, many white southerners who had lost fortune and property relocated to the Chickasaw Nation where, after residing for two years, they could marry a Chickasaw wife and be eligible to own property in the Indian Territory. A group of ranchers, having married into the Chickasaw Nation, ran a cattle operation called the 700 Ranch, which became a hub of activity in the area. It would also become the future site of the town of Ardmore.

The first named thoroughfare in Ardmore was Caddo Street since it was along the wagon trail that led from the 700 Ranch to Caddo Creek. Two blocks of this historic street evolved into one of the wildest areas of the West, ultimately known for its bootlegging, prostitution, gambling, murders, and general lawlessness. Nefarious activities by thieves and gunmen earned this area of Ardmore the nickname "Bloody Caddo". In the book Territory Town, Ardmore resident Ance Rogers, whose family moved from Arkansas to Ardmore when he was three years old, describes the appeal for outlaws to come to this part of the world. "Fellers who had been run out of the States," he said, "all went to Indian Territory where the law wouldn't bother them for any little old thing. We come to this country like the rest of them. My daddy got into some trouble with the law in Arkansas."

As a community, Ardmore, had southern roots. Once-noble families from the war-ravaged South tried to bring a gentrified culture to Ardmore that seems like it would be glaringly out of place in the raw, dusty ranchland of the Indian Territory. Still, education and the arts often soared in Ardmore, more so than other contemporary Territory towns. Victorian-style living rooms, singing soirées, and lavish parties existed in parallel to the murders, gambling, and gunfire happening in Bloody Caddo. To say the least, Ardmore was an eccentric mix.

Honky-tonks were prevalent in the Indian Territory just as they were along the cattle drives down in Texas. This mention of the term "honky-tonk" in a Kansas newspaper defines a honky-tonk as a theater. It also addresses the still unanswered question of the term's origin. From *The Iola Register*, June 23 1893:

> "When a particularly vicious and low grade theater opens up in an Oklahoma town they call it a 'honky-tonk'. The name didn't 'come from' anything; it just growed."

This article characterizes the honky-tonk as a "vicious" place, which seems a particularly harsh word, although probably accurate. As evidenced in this 1894 Washington newspaper article, the honky-tonk's unsavory reputation reached all the way to the Pacific Northwest. From the Tacoma *Daily News*:

> "It's a deadly insult for one Oklahoma editor to say that another has a pass to a 'Honkatonk'."

The honky-tonk's notoriety also traveled the opposite direction all the way to the Northeast. Just before the turn of the century, a New York City newspaper was actually *lamenting* the demise of the honky-tonk in its original splendor, glorifying the institution's inherent connection to the American West. This nostalgic article, which appeared in the December 10th 1889 issue of *The Sun* in New York, describes the indulgent scene inside these bawdy theaters.

"...it is unnecessary at any time to abandon the cigar, and whatever the part of the house, he is expected to be liberal in his expenditure for liquid refreshments."

The Sun article goes on to describe how the cast members traveled and were paid – sometimes in beer.

"The performers do not travel by companies. Every star hustles for himself regardless of all the others, and remains in a community as long as the management will pay him his price, or, if in case of an actress, as long as she is a success at winning checks by inducing her admirers to buy beer."

Sounds like college.

When it comes to citing the locations of actual honky-tonks, the New York newspaper mentions honky-tonks in both Ardmore (my dad's hometown) and Fort Worth (my mom's hometown). Further evidence that honky-tonks are not only built into my family tree, they are in my DNA.

"There is no defined circuit of honkatonks, but the performers swing around a circle of a half dozen theaters which dot Texas and the two territories. The once popular institution is dying off. There is one in Guthrie, one in Ardmore, one in Fort Worth, and a few others further south."

Finally, the article in *The Sun* concludes by perpetuating an age-old myth about how honky-tonks got their name.

"Every child of the range can tell what honkatonk means and where it came from. Away, away back in the very early days, so the story goes, a party of cow punchers rode out from camp at sundown in search of recreation after a day of toil. They headed for a place of amusement, but lost the trail. From far out in the distance there finally came to their ears a "honk-a-tonk-a-tonk-a-tonk-a," which they mistook for the bass viol. They turned toward the sound, to find alas! a flock of wild geese. So honkatonk was named."

Despite this fanciful notion that the etymology of the term honky-tonk derives from the only cowboys in the West who couldn't distinguish the sound of a bird from that of a bar, the origin of the term is officially listed as unknown. There is another popular theory that it came from the Ernest A. Tonk brand of upright pianos that were common in Tin Pan Alley and thus ragtime music. But the company did not start manufacturing these particular pianos – the Ernest A. Tonk model – until 1889. As we've already seen, the earliest recorded mention of the term "honky-tonk" was in the Fort Worth paper on January 24, 1889. So it's nearly impossible that the name brand of a piano from the north could have worked its way into the cultural terminology as far away as Fort Worth in that amount of time.

Another unlikely theory that can't be proven to be either 100% true or false is the notion that honky-tonk is a derivative of the pejorative term "honky" used to describe a white person. While this slang word wasn't widespread until the 1960s, its origins likely date back further. In the 1920s it was maybe-possibly a nickname given to white men in urban areas who would honk their horns to solicit black prostitutes. While the underbelly nature of this theory fits the ill-repute honky-tonks of the plains, the timing eliminates it.

I feigned a scholarly demeanor as I explained all of these theories to my husband and daughter over dinner. But I couldn't remember a particular term I needed in order to explain one more of the etymology options. What is it called when the sound of the word is meant to represent the actual meaning of the word? Thankfully my teenager intervened with her more current English studies and served up precisely what I was searching for: onomatopoeia. The American Heritage Dictionary defines onomatopoeia as, "The formation or use of words such as buzz or murmur that imitate the sounds associated with the objects or actions they refer to." Realistically speaking, "honky-tonk" is most likely an onomatopoeia that sounds like the hippety hoppety musical sounds of the variety shows in the 1800s.

One of the earliest songs to use a derivative of the term "honky-tonk" in its lyrics is the 1914 ragtime tune "Aba Daba Honeymoon", which describes a monkey and a chimp talking to each other and falling in love. Their monkey love story includes them celebrating in a "honky-tonky" way. The title itself is an onomatopoeia of sorts, if one yields to a willing suspension of disbelief that this is what monkeys sound like when they are flirting. It's really a very moronic tune. But that didn't stop ad executives in the 1970s from using it in a television commercial for Frito's corn chips. They kept the melody but changed the "Aba Daba" lyrics to "Muncha Buncha". If you too are a child of the '70s, the irritating jingle is no doubt stuck in your head now. Sorry for that.

Dissatisfied with all of these half-baked theories, I set out to prove the etymology of the term "honky-tonk" once and for all. And while I was unsuccessful, I did uncover a more obscure theory that is infinitely more interesting to me than monkey talk, pejorative slang, and corn chips. And that would be Indians. Perhaps the term comes from the Indians?

I came across a 2005 essay written by a retired lawyer named M. Lee Murrah. The essay is called "The First Honky Tonks" and suggests that the term "honky-tonk" may have its roots in Indian language. First, Murrah cites a series of editorial articles that appeared in an Ardmore, Oklahoma newspaper in 1894 over a period of a few days. The newspaper writer urges Ardmore residents not to attend the "Fanny Hill Burlesque Company" show that was traveling into town. The author claims that upstanding citizens should have nothing to do with "these exhibitors of high-kicking vaudeville proclivities" and derides the women in the show as "painted, padded and brazen harlots who had the unimagined effrontery to pose as examples of legitimate burlesque comedy."

According to Murrah, despite the newspaper writer's self-righteous rhetoric, the people of Ardmore flocked to the show. The day after, the writer attempted to shame the people of Ardmore by calling the show the lowest, most disreputable name he could: a honk-a-tonk. The 1894 *Daily Ardmoreite* article that ran the day after the burlesque show reads:

"The honk-a-tonk last night was well attended by ball-heads, bachelors and leading citizens."

The term "ball-heads" is curious and leads Murrah down an interesting etymological trail. The precursor to modern-day lacrosse was an Indian ball game played frequently in the Chickasaw Nation. Murrah describes their competitions:

"Indian ball games were spectacles. In an era before massive sporting events in the Anglo world, Indian ball games were unique. George Catlin, famous for painting scores of portraits of Indians across North America, stated that he would travel long distances to attend a ball game. To the young men of towns like Ardmore, they would have been an irresistible draw. The games featured large numbers of players. One game in Oklahoma had 1000 players on the field. The games were violent, and broken limbs were common. Deaths were not unheard of."

Murrah explains that these games turned into raucous, multi-day festivals and had all the elements of a 19th century honky-tonk: music, dancing, liquor, gambling, and loose women. To strengthen his hypothesis that the term honky-tonk evolved from these Indian games, he offers three pieces of linguistic data:

1. "Honky-tonk" has a "k" sound (also considered a "hard g" sound) which is prevalent in Indian language, i.e., Oklahoma, Cherokee, Chickasaw, etc.
2. The term honky-tonk is euphonic, which means certain sounds are repeated. Euphony is a common characteristic in Indian language.
3. The Choctaw word for ball field is "hetoka", which is clearly close to "honky-tonk". If you accept the premise that the Indian ball games had similar elements of wild honky-tonks, it's not too much of a leap to see that

the word "hetoka" may have morphed into the term
"honky-tonk".

The terminology may remain a mystery, but the violence of
these Indian games and the intermingling of Ardmore citizens with
the Indian players is a matter of record. In the book <u>Territory Town</u> an
eyewitness account describes one of the town birthday celebrations
that took place circa 1905. Three Indians wandered among the revelers
"smeared with blood", having participated in one of their ball games.
They made a beeline for the trough where there was water for horses
to drink, and they dunked their mouths to quench their thirst. "One
had his eye nearly torn out, another a broken arm or elbow and the
third had a deep gash across his forehead."

Ardmore in the 1800s was hardly suited for the weak. Apparently
there were plenty of people cut from tough stock who managed to
stick it out because the population continued to grow as the town
prospered from one era to the next. The 1900s brought cotton, an Air
Force base, and the Healdton Oil Field. With this lucrative discovery
in 1913 wildcatters raced into the area, bringing their classic reckless
behavior with them. The entertainment scene clipped along, keeping
pace with the ever-changing landscape of this frontier land. It's no
stretch that Oklahoma's Hall of Fame musicians (and those who
should be) were hardly shrinking violets and enjoy a legacy laced
with grit and innovation.

Native American Indians were very skilled fiddle players. In the
1920s a Choctaw from Oklahoma named Henry Hall traveled with his
family to a Choctaw Indian Fair in Mississippi to perform. A promoter
named H.C. Speir heard the family play and secured them a recording
deal with RCA Victor. Just two years after The Carter family famously
recorded its first album, Henry Hall and his family recorded theirs
under the name Big Chief Henry's Indian String Band. On their song
"Indian Tom Tom" the vocals are haunting and clearly evocative of
Native American rituals and music. That said, there is something that
feels similar to old blues recordings as well. The instrumentation (his
sons played guitar and banjo) seems influenced by classic old-time
and gospel tunes of the day.

At the same time Big Chief Henry's Indian String Band was performing, another Oklahoma act called Otto Gray and His Oklahoma Cowboys was making a name for itself. Otto Gray started performing western music in 1924 and some claim he defined the genre of western swing even before Bob Wills. *Whoa, hold on there, compadre, let's not get carried away!* While Gray's music is western and he deserves much credit for being a forerunner, I think Bob Wills' arrangements are more sophisticated, innovative, and light-years ahead in terms of mixing in blues and jazz. When I listen to Gray's "Four Thousand Years Ago", I like it, but it doesn't have the dynamic, get-off-your-bum-and-dance quality that I hear with Wills. So I still give the nod to Bob Wills as the King of Western Swing. That said, Otto Gray did make his mark as a showman. He was the first national act to perform in western clothing and included roping and other cowboy tricks in his act. He was the first western star to be photographed on the cover of *Billboard Magazine*. And his was likely the first-ever group to use custom-made cars to travel while on tour. Gray's personal Cadillac was even outfitted for radio transmission. YouTube videos of Otto Gray and His Oklahoma Cowboys include comedy bits and novelty tricks such as one band member playing another's instrument while the other was still holding it.

Another Oklahoma showman was Gene Autry, who was from Texas. But this singing cowboy television and film star was so beloved and associated with the state of Oklahoma that he is in the Oklahoma Music Hall of Fame and has a town in Oklahoma named after him. Gene Autry, Oklahoma, postal zip code 73436. In the 1930s Autry was part of the Hollywood cowboy phenomenon that turned the nation into crazed fools for the myth of the American Cowboy. Western lapels, bedazzled suits, cowboy boots, and hats. Americans far and wide could not get enough of the image of The Cowboy.

Bob Wills is too Texas to be in the Oklahoma Music Hall of Fame, but his band, The Texas Playboys, was inducted, as was the fabled venue in Tulsa where he set up residence, Cain's Ballroom. Originally a garage in Tulsa, Cain's Ballroom flourished during the Tulsa oil boom in 1924 as a popular two-stepping joint. Daddy Cain bought the building in 1930 and named it "Cain's Dance Academy" where lessons were only ten cents. The "hot string band music" would mature into western swing as The Texas Playboys became associated with the venue and people came from all over the country to see them play.

Life was not all big band bliss in Oklahoma during this era. Because of The Dustbowl, the decade was often referred to as The Dirty Thirties. The Dustbowl represented a period of severe drought and dust storms, particularly in the mid-1930s. This natural disaster devastated Oklahoma and the plains, causing the largest migration in American history in an alarmingly brief time span. Half a million people were left homeless. Roughly 200,000 of these migrants landed in California. This staggering number explains why there are so many figures in music history with ties to both Oklahoma and California. Families moved back and forth for years during and after the Dustbowl. These migrants brought country music to the west coast, laying the foundation for the Bakersfield Sound.

Honky-tonk and rough saloons sprung up in the Bakersfield, California area, catering to agriculture and oil field workers. In the 1950s the musicians playing these joints began to incorporate rock and roll into their honky-tonk country as a blatant reaction to the more restrictive Nashville Sound coming from the East. The first track to be cut from this Bakersfield music movement was "Louisiana Swing" by Bud Hobbs. But it was the guitarist on the song who would serve as the Godfather of The Bakersfield Sound: Buck Owens. Originally from Texas, the Dustbowl forced his family west and he eventually found himself in Bakersfield. Instead of mimicking the cleanly produced countrypolitan sounds from Nashville, Buck Owens fused hillbilly, rock and roll, western swing, and even Mexican polka into his music. His success was contagious as Bakersfield became a hotbed of musical talent.

Merle Haggard was also a key figure in this music movement. Originally from Oklahoma, his family relocated to California during the Dustbowl. Merle had a rough and tumble youth, serving time in San Quentin. He claims a performance by Johnny Cash inspired him to join the prison band. He got his start with a talent show in Bakersfield but is forever associated with Oklahoma based on his patriotic hit "Okie from Muskogee". Haggard is quoted as saying, "I was a transplanted Okie. Just like a godfather to a child, Oklahoma is a 'god state' to me."

Buck and Merle shared more than just a zip code and musical talent. They shared a wife, although not at the same time. Bonnie Owens was a talented singer (also an Oklahoma Dustbowl transplant to Bakersfield) who had her first hit song in 1950 in the form of a duet with Fuzzy Owen called "A Dear John Letter". In 1951 she married Buck Owens, although the marriage didn't last. Several years later in 1965 she married Merle Haggard with whom she performed regularly. Their marriage wasn't meant for the long haul either, although Bonnie continued touring with Merle well after their 1978 divorce.

Unlike all the Dustbowl migrants, Hank Thompson was transplanted in the opposite direction when he moved *to* Oklahoma. Born in Waco, Texas, Thompson was a honky-tonk star that hosted a television variety show in Oklahoma City during the 1950s. He had a huge hit with Woody Guthrie's song, "Oklahoma Hills", and produced an album in 1969 called *Hank Thompson Salutes Oklahoma*. Hank Thompson was a hit-maker extraordinaire whose career stretched across seven decades and yielded over 60 million records. It is said that the movie *Crazy Heart* is loosely based on Hank Thompson, his rough life on the road as a honky-tonk star, and his habit of using local bands to back him in shows.

My dad was about thirteen or fourteen years old when he saw Hank Thompson at the Civic Auditorium in Ardmore, Oklahoma, which would have been around 1962-1963. He remembers Thompson playing all of his big hits like "Oklahoma Hills" and "Wild Side of Life", which is a honky-tonk standard about a wounded husband lamenting his unfaithful wife.

One of my favorite album covers of all time is *Hank Thompson and the Brazos Valley Boys at the State Fair of Texas*. When I was a little girl I would pull it out and gaze at the giant statue of Big Tex, the storied symbol of the State Fair of Texas. On this album, Hank Thompson spent several days at the State Fair and emceed the annual rivalry game between The University of Oklahoma Sooners and The University of Texas Longhorns. Called "The Red River Shootout" this game is always held in Dallas, halfway between Norman, Oklahoma and Austin, Texas. It's played in the Cotton Bowl, right in the middle of the Texas fairgrounds. The album has twelve tracks which include live sounds from the midway, rollercoaster rides, the Longhorn band, and the football game itself. My favorite part is Hank Thompson's color commentary on the game. How much would I pay to wake up every Saturday morning in the fall to ESPN's College GameDay and see Hank Thompson sitting next to Kirk Herbstreit instead of Lee Corso?

We listened to *a lot* of Hank Thompson when I was a child, and there really is no one honkier or tonkier in both sound and story. How can you not smile at his novelty song "Red Necks, White Socks and Blue Ribbon Beer", which is a patriotic anthem for the working man? I love "Six Pack to Go" as he launches into it with a cry out to the bartender before the melody even kicks in. It is a contender for Best Drinking Song of All Time. And then, there's "Honky Tonk Girl". When it comes to broken-hearted cheating songs, Thompson is best known for "Wild Side of Life", but I also really love "Honky Tonk Girl", a kicky tune with rhymes that click into place somewhat predictably, but are also very satisfying. It has an ideal cadence for two-stepping while he croons about a commitment phobic gal-about-town who leaves a wake of fools in her path. "Honky Tonk Girl" is the perfect song to analyze the evolution from western swing to honky-tonk. The elements of western swing are still present as you hear a complex choreography of instrumentals like piano, steel guitar, and fiddle. True to Bob Wills' brand of western swing, it's also very danceable. But honky-tonk slows things down a bit, focusing more on the vocals and the story just as Thompson does in this tune.

Hank Thompson certainly had an ear for honky-tonk girls as he discovered two leading female country singers. Jean Shepard was born in Oklahoma in 1933, but at age eleven her family moved to Bakersfield, California due to the Dustbowl. In high school she started an all-girl band called The Melody Ranch Girls, and they had the opportunity to play with Hank Thompson. He was so impressed with Shepard that he became an advocate for her and helped her secure a recording contract. At just eighteen she recorded a song called "Twice the Lovin' (In Half the Time)". Not only is it a really good song, it was especially racy at the time for a teenage girl to be singing about such topics. Which pretty much symbolizes Jean Shepard's multi-decade career as she was a fearless trailblazer for women in country music. At age seventy-nine, she has been a member of the *Grand Ole Opry* for more than fifty-seven years.

Hank Thompson also helped discover The First Lady of Rockabilly, Wanda Jackson. Wanda Jackson was born in Oklahoma in 1937, and just like Jean Shepard's family and so many others, the Jacksons moved to California in the '40s in search of a better life. But when Wanda Jackson was eleven years old, they moved back to Oklahoma where she later won a talent contest and landed her own radio program in Oklahoma City. Hank Thompson heard her sing and invited her to perform with his band, The Brazos Valley Boys. Jackson began touring as a country singer and later shared the billing with Elvis Presley, whom she is rumored to have dated. Later in life she said in an interview that they did go on dates here and there but it was all very innocent and they were never lovers. Regardless, Elvis did encourage her to break out of her country shell and move her sound toward rock and roll. The result was rockabilly, and it wasn't terribly well received at first. She would cut an album with a rockabilly song on one side and a country song on the other just to get some airplay. Right when she was about to cave and return solely to country, her rockabilly songs took hold and she became a national sensation.

Wanda Jackson brought a feisty spirit to her songs as well as the music industry. Often the only girl touring with all-male bands, she developed a tough veneer, and it translated into her music, both sonically and lyrically. Jackson also infused the entertainment scene with a certain panache as she maintains that she was "the first one to put some glamour in the country music – fringe dresses, high heels, long earrings." In the mid-1960s rockabilly dipped in favor with the listening public, so Wanda Jackson returned to a more country sound. Her voice, personality, and song selections have all combined to make her an enduring success through several decades as she evolved with country, rockabilly, country again, recordings in foreign languages, gospel, live television work, and a popular show in Vegas.

While her legacy is clearly rockabilly, my favorite Wanda Jackson song is one of her country tunes from the '60s called "My Big Iron Skillet". It's about a housewife who is sick and tired of her no good husband's late night carousing, so she declares she is going to whack him with a skillet. She basically decides she's either going to kill him or leave him. A cast iron skillet…there is perhaps a no more poignant or classically feminist image than turning one's stifling domestic circumstance into a deadly weapon. The ultimate power shift. And while I would never advocate any form of domestic violence, much less homicide, I do love how fierce she sounds in this otherwise upbeat ditty. Then again, she is an Oklahoma Dustbowl girl, and that's tough stock. Perhaps the real bumper-sticker advice that we should all heed is *Don't Mess With Wanda Jackson's Skillet.*

Come to think of it, I don't think I would mess with Wanda Jackson either. Or Jean Shepard for that matter. Or Merle…*ever.*

CHAPTER 4 SOUNDTRACK:

Fightin' Side of Me – Merle Haggard

(MERLE HAGGARD)

Wild Side of Life – Hank Thompson

(ARLIE CARTER, WILLIAM WARREN)

Honky Tonk Girl – Hank Thompson

(CHUCK HARDING, HANK THOMPSON)

Twice the Lovin' (In Half the Time) – Jean Shepard

(FLOYD HUFFMAN)

My Big Iron Skillet – Wanda Jackson

(BRYAN CRESWELL, WILDA CRESWELL)

CHAPTER 5

Diggin' Red Dirt

For decades one of Ardmore's long-standing mysteries was whether or not there was a secret tunnel system below the city. Allegedly, after a disastrous fire in 1895, ne'er-do-wells seized an opportunity amidst the chaotic rebuilding phase to dig hidden tunnels that started underneath the popular Dew Drop Inn drinking establishment on Caddo Street. Bootleggers, prostitutes, and pimps, not to mention errant husbands, would have an easy escape route from a pop-in visit by the law, an enemy, or an angry wife. Remnants of iron cots have been seen down there. Gasoline Alley, a prostitute from the early days, explains how "customers" would be lowered down with ropes and charged twenty-five cents a visit. Then they would signal with a bell to be pulled back up by the ropes. As Sally M. Gray writes in Territory Town, "A picture that staggers the imagination is that of Ardmore's matrons, in this very proper, almost puritanical, period riding down Main Street in their carriages, Arabesque in their head-to-toe covering – hatted, gloved and veiled – serenely oblivious to the debaucheries taking place beneath their high button boots."

For decades, eye witnesses who claimed to have ventured down into the tunnels fought the cynics who dismissed them as fiction.

Ultimately the eyewitnesses were vindicated as it has finally been proven that the tunnels do exist.

Just like the puritanical matrons Sally M. Gray describes in their gloves and boots, I was completely clueless about Ardmore's underworld when I was a child visiting my grandparents there. My life was so simple and innocent, and I was wholly unaware that an archaeological dig would require little more than a toothbrush to dust away the surface of this all-American town to reveal a much wilder history. Oh no, my tunnel vision was keenly fixed on my grandparents and all the attention they focused on me.

I loved going to Ardmore. My dad's mother, whom I called Grandmommy, was the sweetest, most gentle woman on earth. Even though she was a commanding six feet tall, she had a kind and warmhearted nature about her. You could tell she was beloved around town from the way people lit up when she walked into a store as they greeted her eagerly, "Well good morning, Mrs. Johnston!" As kind as she was, she had a mysterious method of getting her way without breaking her pleasant veneer. Like the secret tunnels, she had hidden super powers lying beneath her always-friendly character because somehow, the woman got what she wanted. An avid reader, and apparently fairly frugal, one time she took a paperback into the grocery store to return it because she didn't enjoy the ending. The dumbfounded clerk stammered, "But, Mrs. Johnston, you bought it and you've already read it. I don't think I am allowed…" She was calm but unwavering in her criticism of the story, that it was not well-written, and that she deserved her money back. Somehow she walked out with a dollar or so in change – whatever a paperback cost at the time.

It's not that she couldn't control me when I was a toddler – I'm sure she could have if she'd wanted to. She just didn't *want* me to have to do anything I didn't want to do. My parents left me with her for two weeks while they went on a big vacation, and when they returned, I hadn't brushed my hair, and it had become a veritable rat's nest with dried peach juice and marshmallow chunks in it.

On Sundays we'd attend St. Philip's Episcopal Church followed by lunch at the old A-frame style Whataburger. One time in the mid-'70s I remember sitting in church with Grandmommy waiting for the service to start when a real live hippie walked in. This guy was young, probably in his twenties, had a beard and long hair, and was wearing ratty jeans, a sleeveless undershirt, and flip flops.

He was exactly the portrait of the hippie that Merle Haggard describes in "Okie From Muskogee". This was a sensational hit song for Haggard that has survived in popularity despite much confusion about its inspiration and intent. The narrator is a patriotic, freedom-loving, conservative "square" who denounces sandal-wearing hippies, burning draft cards, long hair, and beads. Based on this persona, right-wing Alabama Governor George Wallace even asked Haggard for a political endorsement. Haggard declined because the inspiration for the song wasn't that clear cut. He has said that he wrote the song as a satirical jab at the reactionary mindset of the day. He has also said, however, that it was penned from a place of nostalgia and appreciation for an all-American parochial life. Or perhaps it was inspired just after his release from San Quentin, where he experienced first-hand what it was like to lose one's freedom, suggesting that the song is really about putting independence on a pedestal. Either way, sometimes a song just sticks as a good song because over the years fans and musicians from the right and the left have claimed it and covered it. Somehow Haggard ran the gauntlet with this one and ended up with a hit that people love to its core, regardless of what may or may not be happening below its surface.

When that hippie walked into church and sat alone in a pew, I wasn't thinking about Merle Haggard, I was simply jealous because I was awfully uncomfortable in my starched Florence Eiseman dress. Given how people were always pushing and prodding me into dress-up clothes for church, I assumed looking nice was part of the salvation process. And so I reacted with shocked indignation and pointed the guy out to my grandmother with the subtlety only a five-year-old can muster. She explained to me that God didn't care what type of clothes you were wearing as long as you were talking with him. You could wear anything you wanted to church just as long as you showed up. Seems like an obvious message, but I distinctly recall it was the first time my young mind had ever considered the concept. God didn't care about these clothes? You didn't have to dress up? Society and the dress codes of many church congregations I would experience throughout the years would fly in the face of this basic premise. But my grandmother's compassionate response planted a bug in me early on.

I was over the moon for my grandfather as well. He had movie-star good looks and a swarthy charisma about him. Despite his best efforts to remain crotchety, his charm was irresistible and everyone adored him. On the weekends my grandmother would pull a cookie sheet out of the oven that was covered in warm cake donuts. My grandfather and I would load up as many as we could onto our napkins and venture out for the morning's errands. It's hard to understand how errands, which at this stage in life are nothing more than soul-sucking, spirit-killing, unavoidable tasks on my To Do List, could have delighted me as much as they did back then with my grandfather. I'm not even sure what we did, I just remember I loved it when he would introduce me to his friends around town. I do recall we would always end our outing with a trip to the post office to check his P.O. Box. Years later, when Jerry Jeff Walker came out with his "Pickup Truck Song", I thought for sure he'd written it about me. It was about a Saturday spent with his grandfather running around doing errands, waving at acquaintances, and how, without fail, they always ended up at the post office. It would be too serendipitous except we weren't driving around in a pickup truck.

One of my favorite stories about my grandfather involves my dad's high school football career. My father was a senior, and certain colleges were interested in recruiting him to play for them, including football powerhouse The University of Oklahoma. The head coach, Jim Mackenzie, traveled to Ardmore with his assistant coach Barry Switzer. They sat down with my grandfather and my dad with the goal of getting my dad to commit to Oklahoma. But the conversation became increasingly heated between Coach Mackenzie and my grandfather. Mackenzie was in disbelief, and more than just a little bit enraged, that my grandfather would not influence my dad to sign with Oklahoma. But he viewed football as a means to an end, not the other way around, and believed my dad would have more academic accountability, and thus receive a better education, if he played football at a school like Rice or Vanderbilt.

My grandfather was a man of character in a town full of characters. You don't have to dig too deep before you stumble on numerous stories, told with pride, about the eccentric people of Ardmore. One of the most notorious was Clara Smith Hamon, the secretary and mistress of married millionaire, Jake Hamon. (Clara briefly married her lover's nephew in order to have the benefits of the same last name.) Clara shot and killed Jake, and then fled to Mexico. Ultimately she was tracked down and brought back to Ardmore to stand trial. The national press was present when the jury miraculously acquitted the town's most beloved murderess, citing self-defense. Clara parlayed her freedom into a brief career as a Hollywood actress.

E.B. Luke is another Ardmoreite I find particularly fascinating. Originally from Canada, he arrived in Ardmore in 1893. In 1918 he purchased a property on Main Street with the purpose of opening the first music store in the Territory. He made a trip to Chicago to study a music store called Bing and Goetz to copy their store design – a central glass display, elevated hardwood flooring, and ornate carvings just below the ceiling. At the time, parlor organs were in demand, so he kept six teams of horses on hand to help make his pilgrimages around the Chickasaw Nation. He was a traveling salesman, selling organs and stringed instruments out of his spring wagon. Luke evolved as music evolved, and he began to carry Victrolas, sheet music, and phonograph records. Teens would spend hours listening to music at Luke's Music Store and eventually, E.B.'s son, Edward, joined the family business. The store remained open until October 20, 1981 when two men robbed the store, beat the owner badly, and beat an employee who ultimately died. The store never reopened after that day.

One of my grandfather's friends, Waco Turner, was also one of Ardmore's most illustrious figures. Turner had vast oil wealth, and he spent much of his time and money on golf. While he didn't play the sport, he invested generously to revamp Ardmore's Dornick Hills Country Club and managed to convince the PGA to play a tournament there. He hosted elaborate parties and gave the golfers extravagant gifts, like the time he gave Byron Nelson a palomino horse. But the country club eventually tired of Turner's ornery drinking and pushed him out. So Waco Turner built his own private country club where he hosted the Waco Turner Open, a star-studded Hollywood affair. Turner would patrol the golf course in his Cadillac and fly over in his Cessna, asking his pilot to buzz the players.

Waco Turner died in 1971, so it is unlikely during the one year we overlapped on this Earth that I would have met him during those out-and-abouts with my grandfather. That said, I am pretty sure I crossed paths with at least one of Ardmore's most respected leaders. I know I enjoyed her cooking. Mazola McKerson owned a restaurant called The Gourmet from 1962 until 1977. My grandmother and I would go there regularly, sometimes to dine in, but most of the time we would pick up meals to go. As a black woman during the era of segregation, Mazola was not even allowed to be served in her own restaurant in the beginning. But times would change and Mazola would be a big part of bridging the racial divide.

As a girl she lived in poverty with her aunt who taught her how to do laundry and cook. Mazola became a housekeeper to affluent families in Ardmore. On the side she would make pies and cakes from her aunt's recipes and sell them to women around town. One day one of Mazola's customers raved about her cooking and urged her to start a catering business. Mazola claims she "didn't even know what the word 'catering' meant then." Not only did Mazola start her own catering company, she eventually opened her restaurant, The Gourmet. But her success didn't stop with food. After getting involved with her children's schools, Mazola was elected to the city council in 1977 as both the first African American and first female to serve on the city council. Then she broke more barriers when she was elected mayor of Ardmore. With this she was the first African American female in the United States to serve as mayor of a city with more than 30,000 people. Appropriately, in 1997 she was inducted into the Oklahoma Women's Hall of Fame.

In addition to good food, the people of Ardmore needed places to drink and listen to music. While there have been a number of private clubs, dive bars, and dancehalls through the years, in Territory Town Sally M. Gray notes, "For a town of its size and sophistication, Ardmore has never boasted a really nice watering hole, discounting the well in the middle of Main Street in 1895." The original drinking establishment of Caddo, The Dew Drop Inn, finally closed its doors in 1950. Around this time, The Willow Club had success recruiting national acts to come perform in Ardmore, including Bob Wills and Kitty Wells. Meanwhile, The Avalon, which boasted the largest dance floor in southern Oklahoma, was the place to step out and dance.

For whatever reason, Oklahoma has always been a musical state, and not just through the eyes of Rodgers and Hammerstein. (It should be noted that I did appear in my high school's rendition of the musical *Oklahoma!* when I was a freshman. I was cast as Calico Girl #4.) Music seems to live in the water in Oklahoma, or perhaps it lives in the dirt. Either way it's fascinating to peel back the layers and enjoy the rich musical legacies that have sprung up from this area that was once governed by Indians and later ravaged by drought. Five distinct musical movements have come from Oklahoma, and each one can be traced to a specific venue, neighborhood, or person.

1. Jazz music from the Deep Deuce area of Oklahoma City
2. Folk music with Woody Guthrie and the Dustbowl
3. Western Swing with Bob Wills and Cain's Ballroom
4. The Tulsa Sound
5. Red Dirt music

In the 1920s a jazz movement began in the African American community of Deep Deuce in Oklahoma City. Musical individuals, families, venues, and even street parties in Deep Deuce drove a musical culture that ultimately influenced the Kansas City jazz sound. National jazz and blues bands began to recruit the classically trained talent from this Oklahoma City neighborhood.

The second type of music on the list came from Oklahoma native Woody Guthrie, a folk singer-songwriter who was born in 1912. After his mother died, his father migrated to find work, and Woody was a teenager left on his own in poverty trying to survive with his siblings. He traveled between Oklahoma and California during the Dustbowl years and mingled with other musical migrant workers who played folk and blues. Guthrie began writing songs in this era and earned the nickname "The Dustbowl Troubadour". In the 1940s he moved to New York, where his musical legacy began to expand. It was in New York where Guthrie penned the classic "This Land Is Your Land". He would move on to California and Washington state as he continued to churn out songs that were political, children's tunes, or classic folk. Guthrie wrote "Oklahoma Hills", which was covered by many artists through the years including his cousin Jack, who recorded a western swing version in 1945. Hank Thompson's 1961 version is probably the best known. In the 1960s with the American Folk Revival, Guthrie's music enjoyed a resurgence in popularity. In 1966 Guthrie received The Conservation Service Award from the U.S. Department of the Interior based on how much he loved the land and respected it through his lyrics. Fellow songwriter Bob Dylan was deeply influenced by Guthrie and his music. As Dylan explains, "The songs themselves were really beyond category. They had the infinite sweep of humanity in them." Dylan would regularly visit Guthrie in the hospital through his remaining days. In 2001 the Oklahoma state legislature approved Woody Guthrie's version of "Oklahoma Hills" as the official state folk song.

The third major sound to grow out of Oklahoma was western swing, which flourished when Bob Wills and his Texas Playboys were booked as a regular act at Cain's Ballroom. Granted Bob Wills was from Texas, but his band was incredibly popular during the Cain's Ballroom years, and his musical legacy became tied up with that of Oklahoma.

The fourth musical style that hails from Oklahoma is the Tulsa Sound, which came together in Tulsa in the 1950s and 1960s. It blends rockabilly, country, rock, and blues, boasting music greats JJ Cale and Leon Russell as well as non-Oklahoman Eric Clapton. Leon Russell was the first of the Tulsa Sound gang to work his way into the Los Angeles rock and roll scene. Eventually he purchased the Church Studio in Tulsa, which became his Shelter Records, a veritable hotbed of rock activity. The likes of Clapton, Dylan, and Tom Petty all made their way through this famed studio.

At his core Leon Russell was a trippy rock and roll songwriting maverick. One glance at his album cover for *Carney* gives that away. But at the height of his L.A. rockness in 1973, he released a straight-up country album as alter ego Hank Wilson. The album was titled *Hank Wilson's Back* and just might be my favorite album cover of all time, portraying iconic images of a honky-tonker on stage and an old fashioned radio barn dance in the background. I imagine his alter was a blend of all the great Hanks in country music as there were many: Hank Williams, Hank Thompson, Hank Cochran, Hank Snow, Hank Locklin. Another interesting aspect of this record is that such a prolific songwriter would choose all cover songs *and* sing them very much in the style of their original artist as opposed to his own distinct tone. I suppose that is why he did it under a country alter ego. Despite the seeming lack of originality, there is something incredibly special about it. Perhaps it's the mega-firepower talent he recruited to play on it, including fellow Oklahoman and Tulsa Sound comrade JJ Cale, Billy Byrd who was Ernest Tubb's lead guitar player for ages, and Johnny Gimble who played fiddle in Bob Wills' band, The Texas Playboys. I don't know what the secret sauce is in this musical aberration for Leon Russell, but it works. I just about wore this album out as a child. For years I didn't even know these songs belonged to the likes of Lester Flatt or George Jones. Hell, I didn't know Hank Wilson wasn't a real person. Because in a way he was…through Leon Russell.

Willie Nelson has always been effusive about Russell's immeasurable talent, and in 1979 they teamed up on a duet album called *Willie and Leon One for the Road*. This was another album my parents had in the family collection that I would listen to for hours on end. They cover everything from Cole Porter to Gene Autry to Elvis Presley on this gem, and as only Willie and Leon can do, they pull it off in high style.

The fifth and most recent movement to come out of Oklahoma is called Red Dirt music, named for the rust or rouge colored clay dirt in Oklahoma, reddened by large amounts of ferric oxide. This sound was born near Stillwater, Oklahoma at a place called "The Farm". It was a two-story house located on rural property just outside of Stillwater, where Oklahoma State University is located. In 1979 John Cooper and Danny Pierce rented the house and that's where the lore begins. With no neighbors and just outside the reach of the town's watchful eye, The Farm became a party house. When the Stillwater bars would close, a collective cry would ring out, "Party at the Farm!" Pierce became caretaker of The Farm and Cooper was a musician, so friends and other musicians would convene in the nearby shed and jam until the sunlight hours. According to Pierce, Oklahoma native Garth Brooks would show up as well as Robert Earl Keen. While Pierce wasn't a musician, he lived there for twenty years and adopted the role of unofficial host. "I made sure there was food on the table and beer in the box and the grass was mowed, the bills were paid," said Pierce. "I was the one who charged them their rent." In a 2011 interview with *The Stillwater News Press* he goes on to say, "I never knew what to expect, you know, when I'd come home or whatever. Eventually, it changed over time, but the last 10 years, five years, particularly, the music was just outstanding. Once Bob Childers moved in, he drew people out here."

Bob Childers, an Oklahoma boy, had been in Austin before making his way home and moving into The Farm in 1990. He is unequivocally considered The Godfather of Red Dirt Music. A prolific singer-songwriter himself, earning the nickname "Dylan of the Dust", Childers also served as a muse to scores of musicians who worked out their sound at The Farm. I didn't grow up listening to, or even knowing about, Bob Childers, but when I first heard Childers' music, I got the Dylan in the Dust nickname right off the bat. With his poetry I have the sense he was running around some of the same scenes in the same era as Kristofferson. He has the gravely Americana appeal of John Prine as well as the folksy brilliance of Guy Clark.

Once in Stillwater living at The Farm, Bob Childers played and jammed with friends like John Cooper, the original Farm tenant, and Pierce's 1979 roommate, who had formed The Red Dirt Rangers with Brad Piccolo and Ben Han. Another friend and musical contemporary was Jimmy LaFave. LaFave was born in Texas but moved to Oklahoma at an early age and was deeply influenced by Woody Guthrie, JJ Cale, Leon Russell, and Bob Dylan. In an interview on the Stillwater Red Dirt website he explains the allure of The Farm back in the day. "It was a stopping place for a lot of musicians," recalled Jimmy LaFave. "It was where the drug culture met the cowboy culture...there's a lot of wild stories out of here. But (I remember) the music, the good music, and the feeling of having a tribe of people to belong to."

The generation of musicians who drew off the magic of The Farm started to influence the next pack of Red Dirt artists throughout the 1990s and early new millennium. Cody Canada, frontman for the genre-defying, rocking alt-country band, Cross Canadian Ragweed, was deeply inspired by the Stillwater scene and became a public leader for Red Dirt Music. Cross Canadian Ragweed collaborated with other Red Dirt musicians who were also beneficiaries of Childers and The Farm. Bands like Stoney LaRue, Jason Boland and the Stragglers, and Mike McClure. It wasn't a total boys' club however. Monica Taylor is an Emmylou-esque, beautiful hippie girl from Oklahoma who sings bluegrass with western swing elements. Taylor, who lived under a tarp out at The Farm behind Bob Childers' trailer home, speaks fondly of Childers as both a friend and mentor. "It was just so wonderful," Taylor said. "At night, I could hear people pulling in…and rap, rap, rap on Bob's door. And I'd wake up and go, 'Oh, must be somebody with a new song' and it usually was."

Childers eventually moved on from The Farm. The last resident to live there was Pierce in 1999. While the home burned in 2003, the shed remains and has hosted reunions in recent years, especially to honor Red Dirt's beloved godfather, Childers, who passed away in 2008. The Farm and Childers are no longer around in a physical sense, yet their impact lives on. As a musical genre, Red Dirt continues to thrive.

A new pledge class of Red Dirt artists are keeping the tradition alive. Bands like Jimmy LaFave, Jason Boland and The Stragglers, Stoney LaRue, and Cody Canada. When Cross Canadian Ragweed split up Canada wasted no time putting a new act together called The Departed. Their first album was a tribute to Oklahoma songwriters and was titled *This Is Indian Land*.

As deeply bonded as this community of musicians clearly is, even its most invested artists struggle to define it. As Jimmy LaFave explained in an interview with *Tulsa World*, "It's kind of hard to put into words, but if you ever drive down on the (Mississippi) Delta, you can almost hear that blues sound," he explains. "Go to New Orleans, and you can almost hear the Dixieland jazz. Go to San Francisco, and you get that psychedelic-music vibe. You hear the Red Dirt sound when you go through Stillwater. It has to do with the spirit of the people. There's something different about them. They're not Texans, they're Okies, and I think the whole Red Dirt sound is just as important to American musicology as the San Francisco Sound or any of the rest. It's distinctly its own thing."

If Jimmy LaFave, a prolific Red Dirt ambassador, can't find the exact words, then heaven knows I won't be able to. Though I may not be able to clearly define it, and I am certainly not the best at explaining it, I do know one thing for certain about Red Dirt music: I dig it.

CHAPTER 5 SOUNDTRACK:

Take Me Back to Tulsa – Bob Wills and his Texas Playboys
(BOB WILLS, TOMMY DUNCAN)

Oklahoma Hills – Hank Thompson
(WOODY GUTHRIE)

Home Sweet Oklahoma – Leon Russell
(LEON RUSSELL)

Staring Down the Sun – Cody Canada and the Departed
(BOB CHILDERS, JOHN COOPER, BRAD PICCOLO)

Boys from Oklahoma – Cross Canadian Ragweed
(GENE COLLIER)

The Farm, legendary birthplace of Red Dirt Music, near Stillwater OK
Photo credit and courtesy: The Red Dirt Rangers

CHAPTER 6

From the Beef Trail to the Jukebox

In the foreword I promised not to get too linear during this informal history of honky-tonk music, but I am going to make an exception in this chapter with a broad, brush-stroke account of how honky-tonk evolved from the 19th century cattle drives to the neon, two-stepping music we know and love today. There's more to this story than I could ever possibly tell, but I will highlight some landmark moments in country music's history as well as the dishier points that give it its verve.

In the 1800s honky-tonk referred to the vaudeville style theater shows along the frontier plains of Texas and Oklahoma, ultimately referring to the establishment itself. These lewd Cowtown venues served as beacons to the lonely cowboys traveling along the trail, anxious to drink, gamble, relax, and solicit sex.

Around the turn of the century, the term honky-tonk began to refer to a style of piano playing known for its tinny sound, often on out-of-tune upright pianos. If you're at all familiar with vaudeville and its upbeat piano styling, it's easy to see how the term honky-tonk morphed from variety-theater to this style of piano playing. Honky-tonk piano is very similar to ragtime piano, which was initially played by black musicians in red light districts. Ultimately black and white musicians were both playing ragtime and honky-tonk piano. The distinction between the two styles is subtle at best, but piano experts do identify certain differences, especially as ragtime became more sophisticated. For example, ragtime tends to stick closer to its more complex compositions. Pianist Bill Edwards describes the unique elements of 1950s honky-tonk piano, "It is more often than not played on a prepared piano that has been deliberately altered to sound extra bright, and often detuned in a controlled fashion. There are a lot more tricky flourishes, such as short rolls or crushes into downbeats and frequent novelty piano riffs. The repertoire choice is often towards Tin Pan Alley style rags and popular songs. The pace is usually a bit more brisk than with traditional ragtime performance."

Scott Joplin was a black pianist and composer who grew up in Texas, traveled as far as Chicago and New York as an itinerant musician, and famously lived in Missouri for a short but prolific period of time. Missouri was along the cattle drives, and Scott Joplin would have no doubt played piano in bars and saloons that would have been considered honky-tonks. In 1899 he released one of his most famous compositions, "The Maple Leaf Rag", perhaps titled after the saloon where he played in Sedalia, Missouri, called The Maple Leaf. The piece is credited with launching ragtime music as a popular genre. Hundreds of subsequent rags used it as a model, earning Joplin the moniker the "King of Ragtime Writers".

While the lines between honky-tonk piano and ragtime piano are fuzzy, it is clear this was a wildly popular form of music in the early 1900s. Many black ragtime and blues musicians were referencing the term "honky-tonk" in their lyrics well before white country songwriters would adopt the term. Honky-tonk piano would go on to influence boogie woogie piano, which was predominantly played by black musicians and designed to get people dancing. It had ties to the early Texas railroad culture, and the boogie woogie movement was often nicknamed "fast blues", "fast western", or "fast Texas" music. One of the earliest boogie woogie hits was called "Honky Tonk Train Blues" and was recorded by a piano player and composer named Meade Lux Lewis. (I'm sorry, but is that a cool name or what?) The cadence and pace of the song simulate the sound of a train flying down the rails – hardly the last time a train would find its way into a honky-tonk song.

While honky-tonk piano was gaining favor with listeners in the early 1900s, another external factor drove the popularization of this music in the early part of the 20th century: the process of publishing music.

Much of the folk music swirling around in the 1800s was part of a rarely documented oral tradition, existing before the modern recording industry took shape. Who knows what great songs we'll never hear? For that reason, I am particularly grateful to the more unsung heroes in the story of country music's history, the ethnomusicologists. (Clearly I have been looking for the right opportunity to drop that term on you like a pretentious little bomb.)

John Lomax and Cecil Sharp were two very influential ethnomusicologists. John Lomax was raised on a Texas cattle ranch that overlapped The Chisholm Trail. He grew up immersed in cowboy folk songs and was inspired to publish and promote them. After attending Harvard for graduate school he was backed by two professors to return to Texas and document these western ballads. The Texas State Historical Association describes Lomax's work in detail: "In the back room of the White Elephant Saloon in Fort Worth he found cowhands who knew many stanzas of 'The Old Chisholm Trail'. A Gypsy woman living in a truck near Fort Worth sang 'Git Along, Little Dogies'. At Abilene an old buffalo hunter gave him the words and tune of 'Buffalo Skinners'. In San Antonio in 1908 a black saloonkeeper who had been a trail cook sang 'Home on the Range'." In 1910 Lomax published a pivotal collection titled, "Cowboy Songs and Other Frontier Ballads". Even into his sixties, Lomax traveled and conducted field recordings of white and black musicians throughout the state.

An Englishman named Cecil Sharp did similar work in the Southeast. He was already the premier collector of folk music in England when he first traveled to the United States. In his own words, "Chance brought me to America in the early days of the war...and while here Mrs John C Campbell of Asheville, NC told me that the inhabitants of the Southern Appalachians were still singing the traditional songs and ballads which their English and Scottish ancestors had brought out with them at the time of their emigration." Sharp was taken by the spirit of the Appalachian mountain people and spoke effusively of their character within his 1916 collection of their folk songs. Together, the publications of Lomax and Sharp ignited an interest in white southern folk music.

In 1922 Texas fiddler Eck Robertson was the very first artist to record and release a country song before it was even considered a "country" song. He was a renowned fiddler in the old-time style. At fiddle competitions he included comedy in his routine claiming, "If you don't laugh, we will call the doctor!" He promoted himself as "The World Famous Cowboy Fiddler" and was capable of extraordinary tricks, including tossing the bow or fiddle in the air and resuming play without missing a beat. He could also play behind his back. The one crowd-pleaser he didn't seem to have down was field hollering like his rival John Wills. Both hailing from the panhandle of Texas, Eck Robertson and John Wills, father of illustrious western swing fiddler, Bob Wills, were regular opponents. Bob's father, John, taught his son to fiddle and field holler and did so in his own performances as well. At one competition John Wills beat out Eck Robertson. After the contest someone asked Eck if he'd been out-fiddled. His reply was adamant, "Hell no! He didn't out-fiddle me. That damn old man Wills out-hollered me." Word of this got back to Wills who, bolstered by whiskey, challenged Robertson to another contest later that evening. The two played all night long.

Eck Robertson was a confederate veteran, so he was eligible to play at the Old Confederate Soldier's Reunions across the South, where he met Henry Gilliland from Oklahoma. The two performed together regularly, and on a 1922 tour in Virginia, decided to venture onward to New York City to find someone to record their songs. Gilliland had a connection who got them into the Victor Talking Machine Company, where they sort of forced their way into an audition. I imagine they were hard to avoid as Gilliland was dressed as a confederate soldier and Robertson as a western cowboy. The first day they recorded two songs together, the next day Eck Robertson recorded two songs alone, "Sallie Gooden" and "Ragtime Annie". "Sallie Gooden" was released and is considered the first ever country song.

A year later Ralph Peer of Okeh Records in New York traveled to Atlanta to record Georgia fiddler John Carson. Reportedly Peer was not a fan of Carson's singing, calling it, "pluperfect awful." The public disagreed as all 500 albums sold at one fiddler's convention, indicating to Peer that there was a market for this type of music. Carson's "The Little Old Log Cabin in the Lane" is considered the first country hit.

Unless you're a Vernon Dalhart fan. Because he too is often credited with having the first country hit, and his was a *mega* hit. Dalhart was a Texas musician who trained at the Dallas Conservatory of Music. In 1924 Dalhart departed from his classical training and recorded a hillbilly version of a popular ballad called "The Wreck of the Old 97", which told the well-known story of a fatal train derailment in Virginia. His recording was an immediate sensation, the first southern old-time song to become a hit nationwide. It was a B-side song that made an impression on generations to follow. For example, the current Texas alt-country band, The Old 97s, is named for Dalhart's song, although they admit that they first came to know it via Johnny Cash's popular cover version.

As the first old-time records were being made, country radio began to develop. In 1923 WBAP radio station in Fort Worth, Texas launched the very first barn dance radio show, which featured fiddle and string music. This format was a variety country show. When the Depression arrived, people had less money to spend on records, and nightclubs had less overhead to pay live bands. Radio became increasingly popular entertainment, and barn dance radio shows cropped up all over the country. Saturday night was country night on the radio, from Texas to New York, North Carolina to California. The *National Barn Dance* radio show in Chicago popularized the format when it aired in 1924. Employee George Hay began at the *National Barn Dance* but left after a while and started a similar program in Nashville on WSM radio in 1925. Two years after that, this show would be renamed the *Grand Ole Opry*.

Of course, all these "country" milestones weren't even labeled country at this time. It was all still referred to loosely as "old-time" music. That is, until a band from Galax, Virginia ventured up to New York to record with Ralph Peer. When Peer, the producer, asked what the band was called, their lead guy replied, "We're nothing but a bunch of hillbillies from North Carolina and Virginia. Call us anything." Peer scribbled the band name "Hill Billies" in the margin of his notes. His name for the band inadvertently became the name for this entire genre of music. Ironically, the band members were anything but a group of uneducated, backwood pickers. Among them were a legislator, a store owner, and the son of a justice of the peace, but that didn't stop them from trying to copyright the term "hillbilly" once it took off. It was too late – the term had spread like wildfire. By the mid-1920s hillbilly music was what the industry called music recorded by white musicians, while race music was recorded by the black musicians. This inflexible terminology was dictated by the color of skin as opposed to the sound of the music, so it didn't account for the fact that black music and white music were actually much more integrated sonically than society was at the time. If you closed your eyes and didn't know his skin was white, you might hear Jimmie Rodgers and think you were listening to a black blues musician.

Jimmie Rodgers is considered the Father of Country Music. Born in Meridian, Mississippi, Rodgers began performing and organizing traveling shows by the age of thirteen. His father urged him to work on the railroad, where he learned the picking and vocal styles of the rail workers and hobos. Rodgers became a brakeman on the railroad, which moved him around the country to places like Florida and Arizona, but ultimately he was forced to quit this line of work when he contracted tuberculosis. At this point Rodgers recruited a band called The Tenneva Ramblers to back him on a weekly Asheville, North Carolina radio program.

In 1927 Jimmie Rodgers first recorded with New York producer Ralph Peer, who had left Okeh for Victor. Victor sent Peer to Bristol, Tennessee to conduct a series of field recordings, The Bristol Sessions. These sessions have since been nicknamed "The Big Bang of Country Music" given their profound legacy on the modern country music industry. Nineteen bands played on these recordings, but two in particular maintain a deity-like status in the history of country music: The Carter Family and Jimmie Rodgers.

The Carter Family consisted of A.P. Carter, his wife Sara, and his sister-in-law, Maybelle. The group hailed from Virginia and produced mountain gospel songs with tight harmonies. Maybelle, who became known for her unique style of guitar picking, had three musical daughters, the most famous of whom was June Carter, future wife of Johnny Cash.

Jimmie Rodgers had a tiff with his band, The Tenneva Ramblers, so he showed up to record alone. These recordings launched what is now famously considered the first country solo career. Until this point, hillbilly acts were string-heavy ensemble groups. Jimmie Rodgers was the first hillbilly artist to emphasize the lyrics and vocals of a singular lead singer as well as the first to lead with guitar. Nowadays the image of a solo artist with his/her guitar is so commonplace it's hard to realize how much of a departure it was back then. But Jimmie Rodgers was truly the first country solo star, leading with a guitar no less. Peer was impressed with his Bristol recordings and invited Rodgers to a studio in Camden, New Jersey to record subsequent songs, some of which have become country standards.

Rodgers' one-man persona related naturally to his blues influences as blues musicians were among the first to sing about the individual experience. It also coordinated naturally with the lone western drifter motif Rodgers portrayed in his performances. He was among the first to popularize the cowboy themes in modern country music. He also continued to wear elements of his former railroad uniforms, garnering him the title "The Singing Brakeman".

Packaging aside, there are substantive elements within Rodgers' music that have influenced countless artists, not to mention have given his songs a remarkable shelf life. They just seem to keep re-inventing themselves. Jocelyn Neal is a music professor at The University of North Carolina at Chapel Hill and, as it turns out, is somewhat of a nut for Jimmie Rodgers. In her book, The Songs of Jimmie Rodgers, she analyzes the lasting importance of just three of his songs:

"Muleskinner Blues"
"In the Jailhouse Now"
"Blue Yodel #1"/"T for Texas"

"Muleskinner Blues" was essentially a blues tune that highlighted some of Rodgers' most elaborate guitar solos. In 1939 Bill Monroe and his Blue Grass Boys (the "Blue Grass" is a reference to his home state of Kentucky) would cover this song in Monroe's *Grand Ole Opry* debut. This performance singlehandedly launched the bluegrass subgenre of country music, all from just one Jimmie Rodgers cover song. Monroe's version sped the tempo up considerably, which became typical of the bluegrass sound.

Next Neal discusses Rodgers' hit "In the Jailhouse Now", which he altered from a 1915 black vaudeville song, originally composed to make a statement about racism in local politics. It was popular in New York jazz circles before making its way into the hands of black jugbands. In parallel, Jimmie Rodgers re-worked a version for which his producer, Ralph Peer, aggressively claimed recording rights on Rodgers' behalf. This version has been covered by countless honky-tonk singers. It received an even wider, more mainstream audience when the Coen Brothers included it in their film *O Brother, Where Art Thou*. George Clooney's on-the-run character is trying to pass himself off as a hillbilly singer and chooses "Jailhouse" as the most prototypical southern white man song he can think to perform. But as Neal points out, the choice is ironic given the song has black Northeastern roots: "Like the characters in the film who pretended to be a hillbilly band, and who tied on their hillbilly beards to sing 'Jailhouse', perhaps the song, too, is only masquerading as hillbilly." Neal goes on to suggest that the song "may not, in fact, be any more country than an uptown fox-trot."

Finally Neal discusses my personal favorite Jimmie Rodgers tune, "Blue Yodel #1", more familiar as "T for Texas T for Tennessee". I have always loved this song given my combined Texas and Tennessee roots and used to brag it was about me until I listened to the lyrics more closely and realized the no good woman in it gets killed. Neal explains how and why "T for Texas" experienced a resurgence in the '70s with two different but related musical genres: southern rock and outlaw country. Lynyrd Skynyrd performed "T for Texas" on a 1976 live album, while Tompall Glaser sang it on the *Wanted! The Outlaws* album with Willie and Waylon the very same year. According to Neal, "Lineage and connection, especially to country's roots music, was a critical means of establishing musical legitimacy across the 1970s outlaw and southern rock scenes, each scrambling to reconnect with the image of southern, white masculinity that had been both burden and pride in the region for decades." Southern rock was leaning on Rodgers' blues foundation to set itself apart from the long-reigning British invasion rock bands. For outlaw music, the lyrics were stubborn, defiant, violent, and thus well-suited for their musical revolution against the Nashville music industry.

While I do, in fact, find all of this fascinating, I think Jocelyn Neal is missing a key point. The song is an old-fashioned bluesy, kickass, house-on-fire kind of *fun*. And the '70s rocked it.

But stepping back a little bit…"Blue Yodel #1"/"T for Texas" started a different craze at the time when Jimmie Rodgers recorded it: yodeling.

Can I get a *Yo-de-lay-hee-hoo*!?

Yodeling is often associated with Alpine regions of Europe where early shepherds yodeled in order to call their cattle and communicate with other hilltop neighbors. It is commonly thought that German and other Alpine immigrants brought yodeling to North America. But there are theories that North American Indians were already yodeling when white settlers arrived. Not to mention, black slaves arrived in the early 1600s from an area of Africa where Pygmies and Bantu were also known to yodel.

The Tyrol is an Alpine region in southern Austria and northern Italy. Recognizing the popularity of itinerant Tyrolean singers, Josef Rainer started a family singing troupe in the area called The Tyrolese Minstrels. They toured the United States from 1839 until 1843 and triggered a yodeling trend among black minstrel performers. Some claim Jimmie Rodgers saw one of the many traveling Tyrolean troupes that visited the states. Perhaps, but scholars do agree he was most certainly influenced by the black vaudeville yodeling tradition that emerged as early as the mid-1800s. The black vaudeville performers definitely saw the Tyrolean yodelers visiting from Europe and incorporated yodeling into their performances.

The American Heritage dictionary defines "yodel" as a verb that means, "To sing so that the voice fluctuates rapidly between the normal chest voice and a falsetto." The word derives from the German "jodelin", which means "exclamation of delight". According to Jimmie Rodgers expert Jocelyn Neal, "There are two types of yodeling found in country music. The first one involves quick jumps to falsetto and back within certain words, inserting mini-warbles within a word or line, sometimes merely splitting just one individual word. This was the style Hank Williams was most famous for and the style of so many other honky-tonk singers. The second type of yodeling is stand-alone phrases of complete yodels, nonsensical syllables strung together serving as an interlude in the song. This is the one Jimmie Rodgers (and The Von Trapp Family) mastered."

When Jimmie Rodgers released "Blue Yodel #1" in 1928 his yodeling took the country by storm. White and black musicians alike were imitating him. Suddenly it seemed every hillbilly or cowboy song had to have yodeling in it. Ironic, since the original Alpine yodeler in Europe in fact used yodeling to herd cattle. But instead of evolving through the white settlers and American cattle drives, the yodel came to the cowboy singer through black vaudeville.

And Jimmie Rodgers.

Rodgers never played a major radio show or the *Grand Ole Opry*, but his impact on the history of country music is profound. Not only did he popularize yodeling, he created white blues music, an offshoot of the classic 12-bar blues. His songs are covered decade after decade by artists from various genres. After just six years as a recording star, tuberculosis got the best of him. Rodgers rested on a cot between recordings in New York at what would be his final session. He died two days later at just thirty-five years old. When the Country Music Hall of Fame was created, Jimmie Rodgers was the first performer inducted, posthumously, as "the man who started it all."

From the Swiss Alps to the sandy beaches of Waikiki, in addition to yodeling, the steel guitar, which originated in Hawaii, is another exotic yet signature foundation within honky-tonk music.

Can I get an *Aloha*!?

Around 1889 Hawaiian musician Joseph Kekuku invented the steel guitar in his village on the island of Oahu. The steel guitar is a rectangular guitar played with strings facing up. The name comes not from the material of the strings, but from a steel device that players use to slide up and down the strings while picking with their other hand. Kekuku traveled the Lower 48 as well as across Europe playing with vaudeville theaters. By the 1920s and 1930s the Hawaiian steel guitar was wildly popular throughout the U.S. The steel guitar has three main phases of evolution: the lap steel, which is lain flat in the player's lap; the console steel, which has a frame or base to hold the guitar; and the pedal steel, which added pedals and knee levers. In 1953 a country steel guitar player named Bud Isaacs was the one to add pedals to the steel guitar. He first played the revised instrument on Webb Pierce's 1954 song "Slowly" and revolutionized steel guitar playing in honky-tonk music.

I've always loved the sound of the steel guitar but I didn't know its roots were Hawaiian. Now that I do, the island influence is anything but subtle in many honky-tonk songs. Take a listen to the first few seconds of any of these tunes and you might start hula dancing instead of two-stepping:

"Long Gone Lonesome Blues" – Hank Williams
"There Stands the Glass" – Webb Pierce
"Crying Steel Guitar" – Jean Shepard
"Honky Tonk Girl" – Hank Thompson

And just like that, the neon glow of the jukebox begins to feel more like a Hawaiian sunset.

Bob Wills, who formed his band, Bob Wills and his Texas Playboys, in 1933, the same year Jimmie Rodgers died, wasn't afraid to incorporate yodeling and steel guitars into his blend of jazz and blues. Bob Wills had horns, reed instruments, piano, drums, steel guitar, and by the late 1930s he'd gone electric. He would play off beat and accent the band with his impromptu field hollering, calling out "Play it boys!" or "Ahhh, now!" throughout the songs. His music had so many complex influences it could have been called western fusion instead of western swing. But swing it did because Bob Wills had one goal and one goal only – to get people dancing. Ray Benson of Asleep at the Wheel explains, "It was big band swing as much as Jimmy Dorsey, Glenn Miller, Count Basie, and Stan Kenton. The difference is that Western swing leads with the fiddle instead of horns."

Deeply charismatic, Bob Wills' personality was as much a part of the music as any of the other instruments. Tommy Duncan sang lead vocals while Bob Wills conducted the band with his fiddle bow and called out to The Texas Playboys, highlighting each musician as he had an instrumental solo. "Bob was a stylish western rogue," says Ray Benson. "He danced onstage, he was outrageous. He strutted like a peacock, unheard of back in those days." Wills smoked a cigar on stage, and while off-stage, he chatted with and charmed each and every audience member who wanted to talk after the show.

Drums were an integral part of Bob Wills' big band swing vibe. This was acceptable in Texas and Oklahoma but not so in the Deep South, where drums were considered immoral and had no place in country music. This dates back to the era of slavery when masters and overseers learned that slaves were using drums to secretly communicate with each other. When Bob Wills was finally invited to play the *Grand Ole Opry* he was told no drums, as they weren't allowed on the *Opry* stage. Wills, however, refused to play without his drums, so a compromise was reached: the drummer would play backstage from behind a curtain. At one point during the show, Wills used his fiddle bow to pull aside the curtain and reveal the drummer playing along. *Opry* brass was aghast. Bob Wills and his Texas Playboys never played the *Opry* again. For years after this incident Texas musicians would jokingly claim the *Opry* radio call sign, WSM, stood for "Wrong Side of the Mississippi".

Eventually the conservative *Opry* leadership would change this policy and allow full drum kits on stage. But not until 1974.

As Bob Wills and western swing were cranking up in the 1930s, so were Hollywood western movies. Between Jimmie Rodgers and the popularity of these films, the image of the singing cowboy reigned supreme in the '30s. Gene Autry, who started as a Jimmie Rodgers imitator, became the first singing cowboy of the silver screen. A seismic shift was underway as the image of the Appalachian mountain man was waning in favor with country music singers and fans. It was deemed too primitive while the emerging American Cowboy seemed more sophisticated and embodied the bold frontier spirit that suited the experimental sounds of western swing and emerging honky-tonk music.

This next wave of honky-tonk sound came straight out of Texas. From the vaudeville theater days on the cattle drives to the black ragtime honky-tonk piano era, honky-tonk was about to evolve into its third incarnation: white country music.

When Prohibition was repealed in 1933 people openly visited the beer halls and roadhouses in Texas. In order for the bands to cut through to the hell-raising clientele, they began to slow down their music and play it louder. Compared to western swing, this honky-tonk sound had a slower, driving dance beat with shorter instrumental solos and a greater focus on lyrics. The vocalist began to take the spotlight as the storyline of the song became more important. The 1930s may have brought liquor back, but it also brought the Depression, so working class people related to honest songs about bad luck and hard times. Honky-tonk was shaping its signature "crying in your beer" themes – raw, aching lyrics that were sometimes feisty, sometimes vulnerable, but always spoke the truth. A group of Texas musicians were fine-tuning this honky-tonk sound throughout the late 1930s.

Al Dexter was a house painter who began performing in clubs around Longview, Texas. In 1936 he recorded "Honky Tonk Blues", which is the first white country song to have "honky-tonk" in its title. Dexter would go on to run his own honky-tonk bar where he witnessed antics that inspired his future hit, "Pistol Packin' Mama".

Ted Daffan was born in Louisiana, raised around Houston, and was among the vanguard in the electrification of instruments in the 1930s. He was interested in Hawaiian music and became a steel guitarist. Also a songwriter, in 1939 he penned the first "truck" song of country music, "Truck Driver's Blues".

Daffan's friend, Moon Mullican, a Texas honky-tonk piano player, actually sang lead vocals on "Truck Driver's Blues". Mullican was known for his two-finger right-handed piano playing technique and sometimes recorded straight-up blues. Also a prolific songwriter, Mullican wrote "Mona Lisa", which was a hit for Nat King Cole, as well as "I'll Sail My Ship Alone", which I used to assume was a Hank Wilson/Leon Russell song. It has even been suggested that Mullican helped Hank Williams write his 1952 hit "Jambalaya".

Both Ted Daffan and Moon Mullican played in a western swing band called The Blue Ridge Playboys with another Texas honky-tonk great, Floyd Tillman. Tillman is credited with writing the first country music cheating song in 1949 called "Slippin' Around". It was a hit for Tillman as well as fellow Texan Ernest Tubb.

Ernest Tubb grew up on a cotton farm in Texas daydreaming of being a movie star and singing like Jimmie Rodgers. In 1936 he contacted Rodgers' widow, Carrie, asking for one of the singer's autographed photos. A friendship developed, and Carrie Rodgers took it upon herself to mentor the young talent, open doors for him, and even serve as his manager. Carrie Rodgers was able to secure a record deal for Ernest Tubb and loaned him Jimmie's original Martin guitar, which Tubb used to record and tour with in his early days. Despite two records on RCA, Tubb's career didn't take off. In 1939 he had a tonsillectomy which affected his singing style, taking him from the Jimmie Rodgers falsetto yodels to a raspy baritone. Tubb was just about to give up on a music career altogether when he switched to Decca Records. And then, in 1940 he had a mega hit with "Walking the Floor Over You". This was the first nationwide honky-tonk hit, making Ernest Tubb the first nationwide honky-tonk star.

In 1943 Ernest Tubb joined the *Grand Ole Opry*, often cited as the first to play the electric guitar on the stage of the Ryman, challenging their rule against amplified instruments. He remained a crowd favorite on the *Opry* for four decades, bolstered by hit songs such as "Waltz Across Texas", "Thanks a Lot", "Another Story", and "Tennessee Baby", which he wrote for his second wife. The lyrics include a nod to Jimmie Rodgers' "T for Texas T for Tennessee." Ernest Tubb remained so loyal in his appreciation for Jimmie Rodgers that he didn't even like fans to proclaim he was the greatest country star. Humbly, Tubb always felt that title belonged to Rodgers, and he was quick to point that out.

One time at a family dinner I was waxing poetic about the importance of Ernest in honky-tonk music when my brother-in-law lightly interjected, "Yeah, except he couldn't sing."

I tried not to choke but am sure I gasped audibly at the heresy. Keep in mind I live in Austin, Texas, where it's not uncommon to be sitting at a red light behind a car with a bumper sticker that reads, "What Would Ernest Tubb Have Done?"

Granted, Ernest Tubb was not a master vocalist, sometimes even a tad off-key. Tubb himself was open about it: "I don't care whether I hit the right note or not. I'm not looking for perfection of delivery—thousands of singers have that. I'm looking for individuality." Early on, Tubb figured out what everyone in life should recognize: know your limitations and work everything else to the nth degree. He was a tireless touring musician. He selected hit honky-tonk songs to record. He always appeared in tailored western suits and had his band outfitted to match. Ernest Tubb was known for having the best musicians in the business, and he generously highlighted them in live performances. Taking his cue from Jimmie Rodgers and Bob Wills, Tubb performed with charisma and field hollers, often calling out the name of the band member before his instrumental solo. This casual, fun banter appears on the recorded versions of his songs as well. Just listen to a few Ernest Tubb songs and you will hear him cry out, "And Leon...", "Ahh, Billy Byrd now!", "Pick it out, Smitty…", or "Ahh, do it, pretty son!"

Ernest Tubb is also famous for the record store he opened on Lower Broadway in Nashville, just around the corner from the Ryman Auditorium, where the *Opry* was performed back then. After the *Opry* he would host his *Midnite Jamboree* radio show, which still airs and is the second oldest show on the radio. For Ernest Tubb this was just one outlet where he mentored new talent arriving in Nashville. Tubb plays himself in the movie *Coal Miner's Daughter*, where he is seen helping a fresh-faced Loretta Lynn when she first arrived on the *Opry* scene.

Ernest Tubb also defined what it meant to be a star in Nashville; he set the model for all the celebrities that followed. He was the first to develop a personal relationship with his fans, often staying hours after a performance to speak with each and every one. He came to know many families of the various Texas fan clubs that would come out in droves to see him play. Grateful for his hit song, "Thanks a Lot", and equally grateful for his fans, Ernest Tubb would end a show with a grin as he flipped over his signature guitar that boldly read, "THANKS" across the back of it.

Ernest Tubb brought the Texas honky-tonk sound to Nashville and the nation, and honky-tonk became the prominent sound of country music throughout the 1940s and 1950s. Typically when people today speak nostalgically about "traditional" country music, they are referring to this period of honky-tonk. Soon after Tubb, the Hanks and the ladies of honky-tonk would come down the line. Hank Williams, Hank Snow, Hank Thompson. Kitty Wells, Jean Shepard, Loretta Lynn. Honky-tonk was marked by slow, driving beats, the guitar as lead instrument, louder electrified instruments, pedal steel guitar, string accents, and raw lyrics. In addition, honky-tonk utilized a unique singing style. Voices were stronger and more expressive than in the past, incorporating ornamental tricks and vocal flourishes. Most honky-tonk singers did not attempt the stand-alone yodeling interludes like Jimmie Rodgers and the early cowboy singers did. But they did employ the other style of yodeling with quick breaks mid-word that would transition from chest voice to falsetto for just a quick moment.

I was trying to explain all of this one time around my parents' kitchen island when my mother randomly shared, "Coloratura".

"What?" All eyes turned toward her, fascinated as to how this would be relevant.

"Coloratura," she repeated. "In my opera class, we just learned about this. It's an Italian word which describes a style of opera singing that is very elaborate and uses all these vocal breaks and tricks. Our teacher played Hank Williams in class to demonstrate. He said Hank's yodeling in country music is like coloratura in opera."

So there you have it. Lest the influences of Cowtown vaudeville, Mexican ranchera, old-time fiddling, black ragtime, black blues, Alpine yodeling, African Pigmy yodeling, big band jazz, and Hawaiian steel guitar weren't enough, we have managed to find a way to work Italian opera into honky-tonk music.

Can I get a *Bravissimo*!?

Not just a subgenre of country music, in the mid-1900s the term "honky-tonk" also described the drinking establishments where this type of music was played, either live or on the jukebox. These rough bars catered to agriculture and oil workers in Texas, Oklahoma, and California. Fights were commonplace and bands often played on a makeshift stage behind a screen of chicken wire so they wouldn't get hit by flying beer bottles. But musicians with a sense of perseverance and a renegade spirit embraced these locales and created songs with raw, honest lyrics and bluesy rock sounds.

There's a rich backstory that builds to the Golden Era of Honky-Tonk of the 1940s and 1950s, and a prolific period of country music that follows. I think I was born predisposed to love the sound of yodeling, booming voices, and a steel guitar, so I can talk about honky-tonk for hours on end – listen to it even longer. I love all of the artists who picked and crooned in the honky-tonk heyday, but to a few in particular I would like to give my ERNEST THANKS.

CHAPTER 6 SOUNDTRACK:

Thanks a Lot – Ernest Tubb

(EDDIE MILLER)

Blue Yodel #1/T for Texas – Jimmie Rodgers

(JIMMIE RODGERS)

Walking the Floor Over You – Ernest Tubb

(ERNEST TUBB)

Crying Steel Guitar – Jean Shepard

(DOLLY LONG, SHORTY LONG)

Close All the Honky Tonks – Charlie Walker

(RED SIMPSON)

CHAPTER 7

All Skaters Change Direction

Dallas, Texas isn't widely known for its ability to be subtle. The parties are bigger, the fashions more glamorous, the houses grander, and the cars flashier. My family wasn't a part of such lavish culture with extreme extravagances, but since Dallas *was* my first hometown I am pretty sure it's where I adopted my lifelong philosophy, "If some is good, then more is better." While this attitude thoroughly stresses my husband out and once did cause an inopportune fainting spell (at my own engagement party) as a result of some self-prescribed herbal supplements, all in all I'd say it has served me well in life. What can I say? I'll always have a little Dallas Girl in me.

Long before the world came to know this larger-than-life city through the eyes of the fictional Ewing oil family in all their South Fork opulence, there was a honky-tonk scene rocking the Dallas skyline. At one point, let's say around the 1940s, Dallas was one of the premier recording hubs for country music, which is hard to imagine since now that title clearly goes to Nashville. But a Dallas man named Jim Beck had a studio that was both prolific and prominent during the heyday of honky-tonk music. He discovered local Lefty Frizzell, and together they co-wrote Frizzell's first hit "If You've Got the Money I've Got the Time", which Frizzell recorded in 1950 at Beck's Dallas studio.

Frizzell's career skyrocketed from there, and he is considered one of the kings of traditional honky-tonk as well as one of Nashville's preeminent songwriters of that era.

Beck, who was also a talent scout for the labels, recorded many of the greats such as George Jones, Ray Price, Floyd Tillman, and Marty Robbins. By the mid-1950s Beck had drawn the attention of major record labels Columbia and Decca, both of whom were rumored to be moving their country recording headquarters to Dallas. But this never happened because in 1956 Jim Beck tragically died while cleaning his tape recordings with carbon tetrachloride. Apparently Beck didn't have the studio properly ventilated and the poisonous solution killed him. This marked the end of the country music recording industry in Dallas, and redirected the careers of certain stars like Lefty Frizzell. Once Beck died, the sound of Frizzell's music changed markedly as he began recording in Nashville with Owen Bradley, the patron saint producer of the Nashville Sound. Frizzell would later move to California to be a part of the Bakersfield movement.

Another factor in the Dallas post-war country music scene was a barn dance radio program called the *Big D Jamboree*, which drew remarkable talent such as Webb Pierce, Elvis Presley, and Hank Williams. It was patterned after other successful radio shows like the *National Barn Dance* and the *Grand Ole Opry*. It launched around the same time as the annual State Fair of Texas, and the luck of this parallel timing gave its 1948 debut an exponential boost. The broadcasted show was performed in front of a live audience at a professional wrestling arena called the Sportatorium. In 1953 a rival wrestling promoter is rumored to have burned the building down, causing the *Big D Jamboree* to move venues. While the Dallas-based barn dance radio program never achieved the first-tier cachet of other national shows, the *Big D Jamboree* was an important vehicle for Texas artists, often catapulting them to a much larger audience.

In 1950 Bob Wills partnered with an eccentric Dallas millionaire (and really, is there any other kind?) to open a nightclub called The Bob Wills Ranch House. Wills' involvement was short-lived, just about a year or so, as he sold out and Jack Ruby became part owner. Jack Ruby, later made infamous for killing John F. Kennedy's assassin,

Lee Harvey Oswald, was over-extended with multiple clubs and cashed out of the Ranch House in 1952. Ultimately a local country musician named Dewey Groom bought the place and re-launched it as the Longhorn Ballroom. The club booked country headliners on the weekends like Merle Haggard, Ray Price, and George Jones, and soul acts on Sundays and Mondays such as James Brown and Otis Redding. In keeping with Dallas' penchant for all things over-the-top, the sprawling venue was decorated with elaborate hand-painted western murals. The façade was made to look like an old-fashioned, kitschy western movie set, and the interior columns were designed as cactuses. Once inside, the scene was lawless, with liquor and drugs coming and going freely.

Groom's son managed the Longhorn Ballroom in the '70s and '80s and began to experiment with booking emerging punk acts. In 1978 the Sex Pistols agreed to perform at the Longhorn Ballroom as a part of their manager's marketing scheme to play a string of unlikely Texas honky-tonks for the express purpose of inciting trouble. On January 10, 1978 at the Longhorn, half the crowd was conservative country regulars while the other half of the audience was made up of progressive punk rock fans. Predictably things got out of hand with one woman storming the stage and head-butting bass player Sid Vicious, causing him to bleed profusely. Luckily it didn't stain his shirt, because he wasn't wearing one. So he dipped his fingers in his own head-injury blood and wrote "Gimme" on his bare chest.

Unfortunately I missed this historic show as I was only eight years old at the time. Plus, I had a previous commitment to eat a Salisbury Steak TV dinner with a side of tater tots, served on a TV tray while watching *Love Boat* or a re-run of *The Monkees*. I had to eat in front of the TV for fear of missing a glimpse of those madcap Beatles-imitators, much less the chance of seeing a rare episode with Charo stowing away on Captain Stubing's dreamy cruise ship.

As you can clearly see, I am a true Child of the '70s.

I grew up in a time when the Dallas Cowboys were America's Team, every household appliance – including the vacuum – and all pots and pans were avocado green, and life's most celebrated moments inevitably parlayed into a skating party. Basically there are two types of people in this world: people who know what to do when they hear, "All skaters change direction!" and people who don't. I love just about everything from the '70s. Like the blue jeans of my youth, this decade had *flair*. Not long ago I enjoyed the recurring "Midnight Special" infomercial, and I am still kicking myself for not buying the commemorative DVD set. That Guthy-Renker called my bluff; apparently it actually was a limited time offer.

I love suede vests, bellbottom pants that ring when you walk, fringe, floppy hats, and gold lamé galore. As a little tyke in the '70s my limited social calendar didn't exactly warrant the glam-rock fashions of Studio 54. A big outing for me was when my mom would take me to the state fairground to see the latest Broadway musical. I remember Debbie Reynolds coming out in her bathrobe before her performance of *Annie Get Your Gun* to let us know she was recovering from the flu, and she hoped her performance would be okay.

The 1970s is oft dismissed as a decade of superficial decadence, a pendulum swing from the substantive, mission-driven protests of the 1960s. This fluffy era coincided with my childhood quite nicely, as my early years were marked by blissful innocence, utter normalcy and zero drama. The most exotic thing in my young life was a German teacher at my preschool who taught us to count to ten and perennially sing "O Tannenbaum", the German version of "O Christmas Tree". Texas has a large German immigrant population, so perhaps this was laying groundwork for the many future hours I would spend in Texas' German biergartens, fumbling my way through the Schottische, a popular dance in Texas honky-tonks that hails from the old country. My mother taught at the same preschool, which was around the corner from our house, making our morning commute as simple as possible. At one point she had a student in her class named Michael McFarland. I didn't realize it at the time, but Michael had two family members who would impact my life, one directly, one indirectly. A few years later I would meet Michael's cousin, Mary Terry Benton, in elementary school, and she would become my best friend for life. Meanwhile, Michael's dad, whom I never met, was one of four Dallas promoters who put on the 1972 outdoor music festival that ultimately evolved into the famous Willie Nelson Fourth of July Picnic.

Like every other little girl in that neighborhood of Dallas, Texas in the 1970s, I took ballet from Mr. Bill. Mr. Bill reminded me of The Great Gazoo, that little alien who sometimes appeared on *The Flintstones* in its last, jump-the-shark season. I was elated when Mr. Bill selected me to do a lift in front of the entire class. Until he dropped me. Needless to say I retired from ballet well before I neared the toe shoe stage.

No worries, though, I had plans to fall back on my red-hot singing career, which at that point mainly consisted of singing into my hairbrush in front of a full-length mirror in our hallway. I had plenty of material to choose from as the 1970s produced fantastic music, ranging from rock to funk to country. My parents had all the good stuff in their record collection, while my burgeoning stockpile was anchored by Billy Joel's *Glass House* and Tom T. Hall's *Country Songs for Children*. I couldn't get enough of his song "Sneaky Snake", which, in retrospect, is a mildly concerning title for a children's album. I also had a double LP of the Bee Gees which I treasured. The giant square leaves unfolded to reveal an interior triptych with a headshot of a Bee Gee on each panel. Barry, my favorite, was positioned right in the center with his wild hair flowing and a bejeweled eagle necklace dangling in the vast chasm of his plunging neckline.

When cassette tapes emerged, I rolled along willingly with the new technology, not realizing these fabulous album covers would be threatened, eventually relegated to vintage stores. To reference a Bee Gees' song, it was a *tragedy*. But at the time I was thrilled to receive a cassette player for Christmas, and my first tape was Olivia Newton-John's *Totally Hot*. I was a big fan, having spent most of my time in Mrs. Baughman's second grade class daydreaming about how great I would look in Newton-John's Sandy costume from the movie *Grease* – the black satin pants and stilettos, of course, not the drippy, goody-two-shoes Sandy look. My parents had Newton-John's 1974 *If You Love Me Let Me Know* album, and while I liked singing along to the light beat of the title track, even as a kid I could tell the album was more pop than country. What I didn't realize was the controversy she stirred in Nashville at the time. That same year, in 1974, Aussie-native Olivia Newton-John was awarded Female Vocalist of the Year by the Country Music Association. Painfully, when she accepted she exclaimed how excited she was to be there and that she wanted to meet Hank Williams…who had been dead for twenty-one years. This fanned the already smoldering fire between the emerging pop sounds of the Nashville establishment and the devotees of the honky-tonk classics. Veteran country singer Jean Shepard fired back in the press saying she bet she would have known if one of the Beatles had died. Tensions between the two ideological factions were still high at the CMA Awards the following year. Reigning Country Entertainer of the Year, Charlie Rich, was set to reveal the new recipient, but when he opened the envelope and read the result, he reached into his pocket, pulled out a Zippo lighter, and quite dramatically set the card on fire. The winner was John Denver who accepted, rather ironically, via satellite from Australia.

This saccharine, pop country, tightly controlled by a conservative Nashville power structure, was precisely what the outlaw musicians had been raging against since the beginning of the decade. While the 1970s is typically viewed as a frivolous era compared to the integrity of the cause-driven hippies of the 1960s, the inverse is true of country music. In country music, the 1960s brought the clean-cut, near-perfect Nashville Sound, while the outlaw music of the 1970s swung the pendulum toward raw, poetic lyrics and purposeful experimentation with instruments and innovative sounds. When Willie Nelson was still in Nashville he made friends with Tompall Glaser, Billy Joe Shaver, and Kris Kristofferson, singers and songwriters who were on the fringe of the Nashville machine. They were considered rebels like Johnny Cash and Waylon Jennings. These friendships and collaborations generated some of the most profound songwriting of the 1970s, not to mention electric live performances. The artists called themselves "hillbillies", which connected them back to the early roots of country music. They eschewed the honest, working-man tone of honky-tonk lyrics and incorporated blues, rock, and country into their sounds. Music professor Jocelyn Neal describes their music as "electric blues, southern-fried with a helping of boogie on the side."

Of course there was some boogie. It was the '70s.

Tompall Glaser owned a studio in Nashville nicknamed "Hillbilly Central", which served as the Nashville headquarters for the outlaw movement. Hillbilly Central was a somewhat literal and wholly symbolic fortress among the other industry edifices along Music Row, a place where Glaser, Jennings and crew could retreat from the conservative establishment. It was the studio secretary, Hazel Smith, who first wrote of the group and called them outlaws, coining a moniker for an entire subgenre of country music during a time when country music was experiencing a full-on identity crisis. Ironically, a 1975 article even claimed Waylon Jennings was no longer country as he was introducing a more driving beat that ruffled the feathers of fluffy pop country. Waylon retorted, "Country music is like black man's blues. They are only a beat apart. It's the same man, singing the same song, about the same problems, and his loves, his losses, the good and the bad times." The outlaws were strong, masculine, hyper-sexual, and southern. Their sound was aggressive, hard-driving, and wild. And yet, they were poets. I think it was the most lyrical, achingly romantic era for country songwriting.

They made music for the sake of making music as opposed to being motivated by the dollar. Ironically they sold millions of records and led a rock star life of debauchery on the road. And you know the other thing about all these 1970s outlaws? They all had damn good hair. From Kristofferson's thick mane to Willie's braids and Waylon's wild man look, there weren't a lot of bald outlaw stars. You might even say they were the original hair bands of the '70s.

Like a change in temperature that triggers salmon to start swimming upstream, or the roller rink announcement, "All skaters change direction!", Willie and his outlaw compadres heeded the call to go against the flow, challenging the current. For his part, Willie departed for Austin's already vibrant "cosmic cowboy" music scene in 1971. He describes the Texas culture that drew him in, "There were long-haired cowboys and short-haired cowboys, and the air smelled different." He also noted that "everyone was getting along."

Willie was the mainstay of my family's music in the 1970s – hell, my dad had already been listening to Willie throughout the '60s. But in those Dallas years, Willie was our musical foundation. My mother recalls seeing him live at a concert on the Southern Methodist University campus as well as in the parking lot of an upscale Dallas mall called North Park, where Neiman Marcus was the anchor tenant. The Dallas

Symphony launched a ground breaking series of under-the-stars musical performances, and Willie played with the symphony – which was unprecedented at the time.

When they weren't at Willie concerts they frequented a music dive called the Texas Tea House to hear country singer Will Barnes, a local favorite known for some less-than-politically-correct lyrics and a grumpy stage persona when he didn't feel like singing a patron's request. Like Cinderella, at home with a babysitter and my TV dinner, I was relegated to hearing all their tales the morning after.

While reminiscing about all of this recently my mother had a bizarre disconnect and haughtily asked "You mean you never went to the Tea House?" She looked at me with such shock and pity.

"Yeah, mother…I was like six years old."

Seemingly unaware of the timeframe and also unafraid to pour salt in my wounds, "Oh my gosh, you missed out. I can't believe you never went there. We had the best times. Will Barnes…"

As if I don't already have a heavy enough chip on my shoulder about missing out on all the live music of the '70s. At least my parents played the good stuff around me at home and on vacation. We spent summers road tripping up to Colorado, sometimes staying in cabins, sometimes tents. We looked so scruffy in our bandanas and cowboy hats you would have thought we were traveling on the road with Willie Nelson and his band, The Family. We belted out Willie tunes along the highway, like the classic gospel songs from his *Troublemaker* album. One year we met up with my grandparents, who were vacationing in Snowmass. My mom and dad wandered into a small bar at the base of the mountain one afternoon and liked the singer casually strumming away on a stool. His name was Jimmy Buffett.

I wasn't there for the Jimmy Buffett sighting, but I do remember seeing a lady chasing after her golden retriever outside my grandparents' condo. She shouted after her dog, "Dallas Alice! Dallas Alice!"

"Whoa!" I thought. "Just like the Guy Clark song!"

We listened to a lot of Texas singer-songwriter Guy Clark, who had a song called "Let Him Roll" that tells the sad story of an old man who died while still in love with a prostitute named Alice. She was from Dallas. As a child I didn't understand all of those dynamics, but I always liked the tune. Alice shows up at his funeral and the sad scenario reminds me of a similar unrequited love in George Jones' "He Stopped Loving Her Today". At any rate, shortly after that Colorado trip I got a dachshund puppy for my birthday, effectively kicking my lame Pet Rock to the curb. I named the puppy Dallas Alice. To this day my mother maintains she was named after the golden retriever in Colorado, but we all know the truth. My childhood pet was named after a whore in a Guy Clark song.

In 1972, before I even knew my best friend Mary, her cousin, Michael McFarland's dad, was about to make music history. He was one of four Dallas promoters who had the idea to create a music festival that was a country version of Woodstock. They leased ranch property in Dripping Springs, Texas not far from Austin and spent months outfitting the locale with a stage and facilities. It was called The Dripping Springs Reunion, and Bill Monroe headlined with other Nashville heavy hitters such as Charlie Rich, Buck Owens, Loretta Lynn, Kris Kristofferson, and Waylon Jennings. Willie Nelson also played, but his name wasn't even listed on the front cover. To appease local authorities, extensive security was planned, however as it turned out it wasn't really needed. The promoters ran out of money as the show neared and didn't have enough funds to advertise. The Dripping Springs Reunion was the best kept secret in country music. Accounts vary, but while an estimated 200,000 people were expected, only about 15,000 attended the three day festival. The beefed up security had little trouble with crowd control, save a few cowboys on horseback who had to rope a naked hippie here and there.

It would be easy to label this a failure as I'm sure it was for the promoters' pocketbooks. But The Dripping Springs Reunion served as a catalyst to a series of events that shaped the future of 1970s outlaw music and beyond. First of all, the event brought attention to the central Texas music culture and cemented Austin as a permanent music hub as opposed to a temporal scene and passing fad.

In addition, there was the Billy Joe Shaver and Waylon connection that occurred. Billy Joe Shaver was an unknown songwriter who drove from Nashville to the Dripping Spring Reunion in Texas on a whim. Somehow he found himself performing his cowboy songs – it was his first time ever on stage. Backstage he met Waylon Jennings, who offered to record Shaver's songs. Back in Nashville, Waylon had little memory of this commitment and avoided Shaver's attempts to meet with him. Finally Shaver crashed one of his recording sessions, and Waylon bluntly told Shaver to hit the road. A near fisticuff ensued as Shaver threatened to beat him up if he didn't listen to his songs. Waylon acquiesced, the start of a lifelong friendship developed, and Waylon recorded his 1973 *Honky Tonk Heroes* album. All of the songs on the record except one were written, or co-written, by Billy Joe Shaver. It is one of the greatest Waylon albums of all time and a keystone among the canon of outlaw music.

But the most lasting legacy of the Dripping Springs Reunion would have to be the incarnation of Willie Nelson's now famous Fourth of July Picnic. Before the Dripping Springs Reunion, Willie had never played an outdoor festival (hard for me to believe!), and he was enthralled by the idea of it. He decided to host his own and figured the Dripping Springs ranch was as good a place as any, given it was already outfitted for a concert. In 1974 Willie Nelson hosted the first Picnic with a crowd of 40,000 and music from Waylon Jennings, Kris Kristofferson, John Prine, and Tom T. Hall. Despite critics claiming the event was "moral pollution" and the fact that Nelson was fined $1000 for violating the Texas Mass Gatherings Act, the Picnic became an annual event. Unfortunately, at the 1976 Picnic, with the largest crowd ever at 80,000, things got out of control. There were 140 arrests, four kidnappings, and three rapes. Lawsuits flew at Willie and the event's reputation made it difficult to secure a venue for subsequent Picnics. Through the years it has been held at various places including Luckenbach, Texas and Billy Bob's in Fort Worth. The Picnic routinely drew big name acts from Ernest Tubb to Jimmy Buffett, Ray Price to the Pointer Sisters, and Johnny Cash to The Grateful Dead.

My parents always wanted to go to one of the Picnics but couldn't work it out logistically with a young child in tow. So they started hosting an annual party in our humble Dallas backyard at the same time Willie and friends were rocking down in the Hill Country. They called it The Willie Nelson Fourth of July Picnic Annex, and it, too, was epic in its own way. Preparation took days. My dad had washtub after washtub filled with ice and beer. Speakers were placed out of windows and all around the backyard. We blared Willie Nelson and other outlaw acts for hours as the party rolled on all day and well into the night. I was shocked when my mother, who doesn't even drink, reminisced, "Oh, and we smoked everything!"

"Mother!"

"Food, Christine. We smoked tons and tons of food."

Hmmm, plausible, I suppose. Then again, there was the year Daddy ended up on the roof.

As it turns out, there's not always a big announcement over the loudspeaker when it's time to change directions. Life is not a roller rink and sometimes an era just fades away, seasons change. Cassettes evolve into CDs and roller skates are replaced with rollerblades. But I continue to romanticize this decade of music and musicians and live with a longing ache, a feeling like I missed the party. I was there on a technicality, but way too young to get in the middle of it. Still, I'm lucky my parents introduced me to all of this outlaw music and held in high esteem some of the best values and characteristics of its musicmakers: the importance of creative pursuit, the need for risk-taking, and a spirit of independence, innovation, and benevolence. I may not have been able to boogie down on a ranch in front of Willie and Waylon and Kristofferson, but it was a period of enchanted innocence for me. It was a perfectly protected moment, suspended there in time. Life for me in Dallas, Texas in the '70s was, in fact, nothing short of a picnic.

CHAPTER 7 SOUNDTRACK:

Devil in a Sleeping Bag – Willie Nelson

(WILLIE NELSON)

Black Rose – Waylon Jennings

(BILLY JOE SHAVER)

Honky Tonk Heroes – Waylon Jennings

(BILLY JOE SHAVER)

Let Him Roll – Guy Clark

(GUY CLARK)

Put Another Log on the Fire – Tompall Glaser

(SHEL SILVERSTEIN)

Christine and her parents on a summer trip to Colorado, circa 1976

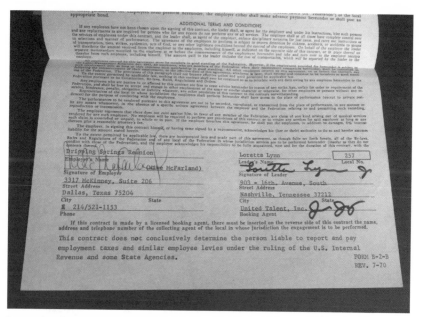

Loretta Lynn's contract from the 1972 Dripping Springs Reunion
Photo credit and courtesy: Michael McFarland

Napoleonic Clear Channel

When it comes to good times, people from Louisiana exist on a whole different wavelength. I've been blessed with many friends from this colorful state through the years and the verdict is unanimous: people from Louisiana are always the most fun people in the room. As the saying implies, they have a *je ne sais quoi* that is hard to pinpoint, much less replicate. Perhaps it's living near swamps and bayous, or maybe it's something in their alligator pie or the Tabasco running through their veins. Whether it's the Creole influence or the sounds of Zydeco, it's plain to see that Louisiana folk are a unique breed. They are eccentric, good-hearted, boisterous, and superstitious. Louisiana people remain proudly tied to their history and traditions, and yet they are anything but closed off, noted for welcoming strangers and visitors with open arms.

Perhaps it's the Napoleonic Code, in part, that makes them different. Louisiana is the only state in the country that operates under the Napoleonic Code as opposed to Common Law, which governs the other forty-nine states. I've made a cursory attempt to learn the difference between the Napoleonic Code and Common Law, but I got about as far as a YouTube clip of Marlon Brando explaining it in *A Streetcar Named Desire*, which I am told isn't entirely accurate.

What I have gleaned is that unlike Common Law, Napoleonic Code isn't mandated to follow precedent; the judge is instead left to interpret the law. Having spent time on Bourbon Street it would seem the judges there take a very *laissez-faire* interpretation of the law. Have you ever had a friend from New Orleans visit you? There's always that awkward first morning when you hand them a muffin with orange juice, and they look at you like a dog that just heard a high-pitched noise as you try to explain that there is no place in your town to get a liquor drink at nine o'clock in the morning that they can then carry down the street in an open container...at least not legally. Is that a result of Napoleonic Code? Apparently this legal system is fairly specific because many Louisiana lawyers displaced by Hurricane Katrina were worried they wouldn't be able to pass bar exams in other states. Obviously I don't know the intricacies of Napoleonic Code, but one thing is clear: like everything else in the state of Louisiana, it's not common.

My friend, Mary, had family from Louisiana, and they were my first introduction to this quixotic state. Mary and I met in the first grade, and while we did have a brief rivalry – a love triangle actually – over a kid from Japan named Michao Fuchuta, we ironed out all of our differences by second grade when we were elected class president and vice-president. From that point on we were best friends and remain so to this day.

Mary was blond, zany, and smart as a whip. Since my failed ballet lift incident I preferred to stay firmly rooted on the ground, but Mary loved gymnastics and was constantly cartwheeling or flipping herself from one side of the room to the other – I pin it on those wacky Louisiana roots. Mostly she was known for her megawatt laugh, which was *extraordinarily* loud and raucous and came from an unbridled spot in her soul way deep down. That laugh drew all kinds of attention our way through the years. Like the time in eighth grade when we decided to learn how to shotgun beers. We'd seen John Cusack do it in the movie *The Sure Thing*, but we had to use 7UP since we were only fourteen. We snuck down to her parents' kitchen at about two in the morning, dressed in towels and bathing suits, prepared for a mess. We punctured those 7UP cans and started guzzling from the bottom, but it never worked quite like it did in the movie and we were covered in 7UP. Mary's laugh was about as discreet as a car alarm going off in the middle of the night, and the next thing you knew, her mother was standing over us in her nightgown and tearing into us, "Makes me feel real good to know I've raised a couple of idiots!"

And that's how close our families were – our parents each helped raise the others' kid. We joked that her parents were my "surrogates" and vice versa. Our parents became dear friends as well, and frankly, we wouldn't be as close as we are without them supporting our friendship through the years. Mary and I were only in school together in Dallas for about four years total as my family moved away, moved back, and then moved away again. We didn't have Internet, email, cell phones, or social media to stay in touch. We wrote letters, talked on the phone constantly, and traveled together as often as possible. Family vacations, spring breaks, long weekends, summer camp. Our families even spent Christmas together a few times. As an only child one might think I had moments of loneliness as a kid or as a teen, but I never did. I had Mary. I had a sister.

Mary's father, Marsh, was an English professor at Southern Methodist University, so her parents' dinner parties were like a salon gathering of affable intellectuals who analyzed literature under the influence and played piano well into the night. Mary's mother, Toni, short for Antoinette, hailed from Louisiana. Mary's grandmother and aunts and cousins all lived in Ruston or Monroe, which are towns in North Louisiana, just east of Shreveport and of a slightly different scene than the Creole culture people tend to associate with the state. North Louisiana is the most typically "southern" part of Louisiana. Which explains why there were so many double names in her family, and if someone didn't have a double name, the middle name was often thrown in for balance. Mary Ansley, Dorothy Dell, Mary Helen. Grandmother was the matriarch and certainly set a standard for Deep South charm. She spruced up every single day of her life, and everyone in the family dressed elegantly for holiday meals as well. But this crowd was anything but stuffy and formal. They rolled into Dallas en masse as theirs were always large gatherings, and they were warm, hospitable, and full of hugs. They were as genuine and expressive as a honky-tonk song….and they certainly knew a thing or two about projection. This group was *loud*. They laughed well, dined well, and of course, imbibed with gusto. At just eleven or twelve years old it was nothing for us to hear Grandmother call out from her throne in the living room to Mary, using her double name of course, "Mary Marshall, make me a drink and let the jigger run over!"

Louisiana brings something special to the table, that's for sure. They even have a term for it along the Gulf Coast, "lagniappe", which means *a little something extra*. As my husband says, "If you can figure out what makes people in Louisiana so unique, you might as well go ahead and find the cure for the common cold." They operate on a different frequency, and they channel their distinct personality right into their parties, their food, and their music. While most people equate Louisiana with Zydeco, the northern part of the state is just as honky-tonk as its Texas, Arkansas, and Mississippi neighbors. It was here in northern Louisiana where a single radio station changed the landscape of country music.

The Red River serves as the border between Texas and Oklahoma and flows into Shreveport, Louisiana before joining the Mississippi River Delta. I think the river must have carried some of the honky-tonk rich sediment from Texas and Oklahoma and deposited it in Shreveport. Because in 1948 Shreveport radio station KWKH created a barn dance country program called the *Louisiana Hayride* that would springboard the careers of infinite music legends – and I mean some *really big ones*. Even if you don't know squat about country music you've heard of these guys. (Teaser: a soft-spoken rockabilly kid from Tupelo, Mississippi predestined to be rock and roll royalty as well as a guy who mostly dressed in black.) With over 600 barn dance radio programs across the country at the time, it's hard to say why the *Louisiana Hayride* rose to prominence as the number two show just behind the *Opry*. Then again, it's Louisiana. Perhaps applying Napoleonic code subconsciously or maybe even on purpose, the *Louisiana Hayride* tossed precedent aside and always did things just a little differently.

Horace Logan was the *Hayride* producer and, toward the end of his life, he wrote a book about the show called <u>Louisiana Hayride Years: Making Musical History in Country's Golden Age</u>. At the outset he addresses a few factors that contributed to the show's success. First, being close to East Texas, they recruited Texas honky-tonk talent and a fan base across the border. Second, the timing seemed right after WWII as people were buying automobiles, living large, and embracing entertainment. Finally, unlike other cities of similar size, Shreveport had KWKH, which was a 50,000 watt clear channel radio station.

Here's my best attempt at explaining clear channel radio. In the 1920s, the broadcast industry was motivated to provide radio to underserved rural areas. Certain radio stations were granted a clear channel license. A clear channel station is an AM radio station that operates at a whopping 50,000 watts. *Yes, that's a lot.* Fans nicknamed these powerful radio stations "flamethrowers". For reasons that scramble the brain (i.e., a more reflective nighttime ionosphere, solar interference during daylight hours, ground waves versus airwaves) the signal of these AM radio stations would span much farther at night than they would during the day. So on a Saturday evening the *Louisiana Hayride* on Shreveport's KWKH reached all the way to the Pacific Ocean and covered most of the country.

WSM in Nashville, home station of the *Grand Ole Opry*, was also a clear channel station. But the *Opry* only accepted a performer who already had a hit song or was a proven star. The *Hayride* was known for sourcing unknown talent, thus young singers were clamoring to get on the *Hayride* from the first moment it aired in 1948.

One of these up-and-comers who hounded Horace Logan for a spot on the show was a lanky kid from Montgomery, Alabama named Hank Williams. Hank's Alabama-based career had garnered a bit of attention, as had his penchant for drinking. Logan gave him a probationary period to stay sober and after a few months of checking in on him, invited him to perform on the *Hayride* on Aug 7, 1948. There was a live audience of 3,800 in the Shreveport Municipal Auditorium, but thanks to clear channel radio, this performance was Hank Williams' debut to a national audience. He sang a tune called "Move It on Over", an uncharacteristically upbeat and lighthearted song in contrast to his well-known canon of sorrowful ballads. The crowd went nuts.

Logan describes Hank as having an elusive sex appeal, an ability to melt women with a single glance, all the while appealing to the male gender as a perennial southern man's man. Perhaps a precursor to the ultimate hip-wiggler that would grace this stage a few years later, Hank gyrated his hips and swayed his knees in a way people had never seen. The reaction from the live audience fueled his performance, which was no doubt felt through all 50,000 watts. Each *Hayride* performer was allotted two songs, encores were dictated by audience applause. On his first night Hank Williams encored *seven times*, a *Hayride* record that would never be broken. According to Logan, the only reason it wasn't more than seven was because the show simply ran out of time. With one broadcast the nation fell head over heels in love with Hank Williams.

Horace Logan offered him a three-year contract on the *Louisiana Hayride*, so Hank moved to Shreveport with wife, Audrey, and her young daughter, Lycrecia. In his touching narrative it's clear that Horace Logan cared deeply for Hank Williams, serving as both mentor and friend. Logan claims that Hank was as gentle and kind as he could be – when he was sober. But his addiction to alcohol, pills, and, frankly, Audrey, made Hank wild and erratic. Still, his performances on the *Hayride* continued to grow his fan base. In 1948 and 1949 Hank Williams and the *Louisiana Hayride* put each other on the map.

Hank's fame reached meteoric proportions with his hit song, "Lovesick Blues". Originally a Tin Pan Alley tune, Hank's version features a Hawaiian-style steel guitar and yodel-rich vocals that he delivered with a writhing little dance on stage. After one performance he commented to the steel guitar player, "I don't know if people really like the song that much or if they just like to see me tie myself in knots tryin' to sing it." Regardless, Hank had a hit song, and the *Opry* came a-calling. Horace Logan wasn't about to stand in the way of such an opportunity and agreed to release Hank from his contract with the *Hayride* on one condition: he had to get sober first. Hank entered a sanitarium, gave a touching farewell performance on the *Hayride*, and made his way to Nashville and epic country music stardom.

Tragically, Hank died on New Year's Day 1953 at just twenty-nine years old. On a personal level, Logan felt that the *Opry* had leveraged the lifeblood out of Hank and then merely spit him out once he was depleted. Logan couldn't reconcile how they worked him to the bone in the face of his obvious health issues, kicked him to the curb, and then after his untimely death, took all the credit for discovering him.

When Hank left the *Hayride* for the *Opry* he established a pattern that would repeat itself time and time again. Horace Logan would source new talent and develop them on the *Hayride*, which then served as a greased pipeline straight to the *Opry*. Logan didn't seem to stand in the way of his talent once the invitations came, but a professional rivalry between the *Hayride* and the *Opry* lasted for years. Logan even joked on air, regularly calling the *Opry* "the Tennessee branch of the *Louisiana Hayride*".

Did I mention that people from Louisiana also have a damn fine sense of humor?

It was another homegrown Louisiana boy who stepped in and filled the void after Hank's passing. When Hank left the *Hayride* many claimed it would be the nail in the coffin for the young show. But a persistent singer from West Monroe, Louisiana proved everyone wrong. Webb Pierce hounded Horace Logan for a shot on the *Hayride*, but Logan repeatedly told him he was just an amateur and needed more experience. Once Pierce had that experience, there still wasn't much Logan could do because the big boss at the radio station held a grudge against Webb Pierce over an incident when Pierce once interrupted a KWKH news broadcast. Ultimately Logan gave Pierce a chance on the *Hayride* by omitting his name from the payroll so his supervisor wouldn't notice. When the bossman figured things out, he went ballistic and demanded Pierce get the boot. Logan quit the *Hayride* and stayed home for a few days until his manager realized there would be no one to emcee Saturday night's show, so he conceded full authority to Logan to make all talent decisions.

Webb Pierce had the first of his many honky-tonk hits with a song called "Wondering". Pierce refused to take singing lessons as he wanted to sound "individual". He tended to raise the pitch of his voice on the final note instead of going down like most singers. His unique vocal style combined with the revolutionary pedal steel guitar sound on his hit song "Slowly" created Pierce's one-of-a-kind sound. After displaying so much perseverance to get into the game himself, Pierce was also known for mentoring younger artists. He brought a whole new wave of talent to the *Louisiana Hayride*, including singer Faron Young from Shreveport, piano player Floyd Cramer, also from Shreveport, as well as famed steel guitarist Jimmy Day. Day came to the *Louisiana Hayride* straight out of high school in Tuscaloosa, Alabama. With countless hit singles, Webb Pierce became known as the "King of Honky Tonk" and ultimately moved on to the *Opry*. Apparently you can take the boy out of Louisiana, but you can't take the Louisiana out of the boy, and Nashville didn't embrace his flamboyant lifestyle. Like other country celebrities, Pierce wore elaborate Nudie Cohn suits. But he also commissioned Cohn to line the interior of two convertibles and "embroider" them with silver dollars. He built a swimming pool in his backyard in the shape of a guitar and charged admission to view it. An estimated 3,000 tourists came each week drawing the ire of his neighbors, including a fellow singer who sued him over the unwanted foot traffic on the block.

In addition, the *Opry* wasn't keen on his enterprising radio investments or sideline music publishing business, so he earned a reputation in Nashville as a rebel. Pierce left the *Opry* in 1956, returned a year later, and then left shortly after for good. His rejection of Nashville prevented his being inducted into the Country Music Hall of Fame in a timely manner. Just before this important musician's death in 1991, he still hadn't received the votes to be admitted. I suppose time heals most wounds as he was finally inducted in 2001. I am a huge Webb Pierce fan and feel it's a travesty that it took as long as it did. There is no greater ambassador for the Golden Era of Honky-Tonk than Webb Pierce.

Horace Logan struggled to find "girl singers", as they were called back then, relegated to singing backup and duets with male acts. The one he did have on hand from the *Hayride*'s inaugural broadcast was Miss Kitty Wells. Born Ellen Muriel Deason, she started her career in Tennessee singing with her sisters until she married and started performing with her husband, Johnnie Wright, and his brother-in-law, Jack. It was standard in those days for women to sing as part of an act, typically a family act. There were no solo female country singers at the time. Johnnie found her given name too hard to remember, so he renamed her Kitty Wells after a character in a folk song. They had a brief shot on the *Opry*, but the *Opry* dropped them, and so they joined the original cast of the *Louisiana Hayride*. When Johnnie and Jack signed with a new record label, they hired a new bass player. But there wasn't enough room in their DeSoto station wagon for this extra body, so someone got the boot – Kitty Wells. Johnnie figured she was tired of performing and was ready to retire anyway. But Horace Logan claims her feelings were deeply hurt, and she asked if she could still sing on the *Hayride* as a female soloist. Who would have known Horace Logan was going to pave the way for the future wave of feminist honky-tonk singers when he made one simple decision…he agreed.

Logan needed all the girl singers he could get, so he arranged for Floyd Cramer and Jimmy Day to back Kitty Wells, which gave her a much more modern sound. After just a few short weeks appearing solo on the *Hayride*, she caught the attention of a Nashville songwriter who asked her to record one of his tracks. It was the first ever "response" song, directed squarely at the lyrics of Hank Thompson's hit "Wild Side of Life". In Thompson's song, the singer/narrator bemoans the fact that his wife was destined to be a cheating honky-tonk angel. Without much thought to the message, Kitty Wells agreed to record the response song, "It Wasn't God Who Made Honky Tonk Angels", which conceded the wife's infidelity but puts part of the blame back on the cheating husband. The message was avant-garde for 1952, but it struck a chord with fans and was an immediate red-hot hit. Kitty Wells was the first woman superstar of country music. From Loretta Lynn to Dolly Parton, there isn't a female country star who doesn't direct all the credit back to Kitty Wells.

I find it fascinating, and deliciously symbolic, that there was no place for a talented girl in the domestic, grocery-getter, housewife *station wagon*. While the girl singer seemed the most expendable, husband Johnnie and brother-in-law Jack were soon backing up the great Miss Kitty Wells, star of the *Louisiana Hayride* and later, star of the *Grand Ole Opry*.

Clearly she didn't hold a grudge since she and Johnnie were married until his death, nearly seventy-four years. Blessed with both marital and professional longevity, Kitty and Johnnie closed their 2001 retirement concert with their 1968 duet "We'll Stick Together".

And just to add to her diverse feminine charm, Kitty Wells was reportedly an incredible cook.

And now it's on to a different Johnny from the *Louisiana Hayride*...no, not that one. Patience, friend. Next I'd like to talk about Johnny Horton, nicknamed "The Singing Fisherman". Horton was from Tyler, Texas, but thanks to DNA passed down to him from his itinerant carpenter father, he was a bit of a roamer. After securing a gig on the *Louisiana Hayride*, he settled down and made Shreveport, Louisiana his home. Johnny Horton loved, and I mean *loved*, to fish. He was so broke during certain points of his career he took a Monday-Friday job at a local tackle store. Despite the hit songs that came his way, he declined invitations to perform on the *Opry*, unlike most of his *Hayride* brethren who had the same choice to make. My favorite Johnny Horton songs are "Honky Tonk Man" and "Battle of New Orleans". Most people probably know Horton's "Honky Tonk Man" because Dwight Yoakam later had a hit with it. If you play Horton's version you can hear the rockabilly bones in the song that likely attracted Yoakam to the tune.

I suppose "The Battle of New Orleans" sounds like a silly novelty song as it tells the tale of defeating British soldiers by shoving ammunition up an alligator's butt as a substitute for a non-working cannon. But this is one of the few songs that will actually get my dad singing, so it's always been considered a family favorite.

Despite professional success, Johnny Horton was weighted down by the eerie connections his life had to that of Hank Williams. Johnny Horton and Hank overlapped briefly on the *Louisiana Hayride*, and as Logan describes it, they shared a mutual respect for one another. Not long after Hank's death, Johnny Horton surprised the music community, and I'm sure many others, when he married Hank's widowed second wife, Billie Jean. While this seems mildly intriguing to me, it's not all that shocking given the circles they all ran in together. But Horton was a spiritual man, albeit governed by a somewhat misguided version of spirituality. He became deeply consumed by premonitions of his own death, convinced he was going to go suddenly. He was obsessed with communicating with Hank's ghost, traveling as far as Mississippi to attend organized séances to speak with him. In 1960 Horton visited fellow *Hayride* musician Merle Kilgore and told him he felt he was going to die within the week, at the hands of a drunk at one of the bars he was about to play in Texas. He gave a guitar to Kilgore, who tried to hand it back to Horton, but Horton insisted he take it.

To some degree, Johnny Horton's vision came true. Horton headed out to Austin, Texas where he played the famed Skyline Club on November 4, 1960. On his way back to Shreveport in the middle of the night, his car was struck by a drunk teenage driver, and Johnny Horton was killed near Milano, Texas.

Johnny Horton had been driving right near Milano, Texas seven years earlier when he received the news that his friend Hank Williams had died. And the last place Hank Williams ever played before *his* untimely death? Also the Skyline Club in Austin, Texas.

The *Hayride* shined bright with the likes of Johnny Horton and Hank Williams, and they each left an irreplaceable void in their wake. That said, Horace Logan wasn't done creating megastars.

Logan says Elvis Presley was an extraordinarily shy kid when he showed up in Shreveport for his first *Hayride* gig. Elvis arrived early on Saturday and asked if he could tour the auditorium so he would have a feel for it before the show. Elvis was notably shaken after his last large-scale performance, which was on the *Opry*. Audience reaction was flat, and the *Opry* execs didn't waste a second scooting Elvis out the door. That was Elvis' one and only *Opry* appearance; he swore he'd never go back, and he kept that promise.

For his debut *Hayride* performance Elvis sang "Blue Moon of Kentucky", a classic Bill Monroe tune. You'd think this would have pleased the country fans, given Bill Monroe was the Father of Bluegrass. But Elvis' version didn't exactly send the audience into a frenzy of applause; he didn't even receive an encore. The country traditionalists in the crowd didn't know what to make of Elvis' oily, combed back hairstyle, his dandy bow-tie, and weathered sport coat. He stuck out like a bull in a china shop, even his sidemen were clad in western shirts. But Horace Logan knew Elvis was already getting a following among younger rockabilly fans, so he kept him on. And sure enough, the young people started coming to the shows. Elvis gained confidence with each performance and soon, Horace Logan was offering Elvis a contract to become a *Hayride* regular. He was so young his parents had to sign alongside his name. Thanks to Shreveport's "flamethrower" radio station Elvis took the entire country by storm and became *ELVIS*.

Like others before him, Elvis asked Horace Logan if he could be released from his contract to chase a bigger opportunity. But instead of Nashville, Elvis was headed to Vegas. Elvis even calculated the number of Saturday nights left on his contract and paid the equivalent $10,000 to buy out his contract. Of course the benevolent Logan released him, but he asked Elvis to come back and play one last grand hurrah farewell show with proceeds going to a local charity. Elvis agreed. They moved the farewell performance to a larger venue, and the show was so well hyped that the crowds were out of control. After the performance, no one would leave for fear they might miss another encore. Women were climbing on cars outside and breaking into second story windows trying to get a glimpse of Elvis backstage or in a dressing room. But there were no more encores coming. Elvis was already long gone and try as he may, Horace Logan couldn't seem to convince anyone of that. Frustrated, he finally spoke firmly into the microphone, "Elvis has left the building."

A simple phrase that would go viral well before the world even knew what it meant to go viral.

Just when you'd think Horace Logan had done his part to source and develop not one but *two* of America's most enduring cult music icons with Hank Williams and Elvis Presley, Logan had yet another brilliant find on the horizon for the *Louisiana Hayride*. The Man in Black.

In 1955 Johnny Cash was still working as a door-to-door salesman when Logan gave him a spot on the *Louisiana Hayride*, which had a wide-spread reputation by this point. In Cash's own words, "*Hayride* had made stars out of long shots and unknowns before – not once but lots of times." Cash himself need look no further than Hank Williams, Kitty Wells, Webb Pierce, Faron Young, and Elvis Presley to know a spot on the *Hayride*, with its national exposure, was just the shoehorn he needed. Cash debuted on the *Hayride* with two songs, and the audience demanded more. He encored with a song that had not yet been released, "Folsom Prison Blues". It was the first time this renowned tune was ever played on national radio.

From this point, his rise was swift. He started receiving *Opry* invitations the following year but stayed on with the *Hayride* through the remainder of his contract. By the time he did move on from the *Hayride*, Johnny Cash was even bigger and grander than the *Grand Ole Opry*. He didn't need it to boost his career, which had already crossed over to genres beyond country. Ultimately he did start making regular appearances on the *Opry*, but maintained his own touring schedule and television show. After Johnny Cash left the *Louisiana Hayride* he bought a full page ad in *Billboard Magazine* that read, "I want to thank the *Louisiana Hayride* and Horace Logan for everything they've done to further my career." Logan shares that no other gesture in the music business touched him so deeply.

The tenderness with which Logan writes about each of these celebrities is heartwarming. Clearly these were much more than professional engagements – they became lasting friendships. He formed a brotherhood with Hank Williams, Johnny Horton, and Johnny Cash. Music has the power to bring people together as family where bloodlines sometimes stop short.

The *Louisiana Hayride* radio show ended in 1958 after 550 consecutive Saturday nights on the air. Horace Logan's book offers an intimate view behind the curtain, a look at the personalities and relationships that brought this program to life. Every Saturday night for 550 weeks straight, they made dreams come true in North Louisiana. And the energy was contagious, clearly highly communicable as it spread easily through the air to the rest of the country. Could the *Hayride* have been what it was in, say, a conservative town like Nashville? A midwestern town like Chicago? Texas produced immeasurable talent – why wasn't the *Big D Jamboree* as successful as the *Hayride*? It launched the exact same year, and it too was a 50,000 watt clear channel. Maybe the *Hayride* was the product of perfect timing, personalities, innovation, and good old-fashioned Louisiana magic. After all these years, I am no closer to pinpointing what makes Louisiana special than I am to curing the common cold. The alligators, the swamps, the spices, the superstitions, Mardi Gras, the roux in their gumbo. Maybe it's all of it, maybe it's none of it. I still don't have a clear grasp on the Napoleonic Code either, but I suppose if I really wanted to understand it I could ask my friend, Mary, to explain it to me. She's turned out to be a successful attorney in Atlanta – I'm quite sure the only tax law partner in her firm with a laugh so loud and booming it could reorganize the ionosphere. She may not deal with Napoleonic Code much in Georgia, but Mary is anything but common law. She has been there for me through every phase of my life, every zenith, every dark valley. We may be states apart, but a quick signal from either one of us and we are on the phone with each other, sometimes for hours on end if that's what it takes. Like the *Hayride* crew, our magic extends well past our geography, and what we don't have in bloodlines, we make up for on the airwaves.

CHAPTER 8 SOUNDTRACK:

Move It on Over – Hank Williams
(HANK WILLIAMS)

You're Not Mine Anymore – Webb Pierce
(TEDDY WILBURN, WEBB PIERCE)

Making Believe – Kitty Wells
(JIMMY WORK)

Honky Tonk Man – Johnny Horton
(HOWARD HAUSEY, JOHNNY HORTON, TILLMAN FRANKS)

Folsom Prison Blues – Johnny Cash
(JOHNNY CASH)

The Louisiana Hayride
Courtesy: LSU-Shreveport Archives and Special Collections

CHAPTER 9

Don't Ask, Don't Rotel

In 1980 my father's bank job transferred him to London, so we left Texas and moved to England just before I started fourth grade. It was the era of hostile takeovers, <u>The Official Preppy Handbook</u>, and trying to figure out who shot J.R. Imagine my surprise to travel all the way across the Atlantic Ocean, the farthest from Texas I had ever been, only to discover that all of Europe had been seized by the "Who Shot J.R." phenomenon. There were stickers in store windows, t-shirts, posters. When people asked us where we were from and we said "Dallas" they crowded around us like paparazzi swarming the royal family. They couldn't separate fact from fiction, curious to know if we'd ever met Miss Sue Ellen or if Lucy was actually that pretty in real life. We tried to deflect attention by vaguely saying we were from Texas and not mentioning Dallas, but that wasn't enough. One of my dad's Texas banking colleagues even considered removing his name, J.R. Erwin, from the nameplate next to the buzzer at his apartment because too many Londoners wishfully read it as J.R. Ewing. I suppose they believed J.R. might really be stashed away inside this London flat recovering from his gunshot wound without bothering to tell authorities the one thing everyone in the free world wanted to know: who, in fact, had shot him. We, too, decided to stay in the closet and not tell people we were Texans. At least for a little while, just until the J.R. storyline calmed down and the Brits could simply accept us as we were.

Maintaining our anonymity meant not ordering chips and queso at tea time. Of course that wasn't a problem because they didn't serve chips and queso at tea time…or at lunch or dinner or at any restaurant ever. Not surprising, but what we did wrestle with was the fact that you couldn't even make do-it-yourself chips and queso at home because (gasp!) the grocery stores didn't sell Velveeta cheese or Rotel tomatoes.

Fine, I'll tell you who shot J.R., just show me where you keep the secret stash of Rotel.

I've come to learn in my later years that not even all Americans know about the culinary treasure that is Rotel. Rotel is a brand of canned diced tomatoes and green chilies that has been a Tex-Mex staple since the 1940s. It starts out perfectly delicious so when you add it to beef or cheese or chicken or a plain chip, it just makes everything that much more delicious. While there is no substitute for chips and queso at a good Tex-Mex restaurant, the best at-home alternative is melted Velveeta cheese with a can of Rotel. We were hesitant to ask American visitors to bring us Velveeta, not wanting to burst their image of us noshing on proper English Stilton while living abroad. But in the end we didn't let our pride stop us. Whenever we could get a brick of Velveeta smuggled in, we would huddle around it like hungry refugees. Luckily Velveeta slices brilliantly into perfect, if not suspiciously square little cubes, making it easy to ration.

When we made the move across the pond, the bank paid to ship our personal belongings, however they imposed a maximum weight limit on the freight we could take. During those final weeks in Dallas, my parents and I crouched down on the tile floor of our little restroom, carefully weighing stacks of records on the bathroom scales. Fierce negotiations ensued as we each pled a case for a certain beloved album to make the trip.

But our things didn't arrive until many weeks after we did. And during our first month in London we lived in a temporary apartment that had minimal furnishings. We didn't have a television, but there was a turntable in the dining room just aching for some vinyl. Since all of ours was still slowly making its voyage across the Atlantic, my dad dipped into his scant spending money and went to a London record store to purchase one album for us. He bought the recently released *San Antonio Rose* with Willie Nelson and Ray Price.

Ray Price had forged a trail from Texas to Nashville just ahead of Willie and served as a bridge from the Hank Williams honky-tonk era to the Nashville Sound (where Ray Price had enormous success) and into the outlaw years. Ray Price, having once roomed with Hank Williams in Nashville, hired Hank's band, the Drifting Cowboys, after Hank died. Later, an unknown Willie Nelson played back-up for Price.

My two favorite tracks on the album, based solely on nostalgia for our London years, are the bluesy song "Nightlife" and "I Fall to Pieces". The latter was a monumental hit for Patsy Cline, of course, but Willie and Ray were anything but shabby on their version. Analyzing how well they may or may not have pulled off her tune was essentially the basis of our family dinner every night the entire first month we lived in England. We didn't know anyone, school hadn't started, and we had no television. After hearing each other's same opinion on the topic night after night we started a new dinner table game where we would go around the room and take turns singing "I Fall to Pieces" until a clear leader emerged, having sung it the best. With each pass the singing didn't get better, it just got louder.

I am sure we pretty much outed ourselves to the neighbors. They may not have realized we were from Texas, but they sure as hell could tell we weren't British.

Aside from the *Dallas* TV show issue, it didn't really matter what state you were from because all British people called all Americans "Yanks". Most of the time they were affable toward us, and we loved our time in England. That said, one time I was roaming around the park near our flat when I came across some boys from the neighborhood playing soccer. Their football, our soccer. I had been playing for a few years back in Dallas and fancied myself quite a good player. Without blinking an eye I tried to join the game, not realizing I was starting a second revolution against Queen and country. They yelled that a girl couldn't play football, much less a Yank.

I was enraged. All of the blood rushed to my face; it was my first experience as the victim of misogyny and such reactionary bias. I shouted at them, they yelled back at me. It went round and round until finally I was exiled from the gardens, shamed into retreating from the stand I had so valiantly taken. They treated me like an untouchable, a veritable pariah. I cried all the way home.

Things improved once school started and we moved into our own flat in South Kensington right across the street from the Victoria and Albert Museum. I *loved* this neighborhood. I could get fish and chips right near the South Kensington tube station where I also liked to pick up my Cadbury Flake chocolate bars. We found a place nearby, Brooks, to get a good burger. There was a Chinese restaurant around the corner from our house where we ate late dinners after the theatre. I would order the crispy seaweed and then promptly fall asleep on my mother's shoulder while the wine and liquor flowed abundantly among the grownups. But my absolute favorite spot in the neighborhood was the Brompton Brasserie where I always ordered the same thing every time: beef bourguignon with pommes frites.

School life was fairly normal. My fourth grade teacher, Sheila Ihde, made a passing compliment about one of my writing assignments, and since I have never met a compliment I didn't like, that is precisely the moment when I decided I was going to become an author. She inspired me to submit a short story to a contest where American students wrote about Halloween, a holiday the British didn't typically celebrate. I wrote a complicated tale brimming with gore, suspense, irony…and then I killed off every last character in the final paragraph. It was O. Henry meets Tarantino. But I tied for first place – which I viewed as outright victory – and was allowed to read my story on BBC radio. It was one of those rare occasions that warranted a long distance call home to the States to share news with my grandparents (as long as you could cover the entire topic in one hundred and twenty seconds or less, *cha-ching*). Needless to say I went as my own inflated ego for Halloween that year.

Knowing we wouldn't be living in England very long, my parents felt we should see as much of Europe as humanly possible while we were there. Every time we hit the continent we transformed into the Griswolds from *European Vacation*. Like the time we were on a ski trip in Austria, taking a nighttime sleigh ride through the Alpine countryside and somehow managed to break the sleigh in half. Or the time we visited a German beer tent filled with thousands of drunkards for Oktoberfest and almost started an international incident over a language barrier miscommunication. Basically my dad tried to ask someone if he had a dog (in German) and accidentally called him a dog.

Then there was the time we spent Christmas in Greece. We wandered into a casual little café in Delphi where *The Dukes of Hazzard* was playing loudly on the television with the voices dubbed over in Greek. It was hard to reconcile that we were eating moussaka in Delphi, site of the most important oracle from all of Greek civilization, while watching Bo and Luke Duke destroy half of Hazzard County in a car chase trying to avoid Boss Hogg. I'm not sure the other patrons appreciated our running commentary, "I don't know, Uncle Jesse, it's all Greek to me!"

Perhaps our most memorable adventure was the road trip to Spain. My cousin Ashton flew over to London to visit during the summer of the Royal Wedding. After we watched Prince Charles and Diana's fairytale wedding and toasted to their happy-ever-after, we loaded up the car and headed for a beach vacation in Spain. To get to Spain from London you have to drive through France, where the travel gods put a terrible curse on our family. We were big fans of Willie Nelson's movie *Honeysuckle Rose* as well as the soundtrack which featured the most epic road trip song of all time, "On the Road Again". The problem was, every single damn time that song played on the cassette tape, our car broke down. It was uncanny, the pattern was glaring. We are still not sure what we did to upset the balance of the universe; it can probably be traced back to our behavior in Delphi, but it was clearly a curse. We spent a quarter of our beach vacation broken down on the side of the road, snapping pictures of French sunflowers and listening to my dad stomp around like Yosemite Sam. We would get going again, car games resumed, the cassette tape would play, and we would forget to fast forward. *The song played.* The final time we broke down in rural France was on a Sunday in the rain. Somehow we found a non-English speaking female mechanic who diagnosed the problem but couldn't translate it to us. She just kept screaming, "Le Ventilateur! Le Ventilateur! Le Ventilateur!"

Le fan belt. My dad figured out a way to rig it so we eventually made it to Spain. For the return trip my parents checked that car on an overnight train to Paris, where we had it fixed properly. But to this very day we still respect the curse. No humming, no mention of the title, certainly no singing it, and we never *ever* play "On the Road Again" while traveling. Just to be safe we've extended the ban to all modes of transportation, including boats and airplanes.

We lived in London less than two years, yet it was one of the most fun-filled, meaningful phases of my life. We loved our time there – the vacation mishaps and the language barriers. The museums, the ruins, and the architecture. I ate fish and chips, seaweed, Greek taramosalata, Austrian wienerschnitzel, and, of course, every combination of Italian pasta and gelato under the sun. I never developed a taste for hot tea, but I loved scones and easily adapted to the rich dairy in England. Plain and simple, their butter ruined me. When we returned to the States everything tasted so flat without that fabulous butter.

That said, every Texan knows how good it feels to come home to chips and queso. Times have changed since the 1980s – I no longer have to live in the shadows of secrecy, concerned what others might think. I will come out boldly, waving the flag and marching with pride to proclaim my inalienable right to melt Velveeta with Rotel. And that's not just the nostalgia talking, I truly love that processed cheese, and I am not afraid to tell the world. *We're from Texas! Remember the Alamo! Pack extra Rotel!*

Oh, and it was Kristin. J.R.'s secretary.

CHAPTER 9 SOUNDTRACK:

London Homesick Blues – Gary P. Nunn

(GARY P. NUNN)

I Fall to Pieces – Patsy Cline

(HANK COCHRAN, HARLAN HOWARD)

Nightlife – Willie Nelson

(WILLIE NELSON)

On the Road Again* – Willie Nelson

(WILLIE NELSON)

Theme from The Dukes of Hazzard – Waylon Jennings

(WAYLON JENNINGS)

* It is not recommended to listen to this song while traveling by car.
And to be safe, probably not by bus, train, or plane either.

The Other Rock City

We weren't home for long before it was time to move again. In the middle of my sixth grade year we moved to Nashville, Tennessee. I was born in Nashville while my parents were young married students at Vanderbilt University, and supposedly I went to Phi Delta Theta fraternity parties before I ever cut my first tooth (which actually explains a lot about my future penchant for late night fun). But I don't remember my early months of life, so when we arrived in Nashville in 1982, those impressions were my first. Having grown up on a plain in Texas with a brief sojourn in the urban mecca of London, I couldn't get over all of the trees. Tall forest-like trees were everywhere. I loved the women's southern accents with all those extended vowels and femininity to spare. Although perhaps my biggest surprise when we moved to Music City – home of the Ryman Auditorium and the *Grand Ole Opry* – was that no one listened to country music. None of my parents' friends listened to country, none of my new middle school friends. None of the moms played Willie Nelson in their car during carpool, which they mysteriously called "hookup" in this new foreign land. How could people in Nashville not listen to country?

The minute we arrived in Nashville my mother decided we needed to attend the *Grand Ole Opry* to embrace our new hometown. In the

1970s the *Opry* had moved out of the Ryman to a new facility called The Grand Ole Opry House, which is a little outside of the city center. I remember thinking it was a lot slicker and more corporate looking than I'd anticipated. I can't remember who played that night, but it was pretty much the last time I would see any country singers around Nashville. Our life was just so separate from the music industry scene, there was very little overlap back then, much different than it is today in Nashville. One time I did see Pam Tillis shopping in a dress boutique. And my mom used to see Loretta Lynn wearing overalls at the frozen yogurt shop near the hospital where Loretta's husband was quite ill.

Once I sat next to Sarah Cannon having lunch at Belle Meade Country Club. If you don't recognize the name Sarah Cannon, perhaps you know her by her stage name, Minnie Pearl. Sarah Cannon was from an affluent family and was related to my Aunt Lillias. Lillias is my aunt by marriage, so sadly I don't share any Minnie Pearl blood. It was exciting to see her lunching so close and looking so elegant. There was no $1.98 price tag hanging from her fur coat. (Yes, $1.98 was the actual price listed on her famous dangling tag all those years.) Apparently she dined there regularly, was always gracious, and was a very cool woman. My father once saw her having lunch at the country club with K.D. Lang ,whose white tank top, blue jeans, and tennis shoes were anything but proper dress code attire and would have no doubt sparked panic and rancor among fellow country club diners had Sarah Cannon not had the clout she did. My dad maintains Cannon made her guest feel right at home as they proceeded to laugh and carry on like schoolgirls, ignoring any onlookers.

While we had a few fleeting run-ins with country stars, I anticipated we would see more. Where was Waylon Jennings? Where was Tammy Wynette? And why weren't any of our friends listening to their music? Obviously there *were* people listening to it, just not the circles my parents and I seemed to take up with. And it's not just Nashville, I have friends from Mississippi, North Carolina, Alabama, and Atlanta, all of whom explain that they simply didn't grow up listening to country music. One of my more honest friends will confess why – they felt country music was for rednecks and hillbillies. Most friends from the Southeast had to go off to college and make friends with people from Texas before they started listening to Willie Nelson and other outlaw music. I don't know when or why country music became a classism issue in the Southeast, but somewhere along the way it did. Perhaps when the image of the Appalachian hillbilly fell out of favor in the 1940s, certain groups in the South wanted to distance themselves from that brand, but somehow they didn't adopt the emerging western/cowboy persona as much as Texas and Oklahoma did. Who knows, these are all generalizations. All I know for sure is the world I fell into in Nashville didn't listen to country – which is not to say they weren't listening to music.

It was all rock, all the time. With maybe just a little pop thrown in for good measure...I did go to an all girls' school after all. When we first looked at schools in Nashville, I balked at the thought of attending an all girls' school with uniforms. I was a free-spirited Texas kid who liked blue jeans and cowboy boots and dreamed of glamming myself up in Olivia Newton-John's black satin leggings and stiletto heels. But by seventh grade I'd changed my mind and enrolled at Harpeth Hall, a girls' preparatory school replete with plaid kilt uniforms and saddle oxfords. *It was happening, I was being domesticated.* Other than the best friends I made, perhaps my favorite legacy as a Harpeth Hall alum is our one-of-a-kind, southern-to-the-bitter-end mascot. We were the Honeybears. Except in middle school, when we were called Honeycubs.

I fell in with a sweet group of Honeybears with whom I am still friends to this very day. I ran with a benign crowd, I have to say our antics were pretty clean. In middle school one of the zaniest things that went down was at my friend's birthday when we accidentally let out all of the animals at the Opryland petting zoo. Opryland was Nashville's theme park, much smaller than Disney and infinitely hokier. We caused quite a scene racing around trying to scoop up baby goats and herd all the rabbits back into their corral. Other than that, middle school was marked by lots of Friday nights watching music videos, beach trips, deep analysis on respective crushes, and an epic Halloween party where I went as a tube of Crest toothpaste.

When we were freshman in high school The Starwood Amphitheater opened, which was a large outdoor performance venue with limited reserved seating and a large sloping grassy hill for general admission. My parents took my friends and me to see Jimmy Buffett, my first big concert. The show was great, we picnicked on the grass and enjoyed seeing my mom's college pledge sister, Marshall Chapman, open for Buffett. I remember she was tall and blond and wearing an all-white outfit, and I thought she had the coolest job on the planet.

Not long afterwards the local rock station 103 KDF was running a promotion for the Steppenwolf concert at Starwood: one ticket per automobile. Someone in our crowd commandeered an extra-long commercial van from her father's business, and we packed about forty-gazillion kids into it, all to split the expense of one ticket. I was so naïve, I couldn't get over how different the Steppenwolf crowd was compared to the Jimmy Buffett scene. It was the first time I realized how some venues were simply a neutral backdrop, their cultures redefined night after night based on the band and its fans.

In high school I started listening to classic rock, which I hope and assume is still a rite of passage for all high school kids. I was into the Stones, the Beatles, Bob Dylan, and the Doors. I also really liked the Byrds and wish I'd known back then how traumatized the conservative country music industry was when they came and recorded an album in Nashville. Being a teenager, I'm sure that would have endeared them to me even more. I railed against my hometown as most teens do, utterly convinced it was too pedestrian for me, which was ridiculous because I was about as Honeybear as they come. I veered slightly off the classic rock track with some safe alternative music such as R.E.M. and 10,000 Maniacs, even a little Dead Milkmen. Plus of course I loved southern rock because it had country bones and underneath my Honeybear façade, an outlaw still simmered.

Ironically I moved to the home of country music in the 1980s, which was a veritable dark age for country music. I'm not going to name names, but let's just say songwriting quality in the '80s waned and it seemed these people were just aching for a rhyme. The Nashville Sound of the 1960s may draw criticism for being overly produced and designed to be crossover pop, but at least it was beautiful and pleasing to the ear, unlike much of the country music of the 1980s. Orchestras, not synthesizers, I say. Did Harold Faltermeyer take the reins of the Nashville studios back then? Because many of those country songs sounded suspiciously like the "Axel F" theme song from *Beverly Hills Cop* with fewer leather suits and more mullets and sleeveless denim.

It was also a time when some of Nashville's archetypal country music attractions were down and out. Tourists today don't realize how bleak it was during this period. Friends who visit now can't comprehend why I have few memories of Lower Broadway, which today is as packed as Bourbon Street on any given weekend. They speak nostalgically about seeing Old Crow Medicine Show at the Ryman and look at me in horror to learn I've never seen a show there. The Ryman wasn't even *open* when I lived in Nashville. And famed Lower Broadway was a desolate, dilapidated area. Once, in high school, my friend Eleanor Jones Murray and I drove down there on a Saturday afternoon to take some artsy photographs. It was a complete ghost town. There wasn't a soul around.

After the *Opry* moved outside of town to the new Opry House, the Ryman Auditorium, aka the Mother Church of Country Music, was essentially put out to pasture and almost faced the wrecking ball. It remained dormant throughout the 1980s, perhaps a symbol of the creative drought that was also happening in Nashville's songwriting. Rumor has it Minnie Pearl helped save The Ryman, teaming up with Oklahoma businessman, Ed Gaylord, to purchase it. Then they invested another 8.5 million dollars to renovate it. But that didn't happen until 1993, after I was long away at college.

So what music genre was experiencing an out-of-character boom in Nashville during the precise years I lived there? Rock. Punk rock, in fact. First on the scene was the Exit/In, a club designed to compete with rock venues in New York and on the west coast. Some big name bands played the Exit/In including the Ramones, Tom Petty and the Heartbreakers, R.E.M., and the B-52s. But they also kept it country with Johnny Cash, Waylon Jennings, and George Jones. Since it opened in 1978 the Exit/In has been a consistent draw for mainstream rock and country.

In 1980 Sid Vicious was dead, and while punk had peaked and was essentially done in Los Angeles and New York, Nashville was largely unaware that it had even ever existed. The former bassist for an early Nashville hardcore band reports, "If you saw a guy walking down the street with a mohawk or a leather jacket, you'd pick him up before some Lynyrd Skynyrd fan hit him with a beer bottle." But a seismic shift happened when a downtown beer joint and hot dog place called Phrank'n'Steins started booking edgy rocks bands. Almost immediately, high school punks and college music lovers came out in droves. While the capacity was only seventy people, they were soon packing 200 or more into shows. Within months Phrank'n'Steins shut down, but a club owner named Terry Cantrell was there to pick up the pieces and keep the movement alive. He took an old Burger Boy restaurant, where it is rumored that both Waylon Jennings and Kris Kristofferson had worked as dishwashers, and turned it into a night club called Cantrell's.

Cantrell's was the epicenter for the emerging punk rock scene in Nashville, fueled by Vanderbilt University's progressive radio station and an underground music magazine called the *Nashville Intelligence Report*. There was considerable overlap between Exit/In and Cantrell's, but Exit/In drew the Vanderbilt fraternity boys while Cantrell's had more safety pins and pink hair. The perennial house band at Cantrell's was a group called the White Animals, who blended 1960s rock with a touch of edgier punk and dub reggae sounds. As unexpected as this scene was in a conservative city built on white man's rural country music, the lead singer of the White Animals was equally ironic. Kevin Gray was a med-school resident when he ditched the white doctor coat to play guitar and sing lead vocals. The band developed an enormous fan base and opened for big name acts such as the Kinks, Duran Duran, and the Talking Heads. Their song "Don't Care" was the first Nashville music video to hit MTV, and it was one of the very first of any indie videos to make it on the music network. While they could never break through to attain their own major label deal, they paved the way for many other Nashville rock bands during this brief but prolific era. Band member Crabtree joked, "If you wanted to get a record deal, you opened for the White Animals."

On the heels of the White Animals came Jason and the Nashville Scorchers. Most people outside of Nashville know them simply as Jason and The Scorchers as their management convinced them to drop the "Nashville". Unlike their punk rock peers who wrestled to distance themselves from the suffocating country shadow of Nashville's Music Row, the Scorchers embraced southern heritage. Lead singer Jason

Ringenberg wore vintage fringed western shirts and shouted Hank Williams songs at mock speed with onstage herkie jumps and other acrobatics. Jason and the Scorchers (they later claim to regret dropping "Nashville" from their name) had brought cowpunk to Cantrell's.

Because the White Animals couldn't seem to nail down a major record deal, they created their own independent label called Dread Beat Records and established a working model for future indie bands twenty plus years down the line. The White Animals put out their own records, performed at credible music venues like Cantrell's, and then played the hell out of every single SEC fraternity party that they could possibly book. They probably toured 366 days out of the year. My friends who went to Alabama claim the White Animals "were this really great Tuscaloosa band." People who went to Georgia think they were from Athens. Ole Miss alums swear they were an Oxford band. I hate to break the news to everyone, but the White Animals were a Nashville band. More specifically, they were a *Harpeth Hall Honeybear band.* They played our school proms, they played our school fundraisers. My mother, along with the moms of some of my friends, even booked them for our 8th grade graduation party in the kids' grill at the country club. Kevin Gray would always hang around after the shows and talk to all of us, kind but cool in his tie-dye t-shirt under a black blazer and adorned with Mardi Gras beads. One time he gave me a few of his rubber bracelets and I slept with them under my pillow. My hair reeked of patchouli for days.

While in high school I did manage to see some White Animals shows at more legitimate venues. One was in a historic auditorium downtown. We were up at the stage when the entire lighting system fell over our heads and into the crowd behind us, sadly ending the show for the night. Then there was the time we took a taxi, which felt very urban, down to Cantrell's to see them play. I don't know how we got in without fake IDs, but I remember how amazing it felt to be smashed into such a small space with extraordinarily loud music. It was way cooler than Starwood Amphitheater. My eyes were opened. I'd been given a glimpse into my future. I am a small venue, live music girl at heart.

Another band I saw play during those high school years was the country duo Foster & Lloyd. Radney Foster and Bill Lloyd released critically acclaimed country hits that drew on the traditions of 1950s and 1960s rock and roll and honky-tonk country. I felt a unique connection to Radney Foster because at the time he was married to my high school French teacher. They shared one car, a maroon Jetta, and most afternoons he would park outside near the Senior Parking Lot, waiting on Mrs. Foster to finish her day. Radney Foster was from Del Rio, Texas, so my parents and I would run into him every so often at the one place in town where Texas expatriates could find decent queso. I felt especially simpatico with this music celeb.

Though I missed Texas, I really loved my life in Nashville, mainly because I was blessed with such wonderful friends. That said, sometimes I felt like I wasn't really *from* there. Eventually I'd been gone from Dallas too long to call it home, but every so often the traditions of Nashville would make me feel as though I was from another planet. More likely it was the fact I was a teenager and predestined to rebel against anything in my path. I had, after all, listened to a great deal of outlaw music when I was little. But when I was a freshman in high school I bucked formality and refused to join a high school sorority. I actually recruited a number of my friends to make a stand with me, which caused quite a stir. It just seemed too ridiculous to further divide an already small group of homogenous girls into sub-cliques. There were only seventy-two in our graduating class for heaven sakes. How many times did we need to slice that pie to feel superior?

I stood alone in my other mini revolution. It was a long-standing tradition that freshman girls would serve as waitresses at the homecoming spaghetti supper of our brother school. I thought that was incredibly demeaning. Begrudgingly, I went to the mother-daughter meeting where we learned the rules and were handed our white organza aprons. That white apron did me in. I protested and wouldn't have a thing to do with waitressing at the spaghetti supper. I couldn't understand why my best friends weren't equally outraged. I realize now they had grown up in Nashville since day one and had probably spent years looking up at all the pretty high school girls on this special night thinking someday that would be them. I didn't have that same cache of memories stored up, so I attended the dinner in plain clothes and my friends had to serve me spaghetti.

I did have comrades in arms when I made another left turn my junior year. I discovered Harpeth Hall had a somewhat latent riflery team that practiced on the Vanderbilt University campus in the ROTC facility. We thought it would be fun to be close to college boys, so a number of us tried out for the team and we all made it. My dad, who is quite the outdoorsman and marksman, immediately had visions of me becoming a biathlete in the Olympics, the event where you cross country ski and then target shoot. So he bought me my very own Anschütz target rifle. Everyone else had to use these dirty, stubby, well-worn rifles that lived in the metal lockers of the underground ROTC shooting range, while I floated in with this sexy racecar of a rifle. It didn't, however, do much to help us meet any college boys. We were already walking across campus in plaid high school uniforms and saddle oxfords, and carrying a gun case wasn't exactly a green light to come flirt. In the meantime, my dad lectured me every which way to Sunday about gun safety and responsibility and demanded that I was not to leave that rifle in my car, explaining that if someone stole my car and shot anybody with it I would be morally culpable. He scared me within an inch of my life.

Unfortunately my social life didn't always permit my making a beeline back to the house directly after those riflery practices. Our favorite hangout was a dive bar down by Vanderbilt. It was gritty, friendly, had a killer jukebox, and they never carded. Hell, we used to drink beer in there in our high school *uniforms*. My friend, Margaret Wirth Ikard, would come meet me there after the practices even though she wasn't on the riflery team. I was terrified about leaving my rifle in the car, so I would haul the massive gun case straight into the joint and they would stash it behind the bar for me. The image of us playing the jukebox and ordering beers in our plaid kilts and saddle oxfords with my rifle behind the bar is a riot...and yet, at the time, I really felt like I was being responsible.

Margaret was also with me on some other high school escapades, namely our senior spring break. We were finally allowed to travel on our own, so I went on a ski trip with Margaret, our fellow Honeybear, Eleanor, and my childhood best friend, Mary, coming in from Dallas. I will never forget my mother's final words to me at the Nashville ticket counter: "Do NOT get in any cars with boys."

We met up with Mary in the Denver airport where the four of us were scheduled to catch a flight to Aspen. Unfortunately, a blizzard rolled in and all flights were canceled, so we were placed on buses. Almost predictably, about forty-five minutes outside the Denver city limits our bus broke down. It seemed like hours that we were stuck there on the side of the interstate. Our senior spring break was tracking to be a total bust. So for kicks, I started thumbing down cars to try to get a ride to Aspen. A few cars stopped but were horrified to hear we wanted to go that far. "There is a blizzard! No one is getting to Aspen today!" Our fellow passengers sat inside the bus mortified at our asinine behavior out in the falling snow. Really we were just thumbing for sport, trying to pass the time. But then a big old Bronco pulled over. I opened the passenger door to find a burly guy in a cowboy hat and yellow aviator sunglasses. I suppose that's the optimal lens color for low light blizzard conditions? At any rate, I asked for a ride to Aspen and he said to hop on in. *Yee haw, spring break is back on!* Mary was totally game, noting that he had Willie Nelson playing on his car stereo, so she knew he was a good guy. My three friends climbed in the back while I rode shotgun with our new friend, Zack, who was a construction worker trying to get to Aspen to clock in for a job. He was part of the crew building the new Ritz-Carlton.

It was slow-going on that interstate in a blizzard, so we had plenty of time to learn a lot I would ultimately forget about ol' Zack. But I do recall his father had been a state trooper, which made us feel safer about our insane decision. Many times we were stopped still on the highway in thick snow with the traffic backed up. Once a trooper came to the driver's side window and greeted Zack by name. We all waved and introduced ourselves. Never once did we feel we were in any danger. At one point Zack needed a little break, so he pulled off and went to this honky-tonk bar. I'd never seen anything quite like it, but I instantly loved everything about it. The neon glow, the pool tables, the brightly lit jukebox. There was equipment that indicated some live music was about to start, and I was dying to hit the small hardwood dance floor. But it was time for us to move on. I'd like to say Zack was just taking a coffee break, but he had already downed at least one beer.

Despite displaying idiotic judgment beyond measure, we made it to Aspen in the middle of the night safe and sound. We spent the remainder of our spring break with other kids our own age, but I never forgot that honky-tonk on the side of the highway. It continued to lure me in well after we moved on.

I suppose I was still country at heart. And so was Nashville. Despite its moment in the rock spotlight, the punk scene faded when Cantrell's closed and the White Animals disbanded in 1987. And Nashville country started to come out of its creative wasteland with a neoclassical singer from Texas who started making waves. George Strait was the Michelangelo of country music, single handedly taking it from the dark ages into a renaissance.

If you listen to George Strait's "If You're Thinking You Want a Stranger", which is from his 1981 debut album, you'll find the synthesized sound is more urban than cowboy. I do love the song even if the intro is a little heavy on the '80s and light on Hawaiian steel guitar. But somewhere along the way he must have received some validation, or simply trusted his own instincts, because by his second album George Strait was delivering the kind of straight up traditional country he'd cut his teeth playing on the Texas circuit. That album produced his first number one single with "Fool Hearted Memory", which I loved and used to play on repeat to practice two-stepping. After George Strait cracked the door, Randy Travis came along with a less Texas, more hillbilly sound. But it was still traditional, and people went nuts. "Diggin' Up Bones" was always a jukebox crowd pleaser and "On the Other Hand" is an old-school honest honky-tonk twang song about love and temptation.

And then came...the one...the only...Dwight Yoakam. Dwight Yoakam was honky-tonk, hillbilly, Bakersfield, cowpunk, and rockabilly all rolled up together. His self-financed debut album struck country music like a lightning bolt and charged it with a whole new energy. The old Bakersfield Sound was new again. People who never listened to country were peering over the fence to see what all the buzz was about. No one had wiggled their hips and legs like that since Hank Williams and Elvis each debuted on the *Louisiana Hayride*. As revolutionary as his first album was, the cover songs he chose were traditional country standards. And the self-penned title track, "Guitars, Cadillacs", was so damn good it blended right in with the other classic songs from veteran country songwriters as if it had been in the canon of country music always.

I subjected my friends to all of this music when they were in my car and I had control of the stereo. But for the most part, I enjoyed this resurgence in country music on my own. I would hear a song on the radio, scribble out a few lyrics, and carry the paper around with me until I had the chance to get to Tower Records in Green Hills and find out who the singer was and the name of the song. This was long before the Internet could have solved this in the blink of an eye. I had to sing the line over and over again for the store employee and describe what plot I remembered from the rest of the song. He would bring someone from the back to listen. Together the three of us would thumb through a giant book that looked like the White Pages until we found a song listing that might be a match. I'd buy the corresponding shrink-wrapped CD and wouldn't have the final verdict until I'd driven it all the way home to play it. Sometimes I would find the mystery song, sometimes not. But typically I ended up with a new album of music that I grew to love.

Occasionally I would see an expert on TV talking about country music history. It was always the same guy on a local Nashville show about music, or sometimes on a country music documentary. He seemed to be the go-to talking head as he shared all sorts of fascinating details on important events such as Kitty Wells' release of the first "response song" and the history of the *Opry* in Nashville. Many years later there was a country version of the reality television show *American Idol* called *Nashville Star*. I stumbled onto the first episode and lo and behold there he was again, this time as judge on this country music contest. By this point I was well armed with the Internet and did my research. His name was Robert K. Oermann, a highly respected country music journalist in Nashville who had written numerous books on the topic.

Not long ago, I had the opportunity to sit down one-on-one with Robert K. Oermann and talk about the history of honky-tonk as a subgenre in country music. We met in Hillsboro Village, a hip neighborhood down by Vanderbilt. I can now relay with firm authority that this man knows more about country music than I can ever hope to. It was fascinating, and I learned so much about the vocal styles of various honky-tonk singers. He told me that famous Nashville honky-tonk Tootsie's Orchid Lounge used to be called Mom's. And he pointed out that all the really old honky-tonks in this conservative town were pushed outside of the original city limits to avoid Nashville's old laws that banned liquor by the drink. He opened my eyes to the real magic behind Jean Shepard and helped me better understand the impact of other Nashville female singers as well as the initial wave of Texas honky-tonk guys who developed honky-tonk from a black ragtime piano style of music into a white country genre. Without blinking, Oermann cited relevant dates, lyrics, and obscure facts from some intricate database he houses in his mind. Scratch that, in his heart. Because it is evident that after thirty-five years in Nashville immersed in the country music business, he truly, truly loves it.

I asked him the one question that surprisingly I had never even pondered growing up in Nashville, having accepted it blindly as the ordained throne of country music. But lately I'd grown curious, "Why Nashville?" Why not Louisiana where the *Louisiana Hayride* was? Or Dallas with its recording industry? Or even Georgia with its early hillbilly recording artists?

Why Nashville?

Oermann was able to quick-draw four distinct answers right from his mental holster.

First, Nashville's WSM (home station of the *Grand Ole Opry*) was a clear channel radio station as early as 1932, somewhat ahead of the clear channel trend, which gave it an early advantage. Still, in the 1940s Shreveport and Dallas both had clear channel stations and popular barn dance radio programs. So other factors came into play that pulled Nashville so far ahead.

The second reason for the city's success was the attitude of *Grand Ole Opry* management. There was always a drive toward excellence in every area of the show, right down to the quality of the velvet curtains. Oermann explained that the *Opry* launched an aggressive talent drive and managed to recruit, mold, and retain top talent in the business.

Third was circumstance. Jim Beck had been the enterprising A&R guy in Dallas who was recruiting a large percentage of the country recording business to his studio in Texas. Pretty much all of the country music was being cut in Dallas and Chicago at this point. When Beck died unexpectedly as a result of a toxic tape cleaning solution, the Dallas recording industry came to a halt. Nashville stepped in to fill the void and producers immediately saw how much easier it was to record where the talent was instead of having the talent travel to a studio.

Finally, the fourth reason: Fred Rose. Fred Rose was a songwriter who had previous music industry experience in California and New York's Tin Pan Alley. While in New York he befriended a western film star and began to see an opportunity with country and western music. He had lived in Nashville briefly once before, but returned in 1942 to make his indelible mark. At the time, Roy Acuff was the biggest star of the *Grand Ole Opry*, and Fred Rose teamed up with Acuff to create the first "secular" (i.e., non-*Opry*) country music business in Nashville. The duo started a music publishing company called Acuff-Rose, which experienced immediate success in large part due to Rose's songwriting protégé, Hank Williams.

I asked Oermann if he thought the rumors were true that Fred Rose had in fact written more of Hank's self-penned tracks than was documented. Oermann proceeded to recite some of the more sophisticated lyrics from "I'm So Lonesome I Could Cry" and affirmed that yes, Fred Rose indeed added to and polished Hank's songwriting. He also confirmed the theory that Fred Rose was a magnanimous older brother to Hank, almost the father figure he never had and truly did his best to care for him and shield him from his own demons. Fred Rose wrote classic hits for countless stars including "Roly Poly" for Bob Wills and "Blue Eyes Crying in the Rain", made famous by Willie Nelson. He co-wrote some of Hank Williams' most well-known songs, including "Kaw-Liga" and "I'll Never Get Out of This World Alive". According to Oermann, Rose also wrote a crossover hit for Red Foley called "Chattanooga Shoe Shine Boy" for which he received no credit at all. But aside from an impressive catalog of meaningful hit songs, Rose, as a publisher, changed the face of Nashville. It's hard to explain how pervasive the songwriting-publishing roots run within this city.

Nowadays it's nothing to hear people talk about "getting co-writes" and "penning tracks" or "sharing rights" on songs. It's not just the *Opry* that sets Nashville country music apart from, say, the live music scene in Austin, it is the business of publishing and owning music. And that is directly traced to Fred Rose. When the Country Music Hall of Fame was founded in 1961, the first three members inducted were Jimmie Rodgers, Hank Williams, and Fred Rose.

From traditional honky-tonk to punk rock to synthesized country to retro rockabilly, the Nashville music community rolls along as various trends and personalities fade in and out. It's crazy to think how one fleeting but fortuitous moment can change it all. A night club opens, a band breaks up, one man dies, another moves to town. They seem like such simple, everyday occurrences, but you never know when one is going to trigger a ripple effect that will be felt for ages to come. I suppose with any music scene, all you can do is drop a little rock in the pond (or maybe even a Rose) and watch how far the circles go.

CHAPTER 10 SOUNDTRACK:

Fool Hearted Memory – George Strait

(BLAKE MEVIS, BYRON HILL)

On the Other Hand – Randy Travis

(DON SCHLITZ, PAUL OVERSTREET)

Guitars, Cadillacs – Dwight Yoakam

(DWIGHT YOAKAM)

Texas in 1880 – Foster & Lloyd

(RADNEY FOSTER)

Don't Care – The White Animals

(KEVIN GRAY, RICH PARKS)

CHAPTER 11

Let's Eat This Peach

It's an interesting thing to have roots in Nashville and a heart for outlaw music. On the one hand I am proud of where I grew up, proud of Nashville's rich country music heritage. And yet, I love every story of every Texas musician who rebelled against the Nashville Machine. I've always been confused by this duality. Am I from Texas or am I from Nashville? Needless to say, the song "T for Texas T for Tennessee" rings particularly true for me given my drifting sense of citizenship. But it runs deeper than simple geography – there are intrinsic attitudinal differences in the way music gets made in Nashville versus, say, Austin. But year after year, new musicians and songwriters flock to Nashville because, setting aside any debate of creative integrity, Nashville makes stars.

Of course I'm not the first conflicted soul to abide in Nashville cycling between a deep sense of municipal pride and frustration with its music industry. Several others come to mind. *Hello, I'm Johnny Cash*. At the end of the day, as much as I love the organic vibe of a live music scene, someone has to put on their big boy pants and go make the cash register ring. And that's Nashville.

I don't typically tune in to awards shows, but when my mother had the opportunity to attend the 2012 Country Music Awards, I watched from start to finish, hoping to see her on TV wearing the accessories we'd caucused about endlessly. I never caught a glimpse of my mother but instead witnessed hours of smoke machines and goofy bands blaring their pop songs and thanking God profusely in pre-packaged twang. I know there's talent galore in this town, but I can't help but feel Nashville country has left me behind for the time being. They say it comes in cycles, and everyone is looking for the next George Strait to get us back on the traditional rails the way he set things straight in the early 1980s. I muscled my way through the entire show, but when an ensemble group won big for their bebop anthem to pontoon boats, it pretty much did me in.

'Til human voices wake us and we drown under the weight of pontoon boat lyrics.

Listen, I'm no Scrooge, I've had plenty of laughs on pontoon boats on a lake on a hot summer day – I get the magic. And I'm all for good-time drinking songs. And it's not that I am above a novelty tune – after all where would we be without "Kaw-Liga" or "A Boy Named Sue"? But I tend to pass on the ones where the deepest, most profound lyrical reference is to a koozie.

Then again, I will admit to having a preexisting issue with koozies, in that I find them moronic. How about just drink your beer faster and it won't get warm? I can't imagine Waylon covering up a good-looking Lone Star label with half-an-inch of factory-pressed foam. I'd have to say the koozie is a fitting image to represent how canned Nashville country muffles the more legitimate honky-tonk sound that lies beneath, suffocating under a layer of made-in-China foam. Sometimes I think if Nashville could figure out a way to outsource songwriting to an overseas sweatshop they would. Heaven help us, maybe they already have.

There were moments of relief during the recent CMAs, like when they did a tribute to Willie Nelson or when Carrie Underwood sang a knockout version of Connie Smith's classic, "Once a Day". The only new material I liked was "Even If It Breaks Your Heart", written by Will Hoge, performed by the Eli Young Band, and a duet between Kelly Clarkson and Vince Gill called "Don't Rush", which had a soulful 1970s feel. Otherwise I was left agog, scratching my head and asking the overwhelming question: "Uh, where exactly is the country music?"

Hell, where is the *good* music?

It's an old grievance that probably dates back to the 1960s and the emergence of the Nashville Sound. Nashville's gone pop, Nashville's not country enough, Nashville just chases the dollar. After watching those CMAs I would kill for the Nashville Sound to come back around. Maybe it was a period of executive-driven song making, but at least some beautiful and sophisticated music came out of that hyper-produced era.

The point is that this debate is not new. Country artists, especially ones from Texas, have always blasted Nashville for being too restrictive, not creative enough, not traditional country, driven by the bottom line, on the "Wrong Side of the Mississippi". Their battle cry is the same refrain year after year: "Modern country sucks." Then again, many of these artists gave Nashville a try of their own free will. Perhaps that is just sour grapes because they couldn't make it in the big league commercial world of country music. Because the fact remains, for every decade since the *Opry* launched in 1925, Nashville has been churning out hit songs and turning singers into celebrities. And we eat them up by the spoonful. It has produced the likes of Waylon Jennings and Johnny Cash, ironically two of the more vocal Nashville rebels. And while they are often associated with the outlaw movement that Willie headquartered in Austin, neither Waylon nor Johnny Cash ever left Nashville, choosing to live out their remaining days there. The debate raged on then, and it does so now. I imagine Music Row will have no problem following this tedious argument like a hazy yellow fog for the rest of eternity.

Or at least until the money runs out.

I was a teenager when I lived in Nashville, so rebelling against my hometown was part of the job description. Then again, just try to keep a teenage girl from falling in love…because I really do love Nashville. If I were a songwriter I'd write a song about it, if I were a poet I'd write a sonnet. But I'm neither, so instead I will just author this list detailing what I cherish the most. A love song, of sorts, to the city where I grew up. Feel free to hum along with any melody you like, traditional honky-tonk, outlaw country, Nashville Sound, or even the computer packaged rock-pop koozie-crap of the moment. Who am I to say what a love song is supposed to sound like? Do I dare to make that call? No, I think I'll just highlight some of the more poetic characteristics of my old hamlet.

Nashville Love...

Hatch Show Print – Boom! I just came right out of the gate with the big guns because The Hatch Show Print letterpress shop might just be one of the absolute coolest things in Nashville. It was founded in 1879 when cattle drives were flowing in the American West, and it remains the oldest continually running letterpress shop in the country. It started out printing posters for vaudeville, circus, minstrel shows, and tent revivals. When the *Opry* came along, Hatch began designing music show posters, creating the iconic color-block, distressed show poster look that so many graphic designers imitate to this very day. I've always had a thing for letterpress printing, so a historic poster shop that combines letterpress and honky-tonk is just about more than I can handle – in my own hometown to boot. When my husband was still my boyfriend, he gave me a Hatch Show Print poster from an old Ernest Tubb show. *Pitter-pat.*

650 WSM – WSM is the 50,000 watt clear channel radio station that has been broadcasting the *Grand Ole Opry* since 1925. It was initially launched and owned by National Life and Accident Insurance Company as they aimed to reach a greater audience through radio advertising. The call sign WSM comes from the insurance company's tagline, "We Shield Millions". When the radio tower was erected in 1932 it was the tallest in North America. It boasts a unique diamond shape design that makes it an architectural and engineering landmark. But its legacy, of course, is that it has been delivering the *Opry* to homes all over America for decades. My dad listened to the *Opry* as a kid in Ardmore, Oklahoma...just like the many stars who gathered around the radio with their families on a Saturday night, dreaming of making it to the *Opry* one day.

Country Music Hall of Fame Rotunda – The Country Music Hall of Fame Museum is an absolute must-see in Nashville for visitors and residents alike. I used to visit the old museum on Music Row, which was borderline pitiful and was ultimately razed. The site is now a parking lot for BMI employees. The new museum is massive and jam-packed with memorabilia and worthwhile exhibits. It's incredibly well done. But the absolute highlight is the grand finale of the tour:

the Hall of Fame Rotunda that displays a plaque for each of the Hall of Fame inductees. If you don't feel awe when you step into this room then you might be reptilian because it conveys almost as much majesty and country music history as the Ryman Auditorium. The dome hints at a cathedral feel, which adds to the gravitas. Jutting down from the center of the dome is a replica of the bottom half of the famed WSM diamond radio tower. And around the edge of the room is the inscription, "Will the Circle Be Unbroken." Goosebumps galore.

Webb Pierce's Swimming Pool – After his neighbors took legal action and prevented Pierce from charging people admission to come see his guitar-shaped swimming pool, he teamed up with investors to create a replica of the pool near Music Row. Ultimately it didn't draw the tourist business they had hoped it would, so it became the pool for the Spence Manor motor lodge. If you are lucky enough to work in the nearby ASCAP building you can still look down on the pool from your office window. Needless to say if I ever have the money to build a custom swimming pool, it will be a knockoff of Webb Pierce's guitar pool.

Ernest Tubb Record Shop – Right around the corner from the Ryman Auditorium is Ernest Tubb's Record Shop which Tubb opened in 1947. More than just a retail location for good country music, it was a meeting place for musicians and fans alike. Every Saturday night the *Ernest Tubb Midnite Jamboree* is still broadcast from the record shop. It is the second longest running radio show in history, also airing on 650 WSM. We already know how much I love Ernest Tubb, so it goes without saying that his record shop ranks as one of my favorite Nashville landmarks. To think of all the honky-tonk stars that made their way from the Ryman to the *Midnite Jamboree…*

Manuel – Manuel is also known as the "Rhinestone Rembrandt" as he has made so many of the flamboyant western suits worn by country stars throughout the decades. He started his career in Los Angeles, but he really hit his stride with Nashville country performers. So he moved his business to Nashville, right on Lower Broadway. He costumed the Man in Black, outfitted all three generations of Hank Williams, and wardrobed countless honky-tonk crooners in brightly colored suits and glittering country couture. Manuel himself is no slouch, often dressed in scarves and geometric western suits that accent his dashing looks and flowing white hair. Manuel is as much a part of Nashville's art legacy as he is its music history.

The Harpeth Hall English Department – Don't be fooled by the saddle oxfords and the Honeybear mascot. I went to a kick ass intellectual high school that didn't offer a hint of anything that resembled a home economics course. It was a rigorous curriculum of liberal arts, and thanks to the Harpeth Hall English Department, I fell in love with literature. My teacher, Gordon Turnbull, opened my eyes to Shakespeare, through which I first came to understand the concept of prayer. We were talking about the point in *Hamlet* where Prince Hamlet, seeking revenge, has the chance to kill his uncle, King Claudius, but finds him on his knees repenting. He decides not to murder him because he doesn't want Claudius to go straight to heaven since he would have died mid-prayer. Ironically Claudius was trying to pray, but he himself knew it was a disingenuous attempt. Claudius says, "My words fly up, my thoughts remain below. Words without thoughts never to heaven go." My heart was stirred by this simple yet revolutionary concept of authenticity over ceremony. In Turnbull's class I also distinctly remember reading the Old Testament as literature, which I found very provocative, as well as T.S. Eliot's "The Love Song of J. Alfred Prufrock", which opened my eyes to the charm and danger of neurotic, self-involved stream of consciousness poetry. I liked how it sort of rhymed, but not perfectly.

The Strict Rules at Belle Meade Country Club – Belle Meade Country Club has all the southern drive-up appeal that any private institution of the Old South should. It is dripping in charm and exclusivity. I like the fact that they don't allow anyone to wear blue jeans and cell phones are 100% prohibited. I imagine some of the members find this irritating and restrictive, but as an infrequent guest, I like it. As casual a life path as I have chosen, it's refreshing to know there are still some efforts to maintain a standard of southern elegance. Brava, Belle Meade.

SATCO – In 1984, just a year or so after we moved from Texas to Nashville, two Vanderbilt graduates from the Lone Star state opened a restaurant called The San Antonio Taco Company, nicknamed SATCO. *Manna from heaven! We weren't going to have to live without proper queso after all!* Needless to say my parents and I were immediate

SATCO regulars, virtually plugging into a Queso IV on a weekly basis. It didn't take long for the rest of Nashville to fall in love with its first real taste of Tex-Mex, and SATCO became a local institution. I can't tell you how many high school weekends I spent with my friends on that outdoor deck. This place has queso and mojo to spare.

Session Musicians – The stars have their faces and names plastered all over album covers and concert marquees and show posters. But perhaps the greatest musical heroes in Nashville are the session musicians. The guitar players, drummers, fiddlers, and pedal steel guitarists who remain nearly anonymous. They are often the secret sauce behind the sounds we fall in love with, sitting in on recording sessions for everyone from Dolly Parton to any unknown kid from out of town who pulls together enough money to produce an album. Session musicians are the real magic in Nashville. They are the ones keeping the legacy of honky-tonk alive. Any one of them could be eating a short stack in the next booth at the Pancake Pantry and you might never know you were dining next to a living part of music history. But they are there, they *are* Nashville.

The Parthenon – I have no idea why we have an exact replica of the Greek Parthenon smack dab in the middle of Nashville, but we do. It is dramatic lit up at night and impressive to walk around during the day, not to mention quite a bit less expensive to visit than airfare to Athens. It's such an integral part of the city I never even question its purpose until someone from out of town looks at me with complete bewilderment expecting an explanation as to why it's there. I don't know what to say. We have a Parthenon. It was already there when I moved to town.

Elliston Place – Elliston Place is a little cut-through street off a major thoroughfare in Midtown, not too far from the Vanderbilt campus and a stone's throw from the Parthenon. This short street packs a punch as it hosts many Nashville landmarks, steeped in character. The Elliston Place Soda Shop is a vintage lunch counter that opened in 1939. It's just as you're picturing it right now. The Gold Rush doesn't exactly have the same charm, but it's a bar and restaurant that has its own staying power, having opened in 1974. It's not particularly fabulous inside, but for some reason it draws the crowds year after year and there is almost always a funny story the morning after a night at the Gold Rush. Also on Elliston Place is the Exit/In, Nashville's preeminent music venue since the 1970s. And last but definitely not least there is Rotier's. Rotier's opened after WWII as a beer and burger joint, but later added southern comfort food. When my parents were in college at Vanderbilt they used to go to Rotier's on dates. It is a warm, cozy dive serving up casual fare and good spirit. Ever since he had his hit song, "Cheeseburger in Paradise", the world wants to know Jimmy Buffett's favorite cheeseburger, and Rotier's is on his list of Top Ten Cheeseburgers in the world.

The Women of Country Music – Kitty Wells, Loretta Lynn, Patsy Cline. I have heard these mermaids singing, and I actually think they do sing to me. Straight to my soul, in fact. The women of Nashville's music industry fascinate me the most. Much more on this in a bit.

The Old Breed of Songwriters – I am probably over-romanticizing the era but I like to imagine songwriter Hank Cochran and Willie Nelson sharing song ideas over a beer at Tootsie's Orchid Lounge. I am also in awe of lesser known greats like Eddie Miller, who wrote some of my favorite Patsy Cline songs such as "Three Cigarettes in the Ashtray", "A Church, a Courtroom and Then Goodbye", and "There He Goes". Then of course, there is the ultimate song writing legend of Nashville, Mr. Harlan Howard. He penned a vast catalog of honky-tonk hits including "Pick Me Up on Your Way Down", "Heartaches by the Number", and "Foolin' Round". Harlan Howard is also famous for laying down the ultimate definition of a country song when he proclaimed, "It's just three chords and the truth." Sounds like a songwriter.

Robert's – Hands down my favorite spot in all of Nashville, Tennessee. Robert's is located on Lower Broadway, just around the corner from the Ryman Auditorium and across the street from the Ernest Tubb Record Shop. Starting in the 1950s the building was home to Sho-Bud Pedal Steel Guitars, which pretty much means it has honky-tonk feng shui deep into the studs. During the 1980s Lower Broadway became a depressing wasteland with triple-X businesses and was considered a veritable red-light district. At that time the place was a liquor store. Then, in the 1990s, Robert Wayne Moore opened it as a western apparel and boot store. He added a jukebox, beer, cigarettes, and pork chop sandwiches. Before long musicians started hanging out at Robert's, picking, drinking, and shopping. He changed the name to Robert's 3 Doors Down (because it is located three doors down from Tootsie's, which he also once owned), and instantly it became a successful live music venue. I remember going to Robert's in the mid-1990s when BR-549 was the house band. In 1999 Jesse Lee Jones bought Robert's, changing the name to Robert's Western World. But that's about all that he changed. The intimate dive bar has a wall of dusty cowboy boots still on display from its retail days. The small stage packs a punch with the house band, Brazilbilly, lighting up the dance floor every Saturday night playing nothing but traditional honky-tonk sounds. With cold PBR, fried bologna sandwiches, and a swinging honky-tonk band, Robert's is unequivocally *the most fun* you can have in Music City, USA. Period.

And that's a mere taste of what I love about Nashville. I've bitten off more than I can chew with this assignment but done so with a smile. Truthfully I've only offered a small peek at how and where this city shines. I am no ordained princess of Nashville, nor was I meant to be, but it turns out I am just as nostalgic as I am rebellious. Love prevails, fuzzy parts and all. Year after year I come back to Nashville with my heart and appetite more and more open; I sink my teeth in and happily sing its praises.

(No koozies were harmed in the making of this list. Unfortunately.)

CHAPTER 11 SOUNDTRACK:

I Love You Because – Johnny Cash

(LEON PAYNE)

I Love You So Much It Hurts – Patsy Cline

(FLOYD TILLMAN)

It Must Be Love – Don Williams

(BOB MCDILL)

I Can't Help It If I'm Still in Love with You – Hank Williams

(HANK WILLIAMS)

I Dreamed of an Old Love Affair – Ernest Tubb

(BONNIE DODD, CHARLES MITCHELL, JIMMIE DAVIS)

The Ernest Tubb Record Shop, on Lower Broadway, Nashville TN

Robert's Western World, on Lower Broadway, Nashville TN

Honky-tonk multitasking. Nashville musician Chris Casello takes a break from his electric guitar to play the pedal steel at Robert's Western World, Nashville TN, February 2, 2013

CHAPTER 12

Eve of Janus

In my teens and college years I seemed to possess an uncanny
ability to botch life's most special moments, those rites of passage that
most girls dream about for which they primp and preen and don carefully
chosen garments in order to look like *better* versions of themselves. I
blame my mother, really. She should have maintained control. Why in
the world was I left with my hand on the nuclear fashion trigger…in
the '80s no less? For example, there was the time I decided, on a whim,
to get a perm and cut layers in my hair on the day of my senior prom. I
looked like a sheepdog who'd met the business end of a Taser, and the
Carmen Miranda flamenco-style dress I'd chosen didn't help matters.

Then there was my 1989 high school graduation. When you attend an
all girls' school in the South, there are innumerable ceremonies through
the years that require wearing a vestal virgin white-as-the-driven snow
dress. I think in a literature class they would call that *irony*. Nevertheless,
we were all white dress experts by the time we were seniors. No doubt
I wanted to go out making a sophisticated fashion statement, so I
convinced my mother to have my graduation dress custom-made. As
it turns out, just because it's made from scratch does not mean it is
couture. I wanted a chiffon flowing gown inspired by Greek caryatids,
and I'm just not sure the Nashville seamstress who had been churning

out the same sweetheart ball gown look for decades shared my inspired vision. The design itself was inherently better suited to a more waif-like girl with the flat chest of a prepubescent boy, and Nashville's own Coco Chanel did nothing to convert the style to my more ample bosom. I looked insane with awkward rosettes on the shoulder that were so tall I felt as if they were grazing my ears. I kept catching sight of them in my peripheral vision, which was quite distracting as I took the stage to deliver my speech to the graduating class.

I was tickled with the multi-layer meaning of my speech, which I titled, "It's About Time". I talked about the past, present, and future we faced together as a graduating class. My message focused on our ten year reunion which would take place in 1999 and, back then, seemed like a sci-fi amount of time off into the future. I was intrigued with fin de siècle themes, not to mention projecting the magic of witnessing a millennium change as we would mark our first decade out in the world. "It's About Time" was a crowd pleaser and the sunny, special day was nothing short of incandescent. But the pictures are too painful to revisit thanks to my swing-and-a-miss dress that made every photo of me look ridiculous.

And then, just when you'd have assumed I had learned my lesson about the risk-reward ratios in fashion decisions, there was my deb dress. Which was nothing short of hideous. By this point it was the early '90s, so I can't even pin it on the '80s. I was at college when I was invited to participate in a Nashville debutante ball called the Eve of Janus. Held on New Year's Eve in the ballroom of a downtown Nashville hotel, the Eve of Janus was named for Janus, the Roman god of new beginnings, transitions, time, gateways, and doorways. In Roman times Janus was often depicted with two faces, one toward the past and one toward the future.

Debutante balls themselves originated in Europe. The Industrial Revolution produced a large, wealthy middle class eager to marry their daughters into families with royal titles. Royal families with pedigrees were eager to share their titles in exchange for access to middle class cash. The debutantes were the young girls being presented to society as eligible for marriage. Deb balls were formal events called "coming out" parties.

None of these archaic marital rituals seemed relevant with Nashville's Eve of Janus Ball in the 1990s. We were there for the party.

I remember racing out the back door with my Hideous Gown over my shoulder, heading to the hotel where I would get ready with the other girls. Based on the week of late night parties leading up to the ball, my mother was warranted in dispensing this last note of caution as I had one foot out the door, "Christine, you all please try and behave yourselves tonight."

Once we were all gussied up we were corralled into the back kitchen of the hotel and arranged in lines with our fathers, who were to present us. The Eve of Janus debs were called "The Signs of the Times" or just "The Signs" for short. The evening began with the "Presentation of the Signs". My dad walked me out of the back kitchen, into the ballroom, across the stage, and down the steps in front of an applauding crowd of men in black tie and women in elegant gowns. Ours was a second-tier deb ball to be sure – we didn't even do a fancy bow like all my Texas friends. But on the upside, it was quick and painless. Once all the Signs were presented, we had to dance in front of everyone to the Tennessee Waltz, and then we were allowed to go upstairs to our rooms to freshen up before the big party.

We'd rented all the rooms up and down one floor of the Vanderbilt Plaza Hotel so debs and their dates were flying in and out of various doors mixing cocktails and cranking music. It was almost a shame we had to leave all this fun for the party down in the ballroom. But someone cried out, "Time to go! They're ready for us down there! Remember to bring extra booze because the lines down there are already getting long!"

With that I tucked a little flask of bourbon into the front of my dress. I jettisoned the heels that were already killing my feet and slipped on my favorite pair of brown cowboy boots. I figured my Hideous Gown was massive enough in every direction to hide both flask and boots. I would be wrong on both counts.

This deb ball may not have had the old-world meaning of Europe's royal court coming out parties, nor did it have the opulence of a Texas deb ball, but I have to give credit where credit is due. While they may not care as much for country music, give Nashville's society crowd a soul band and they will dance until the sun comes up. The ballroom was rocking! The debs – I mean, The Signs of the Times – were boogying down alongside dates, family, friends, and newspaper photographers. By the time I found my parents in the ballroom word had spread throughout the Eve of Janus that "Christine was wearing cowboy boots under her deb gown and she has bourbon in her dress!" They gave me a Whiskey Tango Foxtrot eye roll that conveyed irritation, defeat, pride, and amusement all in one quick glance.

And with that, I made my debut into proper society.

I was home in Nashville not long ago and a crew of my high school friends gathered for a Girls Day/Night on the town. Someone produced twenty-two year old pictures from our Eve of Janus Ball, which could be considered borderline cruel, not to mention blackmail. We guffawed at our hair and dresses, agreeing wholeheartedly that my dress existed alone, in fact, on a whole other plane of hideousness.

By this point I was forty-two years old and had still never set foot inside the famed Ryman Auditorium. So I suggested that we take a tour of the Ryman as a part of our Nashville girls' outing. A little culture before cocktails never hurt anyone, least of all a group of forty-something moms. My friend, Margaret, and I arrived early, so we went ahead and started the backstage tour while we waited for our other girlfriends to catch up.

The Ryman was built in 1892 by riverboat captain and saloon owner, Thomas Ryman. It was called the Union Gospel Tabernacle and was intended to be a house for a popular revivalist preacher, Samuel Porter Jones. A cynical Ryman had attended one of Jones's tent revivals with plans to heckle and make fun of the preacher. But instead he was inspired, converted on the spot, and declared that he would build a tabernacle for Jones. Just one of many examples throughout music history where religion and honky-tonk seem to intersect.

In the 1900s the church structure began hosting other speaker and entertainment engagements, eventually becoming the sixth home of the *Grand Ole Opry*. In 1925 the *Opry* began as a Saturday night barn dance radio show on National Life and Accident's 650 WSM radio station. The show was broadcast from a studio in the National Life and Accident headquarters. Crowds became too large so they built a second, larger studio, but that didn't quell the growing problem. So they moved the *Opry* to the Hillsboro Theater (now the Belcourt Theater), the Dixie

Tabernacle, the War Memorial Auditorium, and then, ultimately found its true home at the Ryman Auditorium. The Ryman hosted the *Opry* during the Golden Era of Honky-Tonk.

The backstage tour began by visiting dressing rooms that were installed after the Ryman's renovation in the 1990s. Each one is dedicated to a significant figure (or figures) from either *Opry* or Ryman lore. The first dressing room we toured was the Johnny Cash room. After finishing his contract with the *Louisiana Hayride*, Cash made his *Opry* debut on July 7, 1956. The word "debut" derives from French language and means "to lead off". Cash led off his inaugural performance on the Ryman stage with "Walk the Line". He received three standing ovations and went on to sing "Get Rhythm" and "So Doggone Lonesome". Carl Smith introduced Cash to the audience that night, which is mildly intriguing since Carl Smith was June Carter's first husband. Perhaps more sentimental, backstage that same evening someone introduced Johnny Cash to June Carter for the very first time. Given that June Carter would become Cash's future wife and lifelong love, it's safe to say the night of Johnny Cash's *Opry* debut was a veritable eve of janus for Cash. He was on the brink of new beginnings musically, romantically, and spiritually.

Three weeks later Johnny Cash performed at the Ryman as a member of the *Grand Ole Opry*. Our tour guide explained that artists can either play on the *Opry* as a guest or as a full-fledged member. Members have voting rights on who performs and who receives future membership, but they also have a contractual commitment to play a certain number of *Opry* shows each year. Back in the day they had to play sixty-two shows annually, which made it difficult to book more lucrative tours on the road. Current *Opry* members are only required to do ten *Opry* shows a year.

Cash resigned from *Opry* membership in 1958 when he relocated his family to California. He continued to make guest appearances until 1965 when he famously devolved into a fit of rage during a performance and kicked out all of the lights along the base of the stage. The *Opry* fired him; Cash was in the throes of his darkest years. Eventually amends were made and he started making guest appearances once again. Roy Acuff later offered Cash membership back into the *Opry*, but he declined due to his rigorous touring schedule. He did, however, film his own television show, *The Johnny Cash Show*, at the Ryman from 1969-1971.

Johnny Cash and the *Opry* enjoyed a messy but loving relationship through the years. Despite the fact his debut song on the Ryman stage was "Walk the Line" the Ryman Auditorium was not featured at all in the Oscar-winning biopic bearing the same name. I know because our tour guide pointed it out several times. She was mighty miffed about it, too, noting in a slight huff, "After all Johnny Cash did meet June Carter here backstage."

The next dressing room we visited was the Hank Williams room. The tour guide announced that Hank's debut on the *Opry* was his first national audience, which wasn't true since he'd previously been starring on the *Louisiana Hayride* to a national audience. But Hank's *Opry* debut on the Ryman stage on June 11, 1949 is something of a legend. He performed "Lovesick Blues" and "Mind Your Own Business" and received six encores from the audience, which is an *Opry* record to this very day. He didn't appear with his own band, the Drifting Cowboys, and had only taught the backing band his music that same afternoon, so they didn't have any other songs to play. He did "Lovesick Blues" over and over and probably would have received additional encores, but he just didn't want to play that same song any more that night. While some Hank experts refute the myth of the six encores, it is fact that he became a member of the *Opry* shortly after his debut. Then they fired him in 1953, exhausted by his drunken antics and missed practices and performances. Our tour guide proclaimed that Johnny Cash and Hank Williams were the only two people ever fired from the *Grand Ole Opry*.

Not only is it interesting that the first two dressing rooms on this retrospective tour are dedicated to two celebrities who got the boot and went on to become cult-status superstars outside the *Opry*, this section of the tour's script was marked with a touch of revisionist history. Cash and Hank weren't the *only* two members of the *Opry* that were fired. On December 6, 1964 the headline of the newspaper in Nashville read, "OPRY DROPS 12 STARS". Management fired the twelve *Opry* members for failing to appear in their minimum number of shows, a rule that had been loosely interpreted up until then. The firings included, among others, Kitty Wells; her husband, Johnnie Wright; Justin Tubb (Ernest Tubb's son); Ray Price; and Chet Atkins. *Opry* leadership had to apologize and retract Chet Atkins' name the following day as it turned out he wasn't even a member of the *Opry*. It would seem they sort of got red-pen-itis on that one. Johnnie Wright claimed he and Kitty Wells weren't fired, but they quit because they were tired of paying the WSM Artists Bureau a 15% booking fee for shows they booked on their own. Some of the fired performers made their way back to *Opry* membership, but others like Ray Price never rejoined, opting instead to stick with more lucrative touring schedules. Many of the fired stars did return periodically to perform as guests on the *Opry*.

Our tour guide also tried to convince us that the Ryman is haunted, a fun little nugget that, in my experience, seems to play well all across America on any given tour that draws an RV tourist crowd. I can't say whether this is contrived or not, but I will tell you while we were on the tour, my friend Margaret's back seized up terribly as we walked into the Hank Williams dressing room. And Hank did suffer debilitating back pain which led to the excessive drinking and pain medication that claimed his short life. Haunted or coincidence?

From there I helped Margaret hobble to the next spot which was the Women of Country Music dressing room honoring Patsy, Loretta, Dolly, etc. Despite her agonizing pain Margaret found the strength to brag about how she had once hung out in one of these backstage dressing rooms with Waylon Jennings. She worked for The American Diabetes Association, and Waylon played a benefit show that she put on at the Ryman. I tried to contain my envy, but I had to admit, that was beyond spectacular. I was turning green.

I think I played it cool, "You know, Margaret, Hank Williams suffered from terrible back pain. I'm pretty sure you're being haunted by his ghost right now."

It's always good to see how a near thirty year relationship has matured since middle school. Luckily our enduring friendship can handle a periodic dose of envy (and sarcasm) because we didn't break into a catfight in the Women of Country Music dressing room.

By the time we arrived at this combination tribute room one of the other tourists in the group had figured out that most of the big female *Opry* stars had to share the honor of this dressing room, and this lady was publically lodging a complaint with our tour guide. I had to agree, clearly Patsy Cline was a star who shined so bright she deserved her own tabernacle, never mind a commemorative dressing room. That said, Patsy was one of the few exceptions in that she was not a star with a big single when she first sang on the *Opry*. On July 1, 1955 Patsy Cline debuted on the Ryman stage. Ernest Tubb introduced her and she sang "A Church, a Courtroom and Then Goodbye". It's a beautiful, aching song that hints at what the world would later love from this incredible vocalist, but the melody was perhaps a bit too languishing for the boisterous Saturday night Ryman crowd. She was crushed by the unenthusiastic applause and felt certain she would never be invited back. According to Margaret Jones' book, <u>Patsy: The Life and Times of Patsy Cline</u>, she cried backstage and told Faron Young, "Oh, I got to be on the *Opry*, but I guess that's the end of it." Faron Young sought out Ernest Tubb who invited her to join the two of them on tour in Memphis two days later.

Patsy did continue playing the *Opry* and had her first big hit with "Walking after Midnight". Patsy was finally invited to become a member of the *Opry* in 1960. I have no idea what took so long because by this point she had been a superstar for quite some time. She approached bossman Ott Devine and asked if she could have an invitation. His response was, "Patsy, if that's all you want, you are on the *Opry*." In July 1961 Patsy rolled onto the Ryman stage in a wheelchair after having been in a hospital for over a month recovering from a near fatal car wreck. She assured fans she would be back performing soon. She was still on crutches the first time she performed Willie Nelson's song "Crazy" on the Ryman stage, which would become one of her greatest hits.

Of course I also love Patsy's good girlfriend, Loretta. In a recent interview celebrating her 50 years in the *Opry*, Loretta recalls her first night on stage at the Ryman. "Me and my husband got in town the night before and we spent the night in the car out front of the Grand Ole Opry, and the next morning, we didn't have any money, so we divided a doughnut and I got my picture made in front of the Grand

Ole Opry." Loretta claims she was so nervous when she debuted on the *Opry* October 15, 1960 with her self-penned single "Honky Tonk Girl" that all she remembers is tapping her toe while on stage. She was invited to begin a tour with Johnny Horton, but he tragically died three weeks later. Her career flourished nonetheless, and in 1962 she became a member of the *Grand Ole Opry*.

The next dressing room was dedicated to Minnie Pearl, who reportedly loved the character she created so much, she crafted an agreement with the *Opry* that there would always be a Minnie Pearl in the cast after she moved on. Sarah Cannon even interviewed the young woman who replaced her as Minnie Pearl. Minnie Pearl was the first woman among the *Opry* cast to perform comedy as she blazed the trail for the likes of June Carter, who was equally famous for her comedy sketches. Not to mention she was instrumental in saving the Ryman Auditorium from the wrecking ball as she mobilized investors to purchase and ultimately renovate it.

The final dressing room was dedicated to another female force of nature within Ryman history, although she was much more behind the scenes. Lula Clay Naff arrived in Nashville in 1904, recently widowed and the mother of a young daughter. Ultimately her career path led her to become Manager of the Ryman Auditorium, and she was shrewd, innovative, and tireless in booking acts. She often introduced herself in correspondence simply with her initials L.C. so as not to draw attention that she was female. In addition to the *Opry*'s long run, Naff was responsible for booking Katharine Hepburn, Bob Hope, political debates, even boxing matches. The Ryman and the *Opry* are so intrinsically linked, it's easy to forget that this venue was wide open six other days of the week, available for additional entertainment to make the cash register ring. Naff would oversee the logistics before each and every performance, standing watch like the captain of a ship in the back of the auditorium. That is, until the lights lowered, the show started, and she slipped away to her office to count the money. During the forty-plus years she served as Manager of the Ryman, she never saw one show.

There are infinite other interesting firsts with the *Opry* and the Ryman. Like the first time Ernest Tubb performed using Jimmie Rodgers' guitar that he borrowed from Rodgers' widow. Or going back even further to DeFord Bailey, the first African American to perform on the *Opry*. Bailey played his signature harmonica on the barn dance radio show in 1925 before it was even called the *Grand Ole Opry*. On December 10, 1927 he played his trademark song "Pan American Blues" on the radio program as the announcer introduced him and subsequently referred to the show as the *"Grand Ole Opry"* for the very first time. *Bailey was the first artist to be mentioned along with the new Grand Ole Opry show title!* Sadly, after performing on the *Opry* for over fourteen years, Bailey was fired in 1941 for seemingly vague reasons. He spent the remaining years of his life shining shoes and renting out rooms in his home to make his way.

Charley Pride is often cited as the first black solo singer to perform on the *Opry* (I suppose because Bailey was an instrumentalist?). Originally a baseball player, Charley Pride pitched four shutout innings in the Negro All-Star victory over the Major League All-Star team, which included Hank Aaron and Willie Mays. But Charley Pride transitioned from baseball to singing and went on to have his first hit single "The Snakes Crawl at Night" in 1965, the song he performed in his *Opry* debut in 1967.

Despite all the history between the *Opry* and the Ryman, in 1974 the *Opry* moved to a new facility about nine miles outside of town, one with air conditioning and cushion seats. The final Ryman show on March 15 was emotional to say the least. Minnie Pearl had to leave the stage in tears and came back out to a standing ovation. Roy Acuff closed the show, "You just don't know how much we do appreciate you people. It's you who have made the *Grand Ole Opry* so successful. Will you not forget us when we move into our new building? You'll love us for being out there and we'll love you for coming to see us. Thank you. God bless you all. Good night."

The Ryman faced years of vacancy, the threat of demolition, and new ownership before it found its salvation in the form of renovation in the early 1990s. When I gave my graduation speech "It's About Time" I obviously didn't have a crystal ball, but I *did* predict something special would happen in 1999. And it was 1999 when the *Grand Ole Opry* finally returned to perform once again in the Mother Church of Country Music, The Ryman Auditorium. It was about time.

After touring the backstage dressing rooms, we were led into the auditorium where we browsed other artifacts and informational videos. I was in awe upon stepping into the main room of the former tabernacle. The stained glass windows, the church pew seating. But the thing that really took my breath away? The stage. The stage where it all happened was right there before me. I had to get up on that stage.

Turns out anyone can get up there, you just have to pay $20 for a souvenir photo. I threw cash at the photographer and snatched Margaret by the arm as quickly as I could, dragging her and her haunted back pain up on stage with me. There were prop instruments available for the photo op. She chose the banjo and I picked the guitar while we posed for our shot. Once the photographer assured us that she had a good one with our eyes open, tummies tucked in, and no double chins, we were free to come down.

But I couldn't. I was standing on the stage of the Ryman Auditorium for heaven's sake. Ernest Tubb was *right here*. And Hank Williams, Patsy Cline and Loretta. Right here, facing out toward all these church pews just as I was. No way was I leaving that stage without…without *singing*.

"Can I sing something?" I asked the photographer, who shrugged back at me.

I looked at Margaret who shut down any notion of a duet. "You can sing, I'm not singing."

I blanked. I couldn't think of any titles of any songs I'd ever heard in my life. "What should I sing?" I was panicking. The glare of the stage lights felt hotter than Hades.

Margaret didn't blink an eye, "Try 'Coal Miner's Daughter'."

I gulped, clutched my prop guitar like a safety blanket, and started singing into the fake microphone. "Well, I was born…" I belted out a few words and couldn't believe how terrible I sounded! I didn't sound this bad in the shower – what the hell? I was screechy and breathy and awkward. I couldn't remember the words to a song I'd been singing for over twenty years. I felt dizzy and started singing louder, which made everything worse. Finally I just hammed it up in one final ridiculous burst and then quit mid-chorus after disastrously missing a few notes.

My debut at the Ryman was unceremoniously met with nothing but silence. A few of our fellow tourists were watching a history video off to the side. Some shadowy figures in the back were checking out Porter Wagoner's Nudie suit in a glass case. Margaret replaced her prop banjo and the photographer was extending her hand, offering us our cheaply printed souvenir photos. Not exactly the vaudeville hook, but I was being led offstage nonetheless. Needless to say, I did not encore.

Perhaps the ripe old age of forty-two is when it's best to quit thinking, "It's just not my time yet" and start to accept the fact that, "It's just not my calling." I'm probably never going to be a singer. Sadly I'm the only one who even considers that a newsflash. Maybe the only thing I am meant to do with a song is listen to it.

Shortly after my dilettante moment on stage, our four other girlfriends wandered up from their tour. I decided we needed a group photo with all six of us and lured everybody back up on stage for a final quick picture. We handed out fake instruments and laughed as we huddled around each other and the microphone. Just after the photographer clicked the picture, one of my friends cried out, "Nobody move! I just lost a diamond earring! I know it's on the floor here somewhere, it just slipped out."

In slow motion we scanned the wood stage floor and quickly spotted it lying by someone's foot, perhaps not far from where Patsy Cline once stood. We had a good laugh about how ridiculously non-honky-tonk we were. We were six forty-something suburban moms, former debs, and aging Honeybears posing with banjos and guitars on the stage of the Mother Church of Country Music. And one of us loses her diamond stud earring. It's almost too poetic for words.

I couldn't resist the near rhyme of it and burst out with, "You lost your diamond at the Ryman!" And then about two steps down from the stage, it hit me, "Hey, y'all, wouldn't that be a great title for a song?"

Diamond at the Ryman. I lost my diamond at the Ryman. I found my diamond...how it shined...brighter than....then I lost it. Lost hope and faith...lost my diamond at the Ryman. Is it a happy song? Lost then found...or a sad song? Found then lost. Diamond...light...within. Hmm...

I suppose there will always be a song inside of me trying to work its way out one way or another, either by voice or by pen. How can you silence hope while standing on the stage of *The Ryman* for heaven's sake? It's hard to comprehend just how many dreams have come true under the watchful gaze of its stained glass windows. The hayseed needles in a haystack, the diamonds in the rough that were discovered under these lights. My friend's diamond wasn't the first star to be found shining on this stage, and it won't be the last. I like to try to calculate the number of Saturday nights that launched the careers of so many performers, standing on the verge of a new beginning. It has been a gateway for legends, to be sure. Fame, no fame. Singer, listener. Either way the Ryman Auditorium will always be a magical place for the hopeful soul. Close your eyes, tap your toes, open your heart, and let faith pour out. Then wait for a miracle. And why not? It did, after all, make its debut as a church.

CHAPTER 12 SOUNDTRACK:

Lovesick Blues – Hank Williams
(CLIFF FRIEND, IRVING MILLS)

Walk the Line – Johnny Cash
(JOHNNY CASH)

A Church, a Courtroom and Then Goodbye – Patsy Cline
(EDDIE MILLER, W.S. STEVENSON)

Honky Tonk Girl – Loretta Lynn
(LORETTA LYNN)

Coal Miner's Daughter – Christine Warren as Sissy Spacek as
Loretta Lynn
(LORETTA LYNN)

The Ryman Auditorium, Nashville TN

Christine in her Hideous Gown (far left) with high school friends
The Eve of Janus Deb Ball, Nashville TN, December 31, 1991
Photo credit: Harkness Brown

On stage at the Ryman Auditorium with good friends from high school
During the Ryman's daytime Backstage Tour, Nashville TN, February 2, 2013

The Gospel of Women

Maybe it's the Honeybear upbringing, but I've always admired women with a spirit of rebellion. Strong but feminine, bold but kind. I think war correspondent Christiane Amanpour is a badass and brings khaki to life like no one else can, not even Banana Republic in the '80s. It's hard for me to reconcile that Julia Sugarbaker isn't a real person, even harder to understand that she and I aren't really sisters. (Her character *was* a Tridelt at UNC Chapel Hill just as I was.) I have a particularly soft spot for the ground-breaking comediennes, making their mark in an industry that's almost as tough on women as country music. Julia Louis-Dreyfus is a hero and not just because people used to say I reminded them of Elaine from *Seinfeld*. And is it completely taboo to say that I think Gloria Steinem is great looking?

Nashville was tough on women. If you dig in and start to understand just how male-dominant this southern traditional town was, then you can better appreciate the early female stars of country, not just for their music, but for their perseverance. It wasn't this hard in other parts of the country. Clearly Horace Logan at the *Louisiana Hayride* was more open-minded. When Kitty Wells asked him if she could sing solo on his show, he made it happen and helped create the Queen of Country. The *National Barn Dance* in Chicago was chock full of female stars like Patsy Montana. If Gene Autry was the ultimate Cowboy Singer, Patsy Montana was the female Gene Autry. When you listen to her best known song, "I Want to Be a Cowboy's Sweetheart", you'll find the lyrics aren't at all about doting on her boyfriend as the title might imply, but are actually about stereotypically male cowboy activities like riding the range, roping cows, listening to coyotes howling. Drifting West.

But conservative Nashville wasn't as receptive to women performers and such bold messaging. Expectations of propriety were paramount for female singers who traveled on the road with their husbands or other family members. In the 1960s Loretta Lynn launched the first wave of feminism in country music, with Dolly Parton sweeping in not long after bringing wave two. Even still, they faced deep-seated chauvinism in the industry. Women weren't allowed to headline on the road and country music radio would not play two female songs back to back. This limited their airplay considerably and stunted their career momentum. A woman had to be twice as good to get just as far.

It was similarly challenging for the women behind the scenes. The Nashville music business was built on the backs of women, women who would take the low paying organizational, administrative jobs. They would nurture a business from scratch just in time for the men to come in and take over once it was profitable.

A look back in time paints a pretty bleak picture for women in this industry – near hopeless. But as my grandfather used to say, "Easter always follows Good Friday." So good news is never far away. And the best news about Nashville is that some groundbreaking angels of honky-tonk came along and carved a unique path for women in country music. Here are my Music City heroes.

When Kitty Wells sang "It Wasn't God Who Made Honky Tonk Angels", it was considered controversial, provocative, and ground-breaking as it not only dares mention the idea of a cheating wife, but defends her. To understand how saccharine pop culture was at this time – the same year that Kitty Wells released it in 1952 – Lucille Ball shocked the world when she appeared pregnant on her TV show. This was unheard of in the early '50s. The fact that Lucy was expecting a baby with her real life husband, who was also her on-screen husband, wasn't enough to temper the sexual nature of seeing a pregnant woman on television.

Kitty Wells faced a similar hyper-moralism with her breakout song. A horrified *Opry* censor claimed, "You can't sing that song on the *Opry* because of the lyrics. You know, that part about the trusting wife going wrong." But the song reached the fans nonetheless and it struck a chord, ultimately catapulting Kitty Wells into celebrity as well as her *Opry* membership.

This was also the first "response" or answer song, a brazen move for the era. The idea that a woman would back-talk in such a way was heady, to say the least. Hers was the first of many answer songs to follow, creating a niche subgenre in country music. Kitty Wells also recorded "I'm Paying for This Back Street Affair" in response to Webb Pierce's "Back Street Affair". And Jody Miller describes the prison of domesticity in "Queen of the House", which was an answer song to Roger Miller's "King of the Road". Roger Miller romanticizes the drifting nature of a man riding the rails while Jody Miller's song brings things right back down to earth, describing the very real, grounded scene of life at home. These answer songs served as a check-and-balance for the suspended reality men often described in their honky-tonk songs of broken hearts and drifting dreams.

Kitty Wells cracked open the door for every female country singer that followed. Loretta Lynn is effusive in giving all credit to Kitty Wells, noting that she is her hero. In her own words, "If I had never heard of Kitty Wells, I don't think I would have been a singer myself."

And yet, Kitty Wells was a transitional figure. She started the revolution but others would carry the torch and see it through. While she was the first female solo artist and had a breakout hit with innovative messages, her vocal style was restricted and very careful. Her appearance remained conservative country feminine. Think gingham dresses. She was happily married to her singer husband, Johnnie Wright, and enjoyed the security of traveling with him and having him serve as her manager. Despite her first feisty hit song, in reality Kitty Wells and her husband were blessed with a long, traditional marriage. Her career stood the test of time as well, yet another testament to her substance as a performer. In 2000, she and her husband Johnnie Wright retired together. They remained in the same house where they lived together for most of their married life and kept their tour bus in the front yard "just in case."

Meanwhile...have you ever heard of Charline Arthur? It's a shame, but not very many people have.

In 1955 *Country and Western Jamboree Magazine* published their DJ's Choice Poll, which listed Charline Arthur as runner-up to Kitty Wells for Best Female Singer. Charline Arthur was born in Texas in a railroad boxcar. She was the second of twelve children and displayed extraordinary musical talent at an early age. At twelve, she wrote her first song, "I've Got the Boogie Blues". She had the opportunity to meet fellow Texan and Patron Saint of Upstart Honky-Tonkers, Ernest Tubb, who inspired her to get deeper into music. At fifteen she landed a gig on a Paris, Texas radio station. When a traveling medicine show blew through town, she left with it. Eventually she married a fellow musician who would help manage her career, although their marriage would not last. Charline Arthur was a honky-tonk virtuoso, not just a vocalist, but also skilled at playing lead guitar, rhythm guitar, fiddle, steel guitar, mandolin, banjo and the harmonica. She played the Texas honky-tonk circuit and ultimately moved to Dallas where she headlined the *Big D Jamboree*, a role that was most unique to women at the time.

While she and Kitty Wells were both venturing into new territory for women, the similarities pretty much end there. First of all, Charline Arthur sang from somewhere deep, deep in her gut. Her voice was loud and expressive, bluesy and booming. And then, there was her wardrobe. She shocked everyone by wearing pants on stage. Charline Arthur wore flamboyant western suits that looked just like the men's suits with fringe and neckties. She was the first woman performer to be photographed with a cigarette. And her stage performances were nothing short of wild, borderline racy. She would jump off amps, sing while lying down, and shake her hips. She herself claimed, "I was shakin' that thing on stage long before Elvis even thought about it." She even toured with Elvis, Johnny Cash, and Jerry Lee Lewis.

So where did she go? Why haven't more people heard of her?

Nashville was not ready for Charline Arthur. She butted heads with RCA producer Chet Atkins, who tried to temper her hard-drinking, brash persona and convert her into a prim and proper lady of country. Unlike others who were just singing honky-tonk, Charline *was* honky-tonk. Although she acquiesced and allowed Atkins to alter her image, the damage was done. She was too outspoken and unsettling for Nashville, and her contract was not renewed. Charline drifted back to Texas, then Idaho, where she lived in obscurity in a trailer, playing rural Idaho clubs to make ends meet until her death in 1987. But her legacy lives on. Patsy Cline cited Charline Arthur as a major influence on her vocal style. She influenced Elvis, too, and is revered in rockabilly circles to this day.

Jean Shepard walks a line somewhere between Kitty Wells and Charline Arthur. Born in Oklahoma, her family was part of the Dustbowl migration to California, where she grew up quite poor. As a teen, she had an all-girl honky-tonk band called the Melody Ranch Girls, which garnered the attention of Oklahoma country and western star Hank Thompson. Thompson went to bat for Shepard with Ken Nelson at Capitol Records, who responded bluntly, "Hank, I don't think there's any place in country music for women."

Hank replied, "But every band needs a girl singer, don't they?"

So Jean Shepard was a girl singer at the start of her career. Despite his initial sexist leanings, record executive Ken Nelson did work with Jean Shepard and served as her mentor for many years. Jean Shepard was just eighteen years old when she recorded her first single, "Twice the Lovin' (In Half the Time)". The lyrics were avant-garde and sexually charged, especially for a teenager. Her first big hit was a duet with Ferlin Husky called "A Dear John Letter". Shepard was too young to leave the state of California to go on tour, so her parents had to sign a document appointing Ferlin Husky as her guardian. Back then all female singers traveled with their husband, a brother, or as a family troupe. It was unheard of for a young girl to be on the road on her own. But Jean Shepard knocked down this and other barriers throughout her career. She was the first female to sing about her own infidelity without pointing the finger at cheating men. Although she did that, too. In "Root of All Evil" she spells out a rather cynical view that men are the cause of all sin, heartache, and cheating, and urges compassion for honky-tonk girls. Her voice was about as honky-tonk as it gets. Bold projection with coloratura yodel breaks, plenty of twang, and countless vocal tricks.

Shepard made her way to the *Ozark Jubilee* program where she met her first husband, musician Hawkshaw Hawkins. She would move on to the *Grand Ole Opry*, becoming a member at just twenty-one years old. Tragically Hawkshaw Hawkins was killed in 1963 in the same plane crash that claimed Patsy Cline's life. For a period of time Jean Shepard was on her own as a working widow in the Nashville country music industry until she remarried Benny Birchfield.

Nicknamed the "Honky-Tonk Heroine" Jean Shepard has made a lasting impact on the face of country music. She was the first woman to record a concept album. Hers was called *Songs of a Love Affair* and each song represents a certain stage in a romantic relationship.

And like a good honky-tonk song, Jean Shepard spoke the truth and pulled no punches. When she first arrived in town she introduced herself to her idol, Hank Williams. He offered, "Well, young lady, they tell me you want to be a country singer."

Jean said, "Yes, sir."

"Ain't many women in country music."

"No sir, but I'm fixin' to change that!"

Hank grinned. "Well, good luck to you, sweetheart!"

Shepard channeled her unedited personality to champion the rights of Vietnam veterans and tried to increase the union pay scale for backup musicians. She was always a stalwart supporter of traditional country music, and sometimes her lack of moderation affected her career. Once, before a concert, she learned that country radio stations were starting to boycott her music. She went on stage and blasted the radio stations, firing up the crowd to call in on Monday morning and request *traditional country music*, maintaining that radio was there to serve them, the fans. Her record company rang up her husband and told him, "You need to tell Jean to tone down her little speeches she's been giving on stage."

Perhaps a student of her song lyrics, her husband Benny Birchfield was too smart to fall into that briar patch and retorted, "I have to live with her! You tell her! Besides that, she believes in every word she says, and who am I to tell her that she's wrong?"

Despite personal hardship and professional setbacks, Jean Shepard has displayed enormous staying power in country music and remains an active member of the *Grand Ole Opry*. She is vehemently proud of her role in the *Opry* and lambasts other members who don't take seriously their commitment to perform their minimum number of shows annually.

I love Jean Shepard. Perhaps it's her unfettered authenticity or the fact that she has picked killer honky-tonk songs through the years. Then again, her vocal prowess stands alone. Either way Jean Shepard is the ultimate honky-tonk heroine who continues to fight the good fight.

Along came Patsy Cline. When Patsy first auditioned for the *Opry* with Texas honky-tonk pianist Moon Mullican backing her up, the result was lackluster. And then of course when she finally did make her *Opry* debut, she left the stage in tears, worried that her song fell flat and she would never be invited back. But there was no way to quell a talent and a voice like the one, the only Patsy Cline. Before her untimely death at the young age of thirty-one, she recorded 102 songs and left an indelible mark on the musical landscape. She was the first female artist to headline her own show, garnering top billing over male performers in the same program. Based on contemporary girl singers, she should have been introduced as "Pretty Miss Patsy Cline". But because of her stardom and stature as a singer she received a more substantive intro similar to that of Johnny Cash and other men in the industry. "Ladies and Gentlemen, the One and Only, Patsy Cline." She was the first woman of country music to perform at Carnegie Hall, and the first to headline her own Vegas show.

Patsy Cline was known for her bravado as well as her voice, but truthfully she just wanted to get along and be a part of the group. Since the group often consisted of male musicians, she garnered a reputation for acting like "one of the boys." She is also described as incredibly sweet and tirelessly generous, especially with young artists arriving in Nashville. She was known to mentor other female singers and even pay expenses while they were finding their way so they could remain in Nashville to follow their dreams. If you were her friend, she called you "Hoss". She referred to herself as "The Cline" which seems mildly cocky, but also quite playful.

What the hell, she deserved it and then some. The world was transfixed by The Cline as she evolved into a country legend and then, posthumously, a figure of cult-like proportion. She started out in western skirts, cowboy hats, and fringe hanging from pretty much any place you could glue gun fringe. Her first label required that she only perform country songs. But once she was released from that contract and Owen Bradley got a hold of her, she began to evolve in both music and fashion into a crossover pop star. She wore more and more glamorous contemporary clothing, including cocktail dresses and evening gowns.

Many have taken a stab at describing her voice, but honestly there are no words to capture its true essence. It was velvety smooth, powerful, sonic, booming. She was capable of so much projection she made a Broadway star look meek. The amount of showmanship and emotion she released through her voice was in sharp contrast to the restrained nature of Kitty Wells. Patsy wasn't a songwriter herself, but she reinvented countless covers as well as performed first-time songs penned by some of Nashville's greatest songwriters. Hank Cochran and Harlan Howard, for example, co-wrote her megahit "I Fall to Pieces". Harlan Howard once commented that he didn't always know what his song was supposed to sound like until Patsy Cline brought it to life. Of all the songs that he wrote and other singers have performed, Willie Nelson maintains that Patsy Cline's version of his song "Crazy" is his favorite.

Patsy is known for belting out sad, slow, weeping, smooth ballads. Owen Bradley cultivated her into a pop crossover star, emblematic of the Nashville Sound. But her voice was incredibly versatile. On certain songs she nailed a typically honky-tonk vocal style, including yodels and her signature "growls". Her version of Hank's "Lovesick Blues" is off the charts in colorful honky-tonk. On "There He Goes" she emotes the power of a true blues singer. Her voice sounds like a pitch perfect organ on the smoother crossover hits such as "Leavin' on Your Mind", "Why Can't He Be You", and "You Belong to Me". I don't know how to describe Patsy Cline's voice any better than those who have come before me. All I know is that when I was a teenager listening to Patsy Cline, her voice sounded the way I wanted to look when I grew up.

On March 2, 1963 Patsy Cline played her next to last performance in Birmingham, Alabama along with Tex Ritter and Jerry Lee Lewis.

After the show she was asked to do a benefit concert the following day in Kansas City to honor radio DJ Cactus Jack who had been killed in an automobile accident. Despite the fact that she had the flu, Patsy did the show in Kansas City, which tragically would be her last. She wore a white chiffon dress as she sang her final song, a Moon Mullican composition called "I'll Sail My Ship Alone". It was also the last song she ever recorded.

While returning to Nashville on March 5, Patsy Cline and other country artists died as their small plane crashed in Camden, Tennessee. Singer Roger Miller and other friends frantically tromped through forested areas until they found the wreckage. Scavengers weren't far behind, looting the crash site and taking personal items found scattered among the leaves and grass. Ultimately many of those items were donated to the Country Music Hall of Fame. The chiffon white dress she wore in her final performance never resurfaced.

One of Patsy's best friends was Loretta Lynn, who famously grew up in meager conditions, the daughter of a Kentucky coal miner. I think I have seen the movie *Coal Miner's Daughter* no less than a thousand times, and thus fell in love with Loretta's music at an early age. Her voice is wholly different than Patsy's. Not nearly as booming, instead marked by an authentic hillbilly accent that could never quite be repackaged or replicated. Loretta was country. Loretta still is country. Her canon of hit songs is vast, but her lasting legacy is the fact that she is a songwriter. Rather unexpected from the fourteen-year old child bride turned girl singer, turned mega star. But it was her songwriting that turned the world of country music on its head and launched a feminist revolution within the industry. Her lyrics were frank and reflected a period when women were fed up and ready to stake claim to their equal rights as human beings. A champion voice for the domestic downtrodden, in ways she was a more effective feminist spokesperson than someone like Gloria Steinem. Because Loretta *lived* her lyrics. She wrote and sang about cheating husbands, divorced women, drinking, carousing, and even (gasp!) birth control.

Ironically, Loretta Lynn didn't consider herself a feminist and even fell asleep on a television talk show once when a women's lib expert was being interviewed next to her. The host asked Loretta what she thought about the woman's remarks. Suddenly startled back awake, her disoriented response was merely, "What?" The audience laughed out loud at Loretta's accidental snub of her fellow guest. Loretta Lynn routinely underplayed her role as a feminist in the country movement, claiming that she simply didn't tolerate double standards for men and women.

Noted country music historian Robert K. Oermann offers an alternate analysis. He feels Loretta Lynn was genuinely naïve, at least in the beginning, and was literally just writing songs about her life. Regardless, Loretta Lynn was hardly a one-hit wonder who got lucky. It's not as if she wrote one edgy hit and pulled back on the throttle from there. Following are just a few of Loretta's self-penned classics:

"You Ain't Woman Enough" (1966) – This famous feisty tune isn't autobiographical. A distraught fan approached Loretta backstage at one of her concerts, upset that her cheating husband had brought his girlfriend to the show. Loretta peeked out into the audience and checked out the philanderer and his mistress, covered in make-up, and promptly told the woman she had nothing to worry about. *She ain't woman enough to take your man away.* It's interesting that in this moment, as in the song, Loretta sets aside the cheating man and deals with the issue woman to woman, claiming there would be victory for true character over superficial fluff. Loretta doesn't indulge in self-pity or allow the cheated upon wife to play the victim. The wife will win over the cheap-looking jezebel because in the end, she has something in her corner that the mistress will never have: she is *married* to him. And that has currency.

"Don't Come Home a Drinkin'" (1967) – Bluntly, this song is about a woman who is pissed off that her husband goes out drinking then comes home wanting sex. The notion that a good girl would talk so openly about liquor and sex was shocking in 1967. But Loretta continued to strike a chord with fans.

"Fist City" (1968) – Country music is no stranger to aggressive lyrics, but in this song Loretta is plainly threatening physical violence against a town tramp who is coming around too close to her man. This gutsy song is highly autobiographical as she was married to a philandering man, which understandably fueled a jealous fire within her. It's pretty powerful leverage to be able to write a song as an admonition, then record it and have it become a number one country hit. I'd say that's quite a dramatic way to send a message to the town hussy. Lynn has confessed to being in a few scrapes in her life, admitting she had to "scratch and kick and bite and punch." Remind me never to get on Loretta's bad side.

"Your Squaw is on the Warpath" (1969) – This is another rant against the drunk husband coming home looking for love, rife with Native American symbolism. The single appeared on an album with this same title that featured Loretta Lynn in a sexy Pocahontas-style Indian costume, looking tan and infinitely sassier than her typical country girl persona. Allmusic.com gives the album four out of five stars and ranks the creative design as "one of the classic politically incorrect album covers." I sometimes use it as my Facebook profile picture.

"Rated X" (1972) – This frank tune discusses the Scarlet Letter that women are branded with after divorce. She talks about the stigma, the stereotypes, and the fact that divorced women can't be friends with men without drawing the ire of married housewives.

"The Pill" (1975) – Talking about birth control was just about as controversial as it could get in country music in the mid-1970s. Here is this southern, married country girl who is talking about how she can enjoy sex so much more now that she doesn't have to worry about getting pregnant...*again.*

It seems Loretta Lynn has remained true to her rural upbringing despite decades of fame and umpteen hit songs. I saw her perform once in Pensacola, Florida, and she exceeded my inflated expectations. She was a vision of lavender in a poofy, highly flammable country ball gown, feisty as hell as she rambled about husband-stealing hussies, was friendly with her fans, and down-home chummy as she bantered with her band. Even in her seventies, her voice was as strong as ever and her songs have stood the test of time. I cried after the show, it was beyond overwhelming to see her live.

The next honky-tonk angel to take Nashville by storm was Tammy Wynette. Tammy was born Virginia Pugh in rural Mississippi. She was married in high school and had three children by the time she was twenty-two. While living in Birmingham, she got her beautician's license to make ends meet because her husband wasn't getting the bills paid. A side interest in music and singing grew until she decided she wanted to go up to Nashville and take a shot at becoming a country star. Her soon-to-be-ex husband was less than encouraging. As she had one foot out the door off to become a star, he shouted at her, "Dream on, baby!"

She dragged her young children all over Nashville as one opportunity after the next ended in rejection. Shortly after producer Billy Sherrill turned her away, he received a phone call from a fellow music executive who was bragging about how he too had kicked her to the curb. Sherrill felt bad for Pugh and brought her back in to test-record the song "Apartment No. 9". The first time she sang it in the studio with the session musicians, she nailed it. Guitarist Jerry Kennedy pulled Sherrill aside and said, "Do you realize what you've got here?" Sherrill signed her and immediately changed her name.

It was 1968 when Billy Sherrill and Tammy Wynette were in the studio recording songs for her fifth album. With one hour left on the studio schedule and all the best session musicians on hand, they needed one more song to round out the record. Quickly, Tammy Wynette wrote her first original composition with Billy Sherrill fine-tuning it. Together they composed one of the most recognized and controversial country hits of all time, "Stand by Your Man". Right away it became a lightning rod issue between conservative southern family values and the growing momentum of women's liberation. Feminists claimed the lyrics were demeaning and encouraged beleaguered housewives to take whatever abuse a degenerate husband was dishing out, no matter the suffering. Tammy Wynette defended the song, claiming it was evocative of the loyal values she admired in her mother and grandmother's marriages, a nod to the traditional upbringing she herself had known.

The issue flared back up nearly a quarter of a century later when Hillary Clinton negatively referenced the song in an interview with *60 Minutes*. In an attempt to quell campaign focus on her marriage and her husband's previous affair, Hillary Clinton famously insisted she wasn't "some little woman standing by her man like Tammy Wynette."

Tammy Wynette saw the interview and was instantly flush with ire. She was less angry about the diss of the song and more offended that she had been called "some little woman."

I hear ya, Tammy. Unfortunately sometimes women who proclaim to be all about women's rights are the very ones who step on other women to get to the top. It's a shame that sometimes the sisterhood looks more like a catfight.

Clinton received backlash, while once again Wynette was in the position of having to defend her simple country song. According to Tammy's friend, Evelyn Shriver, Tammy remarked, "It's unbelievable to me that a song that took me twenty minutes to write, I've spent twenty or thirty years defending."

Personally I don't understand why the song is so unsettling to feminists. I despise sexism, I often fall on the feminist side of issues, and I would certainly never expect a woman to put herself or her children in harm's way by staying in an abusive relationship. But setting aside that extreme example, I think the song highlights the strength of women, not their weakness. Anyone who has been married, oh, I don't know… *ever*, knows there are times it is infinitely harder to stay *in* the marriage for the long haul rather than bail. And the song is about forgiveness, accepting someone you love as human. I don't know about you, but I think forgiveness can be one of the most character-challenging exercises in life. Forgiveness is not for cowards, that's for damn sure.

Ironically, at the time she wrote and recorded the song, Tammy Wynette was in the process of having her second marriage annulled. In 1969 she married third husband George Jones, creating the first megawatt "country couple". Despite the good music they produced together, their relationship was stormy, and the marriage ended in divorce. Tammy had two marriages end in divorce and two marriages end in annulment before settling into her fifth marriage for the long haul.

Tammy's star continued to rise with a slew of hit songs. Her voice was incredible, and Sherrill claimed part of her success was that "she lived every tear everybody ever heard her sing." She was known for her remarkable range, able to travel from low notes to high in the blink of an eye. Sherrill suggested it wasn't so much a wide vocal range as she sang both loud and soft so well. Now who am I to argue with Billy

Sherrill? But I'm telling you, Tammy Wynette had *range*. Just try to sing one of her songs and hang with her note for note.

As dynamic as her voice was, Tammy Wynette wasn't known for her showmanship on stage. She stood like a statue while releasing all levels of human emotion through her voice. Even Dolly Parton marveled, "I could not believe that all of that voice and all that sound was comin' out of a person standin' totally still. I'd think, 'How is she doin' that?' It seems like you'd have to lean into your body or bow down into it or somethin' to get all of that out. I've never seen anything like it to this day. I was in awe of her. I thought she had one of the greatest voices of all time."

Despite hardships of early poverty, four failed marriages, roughly thirty surgeries for various medical issues, and an addiction to pain killers, Tammy Wynette found her way to the top, claiming the title "The First Lady of Country Music". As the very first country musician to go platinum, male or female, I'd say she earned it. One night after a concert Tammy Wynette was signing autographs for fans. She looked up and saw her first husband standing among the crowd, extending his paper for her autograph. Tammy signed it and added, "Dream on, Baby!"

Despite this enormous success, Tammy remained cautious, never forgetting her meager days in the beginning. Every year until her death Tammy Wynette renewed her beautician's license…just in case.

Which brings us to Dolly Parton. Dolly is a quick-witted spitfire a la the late great Texas Governor, Ann Richards, but with a gravity-taunting wig collection that would have rivaled that of Marie Antoinette. In my interview with country music historian Robert K. Oermann, he shared that of all the country stars he's met or interviewed or studied during his thirty-five years in the industry, Dolly Parton is hands-down his favorite. I asked why, and he didn't hesitate, "She is everything you would dream she would be and more."

After releasing a few singles with moderate success, Dolly Parton got her biggest break when she joined Porter Wagoner on his country television show. The two became close friends and were known for a string of popular duets. But just as her wig effortlessly towered over his bouffant, her fame quickly began to eclipse his.

Music professor Jocelyn Neal suggests Dolly Parton ignited a second wave of feminism in country music when she released her version of Jimmie Rodgers' "Muleskinner Blues". Other women had recorded the song but Dolly was the first to sing it straight from the male point of view, singing it as if she were the muleskinner. While this whip-cracking, high energy version of "Muleskinner" certainly energized her growing fan base, Dolly had an earlier single that really laid down the law in terms of feminist messaging. In 1968 she released a tune called "Just Because I'm a Woman", which shuts down the shaming of women for having sexual desire as it calls men on the carpet for perpetuating double standards. Dolly as narrator isn't claiming to be an angel, she's just saying she isn't any worse than a man who behaves the same way. And she also touches on the age-old Madonna Whore Complex, describing men who have no problem cattin' around with women until they are ready to get married, then dump the wilder girl-friend in favor of a more "pure", wife-like woman. It's another edgy, provocative tune, especially in the context of the late 1960s.

In 1974, after seven years on the Porter Wagoner show, Dolly decided to leave to pursue her career in a more independent light. Porter Wagoner was *livid*. Dolly claims she was always upfront with Wagoner, telling him at the outset that someday she wanted to have her own show. But Wagoner fought her tooth and nail, and a nasty legal battle ensued. Industry buzz wasn't on Dolly's side, shocked she would leave such a stable entity and predicting this move would be the nail in her coffin. In the end, Dolly Parton had to pay $1 million to Porter Wagoner (an astronomical sum by any standards, but certainly in 1974) and faced naysayers at every turn.

She proved them all wrong. Dolly Parton was becoming *DOLLY*. Ultimately she was offered a record deal outside of Nashville (Los Angeles) and once again the doomsday chorus claimed Dolly was bound to fail. She was trying to cross over. She was going pop. Dolly Parton was leaving country music. Her response was simply, "I'm not leaving country music, I'm taking it with me." Once again, she shut down her critics with a massive number one hit called "Here You Come Again".

Even after the song was a runaway success, someone pitifully tried to tear her down, suggesting, "Yeah, but a monkey could have had a hit with that song."

To which a good-natured Dolly responded, "Well, a monkey did."

The same year she left the Porter Wagoner show, 1974, she released a self-penned single, "I Will Always Love You", as a farewell homage to Wagoner. When she released it, it charted at number one. Dolly began to hear rumors that one of her idols, Elvis Presley, was interested in recording it. She was elated when Colonel Tom Parker contacted her and confirmed that Elvis did, in fact, want to record her song. But Parker insisted Elvis required her to sign over half of the publishing rights to him. Dolly balked. In her own words after the fact, she explained that she may have considered doing so *if* it had been a new song. However she had already recorded and released it, and the charts clearly demonstrated it was a marketable entity. It made no sense to give away half the rights to a proven success. So up-and-comer Dolly Parton turned down the King while he was at the peak of his living legacy. Dolly was devastated. She loved Elvis and could genuinely hear his voice on her composition. More than that, Dolly was a savvy business woman and trusted her instincts. As historian Oermann explained, "No one is going to own half of Dolly."

I am more intrigued with Dolly as a business woman than I am her music. She bucked the norm and decided not to file the songs she wrote with the Nashville publishing companies. She couldn't understand why she would give away a chunk of the rights to her own music when all it took was a call to a lawyer and a little paperwork. She'd done the heavy lifting, the creative work, the strategic part. Why in the world would she give away partial ownership over the tactical part? I love her for this! Dolly was a self-publishing pioneer. Trusting her instincts in this arena paid off in spades when "I Will Always Love You" was reinvented in 1992. Whitney Houston sang it in the blockbuster movie *The Bodyguard*, which became one of the greatest selling soundtracks of all time, driving Dolly's royalties through the roof. Not that it's all about the cold hard cash, but there is vindication that nearly two decades after denying Elvis songwriting credit – a move considered wildly controversial at the time – Dolly

Parton didn't have to share half of those vast *Bodyguard* royalties with Graceland on a song she had written all by herself.

Not only a shrewd business woman, Dolly is also a generous celebrity who, apparently, isn't one to hold a grudge. Years after her rift with Port Wagoner, she learned that he had fallen on hard times financially. Dolly purchased 200 of Porter Wagoner's songs, a value estimated at $1 million at the time, and signed full ownership of them back over to him for free.

At sixty-seven years old Dolly Parton is still kicking down doors and blazing trails. Age has hardly tempered this singer/actor/entrepreneur/philanthropist/songwriter. Once again, Dolly devotee Robert K. Oermann sums Parton up best as he admires her songwriting staying power, "Most writers run out, but she is still writing."

It's interesting that Loretta and Dolly expressed the most feminist lyrics in their music, yet they were both married to one man throughout their lives. Contrastingly, Tammy Wynette, who had to defend the traditional values she described in "Stand by Your Man", was married five times. All of this just highlights the fact that feminism, as a concept, is as complex as the women who are at the crux of the conversation. Personally, I feel an independent female spirit is to be lauded and is hardly mutually exclusive to a stable lifelong partnership. I believe you can cheer for women without uniformly bashing men. Too often feminism falls prey to living on the extremes and not digging in to the nuances of women and their real-life relationships. I, for one, am a big fan of chivalry and rue the day men look exactly like women and women look exactly like men. Romance and fairytales depend on a certain dose of difference between the sexes. But the common theme among these breakout country females is speaking out against double standards. None of them are trying to sugarcoat sin or excuse bad behavior, they were simply crying out a revolutionary newsflash: fair is fair. In the process they became a new voice in popular culture, a new breed of storyteller bearing witness to a renaissance of sorts. They did so with unabashed charm, talent, and emotion, laying all of their tears and love at the feet of their fans.

So how is one supposed to be a strong, independent, risk-taking, outspoken woman and still maintain an air of femininity? Is that even important? I believe it is. But how is a woman supposed to strive toward her dreams and play through on her ambitions without emasculating the important male relationships in her life? Well, the answer varies from woman to woman and requires a lifelong process of fine tuning. Which is precisely what I think these hinge-point female country singers were trying to do. They were just doing it through their music, in front of a public audience as well as at home with their husbands. I think it is hardwired into our human nature to cheer for these ground-breaking women, whether you are male or female.

Complicated feminist issues aside, the bottom line is it was a chauvinistic, male dominant industry and these women were underdogs. And no other style of music represents the underdog quite as well as honky-tonk. It is the anointed genre of the downtrodden, wronged, outcast, spiritually off-course, and forsaken. Kitty, Charline, Jean, Patsy, Loretta, Tammy, Dolly...I love these honky-tonk angels. I love them for their grit and their perseverance. I love that they chased their dreams while juggling motherhood and real-life marital issues. I love that each one conveyed her own unique brand of femininity, while speaking out against double standards. But most of all, I love them for the songs they have given us. Rock on, sister chicks, rock on.

CHAPTER 13 SOUNDTRACK:

The Root of All Evil Is a Man – Jean Shepard

(JERI JONES)

Leavin' on Your Mind – Patsy Cline

(WAYNE WALKER, WEBB PIERCE)

The Pill – Loretta Lynn

(LORETTA LYNN, DON MCHAN, TD BAYLESS)

Your Good Girl's Gonna Go Bad – Tammy Wynette

(BILLY SHERRILL, GLENN SUTTON)

Just Because I'm a Woman – Dolly Parton

(DOLLY PARTON)

CHAPTER 14

Matriculation

I was really good at college. Having worked above and beyond in high school and having scored fairly well on various tests, I enrolled in college with thirty hours of advanced placement credit. Essentially I was a sophomore on my first day…and yet I barely graduated in four years. Like I said, I was really good at college.

When it was time to sit down with my high school headmaster and discuss where I might apply, the headmaster praised my track record and suggested the school would like to put its full weight behind me as a candidate for an all-women's college such as Wellesley or Smith. *Oh no, I don't think so.* As much as I'd loved my six years at an all-girl prep school, that era was over. I had no problem telling the headmaster thanks but no thanks. I had worked my ass off for six straight years and I was ready for boys, bourbon and football. I set my sights on The University of North Carolina at Chapel Hill, and thankfully the feeling was mutual. I trotted off to Chapel Hill in the fall of 1989 where I pledged a sorority, met the girls who remain some of my best friends to this day, and was indoctrinated into the colorful (nay, vicious) Carolina-Duke rivalry.

During my freshman year I lived in the all-girl Spencer Dorm where I received no less than seventeen noise violations, most of which were due to my singing Patsy Cline too loudly in the shower. A few of the complaints can be attributed to the brief period when I was preparing to audition for the musical *Hair*. I knew the soundtrack inside and out and felt I was a shoe-in. The only issue was the questionnaire they handed out at the informational session. They asked that everyone check a box with a YES or a NO as to whether or not you were willing to appear fully nude in a live show performance. I wrestled with my decision. My friends and family would freak. Then again, it was for the sake of art. And it would likely seal my chances of a better part. Of course I would appear naked! I checked YES.

I wasn't even asked back for a second audition. I tried not to dwell on what that said about my singing, not to mention my potential nakedness.

Chapel Hill was the most idyllic university town, and I loved every second of college life. Sorority rush, Saturday football games which started at "pig-pickin'" parties in front of the fraternity houses. It was a far cry from the beef brisket barbecue I grew up on in Texas, but Nashville had prepared me for Southeastern pork barbecue. I'll never fully succumb to pork over beef but I will say the pomp and ceremony over those pig-pickin' parties was very compelling.

One of my absolute favorite parts of college, an area where I truly shined, was the proverbial road trip. Chapel Hill was well-positioned geographically for road trips to other colleges, D.C., the mountains, and the beach. And we did it all. One of our earliest road trips was a quick drive to Winston-Salem for our Tridelt Pledge Formal my freshman year. We packed up our formal dresses, booze, and dates and settled in to a nice hotel for the overnight celebration. I honestly didn't witness all the drama that caused so much trouble that night, but some of the boys went wild throwing furniture off balconies into the pool below. Firemen came, police were involved, our sorority was placed on probation. I missed all the commotion because I had heard that George Jones was staying in the hotel after his nearby concert and had made it my mission to scour the place until I found him. Unsuccessful, I threw in the towel at about two in the morning and decided to join my date and all our friends at our satellite after-party upstairs. Just as the elevator doors were about to shut, a gravelly male voice asked me to hold it open. George Jones and another guy stepped into the elevator with me. I pressed myself against the back of the elevator in complete silence for the next eleven floors. Eventually I uttered something pointless like, "You're The Possum!" He just looked at me through his aviator sunglasses, said nothing, and walked out once the elevator doors reopened.

I wasn't the only one who had an encounter with a slightly grumpy Possum that night. JP Madren is a wood-working artisan from North Carolina, and he is also a lifelong country music fan. I stumbled onto his George Jones story online while trying to find any record of the set list or other musicians that performed with Jones at this 1990 concert in North Carolina. I was beyond entertained and contacted JP, who recounted his tale to me in detail over the phone.

In 1990, JP Madren was lucky enough to secure front row seats to the George Jones concert as well as a pass to meet him ahead of the show. In preparation he drew a portrait of George Jones and scraped together $49 to have it professionally framed. He also airbrushed a likeness of George Jones on a t-shirt. When The Possum walked into the backstage room to meet the lucky VIPs, JP was excited and nervous. Upon meeting Mr. Jones he showed him the portrait he had drawn.

George Jones was nonplussed. "I hope I don't look like that." Apparently he didn't appreciate the sense of realism Madren captured in the fine lines of his weathered brow.

Fellow musician, Merle Kilgore, walked up to Jones holding the portrait and exclaimed, "George, that young fella nailed you!"

JP Madren was crushed that The Possum didn't care for his artwork. He left the backstage area and found his way to his front row seat for the concert. During the show he met a man named Webb Friend who was managing concessions for George Jones at the time. He was quite taken with JP's airbrush t-shirt and traded him a George Jones VCR tape for the shirt.

Several months later JP Madren and his wife were at a North Carolina music festival where they ran into Webb Friend once again. This time he was manning the merchandise for Lee Greenwood. They struck up a conversation and Friend was quick to update JP on what had happened after the George Jones concert where they first met. Jones was deeply rattled by the portrait JP had drawn. After his performance he polled all the band members as well as the caterers and anyone who had seen the picture, asking if in fact he really looked like that. Everyone confirmed that JP had captured him perfectly.

According to Webb Friend, this triggered Jones to have a face lift which rendered him unable to smile or sing for three months.

No wonder The Possum wasn't chattier when I ran into him in the elevator that night!

No sooner did we end our probation from the Pledge Formal incident than we were facing another crisis. We had teamed up with the ΣAE fraternity to host a barn-themed party. At least that's what we thought it was supposed to be as we arrived in overalls, bandanas, and braids, looking like we fell right off the set of *Hee-Haw*. The boys had bought a bunch of hay bales and chickens and were calling it "An Old Fashioned Chicken Kickin'". A chicken kickin' is an outdated Appalachian game where you stand in a circle and kick a chicken round and round. If the chicken dies in front of you, you're out. The last person remaining in the circle wins. Now I never saw one chicken harmed, but some of the girls flipped their lids when they got wind of the name of the game and called the authorities. All hell broke loose. It hit the news the next day as the animal rights people and the cops tried to match the receipts from the fraternity's chicken transaction, trying to determine whether or not each chicken was still alive. For a brief period the story centered around one missing chicken. Nearby fraternities hosted deck parties to watch the drama unfold at the ΣAE house, which had patrol cars out front. Supposedly they caused themselves even more trouble when someone splattered the fraternity walls with barbecue sauce and the authorities believed it to be chicken blood.

Ultimately all of the chickens were accounted for unharmed. The university paper reported that the final chicken was found in the middle of the night, wandering around in front of one of Michael Jordan's favorite late night eateries, the Time-Out Chicken Biscuit Restaurant.

My sophomore year I was elected Song Leader of my sorority. Basically during rush, all the sororities felt the best way to recruit new members was to dance around like lunatics in the front yard, sing-screaming well known tunes with altered lyrics. We bastardized the likes of Juice Newton's "Queen of Hearts", Sugarhill Gang's "Rapper's Delight", and Kool and the Gang's "Celebration". Even today I have a hard time not slipping into the Tridelt version of those lyrics. Inevitably the show was more fun for us than it was for the poor rushees standing like statues on the sidewalk feigning interest. My job was to ensure we appeared to be having more fun than the other sororities by picking the best songs and writing hilarious lyrics. Having what I believed was a keen intuition for live performance I knew that decibels were king and the louder we were, the more fun we were having. I wanted to drown out the rival Chi-Os down the street as well as the Pi-Phis around the corner. The run-of-the-mill jambox propped in an upstairs window of the sorority house just wasn't cutting it. We needed an *amp*. I am proud to say, like Ernest Tubb on the *Opry*, I was the first sorority song leader at Carolina to get away with plugging in and amping up. I petitioned for some of the house money budget and ran a little sideline fundraiser to get enough cash for a $500 amplifier. The fact that we were located in a historic district and directly across the street from the chancellor's mansion made me about as popular as Bob Wills' drum kit on the stage of the Ryman. The inscription on my tombstone will probably read, "Challenging noise ordinances to the very end."

Hey, if you can't be good, be loud.

My roommates and I were never popular with neighboring apartments either as we played our music extraordinarily loud, and quite often, very late. While my friends at the University of Texas and SMU were all listening to Willie and Waylon and Merle, there weren't many honky-tonk fans at Carolina. We listened to the likes of Guadalcanal Diary, Blues Traveler, and Drivin N Cryin. I was also really into The Band, the Allman Brothers, Janis Joplin, and Lynyrd Skynyrd. Plus I routinely subjected my roommates to endless hours of Willie, Patsy, Hank Sr., Jerry Jeff Walker, and a country band called Highway 101, which was pretty big during the 1990s. The female lead had an over-the-top nasal voice and their records boasted songs written by the great Harlan Howard and even one hit by Justin Tubb, Ernest Tubb's son.

In Chapel Hill we basically saw most of our live music at one of three places: an outdoor dive bar called He's Not Here, a legitimate music venue called The Cat's Cradle, and fraternity houses. We had some good local bands such as R&B classic Doug Clark and The Hot Nuts, a rock band called Dillon Fence that once had Hootie & the Blowfish open for *them*, and The Connells, who attained indie rock success at a national level. One of the Connells lived in my apartment complex my sophomore year, and it was like seeing a celebrity in the parking lot when he would carry his empty pizza box out to the dumpster.

We were lucky to see all the bands traveling up and down the eastern seaboard track. This was the post-R.E.M. era when everyone was either coming out of Athens or wanted to go play in Athens, so there was a well-worn track from Georgia to D.C. with regular stops in Chapel Hill. We saw Phish, Allgood, Jupiter Coyote. Fraternities booked Widespread Panic and Dave Matthews on the front-end of their fame. We saw them so regularly it almost became blasé. Boyd Tinsley was my favorite. He was the dreadlocked electric violin player for the Dave Matthews Band who routinely chatted with me between sets. I thought I was more than just a little bit charming when I jumped on stage and performed my air fiddle routine right next to him. (I am strangely good at air fiddling, but have found it really only appeals to people if it is very late at night.) Once, Boyd Tinsley and I were both wearing suede fringe jackets and decided to trade coats for the evening. If I'd known how enormous the Dave Matthews band was going to become I might have avoided trading back at the end of the night.

Whether we were catching Phish at The Cat's Cradle, boogying down to Dave Matthews on the front deck of the PIKA house, or even springing for tickets to see Neil Young in the Dean Dome, we would wrap up most of our evenings at the Phi Delt house, where they hosted memorable "late nights". Their playlists kept everyone on the dance floor until the wee hours with danceable classics like "Brick House", "Let's Get It On", and all the vintage Michael Jackson you could handle.

Each summer I would find my way back down to Texas to visit family and work as a camp counselor with Mary. In 1991, the summer after my sophomore year, my mother coordinated a family reunion at the beach in Texas, but it rained the entire time. After one too many rounds of Jenga, we ventured out to see the movie *Thelma and Louise*. As the two on-screen heroines walked into a western bar I heard a honky-tonk song that I instantly liked, and I was desperate to find out what it was. After the movie I made a beeline for the record store in the mall and bought the movie soundtrack. It didn't take long to find the song I was looking for: "I Don't Want To Love You But I Do" by Kelly Willis.

Hmm, Kelly Willis? Never heard of her.

Little did I know I was about to become one of the world's biggest Kelly Willis fans, buying every one of her albums and following her music for decades to come.

I was able to get my honky-tonk fix every summer in the Texas Hill Country, specifically about thirteen miles outside a little town called Burnet. That's where Camp Longhorn is located. I was a camper there as was my mother, my aunt, my uncle, and several cousins. Not only was it a longstanding family tradition, this coed camp was *fun*, especially during the counselor years when we had every other night off to carouse the Texas Hill Country. Nights off always began with sunsets and beer and ended with skinny-dipping in the lake. Time in between was spent at one of the local honky-tonk bars.

Our all-time favorite spot, the headquarters for most of our good times during those Longhorn college summers, was the Bluebonnet. The BB, as we called it, was a weathered, Spanish-style, white stucco building that was one of the greatest Texas honky-tonk bars of all time. The burger counter had long since been shut down, although I remember eating there with my family when I was very young. But in our collegiate BB summers it was just the front bar with a jukebox and pool tables plus a large backroom which hosted occasional live music. When there was a band we'd two-step for hours to covers of George Strait songs. Otherwise we'd gather in the front room, everyone vying to prove they were best friends with Joanne. She was the localebrity bartender who didn't take lip from anybody and bristled when some cocky young counselor dared get behind her bar. In reality, she was a total sweetheart and didn't blink an eye the first summer Mary and I were counselors and showed up with the world's dumbest fake IDs. We'd gone to a place in Dallas called the Lone Star Bazaar where you filled out a form on a clipboard and twenty minutes later some dude handed you an extraordinarily fake driver's license. Mary had suggested we hail from L.A., but we misspelled it on the form, so our licenses said that we lived in "Los Angelos, California". We tried to explain to bouncers and bartenders that it was actually a quaint little town in *northern* California, not the L.A. they were thinking about. Imagine how suspicious, not to mention ridiculous, it must have seemed that not one but *two* IDs from Los Angelos, California wandered into the Bluebonnet bar outside of Burnet, Texas.

The jukebox at the BB was the first long term relationship I'd ever had and I loved it with all my heart. The BB is where I turned into a full-fledged jukebox honey. It was chock full of all the greats like Willie and Merle and Waylon. There wasn't a night that passed that we didn't play Marty Robbins' "El Paso" and "A White Sport Coat". The song "Tear in My Beer" always got all the counselors and locals singing together and swaying beers side by side. Hank Williams Sr. wrote and recorded the song but never released it before his death. Years later his son Hank Williams Jr. recorded his own voice with his dad's on the song to create a duet, and his band filled in the instrumentals along Hank Sr.'s lead guitar. It was released in 1988 and the father-son duo "shared" a Grammy win for the song in 1990.

The good times were unstoppable with that BB jukebox. Somehow we even managed to make a beer-drinking anthem out of the maudlin Doug Stone song "In a Different Light". After countless midnight skinny-dipping escapades throughout the summer, it seemed hilarious to scan the crowd of friends while singing Stone's lyrics about seeing someone *in a different light*. When we weren't dialing up tunes on the jukebox, we were blaring CDs in the car as we buzzed around the Hill Country. We sang at the top of our lungs to Jerry Jeff Walker, David Allan Coe, and Kelly Willis.

And so it went, alternating between Chapel Hill and the Texas Hill Country during my college years. By senior year I had every song Kelly Willis had released to date, was a passionate fan, and had already converted several roommates and friends to her music. I was living in the Tridelt house in a small three-girl room with two of my best friends, Meredith Lowder Thomas and Betsy Burchfield Handler. For whatever reason, ours was the only bedroom with a door straight to the outside world, so we were a very popular path for anyone sneaking boys in or out of the Tridelt house. As we were settling in one day after class I distinctly remember one of our sorority sisters wandering around outside with a basset hound she was dog-sitting named Turkey. I thought that was the cutest, most hilarious name for a dog and decided right then and there, someday I was going to have a basset hound named Turkey in honor of Bob Wills' hometown of Turkey, Texas.

My senior year in college was pretty breezy. We'd exercise like fools, walking a big four-mile loop, and then promptly convene on the steps of the Tridelt house to smoke cigarettes in our exercise clothes and plan our evening on the town. I took a very light course load my senior year, including bowling and modern dance, which allowed me plenty of time to cheer for our beloved Tarheels in both football and basketball. Carolina was actually pretty good in football in those days. Mack Brown was our head coach – before Texas hired him away. In the fall I was nominated PIKA Fraternity Miss Beat Dook Runner Up (I may have been runner up to the runner up) which involved sitting on the back of someone's convertible Miata and driving around town in a makeshift parade trying to rile people up a few days before the Duke football game. That spring, we cheered our Tarheel basketball team all the way to the NCAA Final Four and a National Championship win over Michigan. It was pretty unforgettable to have your school win the national championship your senior year of college. We celebrated straight through the night and I remember hopping a ride home at the crack of dawn on the back of a street sweeper cart that had just finished cleaning up the remains of the party on Franklin Street.

Before long it was time to figure out what the hell I was going to do after graduation. I didn't feel the pressure I probably should have under the weight of such a decision. I was too naïve to realize that the first few years out in the real world could set you on a track toward a certain sphere, a certain group of people, a certain lifestyle. I was shortsighted, foolishly thinking I had all the time in the world to try on a few different lives. Part of me wanted to get up to New York City and push my way into the fashion industry. One of my best friends had a sister, a former Carolina Tridelt herself, who worked at Calvin Klein, and I was intrigued with the idea of following in her footsteps. Then again, another part of me wanted to settle in the Texas Hill Country and open a honky-tonk dive that I could manage with my basset hound at my side. I could book up-and-coming outlaw bands and maybe even step up to the mic once in a while myself. Which would it be? Was I going Fashionista or Bohemia? Honky-Tonk or Debutante? Where did I truly belong?

In a sense I split it down the middle with a move that would merely defer judgment on this internal debate, a debate that would rage on within for years to come.

CHAPTER 14 SOUNDTRACK:

El Paso – Marty Robbins

(MARTY ROBBINS)

In a Different Light – Doug Stone

(BOB MCDILL, DICKEY LEE, BUCKY JONES)

I Don't Want To Love You But I Do – Kelly Willis

(PAUL KENNERLEY)

Tear in My Beer – Hank Williams Sr. and Hank Williams Jr.

(HANK WILLIAMS)

Walkin', Talkin', Cryin', Barely Beatin' Broken Heart – Highway 101

(ROGER MILLER, JUSTIN TUBB)

The Bluebonnet Tavern, Burnet TX
Photo credit: Matthew Murray

Queen of Texas, If Only For a Day

People tend to remember exactly where they were when they received shocking, life changing news. First man on the moon, JFK, The Challenger Space Shuttle. And I can tell you that I know precisely where I was the first time I ever heard anyone suggest that pasta was fattening. *Y'all, have you heard? Now we can't even eat pasta anymore! Apparently it's making us all fat. That's what they're saying, I just read all about it.* I was in a state of total shock, as if time stood perfectly still. Certainly this wasn't true. Pasta was making us all fat? What was this woman talking about...carbs? Pasta was my *healthy* choice for heaven's sake.

This was just one of the many myth-busting moments that I experienced in my twenties. As four years of college inched toward an end, everyone started talking career paths. I didn't exactly have a specific job in my mind so much as a lifestyle I could picture. Part of me sincerely believed my life would turn out like that of Hemingway and the Lost Generation in Paris, writing in cafés and running with Bohemian artists and poet friends. Or, on the other hand, maybe I would charge around New York City with other urbane professionals, my finger on the pulse of the latest fashions, galleries, and restaurants. Then again, the allure of returning to Texas was an overpowering draw.

Having spent the halcyon days of summer in the Texas Hill Country every year since moving away made me prone to overly romantic notions of honky-tonks, jukeboxes, and creative circles of songwriters and musicians.

And then, of course, there was young, collegiate romance. I had a boyfriend who wasn't quite wrapped up with things at SMU, so I set my sights on moving to Dallas to be near him. But the only job I deemed exciting or glamorous enough to rationalize moving for a boy was to work in the buying offices at Neiman Marcus. Neiman Marcus stores were dotted all across the country, but in my mind Neiman's was as Texas as Texas luxury could be. It was founded in Dallas and the headquarters were at the top of the original downtown store. Done, decision made. I was going to be a buyer! Paris, Milan, New York. High fashion, and Texas to boot…I would have it all.

Except they didn't want me. Evidently being Tridelt Rush Chair wasn't enough work experience to be an Assistant Buyer at Neiman Marcus, and I was denied an interview. Multiple times. So during spring semester of my senior year I secured a job at a luggage boutique that imported its bags from Italy. It was the most continental gig I could find in Chapel Hill. I networked with anyone who might have any connections with Neiman Marcus. Mary had a bible study leader at SMU who was the toy buyer, so I approached her about an informational interview. A family friend's secretary knew someone who worked there, so I angled in from that direction. My grandmother was a regular customer, having driven over from Fort Worth to the Dallas downtown store to shop for many decades, so I even appealed to her long-time sales associate for support. In fact it was she, Helen Yampanis of the couture department on the second floor of the downtown Neiman Marcus, who finally got me my big break. She secured an interview with her buyer, who was everything you would imagine a couture fashion buyer to be. She was incredibly cold to me, criticized my beige silk suit, and chastised me for wearing my hair down to an interview. But she must not have despised me as much as she professed because she said she would endorse me to HR and believed that I should, in fact, receive a formal interview.

In preparation I spent every waking moment devouring Stanley Marcus' book <u>Minding the Store</u>. Even though he had long since retired as Chairman of Neiman Marcus he was still the soul and the brand of the company, and the more I read about Stanley Marcus the more validated I felt that this was to be my path. He was utterly fascinating. He was a leader in American fashion and luxury retail, an innovator of Texas commerce, a supporter of the arts, a lover of photography and architecture, and had a heart for the written word. Stanley Marcus was a Harvard graduate and a true renaissance man. He was in the Advertising Hall of Fame, the Texas Business Hall of Fame, received the Chevalier Award from the French Legion of Honor, and was named one of the "20th Century Great American Business Leaders" by Harvard Business School. I will never forget a key point in his book, which he wrote in the early 1970s, as he explained his sales philosophy. Every Neiman Marcus sales associate was to treat anyone who entered the store with democratic courtesy. The young, long-haired hippie in blue jeans was to receive the same service and respect as the wealthy Dallas socialite in a full-length fur. I loved and believed every word that Stanley Marcus wrote. I was inspired and longed to be a part of the world he was describing. In truth, it was already a bygone era but no one could have convinced me of it at the time.

Four days after graduating from Carolina I reported for duty in the Neiman Marcus Executive Training Program. I was an Assistant Buyer representing the nearly thirty Neiman Marcus stores across the country. I had a small one-bedroom apartment in Dallas all to myself and a salary that topped my male peers who were going into banking positions in Atlanta or Charlotte. I felt as though I'd been crowned Queen of Texas. Life was starting.

Shortly after arriving in Dallas, the boyfriend and I broke up. True love lasts forever until it doesn't. It didn't slow me down, though, as I was busy competing against every single one of my new friends in my training program to be the very first placed in a buying office. Even after being admitted to the training program, I had to endure more internal interviews as the buyers picked their next assistant buyers from the fresh crop of trainees. I was the second one placed, a decent enough coup, and found myself Assistant Buyer of hats, gloves, sunglasses, and hair accessories for all twenty-eight Neiman Marcus stores. I was an English major with a focus on Creative Writing managing over 200 vendors and a multi-million dollar budget. My buyer was going through an emotional crisis when I was hired, so I was called upon to make buyer-level decisions on a daily basis, which was nothing short of nerve-wracking.

Snobbery was a communicable disease in luxury retail. Buying offices looked down on sales associates all the while sucking up to them to get them to sell their bad merchandise decisions. Meanwhile the older sales associates wouldn't take any crap from the buying offices and pushed back by telling stories of how they worked directly for Stanley Marcus back in the day. "Mr. Stanley" is what they called him. The only other retailers that Neiman's buyers respected at the time were Barneys and Bergdorf Goodman. Saks, Foley's, and Dillard's were all mocked relentlessly, written off as completely bourgeois. I learned to wield arrogant phrases like "fashion forward", "her look was just so Chanel-inspired", "bridge and tunnel girls", and "you are working my last unequivocal nerve." Assistant buyers were a flock of beautiful vultures that spent rare moments away from work exercising employee discounts and shopping for fashionable items that bumped paying rent that month. That said, we really did work like well-dressed children in an Asian sweatshop – we *had* to work 13-14 hours a day because too many people wanted our jobs. Everyone in the industry dreamed of working in a Neiman Marcus buying office, even girls who lived in *Manhattan*. Even factoring in all of their West Village savvy, a Dallas Neiman's Assistant Buyer topped one of those showroom girls from the city. I did go to New York for fashion week and I did attend fashion shows. It was kind of insane to watch established designers in their sixties suck up to me, a twenty-three-year-old rookie. But I was a *Neiman Marcus Assistant Buyer*, and strangely I held a modicum of control over how much we ordered from them. So even I would get wined and dined and photographed by magazines at chic sushi parties at the Guggenheim.

I loathed every second of it. It was all so vapid and pointless. I actually respected the bottom line and the commerce aspect, but all the endless conversations about street fashion and couture trends and hemlines and whether or not animal print was back in or on the way out again were mind-numbing. I couldn't believe how much these people believed their own bullshit. Fashion week trips were so stressful it hardly felt like the fairytale I'd imagined. The industry didn't feel creative and collaborative; it felt mean and elitist. My favorite part of the job, aside from the beautiful clothes, was working with spreadsheets. Sometimes I would spend as many as thirty hours a week in front of a gross margin spreadsheet trying to predict a multi-million dollar buy that had no less than 8400 item combinations. To this day I happen to know that the average glove size for a woman in Los Angeles is 6.5 while in Boston it's an 8. Based on five-year sales data, I had to predict the accurate number of gloves to purchase by size, by style, and by color for each of the twenty-eight stores. And I had to be ready to defend my purchases (and their daily sales figures) to my boss's boss. Turns out despite taking zero math classes in college I was a bit of an analytical savant with a spreadsheet. I liked finding stories in the numbers. Plus I had a keen instinct with new merchandise and promoting it to the sales floor. But spreadsheets were the most relaxing part of my job, and a much needed escape from the lunatic executive personalities of luxury retail.

By day I was an aggressive Assistant Buyer and by night I was a Honky-Tonk Queen. At Carolina we heard a ton of good live music, but it was predominantly progressive rock. In Dallas everyone was venturing out to see Texas songwriters and two-stepping to honky-tonk music. I was unleashed. I think I went out every single night of the week and there was almost always music involved. I was the self-anointed darling of the Dallas music scene from 1993-1995. We followed a local western swing band called The Cowboys and Indians who patterned themselves after Bob Wills and his Texas Playboys. Sometimes they played at a fabulous little dive bar called Naomi's, but it was even better when they played at the Sons of Hermann Hall. Built in 1911, the hall is a meeting place for a German fraternal organization that originated in New York but was prominent among the large German population in Texas. It is an outstanding place to see live music, and thankfully it's still open after more than 100 years.

Sometimes we'd drive over to Fort Worth to see a Kelly Willis show or maybe even Willie Nelson at Billy Bob's. Most of the time, Dallas offered more music than we could handle. On Sunday nights we'd go to a bar called the Ginger Man to hear a western polka band.

We'd dance the Cotton Eyed Joe outside followed by a folk dance that is popular in Texas dancehalls called the Schottische. But if I had to boil it down, the two joints that were the hotbed of Dallas honky-tonk in the early 1990s were Adair's Saloon and The Three Teardrops Tavern.

Adair's was a teeny dive in the Deep Ellum entertainment area of downtown Dallas, the same area where Blind Lemon Jefferson brought blues fame to Texas. Adair's served delicious greasy burgers and had a honky-tonk jukebox when the music wasn't live. Writing on the walls was encouraged, so the interior was layered with graffiti. It was pretty tight quarters, but that didn't stop people from dancing right up until closing time. Texans can lay a piece of typing paper on the ground and turn it into a dance floor; there is no space too small to twirl if the music is good. The Tuesday house band was my friend, Jack Ingram, who had been a summer camp counselor with me at Camp Longhorn. Right after college he released a self-produced album which propelled him into instant local stardom. Of course now he is a full-fledged alt-country music star who appears on satellite radio and grocery store commercials, but at the time, we were all content to be buddies with The Tuesday Night Singer at Adair's. One night pretty late, a drunk guy requested he sing Willie Nelson's "Shotgun Willie". The crowd was thin and I was belting out the beginning of the song while Jack started strumming it. The drunk guy yelled at me to shut up, but Jack defended me, "Naw, man, she's got a decent voice." (I have no clue why he said this. Perhaps he'd been impressed with my rendition of Loretta's "You Ain't Woman Enough to Take My Man" during the camp counselor skit.) And with that Jack invited me to sing "Shotgun Willie" with him. I may not have hit every note, but I can assure you I didn't miss a lyric.

My daydreams of ditching the world of fashion and becoming a regular singer at Adair's never took shape. I stepped up to the microphone at Adair's just once more, on Valentine's Day Open Mic Night. My father was in Dallas on business, so we had made plans to go to dinner. My boss, the Accessories Buyer, was still lonely over a recent breakup, so I invited her to come along. Somehow the three of us ended up at Adair's after dinner, and pitifully we were the only patrons in there. The only other human beings were the barkeep and the guy playing guitar for those who wanted to perform. After several

Lone Star beers, I mustered up the courage to sing Patsy Cline's "Walking after Midnight".

I did not "encore" as they say in the business. But my performance didn't get me fired from Neiman's, so that's not nothing. That was February 14, 1994, and excluding the rare karaoke experience, I am pretty sure it was the last time I ever sang a complete song into a microphone in a public setting.

The place that really set the pace in Dallas back in those days was called The Three Teardrop Tavern, or just "The Three T's" for short. It was a cavernous dancehall located among the bail bond joints of Industrial Boulevard. Every night the proprietor, John, was decked in full western regalia, which often included full chaps and spurs. The man was a shameless flirt and a bit of a sideshow, but he could book the hell out of some good music. Night after night we poured in to see Jack Ingram, Charlie Robison, his brother Bruce Robison. I loved a local singer Ed Burleson, who had been a rodeo cowboy until he hurt himself and took up singing. The Dixie Chicks were a regular big draw. This was well before Natalie Maines joined the group and took them into the national country pop spotlight. At this point they were still traditional country. I saw my first of many Robert Earl Keen shows at Three T's. He closed the show, as he still typically does, with a popular ballad of his which proclaims that the road will go on forever and the party will never end. One listen to the lyrics proves the opposite for its ill-fated lovers, and yet, I too naively believed it could be true. *The party never ends.*

It's crazy to look back on how much good music I saw in such a short period of time in Dallas – not to mention all the good music I saw that I forgot to remember. I do recall getting a group to go see Gary P. Nunn, who wowed with his unique cosmic Texana songwriter style. He wore little circular sunglasses like John Lennon and a hippie vest with his Wrangler jeans, boots, and a bandana kerchief tied tight around his neck like a cattle drover from the 1800s. I also saw Junior Brown many times at the Three T's and couldn't get over how unique, yet traditional he sounded. He was a honky-tonk, Tex-Mex, surfer sound all rolled up into one. He played a crazy instrument that he invented called the guit-steel. It was a double neck guitar, which was part guitar, part steel guitar. We all had a big time at the Three T's when Junior Brown played a themed Ernest Tubb birthday bash. I was thrilled to be back in Texas where people not only *listened* to Ernest Tubb, they threw parties for him! Finally, I was in my element.

Occasionally we'd peel away to the outdoor amphitheater venue to see the bigger name acts. I went to see Alan Jackson with a group of assistant buyers from Neiman's, and it was a fantastic show. I think Texas music snobs (a fraternity with whom I vociferously associate) and non-country fans sometimes dismiss Alan Jackson as being too Nashville country, but I have always liked him. This Newnan, Georgia boy is *country*. His songs aren't on par with provocative songwriting like Kristofferson or Townes Van Zandt, but he picks good covers, churns out one original hit after the next, and keeps most of them straight up honky-tonk. Simple shuffles about love, loss, drinking, cheating, summertime, and closing time. And he certainly has taken a stand for traditional country music. In 1999 George Jones had a hit song called "Choices" that was critically acclaimed, and Jones was asked to perform it on the CMA Awards show. But they wanted to feature younger acts, so they asked him to perform a mere 30-second snippet of the song as the show went to commercial. Jones was livid and boycotted the CMAs. Alan Jackson was slated to perform his hit cover, "Pop a Top" (I love that song!), in its entirety. But in protest, and as a show of support for George Jones, Jackson and his band played "Pop a Top" about two thirds of the way through and then, much to the surprise of CMA organizers, suddenly started playing George Jones' song "Choices". It took the audience a moment to figure out what he was doing, but once they did they were on their feet with a standing ovation. When he finished, Alan Jackson calmly walked off the stage without sticking around for accolades or accusations. Rumor has it he walked straight out the back door of the auditorium and uttered, "Well, that's the end of my career." Hardly. His songs may lean toward the uncomplicated, but this display endeared him to me for the long haul.

Despite his standoffish lack of response to me in the Winston-Salem hotel elevator, I remain a George Jones fan. I listened to a lot of George Jones in those Dallas days. Blared, is more like it. Instead of having to deal with an RA in the dorm for noise violations, I was in an apartment now, so the police often appeared at my parties due to noise complaints. I liked good music loud, and when I wasn't going to see it live, I was playing it. George Jones, Tammy Wynette, Patsy Cline, Willie Nelson, Mark Chestnutt, Jerry Jeff Walker (I hosted an epic sangria party inspired by his song "Sangria Wine". The police definitely knocked on my door for that one.) But there were never any consequences; nothing bad ever seemed to happen back then.

When I wasn't working or seeing music, the only other pastime was Dallas Cowboy football. This was the super bowl winning era of Troy Aikman, Moose Johnston, and my personal favorite, Michael Irvin. The entire city was consumed with Cowboy mania and there were football watching parties for all of the games. One particularly sophisticated girl from the Neiman Marcus training program had the big idea to drive up north to Randy White's sports bar to see if we could meet some of the players celebrating after a big Cowboys victory. Lines were out the door and around the block, but she didn't blink an eye. She marched us straight to the front and boldly told the bouncer we were on Tony Casillas' guest list. (Casillas was defensive left tackle. I have no clue how she came up with that so fast.) The guy was flustered flipping through his clipboard and just waved us in. We successfully used the Tony Casillas guest list trick two or three more times in the 1993-1994 season.

Work, music, football, parties. Work, music, football, parties. It became an endless cycle and I started to feel like I was living in a salad spinner. Something had to give. And of course it would have to be the job. While my father always advised, "Never quit a job without another job," I have never once followed that sage advice. When I left Neiman Marcus I launched a fourteen-year pattern of burning bright and fading fast. I would work like a maniac and then flame out completely, leaving each job in a blaze of glory and myself thoroughly depleted.

I decided marketing, not fashion, was my true path, and to some degree I was right. I would work in the corporate marketing and consulting realm off and on for the next dozen or so years. The first spot was a small direct marketing boutique in Dallas called Narrowcasting. It had four partners and one-worker bee – me. Coincidentally, one of the partners was none other than the man, the guru himself, Mr. Stanley Marcus. And I had the opportunity to work with him personally on a weekly basis. He was everything I had built him up to be. He was the most elegantly dressed gentleman with perfectly tailored suits, pocket squares folded with origami-like precision, a beautiful walking cane, and the most creative cufflinks. He had a soft nature about him, a wise tone, and a sense of humor. At age eighty-nine he didn't drive. His driver would bring him to our offices and drop him off, and he would just hitch a ride from anyone who was available, sometimes even me. It was mortifying to have the most dapper man in the history of the free world piled into my red Honda Prelude with Whataburger bags littered on the floor, but I didn't care because I was always excited to have some one-on-one time with Mr. Marcus. We would talk about computers – he was taking private classes to learn how to use email and the Internet. It was only 1995 for goodness sake – many of my friends were still without an email address! We also talked a lot about Santa Fe. He had a vacation home there and was a big fan of my cousin, a Santa Fe artist who had recently passed away.

As luck would have it we were both going to be in Santa Fe over the holidays, so I blurted out, "Would you like to come over for a glass of wine and see the art in my cousin's house? We'll all be over there on Christmas Day."

He seemed so excited by the idea I thought he was going to leap out of his seat. "Why yes, thank you! I'll just have to make sure I'm back home in time to watch the Cowboys game."

I thought my family was going to fall over when I announced that Stanley Marcus was going to drop by for a glass of wine on Christmas afternoon. There were bets among the crowd to see if he actually showed. And sure enough, *he did*. His wife came in first, followed by Mr. Marcus, who was wearing blue jeans and a Dallas Cowboys sweatshirt. The unequivocal king of cool, he always had a keen instinct on how to dress for the occasion.

One of the last projects I worked on at Narrowcasting (before I burned out and retired for the second time) was to design an invitation for Mr. Marcus' 90th birthday party. I wasn't invited to the lavish soirée, of course, but Mr. Marcus was kind enough to take me out for lunch my last week on the job and presented me with a copy of his new book, signed and inscribed.

I was in the process of relinquishing all my titles…no more Assistant Buyer at Neiman Marcus or Account Executive at Narrowcasting. I even had to step down from my throne as The Queen of the Dallas music scene. I was trading them all in for a new title, Bride-to-Be. And I would be leaving Texas and moving to Boston. Roughly two years after graduating from college I found myself back home in Nashville registering for wedding gifts. I was chatting with my mother and a family friend who owned a gift boutique that was filled with china, crystal, and silver. We were talking about wedding dresses and fitting into them and losing weight before the wedding when she announced the devastating news about pasta. It hit me like a bomb. "Y'all, have you heard? Now we can't even eat pasta anymore! Apparently it's making us all fat. That's what they're saying, I just read all about it."

It was a crushing blow. And yet, I was just beginning to learn the realities of adulthood and the disillusion it exposes. I was just starting to learn that not all fairytales are tangible. I was just starting to learn that the road does *not* go on forever, and that the party sometimes does have to end. Doors close. Bubbles burst. But there were two things that did not disappoint, two things were larger than my most grandiose expectations: Stanley Marcus and Texas.

CHAPTER 15 SOUNDTRACK:

Get Real – Kelly Willis

(JOHN LEVENTHAL, KELLY WILLIS)

Beat Up Ford – Jack Ingram

(JACK INGRAM)

Broke Down South of Dallas – Junior Brown

(JUNIOR BROWN)

What I Like About Texas – Gary P. Nunn

(GARY P. NUNN)

The Road Goes on Forever – Robert Earl Keen

(ROBERT EARL KEEN)

Flying North for the Winter

Freshly married, we moved to Boston in January 1996. All the other birds were flying south by wing or RV while we barreled north against the current. According to the weather reports on CNN, we were traveling along a red swath on the map that had been nicknamed "The Blizzard of The Century". It was an ominous way to kick-start a new life and set up a home in a new city. In retrospect, perhaps it is unwise for newlyweds to cross nature so soon out of the gate.

We lived in Boston until November of 2000, or by my measurement, for four winters. (Not to mention one brutally hot summer.) I look back on my time in Boston like a Dickens novel – it was the best of times, it was the worst of times. In a sense, I fell madly in love with the city. I drank in the European architecture and tried my best to learn all the history. For the majority of our time there we lived in a jewel of an apartment, a light-filled brownstone on fashionable Newbury Street right in Back Bay. I left no stone unturned…gallery openings, new restaurants, bars, and boutiques. I canvassed them all.

Best of all I finally got the beloved basset hound I had been longing for since college. Let me just say, until you have spent a day in Rhode Island at the New England Basset Hound convention, you haven't truly lived. The people-watching was so divine I almost became a documentary filmmaker on the spot. Instead I returned to Boston with the world's most handsome tri-color basset. In lieu of my original plan to name him Turkey, I went with Gus. I was just feeling "Gus" for him, and he owned it. Gus went everywhere with me: the Greek café across the street, the pharmacy, the video store, walks through Boston Common. He became a bit of a celebrity around the city, and I loved him desperately.

On the flipside, there were times when I felt off kilter or as if we had landed on another planet. The husband and wife housekeeping duo I hired quit after just one cleaning because they were deeply offended that I had a zebra rug. At dinner parties, the intellectual snobbery was suffocating. By this point my parents had built a house in Montana and our New England friends looked at us as if they were dogs who had heard a high-pitched noise when they learned we were going to vacation in Montana. I think they imagined us having a secret rodeo life or stockpiling ammunition in our underground bunker while peppering the local community with anti-government flyers. Meanwhile, I was trying to determine without asking outright if any of these new friends actually ever ordered the McLobster Roll, a menu item known only to Boston-area McDonald's and other select regional locations.

My brief two-year stint in the Junior League further highlighted cultural differences. I linked up with a friend from Mississippi and we staged our own fashion revolution at the Junior League Ball by wearing long, sexy gowns and feather boas as opposed to the unspoken uniform of a knee-length, black Ann Taylor cocktail dress.

Come on, girls, it's a ball, not a Harvard Law interview.

Winters were long. It wasn't the intensity of the winters but the longevity. I remember one March visiting Mary, who was at law school in Austin. We lounged on the back deck of Dry Creek Saloon in cutoff jean shorts and drank Lone Star beers at sunset, overlooking Lake Austin. When I returned to eight inches of stale brown slush and biting winds, I was depressed for four straight weeks. That's not to say I didn't enjoy snow. I am proud to have survived the record breaking April Fool's Day Blizzard of 1997 which blanketed the city in a gorgeous, thick snow that was nearly three feet deep. It was a fantastic sight and bonded all of Boston in a unique way. But aside from these fanciful storms, the day-to-day reality of shoveling snow and plowing through wind and sleet to get groceries was a grind. Northeastern winters were hard on a marriage that wasn't meant to last.

But we didn't know any of that in the beginning. At the outset we were filled with hope and energy and dove into marriage and Boston life with gusto. Our first road trip out of the city was to visit a family friend in New Hampshire. We were accustomed to the vast Texas geography where you would drive and drive and drive and would never reach Mexico before it was time to retreat and get back to work on Monday. We couldn't get used to New England where so many small states were clustered together. (Just as New Englanders couldn't believe Texans would actually fly between cities within the same state.) In one fell swoop I glanced down at the map and missed the exit. The next thing I knew we were in Maine.

Damn, that was our exit. Shoot...we're in Maine! That's a whole other state on top of the state we're trying to get to.

I don't know why, but I was surprised no one listened to country music, and I mean not at all. I wondered what the women in my gym would think if they knew I was working out to Asleep at the Wheel's "Across the Alley from the Alamo". I fantasized about singing in an Austin music joint with Willie Nelson. On the treadmill I found myself deep in conversation, at least in my mind, with all my favorite Texas musicians as I begged them, *please please please come to Boston.*

And every so often, they did. We dragged friends to see George Strait in concert. When Jerry Jeff Walker played at the House of Blues, every Texas desperado in New England desperate to hear good Texas music convened at his feet to drink brown liquor and sing along. The fact that he was originally from New York was long since forgiven as Jerry Jeff had been culturally linked to Austin since way back in the day. And much to my delight, Willie Nelson came every summer. He did a show at the South Shore Music Circus, which was a round outdoor venue under a tent in Cohasset, Massachusetts. It was an intimate setting, and Willie would shake hands with fans on his way up to the stage. I couldn't believe how much these non-Texans loved him – just as much as people in the Lone Star state did! They rolled up in RVs and on motorcycles wearing airbrushed Willie t-shirts and singing along to every one of his hits. It was the first time I really understood what a national treasure he is.

I couldn't shake my daydreams of performing so I bit the bullet and signed up for voice lessons. It was a group course offered through a series of continuing education classes. The class was held in a stunning old building on Commonwealth Avenue with high ceilings, glossy wood floors, and intricate molding. There were about ten students and the singing teacher, a woman in her thirties. I arrived donned in cowboy boots and dreams of becoming the next Patsy Cline. It didn't take long to size up the crowd to see that they were aiming less honky-tonk and more Boston Pops. It was a serious lot, save one gregarious woman named Sally, who was warm, outgoing, and had a wide open sense of humor.

The first thing the instructor did was ask us to remove our shoes and sit together on the floor. My face went flush with heat as I remembered my mismatched socks, one of which had a terrible hole. I avoided the directive and sat with my legs crossed atop my cowboy boots, but the teacher caught me, "Please, if you would, remove your boots. We will always remove our shoes for class."

Good Lord.

I can't remember what she blathered on and on about – mostly theory. And then she handed each of us a pencil and a piece of blank typing paper.

"I'd like each of you to close your eyes. Go on, close them. Good. Now imagine yourself singing. Picture yourself, your mouth open, music coming out of you. What do you see? How do you imagine it? Now I want you to open your eyes and quickly, quickly draw what you saw in your mind's eye. How do you picture yourself singing? Draw it on the paper."

I had a very clear picture and began sketching it out as I'd imagined it time and time again. I drew a stick figure with cowboy boots and a retro western shirt. There was a bar with barstools and a longhorn hanging on the wall. In the window I wrote the word "BAR" backwards as if it were a neon sign facing the outside.

I was pretty pleased with my tableau until I heard the fervent sounds of people aggressively coloring with their pencils.

Oh, dammit. Are they shading something? I didn't know we should be…shading. Mine is too simple.

"Okay, everyone. Now let's see what you've drawn."

I panicked as people shared their pictures one by one. They were all abstract drawings with artistic detail and perspective, pictures of wind and oceans and mountaintops. They were practically Impressionist paintings depicting nature and the existential sensation felt as they created music with their own physical instruments, artfully pushing air through their lungs to create harmonious magic.

Nature pictures? They are all freaking nature pictures!

And then there was my honky-tonk stick figure in a beer joint. It was mortifying. I didn't even get a laugh, nothing but blank stares. As we wrapped up class and left for the evening, Sally patted me on the back, "It's okay. You're going to do great."

With that the teacher said to me bluntly, "Please don't pick a country song to work on, it just doesn't lend itself to the beauty of the human voice."

We were charged with picking one song to work on for the remainder of the course. Each week we would sing a little piece of it and receive critical feedback. This would build to the final performance when we would each sing our entire song before the class and judge them based on audience applause.

Needless to say a Loretta Lynn number or a Hank Thompson tune was out of the question with this crowd. I labored over what song to choose and suddenly it hit me. "You Don't Know Me" would be perfect. Originally a country song it has been covered by everyone from Elvis to Willie Nelson to Emmylou Harris to Van Morrison. But it is best known as a Ray Charles R&B song. Fantastic! A sneak attack. I was going to Trojan Horse some honky-tonk on her yet.

"You Don't Know Me", an aching tune of unrequited love, was co-written in the 1950s by Eddy Arnold and Cindy Walker. Eddy Arnold first released the tune, and while he was a big country act at the time, most people typically don't know Cindy Walker. But they should. I am *fascinated* by Cindy Walker. She was one of the most prolific songwriters of the 20th century, churning out over 500 recorded songs, and reaching the top-forty charts over 400 times in both country and pop. Born in Texas in 1918, Walker was just twenty-two years old when she went to California on a family trip and decided while she was there she would pitch Bing Crosby a song she had written especially for him. Miraculously she got in to see him, performed the tune called "Lone Star Trail", and he approved. It became a top-ten hit for Crosby.

Cindy Walker was a bombshell blonde with smoldering good looks and singing talent of her own. But she decided to remain behind the scenes to focus on songwriting. She enjoyed a longstanding collaboration with Bob Wills, who recorded over fifty of her songs. Some of his best known hits such as "Cherokee Maiden", "Bubbles in My Beer", and "You're from Texas" are all Cindy Walker compositions. She even wrote a song about him and his trademark field hollering called "What Makes Bob Wills Holler". Other country greats including Ernest Tubb, Al Dexter, Webb Pierce, Hank Snow, and Gene Autry had hits with her songs as well. She was known for her versatility, able to tailor a tune for a performer's strengths, from country to mainstream pop. She rose at dawn every day to write, typically starting with a title that would bring the song to life for her, and she composed her songs on a pink trimmed typewriter. Despite one interview that references a brief marriage, for all intents and purposes, this Texas beauty remained single throughout her life. She lived most of her years in the small town of Mexia, Texas, known for its unusual pronunciation and another famous blond resident, Anna Nicole Smith. Cindy Walker was inducted into the Country Music Hall of Fame in 1997 along with famed songwriter Harlan Howard, who said that night, Walker was "the greatest living songwriter of country music." She died at eighty-seven in 2006 just nine days after Willie Nelson released a tribute album of her music called *You Don't Know Me: The Songs of Cindy Walker*. Her grave in Mexia is memorialized with a large pink-granite guitar.

Yes, "You Don't Know Me" would be the perfect song for my Boston voice class. Heaven knows they certainly didn't know me at all. They didn't know anything about me or the music I loved. But unlike the forlorn protagonist in the song, I was confident I could win them over. At the next class I presented my song selection and belted out the first verse, incorporating a Patsy Cline growl that I was certain added a powerful effect.

"Don't do that," the teacher chided. "That's called a vocal fry when you do that glottal rattle with your throat. It's terrible for your vocal cord health. It's not natural for your voice to do that."

But imitating Patsy Cline's signature move is my signature move.

"Nope," she insisted. "There will be no more vocal frying."

Subsequent classes followed a similar pattern. I didn't make any friends and the teacher never warmed to me or my song selection. The final performance was terrifying. We didn't have to sit on the floor because there were actual folding chairs, and we were even allowed to keep our shoes on. Of course this gave the whole situation gravitas and charged it with a new formality. Measuring by audience applause, Sally clearly won the top slot right out of the gate with her vivacious, undaunted rendition of the Beatles' tune "She Loves You". A natural performer who sensed an encore was in her future, she sang the chorus several extra times and had the mini audience clapping and singing along. She had choreographed moves for heaven's sake. All I could hope for at this point was runner-up. But I didn't even come close. Places two and three went to two operatic hopefuls. I performed last. People were pretty much buttoning up their coats and wrapping scarves around their necks while I stood there like a statue singing a smoothed out, breathy, saccharine version of "You Don't Know Me" out of key and about two octaves too high for my natural vocal range.

I did not sound like the angel I wasn't.

I tucked tail and returned to my more comfortable role as just a music fan. It took a while, but I finally discovered a music joint called Johnny D's. It had been around since 1969, but I didn't learn of it until halfway through my near five year stint in Boston. This family owned, 300-person capacity venue was the coolest spot in Boston, although technically it was located in a suburb just north of a town called Somerville. With music seven nights a week, Johnny D's hosted everything from rock to zydeco to blues to pop. And they were the only game in town booking the Texas music scene I had left behind. The first time I went to Johnny D's I was going to hear the reformed Dixie Chicks, who had exploded on the national scene with their new singer, Natalie Maines. Ironically she had dropped out of The Berklee College of Music right there in Boston not long before joining the female country act. The Dixie Chicks were a no-show, but I knew Johnny D's was something special. I saw a few acts there, but most exciting was when Kelly Willis came to town.

By the summer of 1999 I was pregnant. In fact I was very pregnant. Boston was experiencing a rare, news-topping heat wave and no amount of money could buy an air conditioning window unit. Every Home Depot in New England was sold out. I was so desperate I considered having my mother drive one up from Tennessee, but miraculously I found one that had been returned to a small family-owned hardware store. The owner took pity on me and turned a blind eye to the waiting list. So I spent the final months of my pregnancy lying on the den floor, covered in wet washcloths, basking in the cool airstream of my 10,000 BTU window unit and blaring the most recent Kelly Willis CD, *What I Deserve*. It was her fourth album and Kelly kept outdoing herself. It featured incredible songs with background vocals by Bruce Robison and Charlie Robison as well as pedal steel guitarist Lloyd Maines, father of Natalie Maines from The Dixie Chicks. I played my favorite song, "Not Forgotten You", at least eighty-five times a day. In the car, setting up the nursery, cooking dinner. It's hard to believe my daughter didn't arrive singing the chorus.

Imagine my delight when I found out Kelly Willis was coming all the way from Austin, Texas to perform at Johnny D's in Somerville, Massachusetts. I bought two tickets and shanghaied a friend to go with me. I can only imagine what fetching maternity outfit I was sporting as we arrived the very moment the doors opened – I didn't want to miss a second. We nabbed a coveted two-top table directly under the main microphone and couldn't have been closer to the stage. The crowds poured in as Bruce Robison opened the show. It was that night I figured out that Bruce and Kelly were a couple. When she came on, I was so excited I almost went into labor. I did worry a tiny bit about how loud it was but figured it was okay since the baby certainly knew all of her lyrics by that point. Willis put on a fantastic show, and I sang every word, lockstep right with her. I was secretly hoping she would notice how well I knew her songs, perhaps even giving me a shout-out, but no matter. I was on cloud nine. This was the closest this baby was going to get to Texas for quite a while. For one night I felt like I was back home in a Lone Star honky-tonk.

But nothing felt like coming home as much as motherhood did. And I was ready. I had made a mixed cassette tape for the delivery room called "L&D Mix" that featured Diana Ross singing "I'm Coming Out". We hung a small Texas flag in the hospital room and snuck a little bag of Texas dirt under the bed. (Big thanks goes to my friend in Dallas who overnighted the dirt to us – it arrived the day I checked into the hospital.) As hard as it was in those early, sleepless newborn days, I felt such a purpose, such a laser-focused sense of unity with my baby girl. Sophie was born toward the end of summer, the last summer of the millennium in fact. People in Texas like the spring because it's not too hot. People in New England like autumn because of the changing leaves. But no matter where I am, I love summer best. I love all the tanned flesh and blockbuster movies and bobbing on a boat on the water. I love the adolescent notion that work hours are merely a suggestion during summer. And I loved my summertime baby. It was the most natural role I had ever slid into. Right from the start we fit together like the moon and the stars. Not to mention I finally had a captive audience to listen to me sing. But no more Broadway-style projection, no more belting it to the rafters. No more vocal fry. These songs were actually *meant* to put someone to sleep. I would two-step her gently around the house singing Loretta Lynn's "Love Is the Foundation". She also liked to be rocked to "Please Help Me I'm Falling". But not the original Hank Locklin version, I imitated the version Loretta, Tammy, and Dolly did on their collaboration album called *Honky Tonk Angels*. I suppose if you can't find an audience, you just have to make one. Because little Sophie loved to hear her mama sing honky-tonk soft and low. Like I said, in some ways it really was the best of times.

But Boston was merely a season as Texas was calling once again.

CHAPTER 16 SOUNDTRACK:

Please Come to Boston – David Allan Coe
(DAVE LOGGINS)

You Don't Know Me – Ray Charles
(CINDY WALKER, EDDY ARNOLD)

Not Forgotten You – Kelly Willis
(BRUCE ROBISON)

Love Is the Foundation – Loretta Lynn
(WILLIAM C. HALL)

Please Help Me I'm Falling – Loretta, Tammy, Dolly
(DON ROBERTSON, HAL BLAIR)

Christine's hand trying to get a high-five from Willie Nelson
South Shore Music Circus, Cohasset MA, circa 1998

CHAPTER 17

Home Is Where the Armadillo Is

The Germans were the ones to kick-start Austin's entertainment scene. In 1866 a German immigrant and Confederate war veteran named August Scholz opened the first Austin bar and café. As its popularity grew, he added an outdoor biergarten. After his death, his family operated Scholz Garten for a couple of years before selling it to the Falstaff Beer brewery in 1893, coincidentally the year the Texas Longhorns had their first undefeated season. (Scholz Garten and Texas football were natural bedfellows as the German tavern was located extremely close to the university.) In 1908 a German singing club called The Saengerrunde (singer in the round) purchased Scholz and added a bowling alley. For decades to follow, politicians, professors, students, and musicians would gather at Scholz Garten for food, beer, live music, and sometimes lively debates. Unofficially the liberals were known to sit outside while the conservative crowd set up camp inside. One century and one year after it opened, in 1967, it was designated a Texas Historical Landmark.

Over on the east side of town, The Scoot Inn opened in 1871. Unlike Scholz Garten, which was nestled between the state capital and the university, drawing politicians and professors, The Scoot Inn was a depot for railroad workers. It sold everything from dry goods to beer and whiskey. The railroad passed just behind the building, so this historic saloon enjoyed a steady flow of visitors through the decades, surviving a reputation that flirted with a seedier element.

German immigrants were also responsible for establishing Dessau Hall in 1876. Originally a gathering place for polka bands and German festivities in the small community of Dessau just north of Austin's city limits, it began to draw performers and revelers from all over. In the 1930s and 1940s, big bands such as Glenn Miller and Guy Lombardo played Dessau. The nightclub burned but was rebuilt in roughly the same location, this time famously with a massive tree growing through the middle of the dance floor. The acts began to lean more toward country and western as Dessau Hall booked Bob Wills, Ernest Tubb, and Charlie Louvin. Saturday night shows were broadcast over KTBC, a radio station owned by then-Senator Lyndon B. Johnson and his wife, Lady Bird. A local band called Jimmy Heap & the Melody Masters was a regular act at the popular but rough Dessau Hall. Their piano player, Arlie Carter, co-wrote the venerable honky-tonk song "The Wild Side of Life" with a man named William Warren. The Melody Masters recorded it first in 1951, the year before Hank Thompson released it and "Wild Side of Life" became a runaway hit.

Dessau Hall drew all the big name acts. Hank Williams, Elvis, Patsy Cline, Loretta Lynn, Willie Nelson, Merle Haggard, and George Strait all played Dessau Hall. It burned again in 1967 but was rebuilt without the tree in the dance floor. This incarnation included a 3,000 square foot dance floor, red velvet wallpaper, and chandeliers. Eventually the Dessau turned into a Tejano club and then made one last Hail Mary as a country venue before it was officially laid to rest.

Another sacred Austin honky-tonk was the Skyline Club, which opened in 1948 at 11306 North Lamar Boulevard, a locale outside the Austin city limits back then. In fact, at the time this stretch of North Lamar was still referred to as "The Old Dallas Highway". Wednesday and Thursday nights were ten-cent beer. The Skyline leveraged the peaking popularity of golden era honky-tonk and booked as many star-studded acts as the Dessau. Hank Thompson said of the Skyline, "It was a small place. You were right there with the audience, and they'd just all gang around. It was a fun place to play from that standpoint.

The ceiling was low and the stage sat only a few inches higher than the hardwood dance floor. At that time it would only hold about two hundred, maybe two fifty at the most. We'd always have it jam-packed with people. It was a very intimate place to play."

The Skyline Club carried on until the 1970s when it was leased out as the new location for another Austin nightspot called the Soap Creek Saloon, which drew Willie Nelson and other Texas country cowboy rockers. By the 1980s it was hosting punk rock bands until it closed its doors in 1989, the same year I was up in Nashville graduating from high school. Today, a CVS Pharmacy stands on the site of the historic Skyline Club. People rush in to buy penicillin and a pack of cigarettes without even realizing they are scuffing their soles on the honky-tonk ghosts of Hank Williams and Johnny Horton.

In 1964, Austinite James White was out of the army and trying to figure out what to do with his life. He longed for the two-stepping heyday of Dessau Hall and decided he was meant to own his own dancehall. He opened the doors to the Broken Spoke, also located on Lamar Boulevard, but way down low in Old South Austin. On opening night, 300 people poured in to drink beer and scoot around its hardwood dance floor. Two years later White was able to book his childhood hero, Bob Wills, and from there other headliner acts followed. Ernest Tubb, Roy Acuff, Hank Thompson, Tex Ritter, Ray Price, Kitty Wells, Willie Nelson, and George Strait have all graced the stage at the South Austin honky-tonk lovingly referred to simply as "The Spoke". In the 1970s the Sunday night house band at The Spoke was called Freda and The Firedogs. "Freda" was a tall female songstress from Louisiana who grew up on Cajun, rock, and blues music, having never sung country songs until she was waylaid in Austin on her way to California. She crooned Loretta's "Fist City" and Tammy Wynette covers like nobody's business. "Freda", otherwise known as Marcia Ball, never made it to California. Austin became her home.

Kenneth Threadgill was busy entertaining people on the north side of town. In 1933 Threadgill was a bootlegger, a yodeler, and a lover of country music when he opened his Gulf gas station just above the Austin city limits. But he always had more in mind than just pumping gas. He stood in line all night and purchased the first beer license in the county. Soon, musicians were stopping by for a drink after a show on their way out of town. Threadgill was also the first to realize that Austin presented a goldmine of an opportunity for an enterprising entertainment impresario: college kids. He catered to the professors and students from The University of Texas. Kenneth Threadgill was a fascinating conduit between Austin's music scene and the eternally re-populating student body. Year after year, decade after decade, Threadgill had a keen ability to stay plugged in with both the music and the university constituencies and managed to keep the two tied into each other.

Clearly Austinites had plenty of places to go honky-tonking and have a good time. Scholz Garten and Threadgill's for cold beer and camaraderie...Dessau Hall, the Skyline Club, and the Broken Spoke for dancing...they all sound fantastic. But honestly they weren't wholly different from other Hill Country beer joints and dancehalls. And there were other Texas cities with similar honky-tonk venues and radio shows that frankly drew big name acts more regularly. Dallas had the Bob Wills Ranch House and the *Big D Jamboree*. Fort Worth had Panther Hall and *Cowtown Jamboree*. Shreveport, Louisiana had the *Louisiana Hayride*. But in the 1970s Austin would take a left turn. It began to stir things up in such a way that catapulted this good-timing honky-tonk town onto the national stage as a music mecca.

Why Austin?

I can't pinpoint why Austin became what it did during the 1970s. It's as mysterious as crop circles, so at some point you have to stop asking questions and enjoy the magic that remains.

But Austin did have two major things going on back then: state politics and a massive university, both of which were seasonal business. The state politicians were largely conservative, representing a conservative state, but their eyes were either on their districts back home or on Washington D.C. Meanwhile city leadership was remarkably loose and laissez-faire. Politicians, lobbyists, students, and professors would ease in and out of Austin as their sessions or semesters dictated. When they weren't legislating or studying, they had to move out of town to find work. Those who stayed in Austin by default weren't terribly ambitious or motivated by the dollar, so a bohemian culture began to take hold. Hippies enjoyed swimming topless in Barton Springs, aimlessly tossing Frisbees, and walking their dogs without leashes. The city was safe, affordable, and people were largely left in peace to have a good time. Austin became a uniquely liberal and progressive city within Texas, the lone blue dot in a very red state.

The whole country was relaxing after the feverish protests of the 1960s and its cause-driven folk music. Everyone was easing into the idea of just having a good time, and Austin was leading the way. It had a mellow pulse to it. Pre-Vietnam War nostalgia churned up a renewed interest in traditional honky-tonk country as well as western swing music. Bob Wills was king once more. And in the early 1970s Texas musicians who had scattered around the country began to return home, convening in Austin. There were no social boundaries in Austin, and so there were no boundaries in the music being played. They began fusing country and western swing with Mexican, blues, and folk music. This "Austin Sound" was a veritable stew of influences. The Austin music of this era was called Cosmic Cowboy, Hippie Country, and Redneck Rock.

Hindsight offers the ability to analyze the impact of certain big-bang moments in music history. Like the Bristol Sessions in 1927 when Jimmie Rodgers and The Carter Family recorded the first official country music. Or in 1951 when DJ Alan Freed popularized the term "rock and roll". Or when the Beatles played the Ed Sullivan Show in 1964 and brought the British Rock invasion stateside. Similarly, Austin, Texas experienced its own big bang moment when Willie Nelson hit town in 1972 and made his debut at the Armadillo World Headquarters.

The Armadillo World Headquarters…sigh.

When a popular rock club called The Vulcan Gas Company was forced to shut its doors, local psychedelic band Shiva's Headband was left looking for a place to play. Around the same time, a few other Austin clubs called it quits, so options were becoming increasingly scarce. The band's manager, Eddie Wilson, spotted an old National Guard armory on Barton Springs Road, just south of downtown and the Colorado River, and decided it would be the perfect location for a new music venue. He named it the Armadillo World Headquarters because he felt the symbol of the armadillo uniquely evoked the spirit of the Texas hippie. It was awkward, regional, and peace-loving, often maligned yet thoroughly loveable. And just as hippies often felt run over by the ambitious forward march of society and progress, armadillos regularly met their fate rather ingloriously on the side of a Texas highway at the hands of high-speeding technology.

The Armadillo opened in August of 1970. (Just one month before I was born.). The cavernous room held a capacity of 1500 people, so Wilson's immediate challenge was to build a regular audience and fill the space. Offering original music was the answer, an alternative to fraternity copycat bands and the country dance halls on the outskirts of town. But sticking with one style wouldn't keep it booked consistently. So he developed a "counter culture honky-tonk" with limitless genres. Country, rock, jazz quartets, classical string ensembles. On Sundays the Armadillo offered ballet, which "even had the blue hairs going home and talking about the place." Wilson concedes it was a constant grind to keep the oversized space filled, but he remained creative in booking eclectic acts. Musicians started helping by referring other musicians. Willie Nelson brought Waylon, who in turn lured Tom T. Hall to the Armadillo. Commander Cody became wildly popular in Austin and recruited Little Feat and Linda Ronstadt to play there. When Bruce Springsteen came to do a two-night gig, Wilson convinced him to add a third Thursday night show and set admission for just one dollar. He was relentless about finding ways to get people in the door, while musicians were starting to fall in love with the place.

The Armadillo also became a hotbed of creativity for a group of nearly a dozen area artists known collectively as "The Armadillo Art Squad". This crew created a new aesthetic for rock-related art, including show posters, paintings and murals. Their work captured the spirit of the '70s and influenced rock art on a national level.

Jim Franklin, a key figure in The Armadillo Art Squad, was an artist roustabout who partnered in the Armadillo by way of moving his mattress into the attic when it opened. He grew up on the Texas coast and claimed his "life was almost ruined by an interest in theater, art, black girls, and drugs." I suppose the most fascinating part of that sentence is the use of the word "almost". He was known to emcee the Armadillo shows in flamboyant costumes and headdresses that rivaled that of George Clinton. This enigmatic figure was intrigued with armadillos because he felt they represented the Texas hippie as they were similarly "reclusive, unwanted, scorned." Franklin was responsible for many of the artistic murals that decorated the Armadillo. Particularly dramatic was the wall art depicting Austin blues musician Freddie King wildly playing guitar while an armadillo exploded from his chest. Another mural featured an armadillo devouring the moon. Jim Franklin also created a vast library of show posters from the Armadillo era, posters that were infinitely trippier looking than the age-old Hatch Show Print posters out of Nashville that had been heralding tent revivals, medicine shows, and honky-tonk acts for decades.

Meanwhile, Willie Nelson had changed quite a bit since touring the Texas beer joints and heading off to Nashville. Long gone were the tailored suits and mock turtlenecks. When Willie took the stage at the Armadillo in the early '70s he was wearing jeans, cowboy boots, and a cowboy hat. He had a beard and a gold earring. His drummer, Paul English, looked like Count Dracula with a pointy beard and cape. There was still the tinny sound of the honky-tonk piano and the driving bass. As fantastic as Willie was as a songwriter, singer, and guitar player, he transcended when he was in front of a live audience. And the audience was as diverse as it could be. Freaks, cowboys, rednecks, and bohemian hippies. They danced and sang along as if they were at a family reunion, which in a sense they were since Willie's band is called The Family and they were, after some long years in Nashville, finally back in Texas. Willie became the unofficial godfather of the Armadillo movement. For someone tagged as an "outlaw" he was just about the least angry rebel you could find. He was peace-loving, inclusive, and mellow. He thrived on stage and fed off the collaboration with other musicians. He had the attitude of the moment plus the honky-tonk chops of old western swing. Just as Austin was an anomaly in the conservative state of Texas, Willie Nelson was a liberal soul in a sea of country music, a genre traditionally connected to conservative white southerners. And yet they all loved him. The musicians and the hippies and the cowboys and the rednecks and the bikers and the grandmothers. Billy Joe Shaver gave Willie credit for starting it all. "Willie laid down such a heavy track record that nobody could ignore him. He's the one that busted it wide open."

As did the Armadillo. It drew musicians that were good enough to go out into the world and land record deals but had retreated to Austin to lick their wounds after tangling with the brutality of the music industry. And it continued to book national talent like Springsteen, B.B. King, Lynyrd Skynyrd, Frank Zappa, Emmylou Harris, and Bonnie Raitt. AC/DC played their first ever U.S. show at the Armadillo. The Grateful Dead did a concert at a nearby venue, and Jerry Garcia remarked how he wished he could play the Armadillo sometime. Eddie Wilson got word of this and scrambled to put together an impromptu show the very next day with Jerry Garcia, Leon Russell, and Doug Sahm. It was on Thanksgiving Day. Another legendary night was Willie Nelson with The Marshall Tucker Band, Charlie Daniels, and Dickey Betts all on stage at one time. Local Austin acts Freda and the Firedogs, Joe Ely, and Stevie Ray Vaughn had the opportunity to open for these big names. The Armadillo became a portal for developing fresh local talent, able to draw on the collaborative vibe as well as springboard off the fame of national bands that played there. Texas singer-songwriter Gary P. Nunn wrote an ode to the beloved venue called "London Homesick Blues" in which he longs to be home in Austin with the Armadillo.

Clearly the Armadillo struck a chord at the right time and created a collaborative sense of community for musicians and fans alike. There was perhaps nothing better than taking a swim at the scantily-clad, hippie-dippie watering hole called Barton Springs, and then wandering down the road to catch a show at the "'Dillo", where the outdoor biergarten was a popular hangout. Wilson says the Armadillo was a "full service honky-tonk" with daycare and incredible food. The shrimp enchiladas were renowned. After Van Morrison played two nights at the 'Dillo, he lamented to the kitchen manager that he never had the opportunity to taste the famous shrimp enchiladas. The kitchen manager assured him he would have a chance to try them the next time he played the Armadillo. The very next day Van Morrison's manager called Wilson and asked if Morrison could come back that Monday and play a spur-of-the-moment show.

The Armadillo sold 1,150 tickets for this last minute performance, promoted totally by word-of-mouth.

Eddie Wilson describes the Armadillo as "a musical petri dish." Musicians met there, joined forces, and created new bands. It was Austin's version of the Fillmore in San Francisco or the Village scene in New York. Even evocative of Hemingway and the Lost Generation in the cafés of Paris, it was an electric and prolific headquarters for creativity and connectivity, helping to put Austin on the musical map.

For example, vagabond songwriter Townes Van Zandt made his way to Austin, living in the Clarksville Neighborhood. It was around these parts that this devotee of Woody Guthrie penned his famous country ballad "Pancho and Lefty".

Jimmy Buffett was around Austin during this time as well. He began to assemble musicians for his Coral Reefer Band, he wrote "Margaritaville" in Austin, and he fine-tuned it after he moved down to the Keys. In his 1974 book, <u>The Improbable Rise of Redneck Rock</u>, journalist Jan Reid claims that Buffett himself, "said he wrote his career-making hit, 'Margaritaville', while hanging out in Austin." Reid also shows a fantastic picture of a young Jimmy Buffett relaxing at a construction site that was to become a music venue called Liberty Lunch. Buffett is drinking Tecate beer, and the caption is quick to point out that the picture was snapped before he was contractually required to promote Corona.

As outlaw music grew in popularity throughout the 1970s, the movement began to connect itself with Austin, no doubt in large part due to Willie making it his home. Although Texas-born Waylon Jennings remained in Nashville, he was largely associated with the Austin music scene. Outlaw musician David Allan Coe once did a 1976 outdoor concert in Austin wearing a sleeveless denim jacket that had motorcycle gang colors and a swastika on it. Bikers in the audience had pistols in their jeans. Not exactly the picture of traditional conservative Nashville country. It's hard to imagine Chet Atkins in a sleeveless denim jacket or Porter Wagoner wearing a sequined swastika on his Nudie suit.

As prominent as it was, the Armadillo wasn't the only game in town. Kenneth Threadgill stood as a link between the nostalgia for traditional country roots and rock music. He was a unique and beloved force in Austin's music history, and drew an eclectic mix of people to his Gulf gas station beer joint. As traditional as his country music roots were as a yodeler, he was very progressive in accepting the edgier rock scene developing in Austin and offered an open mic to anyone who wanted to get up and sing.

Janis Joplin, from Port Arthur in East Texas, came to Austin to attend the University of Texas, where she started performing with folk bands. Kenneth Threadgill first heard her sing country standard "Silver Threads and Golden Needles". But Janis didn't fit the folk singer mold – in fact she didn't fit any molds. She was maligned in high school for awkward looks and befriending African American students. She was chided in college for her promiscuity, and the fraternities cruelly voted her "Ugliest Man on Campus". She wasn't very happy in her own home state, but the best thing that happened to her in Texas was meeting Threadgill. He befriended and mentored her, and she began to play regularly at his gas station bar. Eventually she moved to San Francisco, where she found more national fame and came into her own stylistically, with feathers in her hair and drugs coursing through her veins. Joplin said of Austin, Texas, "They laughed me out of class, out of the town, and out of the state."

Before she overdosed she made it back to Austin to play a large concert in honor of her friend Kenneth Threadgill. She left some scheduled shows in Hawaii and arrived in Texas wearing multiple Hawaiian leis. When she took the stage she proclaimed, "I always promised Kenneth a good lay!" and placed one of the floral strands around his neck. She proceeded to tell the crowd about an up-and-coming songwriter named Kris Kristofferson and sang two of his songs, "Me and Bobby McGee" and "Sunday Morning Coming Down".

It is said Kenneth Threadgill always carried a picture of Janis in his wallet. Given how many people chipped away at her self-confidence in her short life, who knows if she would have gone on to make her mark on the national stage had he not taken such an earnest interest in her talent.

Austin also had the Saxon Pub which started as a burger joint with little flags on the tables to summon your waitress. But it evolved into an intimate music venue that hosted Bob Livingston and Michael Martin Murphey, credited as patron saints of the local cosmic cowboy movement. They were members of the Lost Gonzo Band, a cosmic cowboy group that also included Gary P. Nunn and Lloyd Maines. The Lost Gonzo Band played and recorded with Jerry Jeff Walker and Ray Wylie Hubbard.

Janis Joplin wasn't the only one from Port Arthur, Texas to make a mark on the Austin music scene. Clifford Antone came to Austin in 1968 to attend the University of Texas but dropped out after getting busted for marijuana. At just twenty-five he started a Chicago-style blues club on 6th Street. This stretch of 6th would become one of Austin's premier entertainment districts, sort of Austin's miniature version of Bourbon Street, and Antone's was one of the first music clubs on 6th. Clifford Antone was an advocate for the blues in town, and his club was an anchor for talent. Fats Domino, John Lee Hooker, Delbert McClinton, Muddy Waters, Albert Collins, and B.B. King all played Antone's, helping to establish Austin's moniker, "The Live Music Capital of the World". Antone's moved to a location up north before settling into its legacy locale on Guadalupe Street, also known as "The Drag", near campus. I was visiting Austin one time during high school and snuck into Antone's on Guadalupe – I had landed in heaven. I'd never seen a club so cool. My friends were too chicken to go in and waited for me outside. So I stayed just long enough to have my mind blown by some incredible blues and to buy a too-edgy-for-my-crowd *black* Antone's t-shirt which I sported with pride for years.

The ultimate Texas bluesman, Stevie Ray Vaughn, is mainly associated with two Austin clubs: The Rome Inn and Antone's. Clifford Antone was a staunch supporter of Vaughn's and arranged for him to play on stage with Albert King, which instantly propelled his status as a top blues guitarist. Vaughn's national fame soared with the release of *Texas Flood*, and he was invited to play with Mick Jagger in New York as well as David Bowie and Jackson Browne. Stevie Ray Vaughn was arguably one of the largest musical figures to come out of Austin, eclipsed only by the global fame of Willie Nelson. After kicking a difficult drug and alcohol habit, Vaughn died tragically at the age of thirty-six in a helicopter crash.

In 1974, Jan Reid released The Improbable Rise of Redneck Rock. This book, along with The Armadillo's two-part television show called *The Armadillo Country Music Review* inspired the PBS television show *Austin City Limits*. It began airing in 1976 and is now the longest-running music program in television history. The show featured weekly live concert performances set against a mock backdrop of the Austin skyline. It was Austin's updated version of the *Grand Ole Opry* – but it showcased bands from a mix of genres. What various club owners and musicians put in motion was finally sealed as this television show garnered national attention. Austin was officially "The Live Music Capital of the World". At first they used Gary P. Nunn's song "London Homesick Blues" as their theme song, given its nod to the Armadillo. But Austin musician Charlie Sexton later composed an original score for the *Austin City Limits* theme song.

The Austin music scene could hardly be contained by its city limits, and so it poured naturally into the landscape of the Texas Hill Country. In the 1800s Luckenbach, which is about sixty-nine miles west of Austin, was a trading post for pioneer farmers and Comanche Indians. Fast forward to 1970 when the town was owned by the Engel family… Benno Engel placed an ad in the paper that read, "TOWN FOR SALE".

An eclectic character named Hondo Crouch bought Luckenbach with two other partners. Hondo had been a star swimmer at the University of Texas, where he attended classes barefoot. Once he became Mayor of Luckenbach he printed business cards for himself with the title, "Imagineer". The Luckenbach website explains how the new owners used existing buildings for "anything that smacked of mirth and diversion: 'Hug-Ins', a Luckenbach World's Fair, Ladies State Chili Bust, the Mud Dauber Festival – and daily sessions of song-picking, domino playing and beer drinking beneath the 500-year-old oak trees. Today, over thirty years later, these events are still celebrated and the pickers are still pickin' out under the big oak trees."

Hondo Crouch was a storyteller and all-around cowboy bon vivant who put Luckenbach on the map as a magical place to escape and listen to music in a pastoral western setting. The people-loving, democratic Crouch believed that, "Everybody's Somebody in Luckenbach." Jerry Jeff Walker was one of the somebodies who loved the Luckenbach vibe so much he held his wedding there, and Hondo Crouch officiated. I suppose as the Mayor of Luckenbach he was able to legitimately seal the deal. Even more famously, in 1973 Jerry Jeff recorded a live album at Luckenbach called *Viva Terlingua* backed by the Lost Gonzo Band musicians he'd met at the Armadillo, including Gary P. Nunn. Walker penned about half of the songs on the gold album while others were written by Texas songwriting greats Guy Clark ("Desperados Waiting for a Train"), Michael Martin Murphey ("Backslider's Wine"), and Ray Wylie Hubbard ("Up Against the Wall, Redneck Mother"). Of course it also featured Gary P. Nunn's "London Homesick Blues".

At one point Hondo ran into one of his former college buddies, then-Governor of Texas, John Connally. Connally (famous for being shot in Dallas as a fellow passenger in JFK's car the day of his assassination) asked Hondo, "You still raising sheep around Fredericksburg, Hondo?"

"Yes I am, John," Hondo replied. "What are you doing these days?"

In 1972 the Texas Hill Country town, Kerrville, played host to the first annual Kerrville Folk Festival. Initial artists included Jerry Jeff Walker, Ray Wylie Hubbard, Rusty Wier, Kenneth Threadgill, Michael Martin Murphey, and Townes Van Zandt. Willie Nelson joined in later years, and collectively the Kerrville Folk Festival did much to solidify a body of work known as "The Austin Sound".

Also in 1972, the Dripping Springs Reunion was the ground-breaking, country music festival engineered by four Dallas promoters. The crowd was filled with half-naked hippies who were passionate about both country music and debauchery. Perhaps one of my favorite accounts of this notorious concert was when Loretta Lynn stole the show. In complete contrast to the bare-breasted girls wearing little more than straw cowboy hats and cut-off jean shorts, Loretta Lynn took the stage in layers upon layers of petticoats and full country pin-curled hair. And she brought down the house. Or, technically, brought down the field. She had those hippies dancing and singing and clapping up a storm. They were in a veritable froth as Kris Kristofferson, the closing act, took the stage next and couldn't calm them down. According to Jan Reid, who was at the show, Kristofferson was hoping for more of a "listening audience." He barked into the wild crowd, "Jack off!" He sang just a few more numbers before stomping off the stage in a huff.

Willie Nelson played at the Dripping Springs Reunion around the same time he moved back to Texas. He made his home in the hills just west of Austin. He bought the old Pedernales Country Club and turned it into his own golf course with a recording studio, hence its nickname, The Cut-n-Putt. The course is open to the public and caters to…how shall we say…the more laid-back golfer. Rules allow for "no more than twelve in a foursome." And due to the rugged terrain "in case your ball ends up in an unplayable or merely unpleasant lie, local rules permit you to pick it up and stroll to a more agreeable location for a free drop." That is called The Pedernales Stroll. Needless to say Willie has designed a very loose, inclusive course that highlights fun over form.

On any given day you might see the Red Headed Stranger himself hitting the links. Countless music legends have visited the Cut-n-Putt to record at the studio or even just hang out. In 1983 Merle Haggard arrived to cut a duet album with Willie. They recorded twenty-three very usable tracks, but Willie's daughter Lana, who was managing the studio, felt they were still missing that special song to carry the album. She went home and listened to Emmylou Harris' cover of Townes Van Zandt's "Pancho and Lefty" and decided it would be perfect. She called her dad and Merle back into the studio at four in the morning. They handed lyrics to Merle and together the duo sang one cut of it before retiring once again for the night. Merle woke up a few hours later on his bus and started mulling over the lyrics in his mind. The ballad of a Mexican bandit and his ne'er-do-well running buddy started clicking for Merle as he and Willie had long since been branded outlaws themselves. He busted out of his bus eager to perfect the track and found Willie playing golf. Merle announced that he was ready to properly record "Pancho and Lefty".

Willie chuckled, "Hell, the tape's already on the way to New York."

So the song that reached number one on the country charts was recorded in one take at four in the morning as effortlessly as throwing salt over one's left shoulder…or maybe even picking up a golf ball and dropping it in a better spot. *The Pedernales Stroll*. The album, recorded there at Willie's Cut-n-Putt, went platinum.

I have said it before, and I will say it again: I wish I could have been twenty-two in Austin, Texas in 1972. I ache desperately to have been a part of Willie and the Armadillo and the whole scene. But I was thirty when we moved from Boston to Austin in November 2000. And after all of my moving around, after so many hometowns and so many stopovers, when I landed in Austin I found my soul's true home.

Several of the old hotspots were long gone by the time I arrived. The dancehalls of the honky-tonk heyday like Dessau and Skyline were closed. The Armadillo lived larger than life for one bright decade and then only in folklore after New Year's 1980. Asleep at the Wheel and Kenneth Threadgill were among those who played its final show. After several decades, Kenneth Threadgill faced his own challenges keeping his gas station beer music joint alive. Former Armadillo owner Eddie Wilson purchased it and opened a second Threadgill's in South Austin across from the former site of the Armadillo. Wilson had a dream of serving southern comfort food so he added meat-and-three fare to the live music offerings. I recall many a night as a young mom I was too tired to cook and grabbed a Threadgill's chopped steak to go for my picky little eater.

The oldest bar in Austin, Scholz Garten, is still going strong. I enjoyed several pre-game parties there before walking to the UT stadium to cheer for the Longhorn football team. I've also been blessed to gussy up and attend a black tie private party called The Jingle Ball, which is held annually in the old bowling alley with a large orchestra swing band. The historic Scoot Inn on the east side of town that originally served thirsty railroad workers is also still open for business. Somehow it claims the title "oldest saloon in Austin". I'm not sure how it is that Scholz Garten and the Scoot Inn each declare this label, but the bottom line is that they are both incredibly historic and amazingly still pouring drinks for thirsty, fun-loving Austinites. While maintaining its 1800s dark saloon décor, the Scoot Inn has added more live music through the years as well as a charming outdoor biergarten.

James White and the Broken Spoke are alive and well, serving up chicken fried steak and honky-tonk music. Considered "the last of the true Texas dancehalls", the Broken Spoke is where my heart lies. Neon signs, folding chairs, an incredibly low ceiling. No matter how big the performer, no one who plays the Spoke is too big to cover the standards. On any given night you can hear an Ernest Tubb song or a classic Hank tune. The Spoke is still known as *the* place to two-step and so, no matter who is playing on stage, the dance floor is usually the star of the evening.

Just up the street on Lamar is The Saxon Pub, which continues to book a mix of roots rock, country, and blues artists. It is still a dark, intimate place to see off-the-chart songwriters and perhaps squeeze in a dance on their small dance floor.

By the time I moved to Austin, Antone's was in its fourth location on 5th Street downtown. It was a big, sparse venue that continued to book blues as well as alternative country. Clifford Antone, who also started a record label and record store by the same name, passed away in 2006, which was a blow to the old guard and the entire Austin music community. Antone's moved to the East Side in 2013, the first locale that Clifford Antone wouldn't see in person. And now, new owners have a plan to bring the iconic club back downtown.

We moved into an older neighborhood in South Austin, just below the river and close to downtown. The nearby Continental Club, open since the 1950s, was still rocking on South Congress, perhaps the most vibrant music venue in town at that point. Junior Brown had once been the Sunday night house band but had moved on with fame. Occasionally he came back to play the Continental Club, but the space was so small, they couldn't even advertise his shows. They would simply slip his name onto the marquee that morning and lines would start to form. Lucky for me I lived just blocks away and was pretty quick to see his name and squeezed my way in to a few Junior Brown shows at the Continental Club.

Long since mythologized in Waylon's hit song "Luckenbach, Texas (Back to the Basics of Love)", Luckenbach was still drawing crowds. It was nice to be back in a part of the country where you'd see people wearing t-shirts that said, "Everybody's Somebody in Luckenbach." It particularly made me smile since that was the same slogan my summer camp used, "Everybody's Somebody at Camp Longhorn." It's really no coincidence since Hondo Crouch was a famous swimmer at Texas, and the founder of Camp Longhorn, Tex Robertson, was the swim coach there. I remember one time in college when I was a counselor, I was charged with driving the camp Suburban into Austin to run some errands for the director. Lying on the front seat was a cassette tape with "Hondo Crouch" scribbled in pencil across the homemade label. I popped it in and listened in awe as the renowned Texas storyteller was spinning a yarn right there on tape.

Of course the *Austin City Limits* television show was still airing when I moved to town. In fact in 2002 a promotion company licensed the name and hosted the first annual ACL Music Festival. It launched as one of the top five largest music festivals in the country behind Coachella, Burning Man, Bonnaroo, and New Orleans' Jazz Fest.

After five years in New England I hit Austin and became a veritable food and music glutton. As if just visiting for the weekend I instinctively ate Tex-Mex three times a day, forgetting I lived in Texas again and should probably pace myself. I displayed equal vigor in seeing as much live music as possible. A barely one-year-old baby Sophie stayed with grandparents during the grueling drive from Boston to Austin, so the night we hit town we were free to venture out and went straight to Antone's. The lineup had branched out beyond strict blues and that night presented a Texas country triple threat: Cory Morrow, Pat Green, and Kevin Fowler. The crowd danced and sang every song and it felt great to see guys in cowboy hats singing about how much they love Texas.

It was quite a welcome home.

Not long after that show, I saw Kevin Fowler again at a bar on 6th Street for a Monday night singer-songwriter series hosted by Cory Morrow. The opening act was a young Django Walker, son of Jerry Jeff, who had a fairly popular song at the time. Out of the blue Jerry Jeff Walker himself emerged from the shadows and went on stage to sing with his son and Cory Morrow. The crowd was nuts by the time honky-tonkin' Kevin Fowler was at the helm. He sings fun-loving tunes about beer and bait and quitting your job and loving Texas and having a good old time. The crowd obliged. At one point some girls in John Deere tractor hats stormed the stage and took their tops off. A fight ensued. Kevin Fowler played on and the dancing never stopped. It was quite a scene and yet…just a Monday night on 6th Street in Austin, Texas.

Toto, we're not in Boston anymore.

With a young child and limited babysitting funds, we took turns stepping out on the town. I hadn't really found my best chick friends yet so this was the era when I started going to see live music on my own. I literally could not get enough of it. I recall one Sunday driving down the main street of our neighborhood, South Congress, and there it was on the Continental Club marquee: Junior Brown. I took Sophie to a backyard pool party with toddlers and juice boxes, got her home, bathed and readied her for bed, passed the baton to her dad, and off I went. The place was packed, and while we all waited anxiously for Junior Brown to take the stage I couldn't shake this scruffy older guy who seemed hell bent on striking up a conversation with me. Before you are too impressed that someone was hitting on me, let me paint a more accurate picture. He was wearing jeans and a thin white undershirt on which he'd personally written in purple magic marker, "My face leaves at 10 pm. You better be on it."

His name was Sonny. I know this because, of course, I let him chat it up as I was bored waiting for the show to start. Besides, he was hilarious. I admit I found something admirable in the guy who went to the mall, couldn't quite find the exact sentiment he was looking for at the t-shirt kiosk, took the bull by the horns, and made his own. And they say American ingenuity is dead. China is passing us by. Clearly we just need to clone more Sonnys. Sonny was charming enough company until he had a few too many drinks and got a little excited by Junior Brown's skills on the guit-steel. By the end of the night he was determined to come to my house and rebuild my car and offered to shoot anyone at the Continental Club who was bothering me. Which, at that point, was Sonny. I slipped out and snuck home before the end of Junior Brown.

In 2002 I went back to work full time. I landed a job as a Director in the Creative Services division of a political affairs consulting firm. The company was headquartered in Austin but had offices in Washington D.C., Dallas, and London. I am the least politically-minded person in the universe and rolled my eyes regularly at this male dominant, conservative boys' club culture. I was accustomed to the edgier office scenes at Neiman Marcus and the Boston marketing agency where I'd worked. This place had duck hunting prints on beige walls and giant leather chairs. At the time it seemed many in the firm had a deep-seated disdain for all things advertising and marketing which made it hard to coexist with certain colleagues. As usual, I worked my ass off. I hated the pressure, hated the hours, and hated the over-inflated constant state of urgency. But I loved my clients, loved the projects, and the money was great. I did pretty well for a while and was promoted to Managing Director over all of Creative Services. But the three real highlights from working for this consulting firm were becoming friends with former Texas Governor Ann Richards, getting to see Ray Price play live, and working for the best boss on the planet, Mark McKinnon.

Ann Richards was a spitfire female governor who, in her post-elected official life, enjoyed a near celebrity status on the national stage. She was a *character*. Not to mention a rainmaker, able to open just about any corporate door in the country and get The Meeting. I had the opportunity to work side by side with her on two high profile accounts in New York and had a blast getting to know her. At the end of the day, she was a cool chick friend. She was a mentor to me within the company; I admired her infinitely. Her ability to carry a room of peacock corporate men and never relinquish the upper hand was sheer magic. Plus, sister could deliver a speech.

But at meals she was relaxed and open, sharing tender stories about her family and offering book suggestions. She was a film nut and barbecue aficionado, which gave us endless fodder for conversation. She wasn't afraid to seek out my help on matters either. She was always asking for my feedback on the handbag line she was designing with older women in mind. The idea was to create a fabulous looking handbag that had an interior light that would come on automatically when you opened the purse.

Another memorable snapshot was seeing Ray Price perform. Our chairman was celebrating his 50th birthday so the company threw a party for him at the historic Coupland Dancehall just outside of Austin. Ray Price was the musical guest. He played all his standards, mesmerized the crowd, and was just as charming as he could be. In such an intimate setting I even had the chance to shake his hand after the show.

But the most lasting mentor and friend I made during these fast-paced consulting years was my bossman, Mark McKinnon. Just like Austin was an anomalous island floating within Texas, and Willie Nelson a unique phenomenon within the world of country music, Mark McKinnon was a refreshing creative figure within the conservative firm. He was a nationally recognized media politico having managed all of the advertising for both of George W. Bush's presidential campaigns. A regular on the Sunday talk shows and revered by policy wonks and corporate leaders alike, I simply liked him because he was a music nut, had a killer sense of humor, and was an all-around *good person*.

McKinnon's imaginative and chilled out demeanor is just about as authentic as it gets, and in his former life, he was a musician. As a teenager in Colorado he started a band and managed to get Kris Kristofferson to produce it. He ran away from high school to Nashville where he lived in Kristofferson's apartment and spent a few years camped out at the songwriter's publishing company writing songs for other musicians. McKinnon describes Kristofferson as abundantly generous and patient with a kid who hung around him "like a Labrador puppy."

McKinnon's Texas debut was winning the 1975 Kerrville New Folk Song Writer's Competition. He drove through Austin on his way back to Nashville and was instantly smitten. Nashville had so few places to play live music, and Austin's club scene looked like the land of milk and honey to a young singer-songwriter. He crossed paths with a local musician who bemoaned that "Austin had like fifty clubs with live music, and seventy-five bands."

To which McKinnon replied, "Make that seventy-six bands." Mark and his wife, Annie, decided to make Austin their home.

One of my favorite things about working for McKinnon was hearing intermittent stories about music life in Austin back in the 1970s and '80s. I'd sit politely in his office while he wrapped up a telephone chit chat with the President (of the United States) and then we'd go over my notes in preparation for a big client pitch. In the middle of my presentation, he'd offer a fun anecdote about the days when Uncle Walt's Band played around town. Did I know the country singer David Ball? He had that hit with "Thinkin' Problem"? I did. Well *he* was in Uncle Walt's band. He explained that the young fiddling prodigy, Warren Hood, was the son of Champ Hood, who also played in Uncle Walt's Band. When the elder Hood died of cancer the music community in Austin lovingly rallied around young Warren and invited him right into their scene.

The first time I ever saw Warren Hood play the fiddle I was watching Charlie Robison and his brother, Bruce, at Antone's. They featured Warren early in the night because he was only sixteen years old and had to leave early to study for a math test.

I still love McKinnon's stories from back in the day. He describes it like no other, "Austin in the '70s was just a magnificent explosion of music. People were discovering country music, but they liked it with a little more edge and attitude than the traditional offering out of Nashville. And all the outlaws, rule breakers, and misfits landed in Austin (just like in the 1800s) and started pushing the envelope, creating the cosmic cowboy renaissance."

The cosmic cowboy renaissance. Damnation, I wish I'd been there. But I suppose the next best thing was drinking up the legacy and living in its aftermath.

In October 2003 I was stranded in Dallas for a business trip that was supposed to last a day but developed into a week-long goat rodeo. I was serving as creative director on my first television ad campaign with ads I had conceived and written from scratch. It was intense. We were filming all day and editing all night. I flew back to Austin Friday evening to an empty house – Sophie was with her grandparents again, and her dad on a hunting trip. I thought all I wanted to do was collapse in my bed and watch a movie. But the quiet took hold of me after just thirty minutes and I had to shake loose.

I ventured out to a barbecue music joint called Stubb's to see an outdoor concert with Cross Canadian Ragweed. At this point I had heard a few of their songs on the radio but had never seen them live. They blew me away. Cody Canada smoked on stage and tucked the butt of his cigarette into his guitar strings during his big solos. The crowd was electric and totally wild, and it was clear the band was feeding off the energy. In honor of Johnny Cash, who had recently passed away, they did a killer cover of "Burning Ring of Fire", which lit the place up. At one point they introduced a few players from Willie Nelson's band, The Family, who wandered up on stage and rocked a few numbers with Ragweed. It all felt so unscripted and looked like the party of the year up there. The fans went nuts, strangers were swaying with their arms around each other and toasting and singing at the top of their lungs. And that's when it hit me. *This is what it felt like back then. These are the good old days.*

Whenever people start the old dinner party banter asking everyone to share their first concert, favorite concert, etc., I always include this as one of the best, most exciting shows I have ever seen. Especially since its impact was long lasting. I would go on to see Cross Canadian Ragweed at least a dozen or more times after this. But I will never forget that night, the wild vibe of the crowd, the extemporaneous energy of the band, the breezy Austin sky with a big October moon, and that feeling, that euphoric feeling…I just felt so damn happy. And a part of something. And home.

CHAPTER 17 SOUNDTRACK:

Railroad Lady – Willie Nelson

(JERRY JEFF WALKER, JIMMY BUFFETT)

Gettin' By – Jerry Jeff Walker

(JERRY JEFF WALKER)

Texas Flood – Stevie Ray Vaughn and Double Trouble

(JOSEPH SCOTT, LARRY DAVIS)

Pancho and Lefty – Willie Nelson and Merle Haggard

(TOWNES VAN ZANDT)

On Your Own – Cross Canadian Ragweed

(JASON BOLAND, CODY CANADA)

The Armadillo World Headquarters
Photo credit and courtesy: Steve Hopson, www.stevehopson.com

Mural of blues musician Freddie King, painted by Armadillo Art Squad artist, Jim Franklin;
once on display in the Armadillo WHQ, now hanging at Threadgill's, Austin TX
Courtesy: Eddie Wilson

Armadillo Art Squad artist Sam Yeates designed this poster
for The Armadillo World Headquarters in the '70s
Photo credit and courtesy: Sam Yeates, © Sam Yeates 2013

CHAPTER 18

You Can't Spell Divorce
Without D-I-V-E

When the bouncer cries, "Last Call!" in the bar, you know it's time to go. When fate cries, "Last Call!" in your marriage, it's not always so clear. We tried valiantly to keep it going, but our efforts were in vain. We divorced in 2004.

You don't have to go home, but you can't stay here!

In the months that followed I began to run after live music like a storm chaser racing after tornadoes. While I spent ninety-nine percent of my time single-parenting Sophie and trying to maintain sanity at my pressure-cooker job, I was suddenly free every other weekend. I spent my new and awkward independence dragging friends to dancehalls, honky-tonks, and dive bars, which for the record, are not necessarily all the same thing.

Obviously there is plenty of overlap. A dancehall might be a honky-tonk and plenty of honky-tonks are in fact dives. But a honky-tonk must offer some sort of musical element, typically live country music, at least some of the time. A dive bar is rough around the edges, period. While many bars and watering holes clearly check both of those boxes, there are exceptions. Billy Bob's in Fort Worth is a massive honky-tonk with regular live music, but it is enormous and *nice*, there isn't anything divey about it. And there are certain dive bars that are dicey and full of character. They might even have a fairly decent rock and roll jukebox, but they aren't honky-tonks.

The Oxford English Dictionary explains the term "dive" began to be used in the United States in the late 1800s to describe a "drinking den" or "other disreputable place of resort." The word derives from the fact that these places were often located in cellars or basements and patrons could "dive" down to them without being noticed.

One definition for the term "dive" on the Urban Dictionary website is, "A ghettofied hole in the wall bar where the poor and downtrodden alcoholics of America go to drink discounted mini-pitchers and listen to tired David Allan Coe songs."

Hmm, seems about right.

Another theory is that the term originated in England to describe exotic, surreptitious places where upper crust young men would sneak off to drink away from the watchful eye of their noble parents. These bars offered a retreat from the stuffy propriety of British society. The décor was very relaxed, and patrons lounged on divan sofas. As a reference to this piece of furniture, these establishments were nicknamed "divans" which evolved into the term "dive".

Etymology aside, it's clear that a dive bar is associated with an element of escapism. A dipping down, of sorts. If you consider the vast range of life experience, I suppose subjectivity should allow for anyone to call just about any place a dive, if from their point of view, it feels below their regular comfort zone and more casual than their own daily life. I, however, feel strongly that guidelines should be established.

Word seems to have gotten out that I love a good dive bar, and so friends of friends delight in showing off their favorite dive. I can't tell you how many times I have been disappointed, especially in those early dating months. *Listen up rookies, a sports bar is not a dive!* If you think the twelve flat screen TVs showing sports and the fact that the burgers are served in red plastic baskets make it a dive bar, you need to get off the country club golf course once in a while and start day drinking like a man…in a windowless, cinderblock building with foam duct-taped along the edges of the bar and a weathered, toothless barkeep who seems mildly perturbed to take your order. If the place has a jar of red hard-boiled eggs and a long-defunct Super Bowl pool written in pencil on a fifteen-year-old dusty poster, you're in business. Pool tables are common fixtures, shuffleboard is even better. Darts are cool, perennial Christmas lights are double points, and a jukebox is essential. CD jukeboxes are fine if the selection is good, but a jukebox with old 45 records scores off the charts. A digital jukebox is a travesty. I think digital jukeboxes should be uniformly banned. A bar needs to stand behind its musical offerings, commit to a pre-edited selection of songs, and not let an over-served fledgling ruin everyone else's old school evening with a Sheryl Crow misfire.

A real dive bar has regulars who sit on the same barstool morning after morning starting their day hunched over a cocktail they didn't have to order because the bartender simply knows. Typically these customers are not exactly warm and inviting to newcomers. Kelly Willis has a story about stumbling upon a dive bar near Yoakum, Texas. She was with her husband Bruce (who is very tall), drummer Tom Lewis (another towering figure), and a friend of Tom's. The foursome happened upon a little dive one afternoon during a Texas road trip and wandered in for a beer. Instantly the regular crowd was sizing them up and shooting them dirty stares. After ordering, Bruce and Tom went into the men's room and were followed by one of the crotchety barflies who approached them at the urinal and inquired, "Y'all aren't from around here are you?"

"Uh, no, just passing through. We can't stay long."

To which the unfriendly patron replied, "I think that would be best."

It's a relief that such super cool talented musician types had this happen to them just as I have. It makes me feel better about my inherent suburban-ness.

Grouchy regulars are to be respected, unsavory or dangerous places to be avoided. But the truth is that most of the time, a good dive bar is as warm and jovial a place as you will ever find. Everyone is a friend by the time you leave.

I have spent many hours and incalculable brainwaves trying to nail down the true definition of a dive bar. There are so many intangibles that infuse a place with character that it's hard to create hard and fast rules. How does a dive bar newcomer know if he or she is in a true dive or just a casual bar? Admittedly it can be confusing. But fear not because I have finally pinpointed the definitive, tell-tale sign. The official watermark and universal calling card of a true dive bar is a stained Crock-Pot. Chili dogs, spaghetti, pulled pork…at some point or another a true dive bar is slow cooking some comfort food. Maybe it's for a big bowl game, or a fundraiser to help a beloved patron without health insurance cover some medical bills. Or maybe it's just a rainy Sunday afternoon that calls for tortilla soup and deviled eggs. But at the very core of a dive bar's sense of community lies a Crock-Pot.

The term "dive" took on metaphoric meaning in my life during the year following the divorce. Not only did I spend an increased amount of time every other weekend slow cooking in new-to-me dive bars that suddenly felt more like home than charity events and supper clubs, but my life actually felt as if it were in a free-fall dive. Emotionally, physically, and spiritually I was tumbling without proper anchor, waiting and praying for an unseen parachute to stabilize me. Some days were fine, others found me putting my little girl to bed and sneaking out to the back deck where I would walk around in circles, chain smoking and reciting the Lord's Prayer over and over again. It was hard. Some days I was surrounded by solid friends, good client work, and constructive activities. Other days I allowed a lesser quality of friends to slip into my space while my judgment was blurred. Like most recently divorced women, I spent twelve months manically assuring everyone I was "finally doing fine, finally getting on my feet." Only to realize in retrospect I was still a little nuts. I remember one lonely day after work, when Sophie was with her dad, I literally could not sit alone at home with my own thoughts. I ventured out to a venerable old South Austin dive called The Horseshoe Lounge. It was about six in the evening on a weeknight so there were only three or four other customers. I was naturally temperate with my drinking by this point in my mid-thirties, so I nursed along one beer as I shoved as many dollar bills as I could straighten flat enough into the jukebox and selected a long playlist of Tammy Wynette, Hank Williams, Patsy Cline, Merle, and Waylon. I picked every sad-sack downtrodden tune I recognized and pretty much hijacked the mood of the entire bar. One happy-go-lucky reveler busted into the Horseshoe and called out, "Goddam, who played all this slit-your-wrist music?" I remember growling at him in my mind and cutting him a sour, stand-down look.

It was official. No longer just a fan of classic honky-tonk music, I was actually living out the lyrics. *I was a honky-tonk song.*

Thankfully these hyper-pathetic, solo barfly moments were few and far between because, for better or worse, I fell in with a veritable pledge class of women who were also going through divorce. Some were old friends and some were pass-through friends, but nonetheless I had running buddies both emotionally and socially that kept me afloat during that bizarre phase. One woman who had already survived divorce and landed safely on the other side spelled it out bluntly, "You're going to ride the crazy train for one year."

I don't know what I would have done if I hadn't had Sophie to keep me grounded. Thankfully I remained reliable, up every morning making peanut butter sandwiches, reading to her class, and driving on field trips. It kept me sane. I don't judge grieving women who have a hard time getting the basic parenting tasks done in those early days, I was just lucky that the responsibility actually brought me comfort. But every other weekend when Sophie went to her dad's I nearly lost my mind. It was a quiet, maddening torture with way too much landscape for self-reflection. Anything was an ideal escape, anything to fill that silence.

Buckling under the tedium of negotiating divorce decrees, a fellow girlfriend, also in the midst of a divorce, and I spent one weekend like mental patients holed up at the Four Seasons Hotel wearing white robes and hotel slippers. We went to the spa in our robes, shuffled down to the pool in our robes, and strolled the grounds in our robes. If we hadn't been clutching fruity mojitos we would have looked like a scene from *One Flew over the Cuckoo's Nest.*

She and I were there for each other and Lord knows we covered some ground. We spent our first post-divorce Thanksgiving on the floor, eating off a coffee table in a friend's apartment. In lieu of traditional autumnal décor, we had a bright blue tinsel tabletop Christmas tree as decoration, and we danced to "Nasty Girl" by Nitty as we prepared the turkey. It was actually quite fabulous.

Monday would come and I would get back to real life, back to Sophie. Together we handled life extraordinarily well. We laughed and read together, attended birthday parties, went out for Tex-Mex with other families, connected with my parents. Sophie was so resilient and funny and bright, plugging in with her every day was like mainlining grace. Life seemed normal?

And then another lonely weekend would roll around. Live music filled the dead spaces on the calendar. I dragged friends to see Cross Canadian Ragweed anywhere and everywhere I could: New Braunfels, New Orleans, Corpus Christi, Tuscaloosa, San Francisco, even the San Antonio Rodeo. I saw The Drive By Truckers at Tipitina's in New Orleans, Charlie Robison and Reckless Kelly at the Sticky Fingerz Rock-n-Roll Chicken Shack in Little Rock, Will Hoge at Antone's in Austin, Dwight Yoakam at Stubb's. I even went to see the Gipsy Kings at Bass Concert Hall in Austin and wound up backstage rubbing elbows with Charlie Sexton, then managed to get a lift home on the Gipsy Kings' tour bus.

My biggest challenge was balancing my job, which I no longer enjoyed, with being a single mom. I would fly up to New York for a two-day shoot and end up staying for ten days. I was constantly negotiating with Sophie's sitter to stay longer and begging my dog walker to FedEx me clean underwear. I wanted to spend more and more time with Sophie as she was clipping along into kindergarten and first grade. So I changed the ringtone on my phone to play Kevin Fowler's "I Don't Want No J-O-B", and I quit my job. I was extraordinarily lucky that a steady stream of freelance and contract work came my way. Between that and a small pool of savings I drew down, I was able to keep my house and stay afloat. Budgets were tighter but my chest wasn't. I had more flexibility to be at Sophie's school, get to know the other moms, and work on smaller projects where I could make a bigger difference.

I spent more and more time at my parents' house in Montana. Sophie and I have friends there that we've known for years, so it's a special place for us. And right in the little unincorporated town of Craig, Montana is the greatest dive bar on the planet, Uncle Joe's.

It has a traditional horseshoe shaped bar, a pool table, and a killer jukebox. Joe would make homemade mustard and fix amazing hot dogs. A frozen pizza has never tasted better than at Uncle Joe's. And the Crock-Pot has been known to come out for special occasions. One of the most hilariously fun days of my life was spent at Uncle Joe's with all my Montana friends on New Year's Day. Local character and wandering troubadour, Jimmy, was strumming his guitar behind the bar, taking requests and leading the crowd in a sing-along that spanned the better part of eight hours. I absolutely adored singing with Jimmy. We'd sing at Uncle Joe's, at the campground, on the banks of the river. Originally from Oklahoma, Jimmy knew every single old honky-tonk song on the planet. I couldn't stump him. I loved when he played "Hello Darlin'", "Oklahoma Hills", or "King of The Road".

From the mountains to the beach, I was an equal opportunity escapist and spent a raucous Memorial Day Weekend down on the Texas coast. On the way down we stopped for a beer at a dive bar in South Texas, replete with a Chihuahua named Spike. I was the sober driver and wholly uninterested in the yappy dog, but my friends spent our brief visit petting and cooing over little Spike...who proceeded to give them fleas. That's how the trip began.

I wanted to book a last minute red-fishing guide on a holiday weekend, which seemed impossible. The only one available was a former rodeo rider and male stripper turned fishing guide – I know this because he was eager to share details about his former professions. He proceeded to drink tequila with us most of the day while we were out on our charter. We caught countless speckled trout, but I wanted a redfish. Late in the afternoon we were all out of the boat swimming in our underwear and cutting our feet on oyster beds when one of the rods in the rod holder bent tight and started buzzing. Our guide didn't budge but nonchalantly offered, "Oh, that's probably your redfish."

Willie Nelson's "Whiskey River" was blaring on the radio as I climbed back onto the boat in my sports bra and panties and landed my first ever redfish. Perhaps not the most sporting catch, but the picture was a classic.

We stepped out to celebrate that night but weren't really having much fun in the beach community of Port Aransas. The cheesy western-style dance club wasn't our scene. We were pretty bored, so when two young twenty-something's asked us to two-step, we thought, what the hell.

One of the guys was excessively drunk and rude and barked to my friend, Shelley Schmoker, "I thought you said you could dance."

His goofy wingman was more genteel toward me. "Hey, we've been chilling Jell-O shots all day at my uncle's condo behind the Circle K convenience store. It's the one just diagonal from the dumpster, you can't miss it. Y'all wanna come over?"

Umm, that would be a 'No Thank You'.

Those two brief exchanges threatened to sink us into a serious depression, so Shelley and I pulled the ripcord and went back to the hotel to watch bad TV.

The last night of the trip we traveled over to Corpus Christi to a Robert Earl Keen music festival. We saw Cross Canadian Ragweed, Jack Ingram, Reckless Kelly, Cory Morrow, and Robert Earl Keen. Now *that* was a memorable Memorial day. And once again, music lifted the mood.

Having spent limitless hours sharing and cavorting and laughing and crying and analyzing life with girlfriends, it's clear there are some common experiences which might translate into advice for other women who find themselves newly divorced.

1. Pick parking spaces where you can drive forward and don't have to back out. I logged a high incidence of fender benders during this period, likely as a result of overwrought nerves. I backed into dumpsters, walls, cars. Basically, avoid reverse. Whenever possible, go forward… literally and figuratively.
2. Take vitamins. Exercise. Drink water. Get sleep. (Talk to your doctor if you need a short term prescription.) You don't need to get sick on top of being stressed out.
3. If you have kids, focus on them. When you get to the other side you will feel so much better if you can look back and say you remained a fantastic mom. And, frankly, you will get to the other side faster. Even if you're having a

terrible day and the best mothering you can do is to order pizza delivery for both lunch and dinner while staying in pajamas and watching DVDs all day long…that's fine. Just pile in bed and do it together with your kids.

4. Be aware, you will no longer be invited to as many couple's events or dinner parties, if any at all. No one likes an uneven number at a seated dinner, and by and large people think divorce is contagious. The sooner you accept this the less hurtful it is.

5. Don't talk with someone's husband for too long at a party. Even if you've known him since high school and he's basically a pasty dork and you were maid of honor in their wedding and the wife is one of your oldest friends. If it doesn't bother her, it will still raise other eyebrows around the room.

6. Your goal is TO NOT BE BITTER. Whatever you have to do to get there, do it. Therapy, yoga, religion, meditation, books, movies, steam room, shooting range, pillow fights, Botox, peyote, fake-it-'til-you-make-it. If you spend every day genuinely trying to achieve that goal, you're on track. Don't be right, be happy.

7. Don't drink too much.

8. Don't pee in your own pool. Long distance relationships are best until you get the training wheels off.

9. You know the guy that you started seeing immediately after your separation/divorce? Newsflash, you're not in love with him. You may think that you are, but you're not. In fact, he's most likely a derelict. You have buried all your mourning over your failed marriage into this relationship under the fairytale notion that it was "all meant to be because he's really the one." He's probably not. You're most likely still going to have to walk through a period of being alone, truly alone. You can handle it. But at some point you have to drop transition guy.

10. You get to be nuts for one year. Period. Mark the calendar.

I also have a bit of advice for friends who have a girlfriend going through divorce. It's hard for a happily married wife to know how to be a good friend to someone who appears to have been taken over by alien forces. Not to mention, rants 24/7 about her plight. Or disappears for weeks on end without returning messages (most likely because she's tired of the sound of her own voice and wants to spare you having to listen to any more of her woeful drama). Here are some suggestions if you have a friend who is tackling divorce.

1. Please don't say to her, "Gawd, I am so glad I am not out there having to date again."
2. Similarly, don't say, "Whatever you do, don't do online dating. It's just so creepy. Wouldn't you be scared to have all your information out there?" (If you *do* have the gall to say this, then you'd better not have your own Facebook page with two thousand pictures of your kids wearing all white on the beach and documenting their every move in your hourly status updates.)
3. Never ever say to her, "That custody deal sounds pretty great actually. I could use a few nights off." Most divorced mothers feel a knife cutting through their heart at having to spend this time away from their kids. Please don't romanticize the absolute worst part of the whole situation.
4. Never make the mistake that because a single mother has "time off" when the kids are at their dad's, she has less mothering responsibilities. She's dealing with parenting and co-parenting issues 24/7, many of them incredibly complicated. You may think she spends Saturday nights swinging from a chandelier at a bar downtown, but she's likely at home reading copious books on how to help her children cope while you're at a dinner party with her former social crowd.
5. Invite her to dinner parties.
6. Rest easy, she is not interested in your husband. Unfortunately she's probably got her eye on an utterly

inappropriate, smoking hot, twenty-something musician at the moment.

7. Invite your girlfriend and her kids to do family-oriented activities with you.

8. Call or text her on Mother's Day.

9. Don't enable excessively wild behavior simply because you want to live vicariously through her freedom. Trust me, when she is on the other side she will gravitate toward the more solid, upstanding friendships and will ditch the ones that encouraged poor judgment.

10. Be patient. Love her well. Accept loving her one-way for a little while. Tell yourself she's off doing a tour of duty in the Peace Corps. Don't expect return phone calls or emails. Keep checking in regularly and suddenly, about a year later, you should hear from her again.

I was in New Orleans when my ride on the crazy train expired. It was just before noon on a gorgeous sunny Sunday; I had been out late with friends. Inexplicably I was still sporting a massive and ridiculous blond wig as we poured into one of my favorite cozy, dark French Quarter dive bars, called The Chart Room. Ironic name considering my own internal compass was on the blink. We parked it at the bar and laughed and carried on, having the entire place to ourselves. We weren't there long before my mood began to sink and the blues kicked in.

I skulked off to the jukebox determined to order up the saddest, most depressing song I could find. And I knew just the one: "Sunday Morning Coming Down" by Johnny Cash. I shoved a few dollars in the slot and punched the number for the track multiple times so everyone would have to endure it on repeat.

It is a beautifully lyrical song, with a deceivingly appealing melody. But there is hardly another set of lyrics on the planet sadder than these. You would have to be made of stone not to feel the aching pathos and utter loneliness in this song. It's about someone whose life has drifted toward drinking and drugs, and the story finds him briefly sober and choking on the painful nostalgia of a peaceful Sunday.

I wasn't drinking much at this point in my mid-thirties, but I loved the white noise of a party. I craved the frenetic pace of the nightlife. I had to keep moving to avoid a quiet, truthful moment like this.

We can thank (and blame) the brilliant songwriter poet Kris Kristofferson for writing this tune, which in that moment was serving as an uncomfortable mirror to my soul. The song was originally recorded in 1969 by Ray Stevens, and then Kristofferson himself cut it. But he desperately wanted Johnny Cash to sing it and was having a tough time getting a foot in the door to pitch it to him. After several failed attempts to get the song in front of Cash, Kristofferson pulled off one of the greatest stunts of all time. From his time in the military, he knew how to fly helicopters and was working as a commercial pilot in Nashville. So Kristofferson flew a helicopter to Johnny Cash's house, landed it on his back lawn, and personally delivered a demo tape of "Sunday Morning Coming Down". Needless to say it got Cash's attention.

Johnny Cash *did* record the song and turned it into a massive hit in 1970, the same year I was born. And just two years after Johnny Cash was born again.

After a failed marriage, heavy drug use, and years of painful longing for June Carter, a woman he wasn't allowed to love, Johnny Cash tried to commit suicide. He climbed down into a Tennessee cave where many experienced spelunkers had previously died, unable to navigate its complex layout. He assumed that he too would become lost in its intricate labyrinth and no one would ever find him. He was under the influence of drugs at the time, felt exhausted, dejected, and ready to escape everything. Ready to take the ultimate dive. He passed out in the cave and awakened to feel the presence of God. Henceforth Cash always believed that emerging from that cave was symbolic of his spiritual rebirth.

His true love, June Carter, moved into his home for a month along with her parents. The Carters helped him find both sobriety and Christianity, and Cash referred to this period as his forty days in the wilderness. Later that same year, Johnny Cash proposed to June, and they were married on March 1, 1968. June Carter and Johnny Cash remained married until their deaths and as a couple have become an icon for true love.

Johnny Cash became a devout and active, if not stereotypical, Christian. He developed a close personal friendship with Reverend Billy Graham and attended revival meetings, offering testimony. In Graham's book How to Be Born Again Johnny Cash describes his own imperfect faith walk. After years of emotional darkness and a battle with drug addiction, Cash simply turned it all over to God. He is quick to point out that didn't make his life perfect, but leaning on scripture offered him a new sense of joy and strength. Even with Christ and the positive influence of June in his life, Cash continued to rail against authority and champion the underdog. He never quite fit the mold of the Christian born-again poster child.

In 1983 he angrily tussled with a belligerent ostrich that resided at the exotic animal park behind his home. Now some people may not know what Johnny Cash and I both happen to know, which is that ostriches are mean, fast, and strong. When I was seventeen I was hunting with my family at a ranch in Texas where they had exotic animals mixed in with indigenous game. I was hiking through a field when a rancorous ostrich came after me. I was carrying a rifle, and yet I was so scared that I ran for my life while this gangly, awkward creature came barreling after me with alarming speed. I jumped into the Suburban and slammed the passenger door in the nick of time. The ostrich was so angry he tried to kick through the truck to get to me. Would you believe he dented and mangled the door of the truck? So strangely, like Johnny Cash, I too have gone head to head with an evil ostrich.

And other demons.

Unfortunately Cash's experience didn't end as well as mine. The ostrich battered him so badly he wound up with his stomach and chest ripped open and five crushed ribs. Prescription pain killers triggered a relapse in his addiction. Cash continued to do an addiction-recovery dance throughout the 1980s, but once he accepted Christ in his life, he had a light and a peace within him to fight the good fight.

Known in country music as the Man in Black, Johnny Cash actually wrote a faith-based novel called The Man in White about the apostle Paul. In a separate book called CASH: The Autobiography, Johnny Cash explains why he identified so deeply with this particular biblical figure. Paul had suffered extreme and relentless trials: he was beaten with rods, pelted with stones, and shipwrecked – more than once. Yet with the strength of the Holy Spirit, he persevered, *contently*, and Johnny Cash yearned for a similar peace in his own life.

I wanted some of that, too. Sitting in the Chart Room that particular Sunday I felt as though I had been emotionally beaten with rods, spiritually shipwrecked, and kicked all over by an angry, relentless ostrich. I was tired of trying to outrun my own thoughts and fears – exhausted in fact. I was tired of pulling myself up by the proverbial boot strap and making everyone else feel comfortable about my situation. I was scared I was going to be alone forever. Johnny Cash's voice sang straight into my heart, and the sad lyrics were too honest and poignant to bear. I retreated to the grungy bar bathroom, slumped down into a chair, and cried. I used the long, synthetic locks from my blond wig to wipe my eyes and nose. I loathed where I was, both literally and symbolically. But the man in black was charting a new path.

My ride on the crazy train needed to end, that much was clear. And yet I can't say in that moment I fully recognized all that was stirring within, the subtle tectonic shifts easing me toward a more constructive center. All I knew for certain was that on a Sunday morning, coming down in a French Quarter dive, I found a little slice of redemption in the jukebox.

Johnny Cash saves.

Cigarettes and Coffee Blues – Jean Shepard

(MARTY ROBBINS)

The Wurlitzer Prize – Waylon Jennings

(BOBBY EMMONS, CHIPS MOMAN)

Next in Line – Conway Twitty

(CURTIS WAYNE, WAYNE KEMP)

Rated 'X' – Loretta Lynn

(LORETTA LYNN)

Sunday Morning Coming Down – Johnny Cash

(KRIS KRISTOFFERSON)

Venerable dive bar, The Horseshoe Lounge on South Lamar Boulevard, Austin TX

Crock-Pots by the jukebox at Ginny's Little Longhorn, Austin TX

CHAPTER 19

Remember Me

I had forgotten myself. That Sunday in New Orleans was a
wakeup call that it was time to get back to the real me, back to my
family and friends. It was time to hit the reset button on my value
system. I was done being pitiful, and I was one hundred percent
motivated not to turn into one of those sour divorced women. I saw
something on television about how forgiveness was the antidote to
bitterness, and so without really knowing what I was hoping to find,
I launched a full scale campaign to learn about radical forgiveness. I
scoured the Internet for articles, I searched for stories and testimonies
on Dr. Phil's website, even visited the site of the Queen of Daytime
and self-help guru, Oprah. I followed a website called The Forgiveness
Project. One website would lead to another, which would lead to a
discussion board, which would lead to a magazine article.

I began to understand forgiveness in a whole new light. I learned
that you should forgive someone whether or not they are repentant
because the act of forgiveness is for you, not them. *Hmm, somewhat
counterintuitive, but okay, I'll play along.* I learned to accept that the
one who has grieved you, while disappointing and hurtful, was likely
just doing his or her best. *Hard to choke down, but I will try to see it that
way.* I learned that not forgiving someone, that holding on to bitterness

and anger, is like swallowing a vile of poison and expecting the other person to die. *Well now, that is vivid. I suppose I get it.* I learned that forgiveness was not about forgetting, nor was it about releasing the person from all consequences. It was about relinquishing the notion that you are responsible for making them accountable. It's about letting God determine their consequences on his timeline. I learned that forgiveness is a choice that you often have to make over and over again. I learned it brings extraordinary freedom and peace.

So whom should I forgive?

As I brainstormed answers to that question I realized I was harboring more resentment than I thought. I had to forgive some old friends who seemed to find my divorce uncomfortable and disappeared from my life; and the toxic people who seeped in and filled their void; colleagues who were particularly difficult to work with whom I associate with that negative time; utility companies who annoyingly expected me to pay my bills on time despite what I was going through! But most of all, there was me. The sense of failure was crippling, and the absolute hardest step was self-forgiveness.

I pulled weeds, extricated noxious people from my life, and made room for good friends, old and new. I felt unleashed, hopeful, and light. Of course I had no idea tackling the concept of forgiveness was going to inadvertently catapult me straight into the essence of spirituality. But that's pretty much what happened. It was as if God was tapping me on my shoulder, asking this lifelong Christmas and Easter Episcopalian, "Hey you, remember me?"

Basically I found faith on this Internet rabbit trail. I was an accidental Christian if there ever was one. But the process unlocked a whole new happy life; Sophie and I flourished together, and my social life felt full, bright, and constructive. I was at peace and no longer dreaded time alone. It was a lovely innocent period and my dance card was full. That said, I was determined to keep it all light and not settle down. My girlfriends raved about some of my suitors and chided me for setting my standards unreasonably high. But I stood firm. I was waiting for butterflies. I wanted values, chivalry, and *butterflies*.

My forgiveness quest was hardly the only time I have devoured a computer project, losing myself in the ever-connected tendrils of data and information. I become a veritable crime scene investigator when I want to find out something about a piece of music. The first time I heard the Hank Williams song, "Deck of Cards", I was in the mountains away from a computer but desperate to get to the bottom of something that was curious about this recitation song. In a recitation song the singer speaks instead of sings, and there is background music as he or she narrates. They are somewhat old-fashioned and often associated with messages of faith. "Deck of Cards" is a prime example as it describes a soldier who was court-martialed for looking at his cards during church. He explains to his superiors that each card in the deck represents a biblical lesson for him and he keeps the deck with him always. It is a simple and powerful tale, no doubt, but the first time I heard "Deck of Cards" I was completely distracted by the melody playing in the background. I recognized it. It was another song I knew…but what was it?

That's when it hit me! It was the same melody as the old Jim Reeves hit, "Have I Told You Lately That I Love You". The first time I'd ever heard it was in the movie *Coal Miner's Daughter*. There is a fantastic scene where Sissy Spacek, playing Loretta Lynn, is doing laundry on the porch and teaching herself to play the guitar to the song "Have I Told You Lately That I Love You" while intermittently kicking a washtub. I bought the Jim Reeves 4-CD set just to have his version of the song, not even realizing anyone else had recorded it. But clearly the Hank Williams recitation "Deck of Cards" would have preceded Jim Reeves' "Have I Told You Lately That I Love You". Wouldn't it? Hank Williams' career came before that of Jim Reeves, if only by a small margin. So who wrote "Have I Told You Lately That I Love You"? Did they know Hank Williams used it in his "Deck of Cards" recitation? Was that even a Hank Williams original recitation?

The moment I returned from the mountains and reunited with my computer I was on the hunt for answers. As it turns out, a singer named T. Texas Tyler wrote the recitation song "Deck of Cards" in 1948. He composed the lyrics based on a parable about the soldier and his deck of cards, which dates back to a 1762 book of common-place folk stories that belonged to a British farmer's wife. In addition, poems exist that indicate the story of the soldier may actually trace back as far as medieval times. So T. Texas Tyler repackaged an age-old parable, but did he compose the melody? Did the melody go first with "Deck of Cards", or was it the melody for "Have I Told You Lately That I Love You" first? And who in the hell was T. Texas Tyler?

T. Texas Tyler was a country singer who appeared on the *Louisiana Hayride* and the *Opry* in the late 1940s and early 1950s. I learned he recorded a song called "Remember Me". Certainly it wasn't…it couldn't be the same…not the Willie song? One of my favorite Willie songs of all time is also called "Remember Me".

I thoroughly abandoned the trail for the history of "Have I Told You Lately That I Love You" and became immediately obsessed with knowing whether T. Texas Tyler's 1945 "Remember Me" was in fact the same song that Willie Nelson recorded in 1975. And yes, in fact, it is the same. I had always assumed it was a Willie tune! But Tyler had a hit with it first. So who in the world wrote "Remember Me"? My new rabbit trail continued.

The answer is Scott Wiseman. It turns out Scott Wiseman was one half of the married singing duo Lulu Belle and Scotty. While they were both from North Carolina, they met on the set of the Chicago *National Barn Dance* and married in 1934. Lulu Belle had been a comedic female singer who often performed with Red Foley, but Foley's wife became jealous of their act. So the *National Barn Dance* paired her with new arrival Scotty Wiseman, and the two fell in love. Lulu Belle was the more vivacious showman while Scotty penned many of their songs, including "Remember Me".

And imagine my surprise when I kept reading to learn that one of Wiseman's best known songwriting hits was…wait for it…"Have I Told You Lately That I Love You"! I almost fell out of my chair. I had come full circle and had inadvertently found the answer to my original online quest. Serendipity never ceases to entertain.

In 1944 Scott Wiseman fell quite ill and was in a Chicago hospital for several weeks. One day his wife Lulu Belle was wrapping up a visit and whispered in his ear, "Have I told you lately that I love you?" Wiseman wisely thought it was the making of a great song lyric. He sat in his hospital bed with paper and a pencil, and by the time she returned the next day he had the first verse and chorus ready to sing to her. Gene Autry recorded it first, and then countless others through the years.

I wasn't able to nail down how its melody came to serve as the background music for T. Texas Tyler's "Deck of Cards". But Wiseman wrote "Have I Told You Lately That I Love You" in 1944. In 1945 Tyler covered Wiseman's "Remember Me". So they must have known each other professionally if not personally – or presumably at least known *of* each other. Tyler wrote "Deck of Cards" in 1948, I assume with permission to use Wiseman's pre-existing melody.

It's actually quite common in country music to share melodies, respond with answer songs, collaborate in duets, reference other lyrics, and cover songs by other musicians. Back in the early days when country music was still called hillbilly music, it was regular practice to create lyrics based on a public domain folk song. A.P. Carter of The Carter Family was known to collect old Irish and English folk songs, and he used one as the foundation for the 1929 Carter Family hit, "I'm Thinking Tonight of My Blue Eyes". It's a familiar story of lost love set to a simple melody that resonates. "I'm Thinking Tonight of My Blue Eyes" evolved into four separate country songs, all of which used the same melody, and all of which became hits:

1. **"I'm Thinking Tonight of My Blue Eyes"**
   – The Carter Family 1929
2. **"Great Speckled Bird"**
   – Roy Acuff 1936
3. **"Wild Side of Life"**
   – Hank Thompson 1952
4. **"It Wasn't God Who Made Honky Tonk Angels"**
   – Kitty Wells 1952

Roy Acuff made his *Grand Ole Opry* debut in 1938 singing "Great Speckled Bird". Until the night he sang this song on the *Opry*, instrumental groups were king and vocalists were merely an accessory. Acuff changed all that with his debut performance.

The "Great Speckled Bird" lyrics were written as an allegorical hymn by Reverend Guy Smith. Smith was responding to a controversy in the Presbyterian Church that spanned the 1920s and the 1930s and pitted modern thinking against Christian fundamentalism. In "Great Speckled

Bird" Smith takes the position of the Fundamentalists, basically claiming that scripture cannot be rationalized or marginalized no matter how vehement the outcry of popular modern opinion. The lyrics maintain that the only way, the only path is on the wings of the body of Christ, or the uncompromised church, which in the song is symbolized by the great speckled bird. The avian imagery in the song comes straight from the Bible, specifically Jeremiah 12:9, "Mine heritage is unto me as a speckled bird, the birds round about are against her; come ye, assemble all the beasts of the field, come to devour." This piece of scripture describes an actual phenomenon in nature called mobbing. Mobbing is when weaker, non-predatory birds get together and attack a larger, predatory bird. Basically, it's a power-in-numbers approach. Luke 23:23 describes a human version of mobbing, detailing how public opinion clamored for Christ's demise. "But the mob shouted louder and louder, demanding that Jesus be crucified, and their voices prevailed."

Both scripture and the song express the need to cling to the truth of the great speckled bird, the church, and the body of Christ, and not weaken in the face of mob mentality. The core message of the song is that there is only one truth, and no matter how many mobbing voices cry out against it, no matter how *loudly* they cry out against it, the wings of the bird are the only true path. The essence of the debate within the church was tension over science versus scripture and rationalizing miracles in the Bible. Did they actually happen as real miracles or are they meant to be suggestions of symbolic change? The song the "Great Speckled Bird" clearly sides with fundamental belief, warning in a fiery tone that we shouldn't cherry-pick scripture. We shouldn't believe only the parts that are convenient, easy to follow, and supported by science, while disregarding the messages that are inconvenient, hard, or mysterious to human intelligence. Essentially the song says to wait, be patient, we don't have all the information yet from God to align scripture with science, but stick with the great speckled bird in the meantime. Don't attack her. Have faith.

It's a pretty heady, intellectual, substantive song compared to its much lighter predecessor, "I'm Thinking Tonight of My Blue Eyes", which merely shares a tale of a lost love. But with its third incarnation the melody returned to its roots in old-fashioned heartache. In 1952

Hank Thompson had a smash hit with "Wild Side of Life", which also used this same melody. William Warren, who co-wrote the lyrics, was inspired by an actual honky-tonk girl he'd met when he was young. In the song the wronged husband bemoans the fact that God, much to his surprise, designed some women as honky-tonk angels, destined to cheat and carouse. In his book, <u>The Grand Ole Opry History of Country Music: 70 Years of the Songs, the Stars and the Stories</u>, Paul Kingsbury explains that the song struck a chord with cynical people who "thought the world was going to hell and that faithless women deserved a good deal of the blame."

He also notes that the sweeping gender judgment in Hank Thompson's hit "begged for an answer from a woman."

J.D. "Jay" Miller wrote the answer song that Kitty Wells made famous, "It Wasn't God Who Made Honky Tonk Angels". Ironically Roy Acuff, whose lyrics to the very *same* melody challenged people to ignore a mob of detractors, cautioned Johnnie Wright not to make his wife, Kitty Wells, the headliner of their act. Acuff didn't believe women could sell country music. He couldn't have been more wrong.

In the song, Wells doesn't whitewash the woman's sin; she doesn't deny that the wife in Hank Thompson's version cheated. She is simply pointing out it wasn't God's design. The woman wasn't inherently evil. In fact, the woman strayed because she was hurt first by her cheating husband. Wells' song aims to affirm female dignity by citing nurture over nature. She's not trying to let the woman off the hook as much as she is letting God off the hook and putting the cheating husband on it.

The *Opry* wouldn't let her sing it, and many radio stations banned it from airplay. But it inspired listeners and became a grassroots success. Rarely does an answer song sell better and become a bigger hit than the first song, but Kitty Wells and "It Wasn't God Who Made Honky Tonk Angels" were both blazing new trails.

Four hit country songs, one simple public domain melody. In his 1977 song "If That Ain't Country" David Allan Coe references all four of these songs. Throughout the song he paints the portrait of a white trash redneck who is covered in tattoos and weathered by a rough life. The character cusses and drinks and has a whore for a sister. His yard is littered with attack dogs and broken down vehicles. Of course David

Allan Coe isn't going to portray a saccharine feel-good image of a country farmer and his hard-working family. His version of "country" is rough around the edges and raw. But the outlaw of all outlaws stakes his claim on having traditional country credibility by singing snippets from all four of the country hit songs that share that one melody ("Blue Eyes", "Speckled Bird", "Honky-Tonk Angel", "It Wasn't God") in a descant at the end of "If That Ain't Country". While he first sings an edgy, unflattering portrayal of what is considered "country" he then undercuts himself by referencing four of the most traditional country standards in the history of this music genre.

I suppose sometimes even an outlaw feels an urge to color inside the lines. Even a rebel will crave a sense of connectedness. Isn't the need to connect hardwired within the human spirit? Recycling melodies across these different songs managed to connect wildly diverse storylines and varying points of view. The melodies connected narrators from opposing genders and fans from various decades. Music, especially honky-tonk music, offers a distilled truth that reaches people in a multitude of ways: pathos, validation, inspiration, escape. These common refrains mimic recurring patterns within the human experience. Cycles of sin, love, loss, consequence, forgiveness, and faith. And yet time and time again we are too obtuse to see the cycle or the pattern unfolding in our own life. How hard is it to avoid being hit by a train? Can't you just take one step to the left or one step to the right? For some reason it only feels so simple after you're left to assess the wreckage. I don't have all the answers, but I know I will always try to recognize the power of forgiveness within the cycle. The past may be orbiting around, sometimes threatening our emotional or spiritual well-being, perhaps even whispering a chorus of self-defeat and insecurity, but with forgiveness, the past is relegated to its proper place, which is behind us. A similar melody may play on, but as individuals, we each have the power to re-write the song, we each have control over our own personal soundtrack. We can write our own lyrics *today*, claiming harmony in our lives right this very minute. And we will sing something just a little bit sweeter, truer, than we did yesterday.

CHAPTER 19 SOUNDTRACK:

I'm Thinking Tonight of My Blue Eyes – The Carter Family

(A.P. CARTER)

If That Ain't Country – David Allan Coe

(DAVID ALLAN COE, FRED SPEARS)

Deck of Cards – Hank Williams

(T. TEXAS TYLER)

Have I Told You Lately That I Love You – Jim Reeves

(SCOTT WISEMAN)

Remember Me – Willie Nelson

(SCOTT WISEMAN)

Then he said, "Jesus, remember me when you come into your kingdom."

Jesus answered him, "Truly I tell you, today you will be with me in paradise."

(LUKE 23:42 – 43)

What Can I Say, I'm a Sucker for Spanish Moss

Life was good. Sophie and I were at the top of our game, everything had both a spring and a balance to it. I had two powerful moments of clarity that gave me a sense of direction and peace. The first occurred on the treadmill in my home. It became obvious to me that I needed to be on my own for a while, without a boyfriend or a spouse, because it was time to start writing, time to catapult myself down the creative path I'd always craved. My second vision came during the summer in Montana while I was on a walk. I was jukin' out to Stevie Wonder's "For Once in My Life", entertaining some cows in a pasture, when it washed over me. I knew right then and there I wasn't going to be alone forever.

I wasn't even alone for long. Alabama blew into my life when I least expected it.

Tom Warren was from Mobile, Alabama, and our first official date was camping at a multi-day music festival in Live Oak, Florida. We had originally met while on vacation in Montana and subsequently found ourselves chatting on the phone or by email about fly-fishing, life, and music. At one point he rang me up out of the blue and invited me to a music festival called Springfest.

I flew from Austin to Mobile, and then we drove five hours to the panhandle of Florida to meet up with his friends, who had already selected our campsite. The campgrounds were beautiful, close to the Suwannee River, surrounded by a forest of tall trees, and literally dripping in Spanish moss.

I cannot overstate how much I love Spanish moss. It is so eerie and timeless and Southern Gothic. I wish I could drape myself in it. Spanish moss is my kryptonite, my Achilles heel. It was either a harbinger of good fate, or, at the very least, creating an excessively romantic mood.

After setting up our tent and getting settled, it was time to tackle one of the afternoon stages and hear some live music. We threw our folding chairs over our shoulders and off we went. The amphitheater stage was inviting, the sun was beaming through the trees, and the crowd was mellow and relaxed. We positioned ourselves up front, and the very first act we saw was an Austin-based blues guy named Seth Walker. I giggled at the fact I had just traveled over 950 miles to see a musician who had a weekly gig at the Saxon Pub, just one neighborhood away from my home in Austin. But I'd never seen him before, so I was excited. The very first song he played was "You Don't Know Me", the same song I performed in my Boston voice class. He even introduced it with a nod to venerable Texas songwriter, Cindy Walker. I was in heaven. And Seth Walker blew us all away. He had a retro look with his porkpie hat as he belted out soulful bluesy numbers that transported us to another era.

Despite the fact that we led off with a Texas blues act, the majority of the Springfest lineup was bluegrass music, some of which was traditional in its old-time roots, while some was more rocking, progressive jamgrass. As day melted into night, tiki torches near the stage were lit. The moon illuminated the Spanish moss while we grooved to music under a canopy of stars. People turned on Christmas lights that adorned their campsites. We built a fire. It was a stark contrast to the mega festivals like ACL in Austin; Springfest felt like a throwback. Everyone was wonderfully hippie dippie, either literally or in spirit, people were happy, the crowds were very manageable. The vendors were grassroots…vege-burritos, gyros, homemade hula hoops, and hippie skirts. There wasn't a Verizon booth where you could upgrade your minutes. No one was handing out free samples of Starbucks.

Other Springfest highlights were Guy Clark and Jim Lauderdale, my first time to see both. I cut my teeth on Guy Clark, singing his songs with my parents as we road-tripped to Colorado in the summers. After thirty years of hearing his music, it was wild to see him pick and sing his epic train ballad, "Texas 1947". I knew every word, of course. If you're not familiar with Guy Clark but you're a Jerry Jeff Walker fan, you're likely more familiar with Guy Clark's songs than you realize. He wrote "L.A. Freeway" and "Desperados Waiting for a Train", both of which were made famous by Jerry Jeff. Clark also wrote Rodney Crowell's hit "She's Crazy for Leaving", and Jimmy Buffett covered Clark's "Boats to Build". Guy Clark is a Texas songwriting deity, and I was ecstatic to see him live.

I was also excited to see Jim Lauderdale, especially his flamboyant western outfits that I can only assume are tailored by the famous Manuel in Nashville. Bright orange with flowers and sequins, purple with swirls and arrows, Lauderdale is unafraid and I absolutely love his threads, topped off by his fantastic head of hair. Oh, and he can sing – *and* he's a killer songwriter as well. Lauderdale incorporates some of the old-school *Opry*-style cornball comedy in his act, weaving in some puns between his powerfully poetic songs. After his performance I just happened to be at the side of the stage as he made his way to his merchandise table to sign CDs. I was directly in his path, and he stopped, looked right at me and nodded hello. I choked, I couldn't say a word. I was like a middle school student with a first crush.

Except I wasn't falling for Lauderdale, I was developing a crush on my date. The music, the tiki torches, the Spanish moss, laughing around the campfire…it was beyond dreamy. We had a fantastic weekend. As we were leaving the festival I offered my assessment, "Springfest was like one of those events people would lord over your head and wax on and on about, 'Aw, you should have been there, back in the day, it was magical,' except we *were just there*; back in the day is right now."

Tom and I kept up a little long distance dance with emails and text messages and phone calls. The next time we saw each other was

Memorial Day Weekend. He came to Austin to visit me for a long weekend of live music. His first night in town I took him to eat at Ranch 616 because it is just *so* Texas in both décor and haute ranch cuisine, there's nothing else quite like it. Then we went to Antone's to see Junior Brown. We'd both seen him many times before, and we were both big fans. But I am mildly embarrassed to say I don't think we listened to one song or paid a lick of attention. We parked it at the very back of Antone's and just talked and talked and talked throughout the entire show.

Sorry, Junior. Love the rockin' guit-steel, by the way.

The next day I introduced Alabama Tom to the Texas ritual of the morning breakfast taco. I think he liked them, although at the time I imagine he thought they were a novelty, a once-in-a-while indulgence. I'm not sure he fully grasped it was everyday fare. He was also fascinated by the multiple Latin-style saint candles I had scattered around the house, and I had to explain they were simply the only candles for sale by the cash register at my local grocery store. Living in Austin it's easy to forget how the Hispanic culture weaves its way into daily life so pervasively and beautifully, and how foreign that may seem to someone from the Deep South.

After tacos we loaded up and made the forty-five minute road trip down to New Braunfels and strolled around the nearby historic town of Gruene (pronounced "green", like the color). The cultural anchor of this charming town is Gruene Hall, the oldest continually run dancehall in Texas. Willie Nelson, Jerry Jeff Walker, Charlie Robison, Robert Earl Keen…all the Texas greats have played Gruene Hall. With its stark façade, wide open hardwood dance floor, and twinkle lights strung from trees in the biergarten area, it is the prototypical Texas dancehall.

That night we drove down the Guadalupe River to the River Road Ice house for a large outdoor concert with Cross Canadian Ragweed. The holiday weekend crowd was wild and drunk, many of them having wandered straight off the river from a hot day of tubing. The people watching was hilarious, the energy electric, and the show out of sight. Lead singer Cody Canada was particularly revved up on stage because number one, he lived in New Braunfels and was playing to a hometown crowd, and secondly, it was his birthday. It seemed as if he was having a damn fine time.

Exceptional show, long hot summer night. We were whipped the next day as we limped back up I-35 to Austin. But we weren't totally out of steam. After some white wine sangria in the peaceful courtyard of the Hotel San Jose, I took Tom to one of Austin's smallest and most beloved honky-tonks, Ginny's Little Longhorn. The edifice is nothing more than a burnt orange hut with bright white trim, located on a busy commercial road north of downtown. Every Sunday afternoon the place is busting at the seams as local honky-tonker Dale Watson takes the stage, a term I use very loosely here. The "stage" is nothing more than the corner of the room, and the dance floor is a nine foot square area that has simply been cleared of tables and chairs. Regulars and newbies pour in side by side to two-step and swing and sweat and dance as if they were in a massive ballroom. We squeezed up to the bar, ordered a couple of beers, and settled in. Sunday afternoons are always packed at Ginny's because that's when they host "Chicken Shit Bingo". Basically you buy a ticket with a number on it. At some point the band takes a break and they carry a chicken over to this table that has a cage on top of it. There is a grid painted on the bottom of the cage, and each square has a number written on it. The chicken struts around inside the cage as the crowd gathers around, waiting for it to poop. Cheers and jeers erupt as the chicken teases the inebriated audience. Because ultimately, if it poops on a square with the same number as your ticket, you win.

Just about two feet from the chicken cage is another table with a Crock-Pot. That afternoon they were cooking chilidogs, and we devoured our fair share, chasing them down with cold Lone Star beer in a bottle. It was heaven.

It's highbrow entertainment, no doubt. Austinites would curl up in the fetal position and cry grown-man tears if anything ever happened to Dale Watson and Chicken Shit Bingo Sundays at Ginny's Little Longhorn. It's a rite of passage for locals and newcomers alike.

And that is how my romance with Alabama Tom began. Incredible live music, tiki torches, and flirty text messages that had me racing across the room to grab my phone like a schoolgirl every time it dinged. Campfires, rivers, and honky-tonks set the stage. There was chivalry and old fashioned swooning. We were so hopped up on dopamine we could dance to the band and stay up all night to watch the sunrise. Cupid shot me so full of arrows I must have looked like I was having acupuncture. And at long last, there they were…what I had been waiting for all that time…I finally had them – butterflies.

But let's be honest. It was game over at the Spanish moss.

CHAPTER 20 SOUNDTRACK:

Kick It Around – Seth Walker

(JAMES HUNTER)

Chances – Jim Lauderdale

(ODIE BLACKMON, JIM LAUDERDALE)

Darlin' I'll Do Anything You Say – Junior Brown

(JUNIOR BROWN)

Blues for You – Cross Canadian Ragweed

(CODY CANADA)

Big Town Baby – Dale Watson

(PAUL ANGEL)

Christine and Tom at the annual Springfest music festival
The Spirit of the Suwannee Music Park, Live Oak FL

CHAPTER 21

Lovesick Blues Et Al

Tom and I dated about two and a half years. Our romance was dipped in honey, a modern fairytale of sorts. The more we came to know one another, the more we realized how aligned our values were. We helped each other grow in faith, plus we had *a hell of a lot of fun*. Quite simply, we fit. There was just one massive looming hurdle: geography. I was raising a daughter in Austin and shared custody with her father. Tom owned a business based in Mobile. It seemed we were both shackled to our respective cities. So for two and a half years we fell in love, learned to fight fair and forgive, cooed, courted, and flirted. If I had to select just one word to describe our relationship it would be "resilient". Most of the time we ignored the obvious obstacle that would eventually need our attention. But it was always there, a bittersweet thorn in our side. We were madly in love but quietly sick over the long distance issue. We were lovesick.

Not to mention we were singlehandedly keeping the airline industry afloat, traveling back and forth between Texas and Alabama. Alabama…I was falling for the state as well as the guy. There are just certain regions that have a lot of soul to them, places that have character and characters. And delicious, Dirty South Alabama is absolutely one of those places. With soul comes music, and Alabama has a rich music heritage. Specifically, when you think of honky-tonk you can't ignore the quintessential honky-tonk star, Hank Williams, who was born and raised in Alabama. The moment he debuted on the *Opry* with "Lovesick Blues" he captured the heart of the country and changed music forever. No one before, nor perhaps since, has embodied the raw ache and poetic blues of honky-tonk quite like Hank Williams.

But Alabama didn't stop producing talent after Hank came and left as quickly as he did. There were others, in fact, several others from Alabama who were innovators during the heyday of this genre. Alabama has given us landmark artists who shaped certain subgenres and iconic themes within the world of golden era honky-tonk. If you've spent even a modicum of time enjoying traditional country music, then at one point or another you most certainly have stumbled across:

1. Its flamboyant costumes
2. Brother acts
3. The sound of a steel guitar

You don't know how much it pains me that I can't find a place in my PTA-mom lifestyle to wear a fuchsia gabardine suit embroidered with leather western yolks and ornate embroidered roses top to bottom. I often daydream about rolling up to Sophie's middle school decked out in a vintage honky-tonk costume, kicking back against the side of a 1950s convertible Cadillac with my sequins glistening in the Texas sunlight as I wait for her and her friends to come pouring out of the building when the bell sounds. The mere mention of such a fantasy would no doubt paralyze her teenage constitution with mortal embarrassment as I would no doubt be sporting a rainbow of preposterous colors and an over-the-top amount of rhinestones illustrating various western images on my lapel and all the way down the sides of my pant legs. And there would be fringe. So much fringe. It's no wonder honky-tonk singers wore as much fringe as they did, given how they sang about the disenfranchised, appealed to outlaws, and often lived their own lives on the very fringes of society.

The colorful cowboy costume trend in country music began in California in the 1930s. A Polish immigrant tailor named Nathan

Turk was making ornamental suits and stage wear for on-screen singing cowboys like Gene Autry and Roy Rogers. Turk had always loved western movies and created fine gabardine suits with arrowhead smile pockets and other classic western detailing. The motion picture cowboys may have started with Turk suits, but it was a family band from Alabama that ignited the trend among hillbilly musicians. In 1933 Lula and Charlie Maddox took their children from Boaz, Alabama and rode the rails all the way to the San Joaquin Valley of California. Here they made a modest living as migrant fruit pickers, all the while trying to get a music career going. Five of the sons and one daughter comprised the family band, The Maddox Brothers and Rose.

They began to receive airplay in Modesto, and Lula, who was both mother and manager, decided she wanted the band to be the best dressed in the business. She received a referral from Roy Rogers who sent her to his tailor, Nathan Turk. And that's where it all began. Immediately known for their cowboy couture, they earned the nickname "America's Most Colorful Hillbilly Band".

In her book, <u>Hillbilly Hollywood</u>, Debby Bull explains, "The outfits Turk made for the Maddoxes were the first of their kind: embroidered, flashy, brightly colored, and, because they were so beautifully tailored, a little elegant, as well."

Rose Maddox is quoted in Bull's book, explaining, "Nathan Turk made all of our clothes. It was my mother's idea to dress us up like that. She was the boss of the band, the head of the herd. We gave him an idea, and he took it from there. It was something people had never seen before, a whole group dressed alike in those wild clothes."

The band's music was equally colorful and upbeat. They performed country boogie with unprecedented vigor, which has led many music historians to consider The Maddox Brothers and Rose to be predecessors of modern rockabilly. Their fame soared as they played more shows outside of California. Rose Maddox remembers touring with their trendsetting costumes, "We traveled on the road in four or five matching Cadillacs. There was no such thing as tour buses back then. We never ironed the clothes out on the road. There was a rod that we hung across the back of the car, and we kept the clothes on hangers in the car. We would take about six outfits along, enough to last for the length of the tour."

When my daughter, Sophie, turned one, we had to be in Fort Worth at a wedding on the weekend of her first birthday. So I invited all of Sophie's family to town as well as a few of my friends and people who were attending the same wedding as we were, and we celebrated Sophie's birthday at the world's largest honky-tonk right there in the Fort Worth Stockyards, Billy Bob's. There was cake for the little ones, beer for the grownups, and plenty of photo ops on the mechanical bull. But hands-down my favorite part of the party was the cake. It was decorated with a black and fuchsia cowgirl outfit inspired by a fringed Rose Maddox costume.

Nathan Turk in buttercream icing. Does it any get better than that?

As biased as I am, even I can see that The Maddoxes' legacy is much greater than Sophie's first birthday. They influenced all of the hillbilly singers of their time. Everyone wanted to dress as flamboyantly as they did. There was so much demand from honky-tonk musicians that it wasn't long before Nathan Turk had competition. Nudie Cohn was a Ukraine-born immigrant tailor who also made his way out to California. And he, too, began making wild and colorful suits for singing cowboys and honky-tonk performers. Roy Rogers had him add more and more rhinestones to his costumes so the people in the cheap seats of the largest arenas could always see him. Nudie Cohn would customize the imagery on the suits for the artist. Porter Wagoner had sequined wagon wheels. Hank Thompson had golden nuggets as he was the first country star to play in Las Vegas at the venerable Golden Nugget. He also had a humpty dumpty suit for a song he did with the nursery rhyme theme, as well as an airplane suit because he enjoyed flying. Hank Thompson liked buying Nudie suits because they were less expensive than a Turk, so he could get several at a time. With the help of his wife, Bobbie, Nudie Cohn outfitted all the singing cowboys as well as the great honky-tonk stars of the day. Roy Rogers, Dale Evans, Hank Thompson, Hank Snow, Webb Pierce, Porter Wagoner. Hank Williams had a white Nudie suit with black musical notes embroidered down the sleeves. Nudie even created Elvis' famous gold lamé suit, which he wore on the cover of his album *50,000,000 Elvis Fans Can't Be Wrong.*

Gram Parsons and the Flying Burrito Brothers all wore Nudie suits on the cover of their 1969 album *The Gilded Palace of Sin*, notoriously featuring sequined images of marijuana leaves.

According to Cohn family folklore, Nudie's wife, Bobbie, surprised him one time when she wandered into the room wearing nothing but a cowboy hat, boots, and a holster. The self-proclaimed "Rhinestone Cowgirl" quipped, "When are you going to make the rest of the outfit?" This inspired the first logo for the tailoring company which featured a bare-breasted cowgirl kicked back on a fence and twirling a lasso which spelled out the company name "Nudie's Rodeo Tailors". Nudie Cohn converted to Christianity in the 1960s and redid the logo with a more modest, clothed cowgirl. Today, Nudie suits bearing the original *nude* Nudie label are considered prized collectibles.

The third tailor to shape the heritage of honky-tonk costuming was, and continues to be, Manuel. Manuel Arturo José Cuevas Martinez was born in Michoacán, Mexico, the fifth of eleven children. He was taught to sew at the age of seven, began making all of his own clothes, and went on to master leather working, hat making, silver skills, and boot making. He made his way to California and in the 1960s became head tailor for Nudie Cohn. Manuel worked for Nudie for fourteen years, serving as head designer and even marrying Nudie's daughter, Barbara.

But when they divorced Manuel went out on his own to start a shop. Around this time Nathan Turk was closing his business for health reasons, and Manuel bought up everything he could from the esteemed tailor, including sewing machines, patterns, even his scissors. Manuel wrote Turk a blank check and told him to calculate it up and simply fill in a number. In a generous and gallant gesture, Nathan Turk never cashed the check. In the 1980s Manuel moved his operation to Nashville where to this day he continues to create western couture garments for country stars and those with stars in their eyes.

Lula Maddox from Boaz, Alabama started something monumental when she set out to costume her family band in upbeat, vibrant clothing. It seems only fitting that fellow Alabama honky-tonker Hank Williams was buried in Montgomery in a Nudie suit, keeping the traditions of color and pageantry safe there in the soil of Alabama, and in its soul.

Brother acts began popping up in the 1930s offering a polished sound that stood in sharp contrast to the raw, earthy Appalachian hillbilly music. Sibling singers often possessed a common vocal timbre which made their harmonies so close it almost sounded like one person singing. However, their close-knit harmonies were the antithesis of the strife and conflict that typically played out between the brothers off stage.

The first successful brother act came from Alabama. Alton Delmore and Rabon Delmore, known as The Delmore Brothers, were born into rural poverty in Elkmont, Alabama. The Delmores grew up in a religious and musical family as their mother wrote and sang gospel songs for the church. The Delmore Brothers would blend this gospel foundation with folk music and blues to create a unique sound in a still-evolving country music genre. They were among the first stars on the *Grand Ole Opry*, joining in 1933 and headlining as crowd favorite by 1936. A dispute with *Opry* management forced the brothers to leave the show, after which their success plateaued despite years of additional performing. They wrote over a thousand songs together, one of which, "Blues Stay Away From Me", was later covered by another brother act, The Everly Brothers. Some consider the Everly version to be the first rock and roll record.

My *favorite* brother act also hailed from north Alabama. Ira Loudermilk and Charlie Loudermilk were born in Henagar, Alabama and grew up picking cotton and singing gospel. As they perfected their harmonies they realized music was their ticket out of the cotton fields. They took on the name The Louvin Brothers, and their first paying gig was $50 on a mule-drawn merry-go-round at a Fourth of July celebration. It proved to be their independence day as they soon broke free from the rigors of picking cotton. Other performances followed for the teens, including a 4:30 a.m. regular appearance on a Chattanooga radio show.

At a show in Arkansas Charlie Louvin took pity on a thirteen-year-old kid who didn't have enough money to come into the show, so he let him sit on a bench near the stage and watch. That kid was Johnny Cash. Years later, when Cash and Charlie Louvin became friends, Cash confessed that he watched Charlie Louvin eat some soda crackers that night before he went on stage and so for years Cash always ate soda crackers before his own performances. He believed that's how Louvin achieved his incredible singing voice.

In 1955 The Louvin Brothers finally had their long-awaited shot at the *Grand Ole Opry*. A mutual friend got the ear of the program director who had routinely been turning them down and told him The Louvin Brothers had an offer to join the *Ozark Jubilee*. There was no such offer, but *Opry* brass was viciously competitive with the *Ozark Jubilee* and took the bait. The Louvin Brothers were immediately offered an *Opry* audition. Charlie Louvin maintains that Jim Denny, who ran the *Opry* at the time, never really took a shine to The Louvin Brothers. At their first meeting with them he said, "Boys, y'all are in tall timber, you better shit it and get it." They must have, because they were placed on the Friday night *Opry* show and, eventually, the regular Saturday night performances.

When I first started watching YouTube videos of The Louvin Brothers I couldn't get over how two guys whose voices were so perfectly matched could be such different heights. Ira was super tall and lanky, while Charlie was very short. How could they even share the same mic? But they did. And their harmonies are like none other. I don't know enough about vocal skills to understand it myself, but those that do rave about The Louvin Brothers. Experts marvel at the super-human sounds that Charlie and Ira were able to produce with their voices, but also the fact that they would switch the melody and harmony parts back and forth several times *during one song*. Apparently that is incredibly difficult to do, and they did it seamlessly. I like their music because it offers the incredible harmonies you expect from a brother act, yet their songs seem more powerful and the lyrics more relatable. To me they have more bite than the typical brother act.

For years The Louvin Brothers only recorded gospel music, but once they joined the *Opry* they introduced secular tunes into their repertoire. They are probably best known for their 1959 album, *Satan Is Real*. The album cover routinely lands on a sundry of "Best Of" lists: "Best Album Cover of Country Music", "Best Bizarre Album Cover of All Time". It features Ira and Charlie clad in white suits, standing in a hellish scene with fire and brimstone and a giant red devil lurking over their shoulders. Since this was long before Photoshop, to shoot the artwork they actually stood in a rock quarry among burning tires and a 12-foot tall plywood painted devil. The album cover continues to attract its own cult following, the subject of regular Internet memes and blog conversations.

Ira designed the cover. And unfortunately for Ira, Satan was very real. As their fame grew, Ira's drinking and temper became unmanageable. He was prone to fits on stage where he would bash his mandolin to pieces. He married and divorced multiple times, and the *Opry* placed him on probation after one particularly dramatic domestic dispute. One of his wives shot him six times after he tried to strangle her with a telephone cord. He survived, but the scandals continued. Once, while on tour with a young Elvis, Ira flew into a rage, calling Elvis all sorts of racial epithets and claiming his music was trash. Charlie, a sober and focused soul, witnessed so many outbursts that it began to take its toll. The two brothers who were so close in their vocal harmonies couldn't have been more different in real life. Eventually Charlie had to call it quits with Ira and perform alone.

Ira was 41 years old when he and his fourth wife were killed by a drunk driver in 1965. Ironically, at that time there was a warrant out for Ira's arrest for a DUI. Ira was yet another musically creative talent tortured by darkness and conflicted by the polarizing pull of good versus evil.

Charlie lived until 2011. In one of his final on-camera interviews, he said the pain of his brother's tragic death still rattled him. In the footage, which was shot for a documentary called *It Goes a Little Somethin' Like This, The Greatest Songwriters of Our Time*, Charlie explains that Ira had always wanted to be a preacher and that he lived a "miserable" life because he never became one. Just before his fatal accident, Ira decided he was going to buy a tent and start preaching. But as Charlie concedes, "The bossman upstairs knew he couldn't drop his drink."

The Louvin Brothers, as well as Charlie on his own, made an indelible mark on country music, and their legacy lives on in the countless covers that other musicians have done of their songs. Emmylou Harris had a hit with "If I Could Only Win Your Love", written and originally recorded by The Louvin Brothers. The Byrds and Johnny Cash also covered Louvin songs which further fueled a cult following of Louvin Brother music among the more modern alt-country fans. When T. Bone Burnett and Stephen Bruton managed the music for the 2009 film *Crazy Heart*, they included one of my favorite Louvin Brothers songs on the soundtrack, "My Baby's Gone". And in his 2012 book, Roll Me Up and Smoke Me When I Die, Willie Nelson includes The Louvin Brothers on his list of "Good Pickers". Kris Kristofferson wrote the foreword to Charlie Louvin's autobiography. The Louvin Brothers may not be a household name among today's Nashville country fans, but some of the best musicians in the world still admire and respect their work, and I am following their lead. I'm stickin' with the ones who brung me.

Just when you think Alabama has done enough, paid at the gate, contributed more than its fair share to the good cause...there is more. Two of the most legendary steel guitar players came out of Alabama. The first, Don Helms, was born in New Brockton, Alabama and started playing lap steel guitar as a boy to emulate his idol, Leon McAuliffe. McAuliffe had played steel for Bob Wills and his Texas Playboys. At just seventeen years old, Helms joined Hank Williams' band, The Drifting Cowboys, and played gigs all over Alabama and the Southeast. After Hank debuted on the *Opry* with "Lovesick Blues" he relocated to Nashville and invited Helms to be a part of a new incarnation of The Drifting Cowboys. Don Helms played steel on over a hundred of Hank's songs including "Your Cheatin' Heart", "Cold, Cold Heart", and "I Can't Help It If I'm Still in Love with You". In 1950 he started playing the Gibson Console Grande, a table-style steel which produced the sound most associated with Hank's songs. Helms favored the treble strings and played high on the neck. Producer Fred Rose encouraged this technique because it created a strong, penetrating sound that could cut through the noise and chaos of the wild dancehalls where Hank often performed. Don Helms is widely regarded as having defined not only the significant music of Hank Williams, but also the quintessential sound of the honky-tonk genre as it moved away from the old-fashioned string music of the 1930s to the more electric, powerful, bluesy music of the 1940s and 1950s.

Eventually Helms began to play a pedal steel guitar, but he always kept the prized Gibson table steel under his bed, pulling it out for special occasions.

Don Helms played on Hank's final recording session, which included the famed song, "Your Cheatin' Heart". Helms recounts, "I played him an intro, and we sang the song through one time." Helms never saw Hank alive again after that session. "Your Cheatin' Heart" was released after Hank died.

After Hank's death, Don Helms and the Drifting Cowboys joined Ray Price's act. In addition, Helms went on to play steel for Ernest Tubb, Patsy Cline, Johnny Cash, Webb Pierce, Ferlin Husky, and many others. He died in 2008 at the age of eighty-one, the last surviving member of the original Drifting Cowboys lineup.

Jimmy Day is another venerable sideman steel player to come out of Alabama. He grew up in Tuscaloosa and was performing at area honky-tonks by the age of sixteen. He auditioned for a spot on the *Louisiana Hayride* where he met and played with Webb Pierce. He also landed a six month gig with Hank Williams, who was so impressed that he asked Day to be a part of a new band he planned to assemble the following year. Unfortunately Hank died before this came to fruition. In 1956 Day began to play the pedal-style steel guitar exclusively, picking steel on Ray Price's cut, "Crazy Arms". Day was instrumental in urging Shot Jackson to start his own brand of pedal steel guitars, which he did. Jackson teamed up with Buddy Emmons to launch Sho-Bud, the first electric pedal steel guitars. Jimmy Day's personal Sho-Bud steel was famously nicknamed "Blue Darlin".

Jimmy Day played regularly with Ray Price along with the young bass player in the band, Willie Nelson. When Willie left Price to go out on his own, Day went with him. Jimmy Day went on to play with the likes of George Jones, Leon Russell, Charlie Louvin, Don Walser, and Charlie Walker. Day played steel on Charlie Walker's honky-tonk hit song "Pick Me Up on Your Way Down", which has been covered by country artists from almost every generation.

Steel guitar trailblazers, harmonious brother acts, outrageous costumes. When it comes to Alabama's honky-tonk pedigree, there's clearly more to adore than Hank alone. Hank is undeniable, but there are others. Frankly there's so much to enjoy within Alabama you could almost forget about "Lovesick Blues" for a little while.

Almost.

Because one can only elude the lovesick blues for so long.

CHAPTER 21 SOUNDTRACK:

Honky Tonkin' – The Maddox Brothers and Rose

(HANK WILLIAMS)

While You're Cheating on Me – The Louvin Brothers

(CHARLIE LOUVIN, IRA LOUVIN)

If I Could Only Win Your Love – The Louvin Brothers

(CHARLIE LOUVIN, IRA LOUVIN)

Your Cheatin' Heart – Hank Williams

(HANK WILLIAMS)

Pick Me Up on Your Way Down – Charlie Walker

(HARLAN HOWARD)

Sequins, satin, neck ties, and wagon wheels...
A typical western performance costume from the Golden Era of Honky-Tonk
On display at The Ryman Auditorium, Nashville TN

Elaborate western tailoring is still a tradition in country music.
Jim Lauderdale at the annual Springfest music festival
The Spirit of the Suwannee Music Park, Live Oak FL

CHAPTER 22

Must Be Mobile on
the Road to El Dorado

As much as I have moved and traveled, I don't exactly have a mantle over the fireplace lined with trophies exalting my lifelong excellence in geography. I am notoriously obtuse in this department. Back before I started dating Tom or first visited Mobile, Alabama, I hadn't a clue it was on the coast. Growing up in Nashville, I would hear mention of Mobile and promptly pictured an industrial, grey-toned place, sort of the Dirty South version of that town in the 1983 Tom Cruise football movie, *All the Right Moves*. I think I imagined Mobile landlocked with a skyline of endless refineries because I made a subconscious, and erroneous, connection to Mobil Oil.

That changed around 2001 when Junior Brown released a song called "Guitar Man". In it he chronicles the character's woes traveling from the north and throughout the south, trying to land a gig as a guitar player. He spends the night at the YMCA in Memphis, hitchhikes to Macon, Georgia on a poultry truck, wanders to Panama City, and sleeps among hobo jungles, trying to find a place that would hire him as a guitar player. The odyssey ends in Mobile, Alabama where the song's narrator finds a gig at a club called Big Jack's. He describes the club as a jumpin' juke joint with a swinging five-piece band right by the ocean. It was on the Gulf Coast where he finally found his home, lived his dream, and could stop wandering.

I thought Big Jack's sounded like nirvana! Ocean breezes, a rocking club, and happy regulars crowding the dance floor. I wanted to go to Big Jack's or a place like it. I wanted to have a carefree night like that.

I later learned that Junior Brown's song was in fact a cover, and he wasn't even the first to cover it. Elvis had a pretty solid hit with it in the late 1960s. But it was originally a Jerry Reed song. (The same Jerry Reed who played Cledus "Snowman" Snow in the movie *Smokey and the Bandit*.)

At any rate, through the years of listening to both Junior Brown and Jerry Reed's versions of the song, I would often daydream of the club by the ocean called Big Jack's. It morphed into a tableau of sorts in my mind, the snapshot of a warm, breezy moment in time. It embodied that rare but familiar mood of feeling *good*. Dancing the night away, laughing, and swirling. Willing suspension of disbelief, backed by a five-piece band.

Big Jack's was just one of the many escapism scenarios I conjured up in my mind's eye during those less happy days around the start of this millennium when my marriage was unraveling. Daydreams and El Dorados kept hope afloat. El Dorado…

Folklore teaches us that El Dorado is the mythical South American city of gold that lured countless European explorers to travel great distances to find it. The geographical location of El Dorado has shifted so many times throughout the centuries of failed expeditions that the term has evolved to more broadly represent a symbolic source of immeasurable treasure. El Dorado is often considered a subjective holy grail, interpreted by the respective beholder. It might be the font of endless wealth, a quest for ultimate happiness, or the wellspring of true, unending love.

It's everything, or maybe nothing. It's the ultimate.

Edgar Allan Poe wrote a slightly mocking poem in 1849 titled "Eldorado" in which he suggests that to find the mythical city of gold one must travel to the extremes:

'Over the Mountains
Of the Moon,
Down the Valley of the Shadow,
Ride, boldly ride,'
The shade replied,—
'If you seek for Eldorado!'

Ride, boldly ride.

Mock if you will, Mr. Poe, but Tom and I logged so many hours flying between Austin and Mobile that we likely earned enough points to travel over the mountains of the moon and back. And we did it for something wildly better than gold, and for something much more elusive. We did it for love.

So we decided we'd keep on doing it 'til death do us part.

Ride, boldly ride.

Tom proposed in 2010 and we married three months later. Our dual-state challenge hadn't changed, but our attitude about it had. Like the Guitar Man in the Junior Brown song, we weren't going to let geography wear us down or keep us from our dream. So we would stop our wandering but keep on traveling. Tom moved to Austin where he works via telecommuting and on a remote computer linked to his desktop files in Alabama. Every other week he commutes between Texas and Alabama. Roughly once a month I travel to Mobile for about six days when Sophie is with her dad. In the end, Tom and I are only apart about seven or so days each month. I always remind Sophie that this is less than some families that have a parent who travels for a consulting job clear across the country. Some people travel for work; we travel for love. The trick is to be flexible, communicate constantly, and get really organized with the calendar.

And for the record, there is no calendar program on the market that can accomplish the complex scheduling nuances I deal with on a regular basis, so I built my own. NASA should hire me for my custom calendar with its shading and linking and highlighting. It's a masterpiece.

My roots remain in Austin with Sophie, but I get to sprout wings each month and flit over to Mobile, which I am delighted to report is absolutely nothing like my early, ignorant impression. It is *gorgeous*. It sits on the Gulf Coast on the west side of Mobile Bay, which offers temperate climates and lush vegetation. Johnny Cash recorded a wonderful song called "Mobile Bay" about a homeless wino in Chicago in January, pining for the warm ocean breezes of Mobile and its magnolia trees. It really is that dreamy. The tropical temperatures and coastal humidity create a mix of bright pink azalea bushes, camellias, palm trees, magnolias, massive oak trees, and of course my personal favorite, Spanish moss.

The architecture reflects the early Spanish and French settlers, with charming brick buildings downtown that have wrought iron balconies that rival New Orleans. Residential homes in older neighborhoods are anything but cookie cutter. You'll have a Spanish stucco house next to a Greek Revival next to a Tudor. There is history, character, old squares, and southern churches.

And people in Mobile are *fun*. Our pre-marital counselor in Mobile explained to me with a slightly cautionary tone, "Mobile is a coastal town. People from coastal towns are wild. New Orleans, Savannah, Charleston, Corpus Christi, Mobile – people from these places like to have a good time. I have counseled many couples where one was from Mobile and the other wasn't, and it can be problematic if you're not on the same page. If you're not from here, it's hard to understand how much people in Mobile really like to have fun."

I couldn't tell if she was giving Tom some antiquated hall pass to behave however he wanted or if she was challenging me to put on my big girl panties and step up my game. Regardless, I felt like I had this one in the bag. Fun and I are old pals from back in the day.

I also had to convert from any tourista mentality and uneducated notion that Mardi Gras is a New Orleans thing. Instead, when I married Tom, I accepted Mobile Mardi Gras as the one true original Mardi Gras. You see, the first mystic societies to celebrate Fat Tuesday with elaborate parades were founded in Mobile, and Mobilians proudly defend their Mardi Gras as the oldest in the Unites States. Now if you were the adolescent prankster in high school who liked to plant a burning bag of...defecation...on someone's doorstep and then hide in the bushes to watch chaos erupt as your victim discovered it, then you would probably also enjoy announcing to an entire party full of people from Mobile that Mardi Gras started in New Orleans.

Let me know how that turns out.

I love Mobile Mardi Gras, I love watching Tom ride in the parades in his elaborate satin costume accented with a mask and plumes. Pledging my allegiance to Mobile Mardi Gras over New Orleans was an easy commitment, especially since there were so many other loaded topics we had to handle delicately with compromise and flexibility once we were married. We were a true blended family in terms of natural parents and step-parents, but we were also blending geographies, cuisines, home décor, cultures, and traditions. I struggled to explain to Tom that duck hunting was a sport, not an interior design style. His aesthetic was decidedly traditional while mine was more eclectic. Meanwhile Tom couldn't fathom how much – and how often – Sophie and I could eat queso, while I tapped out on fried okra much sooner than he would. Tex-Mex was a part of our daily cuisine, and yet he started to twitch if he went too long without a southern style meat-and-three meal. And of course there was the barbecue issue. We really wanted to make the marriage work, so we lovingly agreed to embrace both southern *and* Texas barbecue in a democratic fashion and forgo trying to win the age-old battle about which is better, pork or beef.

(Beef.)

I swooned for Mobile from the start. Tom's family welcomed me with open arms, and I made wonderful friends. I asked Tom repeatedly, but he simply had no recollection of a club in town called Big Jack's. I suppose it was fictitious, made up for the song. It didn't really seem Mobile was much of a honky-tonk town anyway. They marched to their own beat down there on the coast, and the more famed honky-tonk scene unfolded farther north in Alabama, up around Montgomery. Mobile was more of an R&B, blues, and rock town. They love the Allman Brothers, which is fantastic. Jimmy Buffett went to high school there, so there's plenty of well-earned Parrot Head pride. And a great 1970s southern rock band called Wet Willie is also from Mobile.

But you just might stumble upon some old-school honky-tonk when you least expect it, and in the most unlikely of places. Not long after our small, family-only wedding, some good friends in Alabama threw us an after-wedding celebration at the country club. In perhaps one of the most gracious gestures of all time, they booked a local honky-tonk band knowing how much we would enjoy it.

The band was The Modern Eldorados, and lead singer Gretsch Lyles shined with lively renditions of country classics such as "Kaw-Liga", "Jackson", and "Cocaine Blues". I think anyone in attendance that night will concur, it was a big, big time. Women in lovely pantsuits and cocktail dresses boogied down next to all the dashing men in their blue blazers and loafers. High heels were kicked off in favor of cowboy boots, and ties were lost or loosened as we collectively bum rushed the stage begging for encores. The irony tickled me to no end…that my first encounter with real, old-school honky-tonk music in Mobile was at a *country club*. And it was an epic bash. Just goes to show, sometimes honky-tonk transcends its physical surroundings and is more a state of mind.

I loved that night.

After that, Tom and I leapt at any chance to go see The Modern Eldorados whenever we were in town. Eventually I wheedled my way into becoming buddies with Gretsch, lead singer and all-around great guy. We met at a coffee shop one afternoon and waxed poetic for hours about country music.

We went deep into the history of honky-tonk and shared similar stories of how we each cut our teeth on venerable greats such as Webb Pierce, Ernest Tubb, and Hank Thompson. We both grew up in homes that had extensive vinyl collections and with parents who loved this music. The difference is that Gretsch has actual musicians in his family tree. His grandfather had a band in Mississippi in the '30s and '40s called The Lyles Brothers. It was his grandfather who started their record collection, and then Gretsch's dad added to it with 8-track and cassette tapes. Roy Orbison, Conway Twitty, Marty Stuart, Dwight Yoakam…we both grew up listening to these sounds, not to mention, devouring the images on the album covers.

Hence, the inspiration for Gretsch's fabulous western jackets and suits. He has many of them custom made by Manuel in Nashville, like so many other great country stars. Compared to these elaborate and eccentric fashions, his philosophies are laser-focused and delivered plainly, "It's the music I like and that's what the country singers wear."

And he backs up those Manuel suits with talent. I don't know how anyone could see Gretsch Lyles perform live and be in a bad mood. He sings, plays guitar, wriggles around the stage a la the greats of stage wriggling: Hank, Elvis, and Dwight. But he also has his own signature tai chi style of leggy balance moves, all the while picking and singing.

Gretsch talked about an Austin band from the '80s called the Wagoneers and its frontman Monte Warden, who was one of his greatest inspirations as a songwriter. I learned he loved Kelly Willis as much as I do. And he told a fantastic story about one of the guys in his band whose wife had given him a Buck Owens CD set for Christmas one year. When his house caught fire he ran back inside just to save the Buck Owens box set.

As if it can't get any better, Gretsch owns a 1960 Wurlitzer jukebox. He likes to turn it on and wait and wait until its tubes get really hot which alters the tonality and makes the honky-tonk songs sound even more like the old days.

Most of all I learned what a great guy Gretsch is. He has the most gentle demeanor and exudes kindness. In addition, he expresses so much respect for those who have inspired and mentored him, such as Hank Williams, songwriter Jim Lauderdale (whom we all know I love from Springfest), and even local Mobile country singer Jack Cardwell, who was friends with Hank Williams. Gretsch goes on to explain how he pays his respect to Hank. Any time he and the band are in the Montgomery area, he stops by Hank's grave and leaves him a guitar pick and a pain pill because he worries "Hank still might be hurting a little."

Growing up Independent Baptist, Gretsch is a deeply principled man, having never had a beer, cigarette, or illegal drug in his life. This is particularly impressive considering he has spent the past twenty-two years playing bars and nightclubs almost 200 nights each year. Simple math puts that at an estimated 4,400 gigs. Yet he shares repeatedly, "I have never had a bad show." He is wholly committed to playing honky-tonk music, and he is grateful that he has "never had to play 'Brown Eyed Girl' even once." When it comes to the fans he always takes time to shake hands and talk to anyone after a show who wants to chat. He offers, "I always have time for those people because you never know what they're going through."

It's clear to me Gretsch knows two things on a very deep level: the power of music and the power of kindness.

Gretsch represents the current honky-tonk scene in Mobile, and no doubt the future, but I learned there is a bit more of a past than I'd previously realized. Jack Cardwell was a prominent figure around town and an effective ambassador for country music. The year after Hank Williams died, he released a tribute called "The Death of Hank Williams", which sold over a half million records. It is perhaps slavishly imitative of Hank Williams' style, but that's excusable in my mind since Cardwell and Hank were friends, and Cardwell's genuine sorrow comes through in the song.

Jack Cardwell was probably best known as a country DJ for years on various Mobile radio stations. His father was a reverend, and he too served as interim pastor for a Mobile church in the 1960s. One of his greatest legacies was the "Hillbilly Christmas Party" he hosted annually to raise funds for poor children in Mobile. He recruited some of the biggest names in country music and put on a concert in Ladd Stadium in Mobile. Admittance to the show was to simply bring a toy to donate to a child in need. Jack Cardwell was connected enough – not to mention charming and inspiring enough – to convince headliner country acts to contribute time *and* travel expenses to this annual event. Oh, and they were each required to donate a toy as well – no exceptions.

Cardwell did a great deal to promote country music and support the genre around Mobile. He started the Mobile Country Music Association, which still exists, and mentored younger artists in town. One of those notable musicians was a young Mobile talent named Lawrence Reynolds. Jack Cardwell co-wrote a hit song with Reynolds called "Jesus Is a Soul Man". It was suggested to me by a well-informed little birdie (who knows everything about everything about music) that Reynolds really wrote the whole thing while Cardwell merely lent his name to give it more cachet within the industry. It must have worked because Reynolds was invited to perform the hit tune with Johnny Cash on Cash's TV show. Several other musicians have covered it since, including Conway Twitty. Andrew Lloyd Webber and Tim Rice have even stated in interviews that this song was, in part, the inspiration for their smash Broadway musical, *Jesus Christ Superstar*. Reynolds had a hit song, was a prolific songwriter with hundreds and hundreds of self-penned tunes, received powerful endorsements from Nashville heavyweights like Johnny Cash and Harlan Howard, and was a looker to boot. But he never really took off and is hardly a household name these days. I questioned this once, and the same, well-informed little birdie explained to me that Reynolds suffered a volatile demeanor that made it difficult to work with him, and as a result the industry passed him by.

Curtis Gordon was another influential country figure in Mobile. He was from Georgia but came to Mobile to perform for thirteen weeks on the *Dixie Barn Dance* program. Then decided to stay. Gordon opened the largest night club in Mobile called Radio Ranch on Dauphin Island Parkway. Gordon played there with his own band as well as booking other big name acts like Jerry Lee Lewis. Elvis Presley played The Radio Ranch three times in 1955 sharing the billing with Curtis Gordon and his Radio Ranch Boys.

Elvis also played at Ladd Stadium in Mobile in 1955 as part of a tour with Hank Snow. While the local paper said "Elvis Presley and his sidekicks Bill and Scotty" would be part of the performance, their names didn't even make the show poster. Presumably they were among the "many other great recording artists" referenced.

As an aside, Ladd Stadium was not only the site of an Elvis show and Jack Cardwell's "Hillbilly Christmas Party", but also hosted college football games. In September 1958, over thirty thousand people wedged into Ladd Stadium to watch Alabama play LSU. Recent rains had soaked a section of wooden bleachers in the north end zone and they collapsed in the middle of the first quarter. The game was delayed while ambulances were scrambled to the scene to tend to the seventy or so who were injured. Luckily no one was critically wounded. Alabama went on to lose that game 13-3. It was Bear Bryant's first game as head coach of the Crimson Tide.

At any rate, Elvis played Mobile several times, and three of those times were at Curtis Gordon's club. Gordon himself switched record labels a few times and found more creative liberty with Mercury, where he was allowed to cut a few original tunes with his trademark "Gordon

Sound". This coincided with the nation's fascination with rock and roll, and Curtis Gordon recorded faster, edgier country numbers. Gordon is often hailed as one of the forefathers of rockabilly music.

Curtis Gordon sold Radio Ranch in 1959, and unfortunately it burned not long after.

Jack Cardwell, Lawrence Reynolds, and Curtis Gordon may not be household names today, but they held their own during the heyday of traditional honky-tonk music. They carved a path for the country genre that typically played second fiddle in Mobile to the likes of soul, blues, and R&B...not to mention occasional visits from the king of rock and roll.

Speaking of honky-tonks, the king, and Mobile, the king of honky-tonk himself, Hank Williams, actually spent a chunk of time in Mobile. Little is known about this period of Hank's life. There are volumes of biographies about Hank Williams, his music, and certainly his death, but much mystery hovers over his time in Mobile. Was it two years or a few weeks? Different people offer different theories. His mother claims it was only a few weeks, but her version of things almost always comes with an asterisk next to it. Presumably, he became discouraged grinding it out with dicey honky-tonk gigs and decided to quit music all together. He had relatives in Mobile and came to work at a shipbuilding company until his domineering stage mother yanked him by the ear and urged him back to performing.

Or he went back to music on his own, who really knows. While her influence on his career was domineering and borderline greedy, she may have overinflated her savior-like status as she describes herself swooping in and bolstering his ego until he returned to the stage.

Did he play music at all while he was there? I find it hard to believe he turned it off like a spigot. Especially since his buddy, Jack Cardwell, was there. Did they ever pick together?

I scoured the Internet for details about his time in Mobile with little result. I did learn the shipbuilding company where he worked was Alabama Dry Dock and Shipbuilding Company (ADDSCO), the largest employer in South Alabama around the time of WWII. And I stumbled onto a cached version of a defunct blog that had a story about Hank Williams and his employment at the shipyard. It seemed to describe a fantastic tale about a piece of Hank Williams memorabilia. I put my online sleuthing skills on overdrive and found the author of the piece, a man named Bob Wilson who lived in Mobile.

Bob was kind enough to meet me for coffee and we had a sensational conversation about music and Mobile and music in Mobile. I learned a great deal from him. I also heard one of the greatest fan stories *ever*.

Bob grew up in Mobile listening to Hank Williams and Jack Cardwell, whom he described as the "staples" of the day. He recalls his housekeeper introducing him to Elvis' music for the first time. And in the 1950s he began hearing Johnny Cash, which inspired him to start playing music himself. He and other high school friends would gather to play guitar and sing, getting more and more into the popular folk music of the late 1950s and 1960s.

In 1962 Bob was a freshman at Auburn University. Right away he could tell by the radio stations that country was more popular in that part of the state than it had been in Mobile, where R&B prevailed. He was listening to the Kingston Trio and other folk artists. One balmy afternoon he was in his dorm room, trying to cool off between classes under an oscillating fan with the radio playing. The DJ played a few songs from a new artist named Bob Dylan. The record was his self-titled debut album. Bob Wilson was transfixed by what he was hearing. The song "Baby Let Me Follow You Down" featured guitar and harmonica work that woke him from his Kingston Trio folk coma and catapulted his musical interests in a totally new direction.

Bob Wilson was an instant and passionate Bob Dylan fan.

Like good fans do, he became a student of the musician as well as the music. In those days, well before the Internet, Bob would spend free time in the library scouring *TIME Magazine* articles about Dylan and other newspaper clippings. He learned that Dylan considered Alabama's own Hank Williams to be one of his greatest influences.

We meandered away from Bob's story for a few minutes to talk about Dylan and Hank and the overlap in their music. I challenged Bob to explain to me how to hear Hank's influence in Dylan's music. His reply was to go back and really listen to that debut album, *Bob Dylan*. We talked about how Dylan felt a connectedness to Hank Williams as a songwriter, and identified with the pathos in his voice and in his music. At the end of the day they really were both singing the blues. We discussed the relatively recent 2011 album *The Lost Notebooks of Hank Williams* that Bob Dylan championed and helped to produce with various artists performing never-before-heard tunes that were written, or in some cases half-written, by Hank. Bob and I both agreed one of the most beautiful songs on the record was performed by Holly Williams, Hank's granddaughter. Particularly special is the Vince Gill and Rodney Crowell track called "I Hope You Shed a Million Tears" because Hank's original steel guitar player, Don Helms, played pedal steel guitar on the recording. This would be Helms's last recording session before he passed away.

By the early 1970s Bob Wilson was back in his hometown of Mobile, working at a downtown engineering firm. A friend of his worked at ADDSCO, the shipbuilding company, and called him about an intriguing situation. The friend worked in the office with Peets Buffett, mother of Jimmy Buffett. While cleaning out some old files they uncovered what they believed might be Hank Williams' original job application, including a photograph. The friend called Bob to see if he could confirm it.

Bob Wilson took one look at the application and the associated work photo and confirmed that the picture was, in fact, Hank Williams.

They had found Hank's original job application, filled out in pencil. Attached to it was a black and white photo of Hank that Bob said looked like a mug shot. There was also a negative of the photograph. Since they were clearing out all these files anyway, the friend allowed Bob to make a photocopy of the job application and gave him the negative of Hank Williams' official ADDSCO work photo.

I can't imagine how cool it must have been to see Hank Williams' actual handwriting. To hold it right in your hand and know he held the same piece of paper decades before. The job application was filled out in 1942 when Hank was nineteen years old. On the application Hank listed his birthplace as Flat Rock despite the fact most biographies cite him as being born in Mount Olive, Alabama. He wrote that he had relatives in the area with the surname Skipper. Next to address, he replied "none yet". When asked if he had ever had a physical exam he replied that he had not. He responded that he was 136 pounds "without overcoat or hat", as the form required. He listed his eyes as brown, his hair as brown, and his complexion as "sallow".

A particularly odd reply. *Sallow*?

Question #23 asked if he had ever been arrested and he replied honestly, "Yes. Suspicition [sic], last year. Montgomery, mistake."

Question #25 was designed during wartime to flush out enemy sympathizers that they certainly wouldn't want working in the shipyard of a port city. It asked if the applicant had ever worked in a foreign country. Hank answered, "Yes. In Mexico in 1940 as a musician."

Hank was fascinated by cowboys, and I imagine he visited Mexico around the same time he went off to Texas, where he tried his hand at riding in rodeos. He suffered a bad rodeo fall, which exacerbated the back pain that would ultimately lead to pain pill abuse.

Bob Wilson kept his treasured photocopy of the original job application in a file in his office along with the negative of the picture of Hank. He doesn't recall why, but a few years later on April 29, 1976 he had the photo negative in his wallet instead of locked away in the file cabinet. He remembers the date because it was the day Bob Dylan was performing two shows in Mobile as a part of his Rolling Thunder Revue tour. Bob had plans to attend the second show that evening.

He was driving back to his downtown office after lunch, heading east on Dauphin Street. He reached Cathedral Square and saw a man in a white bandana and leather jacket walking with an attractive brunette. They were standing right where the Spot of Tea restaurant is currently located. It didn't take this music fan long to recognize that it was Bob Dylan. Bob felt a sense of urgency…what should he say…they were walking past…he was in the middle of a busy street…but this was a once in a lifetime moment.

And then it hit him. The Hank Williams negative. He knew Dylan was a Hank Williams fan.

So he stopped his car in the middle of Dauphin Street and called out through his driver's side window to Dylan, "I've got something to show you!"

With cars navigating past them in the middle of the street, Bob dug out the negative of Hank Williams and passed it through the car window to Dylan, who held it up to the sun.

Bob pointed to the negative, "That's Hank Williams."

"No kidding?"

Dylan listened with great interest as Bob told him the complete story about the friend at ADDSCO and the job application. Then Bob made a generous gesture, offering the negative to Dylan.

"Are you sure you want to give this away?"

"I will give it to you."

They kept chatting and Dylan seemed keen on seeing the copy of the job application. Bob explained he was planning on attending the second show that evening, so Dylan instructed him to come backstage and ask for his Road Manager, Mike Evans. He wanted to take a quick look at the job application before the show.

Bob was on cloud nine. He grabbed his friend Lewis to go with him to the concert, and he took the copy of the job application to show Dylan. They proceeded to a large tent that had been erected behind the Mobile Civic Center and Expo Hall which served as a restricted backstage area. They found Mike Evans who was expecting Bob. He showed them where to sit under the tent and took the job application. They waited patiently until a back door of the Civic Center opened and Bob Dylan came out. He had the job application in his hand and was walking over toward them. He walked right up to Bob and his friend Lewis, stopped, looked at them, then abruptly turned around and inexplicably walked back inside.

Still holding Bob's only copy of Hank's job application.

They waited about thirty minutes, but he never returned.

Bob Wilson has spent all these years since 1976 wondering what happened. He knew as much about Dylan as any fan could and understood he was a private, press-shy musician. Perhaps he saw Bob's friend Lewis and was turned off that he brought an extra person along. Perhaps he thought Lewis was a journalist trying to get a scoop. Perhaps he was just behaving like an eccentric musician right before a big performance.

A different friend who attended the afternoon Dylan show told Bob that Dylan commented to the early crowd, "I found Hank Williams today." There was no such mention in the evening concert.

Bob had not intended to give Dylan the copy of Hank's job application along with the negative, he was simply going to show it to him. Still, Bob says he is not at all resentful that Dylan kept it. He remains a devout Dylan fan and only has one lingering question. He's curious if Dylan still has the negative of Hank Williams and the job application.

Meanwhile I had just one more question of my new Mobile friend: "Was there ever a club in town called Big Jack's?"

"I don't think so, never heard of it."

I suppose some things are meant to remain a myth. Some riches are eternally elusive, seemingly just beyond our reach. Others are fleeting and pass through our hands for a brief moment in time. But thankfully my odyssey ended with a lasting, immeasurable treasure. I did find true love, a second shot at a happy marriage. El Dorado, Mr. Poe. It's real.

CHAPTER 22 SOUNDTRACK:

Guitar Man – Junior Brown
(JERRY REED HUBBARD)

Mobile Bay – Johnny Cash
(CLAUDE "CURLY" PUTMAN JR., DAVE KIRBY)

The Death of Hank Williams – Jack Cardwell
(JACK CARDWELL)

Let's Have a Rendezvous – The Modern Eldorados
(GRETSCH LYLES, CHRIS REID)

Jesus Is a Soul Man – Lawrence Reynolds
(LAWRENCE REYNOLDS, JACK CARDWELL)

Gretsch Lyles and The Modern Eldorados playing at a wedding party
for Christine and Tom, Mobile AL, February 2011
Photo credit: Amy Thompson

Chiaroscuro

Social stationery and breakfast tacos are pretty much the only way I can begin to wrap my head around the simple but lasting genius that is Hank Williams.

I can explain this. (I think.)

Years ago during one of my temporary retirements from corporate life, I started a stationery design business with an offering of party invitations, wedding stationery, birth announcements, and so forth. I had stars in my eyes for exotic imported papers from Germany and silk bows and elaborate bells and whistles. But as I sat down to establish retail pricing, I quickly learned that my at-home cottage industry couldn't afford such sophisticated trimmings. I had to pre-order large quantities of basic white cover stock and bulk envelopes, all the same size. Suddenly all of my designs were limited to a four-by-six inch box with a plain white background.

At first I was disappointed and feared I would suffocate from the monotony, but I was shocked at what transpired during the months I spent designing the stationery line. My graphic design skills became much stronger. Setting aside the pretense of humility, I have to say the designs were wholly unique and like nothing else on the market at the time. Because I began with a bland backdrop, I had to differentiate my work based on the quality of the images, witty copy, graphic creativity, and attention to the most miniscule details of the layout. Negative space was my secret weapon, and often just airing out a millimeter of space would make a world of difference. The confines of thinking inside the box were actually making me better. Each design began with the same simple, blank slate, the same familiar framework. What happened from there had to be loaded with precision, power, and uniqueness.

This is exactly what Hank mastered, but on a much deeper level.

Similarly, my favorite breakfast taco is a simple bean and cheese breakfast taco. I maintain this makes me the best judge to evaluate the millions of taco stands around Austin because my straightforward order can't be doctored up with fancy, foodie, hey-look-at-the-light ingredients like tempura-fried avocados, tomatillo sour cream sauce, or grilled pork bellies. All I need is a corn tortilla, refried beans, and cheese. Three simple ingredients. My taco orders always begin with the same simple blank slate, the same familiar framework. Yet they taste wildly different at different restaurants! How it varies as much as it does remains a head-scratching mystery, but it certainly highlights the places that do it best. How does one place make such a simple taco so much more delicious? Homemade corn tortillas? Putting the beans on the griddle? Some secret lard infused into the cheese? I don't have the answer, I just know that when limited to the most elemental ingredients, the ones with the most talent step up to the plate and shine above the rest.

Just as Hank did.

Hank Williams' songs became a template for traditional honky-tonk tunes with basic construction, few frills. Yet they were anything but austere or sparse. He filled the framework with his bold, clear, powerful voice. The stories were potent and packed with emotion. His keen sense of timing with partial yodels and coloratura vocal breaks wound the pathos springs exponentially tighter, then tighter still. He was stirring, he was raw. There was a realness that brought him down to everyone's level, and yet a lonely place deep within that no one could reach. Hank's steel guitar player, Don Helms, was nothing short of sheer brilliance, and yet Hank's own voice emoted more sorrow than the pedal steel itself.

I mean really, what more do you need in a honky-tonk song?

His canon of music continues to weather the test of time and remains a classic standard within the country genre. I am just one among millions of Hank's legions of fans. And I'm hardly an expert on this hillbilly virtuoso. Only recently did I learn that in addition to his vast body of work he also recorded under an alias, Luke the Drifter. It was the worst kept secret in Nashville at the time. He yearned to sing darker, sermon-like songs about evil, righteousness, sin, and redemption, but his management wouldn't allow it. They knew the honky-tonks were his bread and butter, and people didn't want to hear depressing, moralistic songs while they were drinking beer and carousing. Eventually Hank's fame was too powerful to ignore so they permitted him to record fourteen of these musical missives as Luke the Drifter, completely separate from his career as Hank Williams.

I am fascinated by the notion that an already tormented and troubled man who lived his life between the grandiose extremes of public fame and private pain was forced to adopt yet another double identity, this one a result of marketing and branding objectives. While I genuinely believe his publisher, Fred Rose, was nobly motivated to protect Hank's career, retrospect offers me the ability to question the psychological effect this added layer of duality may have had on an already fragile soul. And did Hank pick the name "Luke the Drifter" or did his management team? I'm not entirely clear on this. The only reference I have found suggests his team selected this nom de plume on his behalf. On the 2009 liner notes that accompany Disc 3 of a Hank compilation called *Revealed: The Unreleased Recordings* Brian Turpen writes that "Hank once stated he didn't know where they got the 'Luke' part, but knew where the 'Drifter' part came from."

As a relatively new, part-time Alabamian I decided it was my duty to learn everything I could about Hank/Luke. I was pouring over notes and biographies when, in what can only be described as fortuitous timing, I received a call from my Mobile girlfriend, Ginna Inge. She randomly shared that she had just been on the road back to Mobile and stopped in at the Hank Williams museum on a whim.

It was a sign!

A sign we needed a road trip. A Chicks Road Trip, that is.

I sounded the call and miraculously managed to recruit about six of my girlfriends in Alabama to commit to a day trip to visit Hank's museum. Logistics were mildly tricky to hammer out in order to accommodate dropping off kids at multiple schools with various start times. And there was some debate over which museum we would visit. We finally agreed on the Hank Williams Boyhood Home and Museum in Georgiana, Alabama because it was the one Ginna had just visited, plus it was closer than the big one in Montgomery. This would allow everyone to get back home at a decent time to tend to husbands and kids. To add to the confusion, half the group was traveling up from Mobile while the other half was coming from the Eastern Shore over Mobile Bay. Tom helped me map out a meeting point at a truck stop in Stockton, Alabama where we could pile into one car together for the drive up to Georgiana.

I wish I had been a fly on the wall at that truck stop when six outgoing midlife moms in cowboy boots charged inside full force to exchange hugs, use the ladies restroom, refuel on coffee, laugh hysterically, and kick start the day trip. We weren't exactly understated.

As we barreled north on the highway, conversation in the SUV evolved naturally into a dialog about the Gospel of Luke, partially because I had teased the women with Hank's story of Luke the Drifter, and also because this crew meets regularly as part of a larger women's bible study. It was particularly poetic considering the Gospel of Luke is often referred to as the gospel of women and this was most certainly a carload of strong, bright women of character. As chick-friend Amy Thompson always describes this group, "We're like a river, sometimes we're shallow, and sometimes we're deep."

In response to the intriguing fun fact that Hank had an alter-ego recording persona, bible study leader Robin Minton explained that, similarly, it is remarkably common in scripture for God to dramatically change the names of key biblical figures. But one of the more mysterious name changes is Saul, who later simply goes by Paul. There is no major proclamation from God, and the Bible offers little explanation. Acts 13:9 states "Then Saul, (who also is called Paul,) filled with the Holy Ghost, set his eyes on him."

Did God change his name or did Saul pick Paul? Did Fred Rose change Hank's name or did he pick Luke the Drifter himself?

In Corinthians 9:22 Paul does explain the benefit of having multiple names and personas, "To the weak I became weak, to win the weak. I have become all things to all people so that by all possible means I might save some." It's as if Saul/Paul and Hank/Luke needed an extra name that was a better fit for their evangelistic messaging. Whether Hank came up with the name Luke the Drifter on his own or whether Fred Rose and team proclaimed it would be his new alter persona, it clearly suited him. He always identified with the western imagery of the lone drifter, naming his band the Drifting Cowboys. He himself was a wandering soul, searching for anything on this earth to ease his loneliness. But while "drifter" seems an obvious tag, the name "Luke" is an even better fit for Hank Williams. The Gospel of Luke is flush with redemptive, non-judgmental stories about some of the most broken, marginalized figures in the Bible. It offers an honest look at the faithful inner heart of outcast characters that society otherwise deemed worthless based on superficial, two-dimensional assessments. Plainly, the Gospel of Luke is the gospel of the underdog. It reveals the true heart of the outcast, the outlaw, and the untouchable. And this was Hank's music, it was Hank's audience.

It was Hank. It was Luke.

§

Hank Williams was born Hiram Williams in rural Mount Olive, Alabama in 1923. His name was misspelled as "Hiriam" on his birth certificate, which was, perhaps, a harbinger that life on Earth would always be a tad off kilter for little Hiram. He was born with an undiagnosed case of Spina Bifida which would ultimately contribute to his addiction to pain pills. As a child he was unable to participate in logging and other common physical endeavors, so he turned to music – and drinking, quite early.

Hank's father, Lon, went away to fight in World War I and returned shell shocked with injuries of mysterious origin. Maybe a truck incident, maybe German bombs, or perhaps a bottle cracked on his head in a dispute over a French girl. Regardless, at some point Hank's mother, Lillie, carted Lon off to a veteran's hospital indefinitely and managed to collect his disability pension. Hank would see his father just two times in the next seven years, which no doubt left a psychological and emotional void that scarred him throughout his brief life.

Lillie moved Hank and his older sister, Irene, to Georgiana, where she opened a boardinghouse. This is where Hank met a black blues street singer named Rufus Payne, nicknamed Tee-Tot. Tee-Tot sat on the front steps of Hank's home and taught him how to play guitar, which in turn helped Hank overcome his innate sense of shyness. Without question the blues that permeates Hank's music is Tee-Tot's direct influence. Hank, who never graduated high school, once claimed that Tee-Tot was his only teacher.

Eventually Lillie relocated her family to Montgomery where she ran another boardinghouse and served as the ultimate overbearing stage mom to Hank's budding honky-tonk career. He soaked up all the music he heard on the radio, including Ernest Tubb, Roy Acuff, and the popular "Texas Drifter" who performed spoken recitations, poetry set to music, and dynamic yodeling ballads. Hank may have crossed paths but almost certainly was influenced by Alabama musician Rex Griffin, who had already recorded the song "Lovesick Blues".

But first, Hank had to do his tour of duty around the rough honky-tonks of Alabama and the South. At one point he ran off to Texas to join the rodeo, but he took a terrible tumble and injured his already fragile spine. Again, this would compound his future issues with back pain and medication.

At one point he quit music entirely and moved to Mobile (at least once, probably twice), where he lived with extended family and worked in the shipyards. Apparently he couldn't make a clean break from music any more than he could make a clean break from drinking, and he played in clubs around Mobile. Fiddle player Freddie Beach worked with Hank during those Mobile days and recalls two things: Hank was determined to get back to performing, and he was an extraordinarily bad driver. Mother Lillie claims she swooped in and rescued Hank from the grind of the shipyards and lured him back to music. Then again, Hank's first wife, Audrey, claims that she is the one who pulled him away from the mundane work as a ship builder's assistant and encouraged him to perform again. This is just one of many examples of the ongoing clash between Lillie and Audrey in their respective, ambitious quests to manhandle Hank's career. And future fame.

Hank and Audrey were married in a filling station just ten days after her divorce from her first husband was finalized. So based on the sixty day waiting period in Alabama their marriage was technically not legitimate. Audrey already had a young daughter from her first marriage, and by all accounts Hank accepted step-daughter Lycrecia in a fatherly fashion and with a wide-open heart. Audrey took on the management of Hank's career with an open heart as well. Somehow she convinced him that she, too, was a singer, wheedling her way into the Drifting Cowboys band as an occasional female vocalist. I have yet to find an eyewitness account that praises her vocal skills.

According to esteemed biographer Colin Escott, rumors have endured throughout the years that Hank was also a parent when he married Audrey. Hank was close to his first cousin Marie, two years his elder. She lived with Hank and his family at the boardinghouse in Montgomery, and the two may have had a son together. Marie gave birth to Lewis Fitzgerald in 1943, and when Hank visited him in the hospital, he quickly referred to him as "my Butch". Later in life Butch shared that there were many hints through the years from his mother and others that Hank was his father. He also indicated that Hank was more attentive, protective, and involved than a typical extended family member. He even claimed that Hank's own mother, Lillie, found Hank and Marie naked in bed together on more than one occasion.

Hank never confirmed or denied the rumors, but he continued to treat Butch (or Lewis, which was his given name) in a consistently paternal manner.

Hank, Audrey and Lycrecia made their way to Shreveport, Louisiana when Hank was offered a contract to perform on the *Louisiana Hayride*. Radio program director Hoss Logan became very close with Hank during this period, praising his supreme talent, while scratching his head over his volatile marriage to Audrey. In his memoir, Logan seems frustrated that Audrey was constantly trying to finagle her way onto the show and into Hank's act. He didn't completely see the attraction, although he recognizes it was there, and that it was deep. Logan says, "Beyond the slightest doubt, Audrey was the inspiration for many of Hank's greatest songs. The emotional torment embodied in such tunes as 'Cold, Cold Heart', 'You Win Again', and 'Your Cheating Heart' was distilled from real life – the direct by-product of his relationship with Audrey. If she'd been a more amiable person, those songs might never have been written."

Hank toured aggressively but was back in Shreveport on Saturday nights to perform on the *Louisiana Hayride*, where he was a beloved star. Hank put the *Louisiana Hayride* on the national map and vice versa. But Logan worried about his drinking. There were periods of sobriety in which many describe Hank as sweet, sensitive, friendly, and charming. But the mood would swing abruptly and dramatically with his drinking. Logan was responsible for helping him get help in Shreveport, where he checked into the local sanitarium on more than one occasion to try to rid himself of the stranglehold of addiction.

Fame was a bright light that beamed down on Hank with extreme glory, intensity, and heat. The unavoidable flipside of such a linear ray of light is the shadow it creates behind you. Over Hank's shoulder trailed an obscure figure shaped in his own image, and he couldn't help staying lost somewhere in this dark shadowy version of himself.

Audrey gave birth to their son, Hank Jr., while they still lived in Shreveport, and Hank was determined to be the father figure he ached for when he was growing up. By this point Hank was a major celebrity on the national stage, and the *Opry* came calling. Hoss Logan released Hank from his contract and allowed him to move with his family to Nashville, where he set the audience ablaze with his debut performance and joined the cast of the *Grand Ole Opry* in record-breaking fashion.

In Nashville, publisher Fred Rose continued the paternal role Hoss Logan had assumed in Shreveport. Rose was publisher, manager, friend, brother, and father to Hank. He cared deeply about Hank's career and about him as a person. It is long rumored that Rose, a prolific songwriter credited with countless hits, was actually the brains behind Hank Williams songwriting prowess. Most people in the know, including country music historian and journalist Robert K.

Oermann, believe that Hank really did write his own songs, but Fred
Rose "polished them up" here and there.

Hank had a great deal pouring out of him, and it seemed songs
were the best, most constructive place for him to channel his emotions.
Like many country singers raised in the rural South, Hank grew up on a
steady diet of both white and black gospel music. Unlike hymns, which
were designed to be sung prayerfully and directly upward to God,
gospels were songs of public proclamation, unabashed testimonies
sung from one human being to another. The open, storytelling nature of
gospel music dovetailed naturally with the unedited, honest storytelling
nature of honky-tonk. Early gospel songs, often called "blood songs",
were unflinching narratives of sin, damnation, and the dark side
of human nature. Hank Williams felt called to sing the sermon-like
messages found in these bloods songs. He ached to expose and unearth,
musically, the unattractive but real aspect of the human condition.

As Luke the Drifter he was allowed to record a small collection of
songs, mostly recitations spoken to background music. Recitations are
also considered "the talking blues", which is a musical style descendant
from the vaudeville era. The album *Beyond the Sunset* is a collection
of Luke the Drifter tunes, many written by Hank Williams and/or Fred
Rose. My favorite piece is called "Pictures from Life's Other Side",
which is actually not an original Hank Williams composition. (I am
not certain how, but Hank Williams does receive songwriting credit
on this song on the album.) In fact it was an old Victorian parlor song,
a fable about morality. With pathos and pain, Hank/Luke claims it as
his own. The story explains that behind the gallery of photos which
celebrate happy moments in life, there are hidden images of people
in pain, outcast and unloved. There's the destitute gambler who bets
away his dead mother's wedding ring and then dies from shame. And
there's the once happy, desirable young woman who later finds herself
so alone, outcast, and unloved (presumably for being unfaithful?) that
she leaps to her death with her baby in her arms. Not recorded on this
album, an extra verse describes two brothers who took completely
different paths in life, one an honorable, wealthy man, the other a
thief. Unknowingly, they meet on a highway and the thief robs his
own brother and stabs him to death.

Heavy stuff, to say the least. The first time I listened, I mean really listened, to Hank Williams sing "Pictures from Life's Other Side" all I could think was…this was a man who was intimately familiar with pain. He knew darkness all too well. Ironic considering he is perhaps best known for his hit song "I Saw the Light".

Some claim his grim Luke the Drifter songs reveal the *true* Hank. Others either optimistically or naively cling to the upbeat gospel "I Saw the Light" as the real version of Hank Williams. I believe the magic he put into his music was neither one nor the other, but both. The very internal war between the dark and the light was what made Hank Williams so potent, so multi-dimensional, so realistic, and sadly, so short-lived. To ache that deeply over conflicting powers within one's own soul makes for great art but bad living.

Friends and family claim that when Hank was sober, he was soft-hearted, loving, and exceedingly generous. Though not Catholic, he privately gave significant donations to a Catholic orphanage in Montgomery without fanfare. Perhaps he felt a deep ache at not growing up with his father in his life, perhaps he was in fact the parent of young Lewis "Butch" Fitzgerald and felt guilt over not being his dad. He was known to emphasize family and encouraged his band members to spend time with their loved ones. He was also generous musically, often allowing his band mates to enjoy the spotlight, which no doubt improved their skills over time.

But when he was drinking and taking pain medication he was prone to ugly antics. Some claimed he drank beer after beer, while others say he really didn't have much to drink, and just the smallest amount affected him. Regardless, he was known for infidelity, brash arguments with his wife, and lunatic public drunkenness. Police were often called to his hotel rooms, sometimes to find him racing around with a nude woman, other times because he'd shot the place up with one of the guns he'd started collecting.

The *Opry* was unrelenting with Hank's schedule. He performed the regular show in Nashville as well as hitting the road for *Opry*-promoted tours. It's as if they had a crystal ball that told them he wouldn't live much longer, and thus they were trying to squeeze every last drop of blood from their prized turnip. Audiences across the nation ate him up. No one had ever seen a performer as engaging and mesmerizing as Hank Williams. In his book, <u>Sing a Sad Song</u>, Roger M. Williams highlights reactions from other musicians who performed with Hank. At the height of her career, Minnie Pearl played a show with him. She was to follow him on stage, but the audience simply wouldn't let him off. She was plumb embarrassed and told the promoter, half joking and half truthful, "I don't ever want to follow this man again."

Another *Opry* colleague who shared many a stage with Hank was Little Jimmy Dickens. "He just seemed to hypnotize those people," shared Little Jimmy. "You couldn't put your finger on it. Simplicity, I guess. He brought the people with him, put himself on their level."

His old friend from the *Louisiana Hayride*, Hoss Logan, received a late night call from Hank one time, while Hank was traveling in Cincinnati. Wistfully, Hank invited Logan to come up and visit him during the recording sessions. Hank continued, "I recorded the saddest song today I ever wrote in my life."

Logan remembered the time Hank cried genuine tears when he sang a maudlin tune called "Wedding Bells". He asked him if it was sadder than that one.

"Aw, yeah, it's a lot sadder'n that. It's called 'I'm So Lonesome I Could Cry', and I'm telling you, it's gonna tear people up when they hear it. If it don't make you cry in your beer, nothin' will."

It seems Hank Williams was one of those singers who lived and felt the lyrics of every one of his songs every time he sang them. Which explains why they all seem so authentic, but it also seems exhausting. And hardly sustainable. But I imagine that was the only way he knew how to make and share music.

Life began to unravel for the lonely celebrity. Audrey finally divorced him, and he struggled being away from his young son. He briefly became roommates with a young Ray Price, but Price moved on. While they remained friends, Price needed a more stable environment. Then the *Opry* fired Hank over his repeated drunkenness. Ernest Tubb was in the room when *Opry* exec Jim Denny made the call and fired Hank over the phone. Tubb later claimed that while Denny showed some remorse, Tubb was quick to point out that he had been urging Denny to give Hank a break for months.

Once again, Hank called his old friend in Shreveport, Hoss Logan. This time he was asking for another shot on the *Louisiana Hayride*. Logan agreed wholeheartedly and signed him to a three year contract. When Hank returned to Shreveport he was a mess, but had a new fiancée on his arm. She was a very young girl named Billie Jean. Hank had first spotted her in Nashville with Faron Young and announced to Faron that they were switching up their dates. Hank then pointed a gun at Faron to further emphasize that he didn't want Faron to date Billie Jean any more.

Hank and Billie Jean were married in the fall of 1952 despite a rocky engagement that included a few trips to the sanitarium for Hank to dry out and Billie Jean leaving him at least once. Hank had put on about thirty pounds, which some now ascribe to edema from a heart condition as well as his drug use. Billie Jean maintained it was due to her superior cooking and that he simply hadn't eaten well until he took up with her. Hank's drinking was so bad that it was profoundly affecting his performances. Even the audiences were beginning to turn on him, booing when he tripped over the wrong lyrics to some of his classic tunes. He had lost control of his bladder and bowels and would soil his pricey stage costumes so badly they couldn't even be cleaned. They would have to be thrown out. He was constantly napping or passed out, in which case he would wet the bed. Hoss Logan seemed very impressed with Hank's young bride, noting that she must have cared for him deeply to put up with so much as a young newlywed.

Conflicting reports and questions remain about Hank's final weeks in December of 1952. He was scheduled to play a week-long tour in Texas and would travel with Toby Marshall, a man Hank had hired to be his personal physician. In fact, Marshall was a shady quack with no medical credentials.

After the Saturday night show on the *Louisiana Hayride*, Hank set out for Houston in the backseat of a car with brother-sister act Tommy Hill and Goldie Hill, who were booked on some of the Texas dates with Hank. They had agreed to drop him in Houston on Sunday. Somewhere during the drive, they realized Hank was slumped over in the back seat with his head between his legs and he had turned black. Hank had stopped breathing. Goldie was screaming. Tommy pulled over, hoisted him out of the car and revived him by walking him back and forth. Hank refused to go to a hospital, so they checked him into the Rice Hotel on a stretcher. He made it to the show at a venue called Cook's Hoedown, but he was such a mess the audience booed him off the stage. He downed a few cups of coffee and took the stage once more. But they booed him off again.

Hank was unable to perform at the Monday show in Victoria, Texas. Toby Marshall merely claimed that he was "too goofed up" to play, but it is likely Hank either overdosed or had a heart attack in Victoria. Marshall did reach out to Hank's mother at this point and summoned her to meet the outfit in San Antonio.

Singer Tommy Hill, who was along for much of this Texas tour, describes Marshall's sickening method of treating his fragile, alcoholic, overwrought patient. Right after Hank woke up he would give him a few beers, then make him take a drug to induce vomiting, then make him down several cups of coffee. Then he would give him Dexedrine tablets. After the show he was given more beer, then downers. Marshall was sticking him with needles every hour. There was an injection to rev Hank up for a performance, then another to take him down until the next show.

When they arrived in Dallas on Wednesday, Hank ran into his old Nashville buddy, Ray Price. Price invited Hank to spend Christmas with him and his family, but Hank declined, claiming he wasn't sure what his plans were for the holidays. They agreed to meet up for lunch in Ohio after their upcoming New Year's gigs. By all accounts Hank did all right at his show in Dallas as well as at the Thursday show in Snook, Texas.

On Friday December 19th Hank and his entourage arrived in Austin to perform at the Skyline Club. This would be Hank's final public performance. Despite widespread reports of his drinking and erratic show attendance, this fallen-from-grace star drew a huge crowd that night. The Skyline Club was well over capacity, and owner Warren Stark was crossing his fingers the fire marshal wasn't among the audience. Hank was disheveled, had a runny nose, and appeared sweaty, likely from a persistent fever. Accounts of his performance vary. Tommy Hill and sister Goldie shared the bill that night, and Tommy claims Hank gave one of his best performances ever, singing until about one in the morning. He did gospel tunes and all of his hits, some more than once.

Hank wasn't traveling with the Drifting Cowboys on this tour, he was performing with local house bands. Austin steel player Jim Grabowske remembers things a bit differently. In a 2010 interview with writer Rush Evans for *Goldmine Magazine*, Grabowske claims Hank was shaky and had a difficult time getting through his second set. He says club owner Warren Stark had to sneak off and call an ambulance. Hank slipped off stage while the band continued to play for the crowd, and he left the Skyline Club in an ambulance for Breckenridge Hospital in downtown Austin. Apparently Warren Stark commented to another Austin musician, Bobby Earl Smith of Freda and the Firedogs, that Hank Williams' Cadillac was left behind at the club that night and remained there for some time.

Hank's possible hospital visit in Austin doesn't appear in most biographies and to some degree is a moot point. The reality is, if he didn't go to a hospital that night, he probably should have. He was sick, he was stoned, he was exhausted. And he was in the care of a miscreant faux-doctor who was simply motivated to get his meal ticket to the next gig.

Hank returned to Shreveport after the Austin show and checked into a hospital to be treated for pneumonia. Hoss Logan spoke with Hank's mother and agreed that he should take a little time off and return with her to Montgomery to rest over the holidays. Logan emphasizes this was a "leave of absence" for illness not a release from his contract, a point that would become pivotal very soon.

During the holidays, Hank and Billie Jean set up camp in Montgomery at Lillie's boardinghouse with Lillie, Hank's cousin Marie, and her son, Butch. Hank and Billie Jean traveled around Alabama, introducing Billie Jean to Hank's extended family. Some of his family expressed that they liked Billie Jean a great deal; she was beautiful and eager to help with cooking and cleaning unlike Audrey, who rarely stepped out of the car to visit with them. They tried to visit Hank's father Lon, but he wasn't home. Hank left him a note on a piece of wrapping paper, and Lon was so traumatized to have missed

Hank's visit he had trouble leaving his house after Hank died, always worried he might miss another important visit.

Hank and Billie Jean attended a music industry dinner on December 28th in Montgomery, where Hank sang a few songs. While a private industry function, this was in fact Hank's last performance. It's also clear that Hank and Billie Jean argued while in Montgomery, as they did regularly. Billie Jean showed great affection and love for Hank, but she was also feisty, another strong willed woman in Hank's life. There are theories (mostly supported by Audrey) that Hank still missed Audrey a great deal. But he also showed great tenderness toward Billie Jean when they weren't fighting. Hank definitely ached for his three-year-old son in Nashville whom he'd only seen one or two times since September. Meanwhile, Hank's mother and cousin made Billie Jean feel unwelcome, which created constant tension in the household. While all of this was going on, a secretary from Nashville, with whom Hank had a fling, was about to give birth to a baby she claimed was his.

His life was complicated, to say the least. It's no wonder Hank was strung out and overwrought.

Despite his leave of absence from the *Louisiana Hayride*, Hank was booked for two shows by a separate promoter who wouldn't let him out of his commitment. He was scheduled to play a show in West Virginia on December 31st and then Canton, Ohio on January 1st. Dicey weather threatened flight plans, so at the last minute Hank decided to travel in his Cadillac and hired a buddy's son, college student Charles Carr, to drive him. Billie Jean opted out of the road trip and decided to meet him in Ohio after the first of the year.

Winter conditions made driving a slow grind. By Knoxville, they decided they would have to fly in order to make the West Virginia show. Hank and Carr boarded a flight which had to turn around and go back to the Knoxville airport due to bad weather. Carr checked them both into the Andrew Johnson Hotel in Knoxville and called to let the promoter know they couldn't make the West Virginia show. The promoter insisted Hank honor his Canton commitment.

They ordered steaks in the room, and Hank ate very little before experiencing a case of hiccups. He lay on the bed, sliding off one time, and waited for a doctor to come to the room. The doctor gave him morphine and a shot of vitamin B12. At about 10:45 pm Carr checked them out of the hotel to continue the drive to Canton, Ohio. Hank left in a wheelchair, and there has been much speculation after the fact about whether or not he was already deceased when he was carted out of the Knoxville hotel. Most researchers believe he was still alive.

Carr maintains he was definitely alive leaving Knoxville and claims Hank got out and stretched his legs at a stop in Bristol, just over the Tennessee-Virginia border. But he later changed his mind and said that it wasn't Bristol, but Bluefield, West Virginia where Hank stretched his legs. At some point Carr was pulled over for reckless driving, and when the officer noticed Hank in the rear of the car he asked if he was dead. Carr explained that Hank had been drinking a few beers, was asleep, and was not to be bothered. The officer always maintained that Hank was dead when he saw him, and that there was a uniformed co-driver in the passenger seat. No such co-driver has ever emerged from this incident. And it seems odd to me that a police officer would allow a teenage college student to pay his fine and then simply drive away with a famous corpse.

At some point, Carr did recruit a relief driver along the route. Don Surface joined them on the quest to get to the Ohio show. They claimed they stopped around six in the morning for coffee at a place in Oak Hill, West Virginia called the Skyline Drive-In, where they discovered Hank was dead. If accurate, it's incredibly eerie considering Hank's last show was at the Skyline Club in Austin. But the Skyline Drive-In was about three miles from where the rest of the story unfolds, so it's hard to know if that data point is correct. Regardless, at some point, Carr claims he reached toward the backseat to put a blanket back on Hank and felt that his arm was shockingly stiff. They sought directions, likely at a gas station, and took Hank to the hospital in Oak Hill.

Or maybe they discovered his deceased body slightly sooner in the trip? A doctor at Beckely Hospital about fifteen miles earlier on their route claims Carr wheeled into the emergency room and showed Hank to him. This doctor said that he was dead, but explained there was no coroner on staff at that hour so they would need to go to Oak Hill.

According to biographer Colin Escott, "Carr and Surface were nervous enough to invite suspicion that foul play had been involved in Hank's death; that suspicion was reinforced by a welt on Hank's head." It's forever a mystery whether Hank died in the late hours of 1952 or the early hours of 1953, although most concur he died early January 1st 1953. Carr's road trip seems riddled with conflicting details and sliding facts, but overall the end result is the same. And very sad. The autopsy cited that Hank died from "insufficiency of right ventricle of heart due to the high position of the diaphragm." Escott interprets the medical jargon and explains that Hank's slumped position in the car, combined with respiratory depressants he had taken, plus an already compromised heart is what killed him. There were traces of alcohol in his system but they did not test for drugs. The autopsy did show that Hank had recently been severely beaten and kicked in the groin, but no one ever emerged with a confession or as a witness to shed further light on this.

The show went on in Canton, Ohio. When they announced that Hank Williams had died the audience didn't believe it at first, assuming Hank had once again missed a performance due to drunkenness. Once they realized it was true the crowd sang along as the band played "I Saw the Light".

The young driver, Charles Carr, who was paid $400 to drive Hank on that final ride, was tight lipped through the years about the experience. He went on to become a successful businessman in the Montgomery area and remained private despite a constant onslaught of questions. The details around Hank's final days became grandiose folklore.

Hank Williams did not have a will, which means by default his estate would go straight to his widow. Seems straightforward enough, right? Hardly. First wife Audrey came out of the woodwork claiming that the *Opry* was in the process of hiring Hank back, that he was making plans to return to Nashville, and that they had decided to reconcile. She believed she was Hank's rightful widow and heir to his estate. While there wasn't much cash or many possessions remaining at the time of his death, the real value was in the royalties, the copyright ownership to his library of songs. Of course Billie Jean was his wife at the time of his death, claiming she was the obvious widow and owner of the estate. Hoss Logan had to testify more than once that Audrey's claim was untrue, at least the part about Hank leaving the *Louisiana Hayride* and returning to the *Opry*. He testified that he had no intention of releasing Hank from his three year contract at the *Louisiana Hayride*. Not again, not after what Nashville had done to him the first time.

Unfortunately for Billie Jean her marriage to Hank was ruled illegitimate as she was still legally married to someone else at the time of the wedding. (I don't know why it was overlooked that Audrey's marriage to Hank was also a paperwork illegality, since her first divorce had not surpassed the mandatory sixty day waiting period Alabama required when she and Hank wed.) But for a payout of a mere $30,000 Billie Jean acquiesced. She relinquished the right to use the name Mrs. Hank Williams as well as any claim to the royalties on his music. Audrey received fifty percent of the royalties, and their son, Hank Jr., received the other fifty percent.

But about twenty years later, in 1973, Billie Jean armed herself with a new legal team focused on proving that she was, in fact, Hank's wife at the time of his death. This time the court upheld her legal claim as his rightful widow. Two years later she took Audrey by complete surprise with a swift and unexpected legal maneuver. When Billie Jean accepted the $30,000 and agreed to walk away from the music royalties over two decades prior, she never agreed to walk away from the *renewal* rights. In 1975 the copyrights were up for renewal and Billie Jean, now rightfully considered Hank's widow, was awarded half of his music estate. The fifty percent originally given to Audrey was transferred to Billie Jean.

You'd think that would be enough post-mortem melodrama, but there was yet another soap opera unfolding on a separate track in the wake of Hank's short life. Somewhere between, during, or overlapping his marriage to Audrey and his engagement to Billie Jean, Hank fooled around with a Nashville secretary named Bobbie Jett. She became pregnant, ostensibly with his child. So during the summer and fall of 1952, while Hank had his hands full getting fired from the *Opry*, rejoining the cast of the *Louisiana Hayride*, and planning a wedding to Billie Jean, he was also dealing with a secret baby. It's not 100% clear beyond a shadow of a doubt whether the baby was his, but all signs indicate that it was. At least he was accepting it as such. Hank agreed to give Bobbie Jett enough money to get herself out West if she would have the baby in Montgomery and grant him full custody. He had a legal custody document drawn up that arranged for the baby to stay with his mother, Lillie, for two years, after which he would maintain custody of the child. Some say Hank was determined to get cleaned up, was self-aware enough to recognize his drinking problems weren't ideal for a newborn, and he was giving himself two years to pull himself together. Then he would raise the child himself.

Bobbie Jett gave birth to a baby girl on January 6, 1953, just five days after Hank died. She was first named Antha Belle, but Lillie legally adopted her and renamed her Catherine Yvonne. Lillie died two years later in 1955, and the baby went to Hank's sister, Irene. But Irene saw the two year old as yet another threat to Hank's estate and conspired with an attorney to give the child up for adoption and have all the records sealed.

Damn! Sorry, but I mean really? That is low down.

Little Many Names was adopted by a family in Mobile, where she was once again renamed, this time Cathy Louise. Many years later she was a college student at the University of Alabama when her adopted parents arrived unexpectedly with bizarre and life-altering news. She had received a small sum of money from Hank's deceased mother who had pre-arranged for the gift to reach the child on her 21st birthday. (Which means the state records weren't all that sealed because *someone* from Hank's camp knew where to send the money.) It seemed that Hank Williams might be her biological father, but they couldn't prove it.

That didn't stop her from trying. Cathy Louise spent well over a decade working legal avenues, talking with Hank's family and friends, and trying to get her adoption information from the state. Ultimately she sought help from a lawyer in Washington D.C. (whom she later married), who was able to lay his hands on irrefutable evidence that no one else had unearthed. He found a copy of the pre-birth agreement that Hank Williams drafted and signed with the birth mother, Bobbie Jett.

The child, now a grown woman, changed her name to incorporate the surnames of both of her birth parents and now goes by Jett Williams. She was able to legally prove that her Aunt Irene conspired to keep her from her rightful claim to Hank's estate. So she sued for her portion of his royalties, which was half of what Hank Jr. had been enjoying all those years. He countersued and lost. He famously denounced her, refusing to accept her as part of the family. Recent accounts indicate he has softened slightly although it doesn't sound like he is setting a spot for her at the Thanksgiving table.

Almost predictably Jett Williams launched her own music career. She hired as many living members of her father's Drifting Cowboys band as she could find and started touring with them. In 1993 she made her debut on the *Grand Ole Opry*, forty-four years after her father did.

Clearly the tradition of music carried on in the family after Hank's premature departure. His son, Hank Jr., has enjoyed a multi-decade career. Two of *his* children have made names for themselves as performers, including the edgier Hank III (who also goes by Shelton), and daughter Holly, a Nashville Americana artist. Jett Williams continues to perform and hosts an annual Hank Williams tribute concert in Georgiana every year. Hank's widow, Billie Jean, married Hank's fellow *Louisiana Hayride* singer, Johnny Horton, and released an ill-fated album of her own, titled *Octopus*.

Trying to nail down immutable biographical facts about Hank Williams can be frustrating because it seems much of his life is recorded via oral history…and in triplicate. There are at least that many conflicting versions and stories from family and friends and fans about even the most miniscule detail. But the most important aspects of this man transcend eyewitness accounts and legal wrangling. He was uneducated, yet brilliant; sweet and then a scoundrel; masculine and shockingly passive; unfaithful and yet broken hearted; deeply spiritual and wholly tormented. He was intuitive, addicted, lonely, and talented.

Beyond the myth and the melodrama there was the music, the real legacy that plays on after his tragic demise. Bob Dylan has expressed many times that Hank Williams inspired him to become a songwriter. Willie Nelson closes his shows with "I Saw the Light". There are so many songs that I grew up listening to, perhaps on a Leon Russell record or a Patsy Cline album, and I didn't know for years they were Hank's songs. I would sing them in the shower, trying to sound like

Patsy, not knowing I was carrying the Hank tradition forward. His music is timeless and nimble, and it lives well beyond the boundaries of decade, fashion, and genre.

§

The Chicks and I rolled up to Hank's boyhood home in Georgiana mid-morning and took the sleepy neighborhood by storm. I found it poetic that the house was located at 127 Rose Street, as I couldn't help but think about Fred Rose, who had such a positive impact and influence on Hank's life. Turns out the house was once owned by a prominent local businessman and bachelor, Thaddeus Rose, who took pity on single mother, Lillie, and her children after their first house in Georgiana burned to the ground. He allowed them to stay in his rental property, the home at 127 Rose Street. Fascinating that Hank had not one but two benevolent Roses in his short life.

The only employee at the museum was a lovely woman named Leona who let us browse the small house freely, but was quick to offer additional history and anecdotes. She knew *a ton*. She hadn't grown up knowing so much about Hank, but like me, once she got into it she got really into it. She read every biography she could get her hands on, interviewed family members, friends, his band. It was endearing to hear from someone so informed who spoke about Hank with such loving passion and respect. I didn't wrap up any outstanding mysteries about Hank's life, but I did glean quite a few new nuggets. According to Leona:

- With such a reputation for alcohol and drug use, it's fascinating that Hank didn't really drink as much (in terms of sheer quantity) as we might think. He would sometimes go for long periods, six months or longer, barely drinking at all. And people also claim he actually had a low tolerance for alcohol. It didn't take much.
- Hank was all about family, family, family. He was a good-hearted guy who respected his band members and was very generous with them on stage, allowing them to showcase their talents. Supposedly the only time he

was cross with them was if they interrupted him while he was deep in songwriting mode. Perhaps it was this musical generosity that helped band members like Don Helms become such masters at their instruments, thereby helping to shape the honky-tonk sound.

- Hank's mother was nothing shy of a battle axe and ran her boardinghouses as part-time brothels.
- Hank's father, Lon, claimed he was kept in the veteran's hospital against his will and that Lillie had told his family members he was dead, also telling the hospital she and the kids were his only family. Lon repeatedly tried to convince the hospital staff he had a brother and a sister, but no one believed him. Finally he persuaded a fellow patient to write a letter to his sister, Bertha. Upon learning he was alive, Lon's sister, Bertha, and brother, Mack, appeared at the hospital with affidavits to secure his release.
- Leona didn't seem particularly fond of Jett Williams' singing career and griped at the fact that Jett would never take a DNA test. "Why would she, the courts gave her the estate. Why would she risk losing it?"
- Then again, Leona shared that she personally spoke with Hank's granddaughter, Holly (Hank Jr.'s daughter), who seemed frustrated that her father wouldn't accept Jett as his sister. Leona told us that Holly felt Jett looked exactly like Hank Sr.
- On our way out the door Leona proudly showed us one more picture of young Hank in a dark-colored cowboy hat. "This is the only picture you're gonna see of Hank in a dark hat, he only wore white ones after this."

I suppose when it came to hats he didn't have as much trouble choosing light over dark as he did in other areas of his life.

After buying scads of Christmas presents in the small gift shop, we gathered on the front steps to get a group photo before parting ways with our host, Leona. I couldn't help but imagine Hank as a young boy sitting on this porch while Tee-Tot Payne taught him how to play the guitar. We approved a group shot where all of our eyes were open, and were saying our farewells to Leona when a train went charging loudly by on the nearby tracks. It was a gripping and eerie punctuation mark to end our Hank pilgrimage. To think, he would sit right on these very same steps and hear that locomotive every day. If you glanced down Rose Street you could see flashes of sunlight reflecting off the train's dark metal sides as it roared by; trees obscured it from view from there. But you could still hear the low rumble and feel the power, the velocity moving on down the line. No wonder Hank Williams traveled this earth with a drifter's soul.

Just as fast as that train came, it was gone.

CHAPTER 23 SOUNDTRACK:

Ramblin' Man – Hank Williams

(HANK WILLIAMS)

Long Gone Lonesome Blues – Hank Williams

(HANK WILLIAMS)

Cold, Cold Heart – Hank Williams

(HANK WILLIAMS)

Take These Chains from My Heart – Hank Williams

(FRED ROSE, HY HEATH)

A Picture from Life's Other Side – Hank Williams

(HANK WILLIAMS)

Christine at the Hank Williams Boyhood Home & Museum, Georgiana AL
December 5, 2012

"The Chicks" on the porch where Hank learned to play guitar with Tee-Tot Payne
The Hank Williams Boyhood Home & Museum, Georgiana AL, December 5, 2012
Photo credit: Amy Thompson

Extend Yourself

Generally speaking, extensions are a positive thing. Who hasn't been saved by an extension when filing taxes? A gracious person extends his or her hand for a polite greeting. Every prima ballerina strives to achieve a higher, more beautiful extension, stretching her leg farther and farther up into the air. And it's hard to avoid the late night television infomercials for ExtenZe, an herbal supplement with ads that convey, through euphemism and celebrity spokespeople like former football coach Jimmy Johnson, that ExtenZe will extend a penis. A Hail Mary catch in the end zone is perhaps one of the most exciting examples of someone extending their reach and finding much needed extra inches to claim victory. And of course there is the extension ladder which supports my lifelong philosophy, if some is good then more is better.

Yes, extensions are a good thing, which is why I started getting eyelash extensions years ago. I found a small, chic boutique spa in Austin called Betty Lash, where they specialize in lash extensions. During my first visit, the owner, Kate Merrick, personally applied my gorgeous set of lush, natural-looking longer eyelashes. We chatted all through the appointment and I learned that Kate is from Ardmore, Oklahoma, my dad's hometown. Over the course of subsequent visits we figured out that our fathers knew each other in high school in Ardmore, and we commiserated about dating life and shared respective joy as each of us fell in love with the men we were dating and planned weddings. I have enjoyed watching Kate have her baby son and grow her business. There are several young women who do lash extensions now, and others who provide other day spa and beauty services.

But I am loyal to my eyelashes, nearly religious in my monthly appointments, which always involve fun banter. I guess you would say it's my version of the old fashioned beauty salon experience; the talking is as important as the vanity-boosting end result. One day I found myself lying down, eyes closed, while my sweet friend, Ashley, was working her magic on me. I rambled on about some of the honky-tonk research I'd been working on, and she quickly suggested I talk with Tiffany.

"Tiffany…who's Tiffany?"

"You don't know Tiffany? She works here, she does make up."

"Oh, well I only come for the lash extensions, so I guess that's why I've never met her."

"Well, I think she could help you with your research. She probably has some pretty good stories."

It seemed so implausible, a long shot that this friend of a friend in this utterly feminine day spa would have some insider track information about honky-tonk. But then again…what if I put myself out there and stumbled on a gem?

"So why would Tiffany have stories about honky-tonk?"

"Well, her family. She's working on a movie about her family in fact."

"Who's her family?"

"Her grandparents are June Carter and Johnny Cash."

Whoa! Are you kidding me? Country music royalty right here at Betty Lash?

"ASHLEY! PLEASE REMOVE ANY SHARP INSTRUMENTS YOU MIGHT HAVE NEAR MY EYEBALLS AT THIS VERY MOMENT BECAUSE I AM FREAKING OUT AND NEED TO SIT UP!"

She giggled, anticipating my excitement. "Yeah, she'll talk with you. She is super sweet."

The original Carter Family included A.P. Carter, Sara Carter, and Maybelle Carter. Maybelle's daughter, June, was just one member of the next generation to join The Carter Family band. Before she and Johnny Cash found their way to each other, June Carter was married to country singer Carl Smith, and they had a daughter, Carlene, who would become a performer in her own right. Carlene was quite young when she had her first child, a daughter named Tiffany. Tiffany was about seven when her mother married her stepfather, Nick Lowe, who had the strongest role in raising Tiffany as a father. In fact she takes the surname Lowe as her own. Nick Lowe is a famous English rocker and producer (his most well-known hit is "Cruel to Be Kind"), so Tiffany lived in London as a child, raised among British rock stars and attracted to the punk rock of the '80s. It was quite a culture shock when her mother, Carlene, decided to focus on her own career and moved Tiffany to Hendersonville, Tennessee to live with her grandparents, June and Johnny Cash.

Ashley connected Tiffany and me, and we scheduled a lunch to meet in person. I was dumbstruck when she appeared, taken aback at how much she favored her grandmother, June. Tiffany is tall and statuesque with dark hair and gleaming olive skin. Sort of like Sophia Lauren meets June Carter Cash. And Ashley was right, she is super sweet. We had a ball talking about life and music and motherhood; she has a young daughter and son. We figured out that we both lived in London at the same time, and we both attended the American School in London. And we both moved to Nashville in our middle school years, remaining through high school. It was pretty heady to listen to her Nashville high school stories, reminding myself that when she referenced her "Grandma" or "Grandpa" she was talking about *The* June Carter Cash and *The* Johnny Cash.

Tiffany's earliest memory of "getting to work with the family" was being on stage at about five years old. She appeared on television on *The Johnny Cash Show*, marching into the auditorium and up the aisles to the tune of "Onward Christian Soldiers". Then she joined her family on stage in front of all the lights and TV cameras.

Tiffany shared lovely stories about her grandmother, June. She urged me to spend some time on YouTube watching sketches between

June and her Grandpa Carl. "Their comedy routines are incredible! He was so handsome, too. Did you know he quit country music at the peak of his career to show horses? He was remarried then to my Grandma Goldie. Grandma Goldie was very beautiful." She was talking about *Opry* star Goldie Hill.

I asked if June incorporated comedy into her act in keeping with the old vaudeville and early *Opry* traditions. "Oh, Grandma was funny to make up for the fact she felt she couldn't sing all that well. She had the fastest comebacks. She could think on her feet real time. She wasn't afraid to play the fool."

June's granddaughter wasn't the only one who found that light heartedness endearing. Apparently Elvis, who was a close family friend, had a long-standing crush on June Carter. Once, Elvis dropped by to visit June, who wasn't home. He made himself quite at home, however, making biscuits, a big mess in the kitchen, and then settling in for a nap. Estranged first husband, Carl Smith, also cruised in for a visit and found Elvis napping in June's bed. Elvis woke up to Carl's pistol pointing straight at him. According to Grandma, Carl then chased Elvis around the backyard with the gun. However, Grandpa Carl said he and Elvis simply had a big laugh about it.

Johnny Cash was also jealous of Elvis' affection for June. When they married he asked her to get rid of any gifts that Elvis had given her.

June was more flexible and forgiving with the relationships that came in and out of her blended family. Tiffany says June maintained an open door policy with all of her former sons-in-law, a list which includes country greats Rodney Crowell and Marty Stuart. Both Crowell and Stuart performed on her Grammy-award winning solo record, which was titled *Press On* and released in 1999.

Tiffany and I were having lunch alfresco at a food trailer. But I was much too intrigued with the conversation to bother with my pressed pork Cuban sandwich. Curious, I asked her how accurate the movie *Walk the Line* really was.

"Oh, very. I reviewed the script. My uncle was involved in the film." Her uncle, John, is the only biological child between June and Johnny and is very close in age to Tiffany. In fact they both grew up under the same roof through their teen years, effectively sharing June and Johnny as parents during that era. "You know, Grandma knew Reese Witherspoon was going to play her before she died."

"So were June and Johnny really the great love story we all think they were?"

"Oh, yes, with them, love always prevailed. He was very dependent on her. He called all the time when they were apart. When she died, a light went out of his house. What she lit up inside of him was crushed, the light went out. I just can't imagine one of them living without the other."

"Were they really as spiritual as I've read?"

She laughed and nodded in agreement as her eyes seemed to drift off to some happy memory. "They definitely had a direct line to God. Their prayers got through."

At the end of that first lunch Tiffany shared a last minute anecdote, practically an afterthought, which I found the most fascinating of all. Apparently Johnny Cash loved the movie *Gladiator*. A mutual friend of the family arranged for *Gladiator* star Joaquin Phoenix to join the Cash-Carter clan at one of their Los Angeles homes for dinner one night. (This is before Joaquin Phoenix was slated to play Cash in *Walk the Line*.) Phoenix was understandably nervous to be summoned for dinner with The Johnny Cash, but what he didn't know was that Cash was even more nervous to meet him. The Man in Black dealt with his jitters at the dinner table by reciting almost every single line from the movie *Gladiator*.

"Joaquin Phoenix's eyes were just wide open!" Tiffany laughed. "After dinner we had a guitar pull…that's when we pass around a guitar and each person does a song or poem or joke, whatever their talent is. I sang a song I had written about Grandpa. Grandpa sang something. And then he handed the guitar to Joaquin, and Joaquin just sort of shook his head politely. He just couldn't do it."

"Sounds like quite a night for both of them."

"Oh it was. And you know Grandpa died without ever knowing Joaquin was going to play him in *Walk the Line*."

Tiffany is a talent and a treasure in her own right. In addition to the makeup services she does for individuals, music videos, and film, she is a writer, singer, and songwriter. She's even had one of her songs,

"Queen of Everything", included in a motion picture. I have loved getting to know her. So one day I tossed her a crazy idea, "Hey, Tiffany, do you want to write a song with me?" Much to my delight she was all over it. We've had fun lunching on tacos and sharing a few ideas, but we are both busy moms, so it's been hard to reconnect and hammer it out. We have decided it's going to be honky-tonk. And we know the title includes something about diamonds and The Ryman (inspired by my brief moment on the Ryman stage when my friend dropped her diamond stud earring). But time will tell if it's going to be a happy song, a sad song, a song about love, or a song about loss. It's a work in progress. But sometimes I have to pinch myself and remember we are working on a song about The Ryman, the very place where all four of her grandparents met and fell in love.

To think I have Betty Lash to thank for this fun, talented chick friend. Honky-tonk shines in the unlikeliest of places. In fact, Tiffany isn't the only musical friendship that this boutique day spa has given me. Ashley also suggested I meet her buddy, Tex Smith, a singer-songwriter trying to make it in the Austin music scene.

As I was batting my new longer eyelashes at the register, Ashley rang me up and encouraged me to follow up on this idea. "Christine, you have to meet Tex. He's got the whole honky-tonk thing going, I think you'd enjoy his music. Such a good guy."

Tex had a Tuesday night show at a joint called Sam's Town Point and invited me to come see him play as well as sit down and talk for a bit. Tex looks as honky-tonk as Sam's Town Point. He has the pointed cowboy boots, carefully shaped hat, sideburns, and western shirt. That said, his sound is more Americana eccentric than it is straight-up honky-tonk. He reminds me so much of Townes Van Zandt – seemingly simple but emotionally complex. The rhymes don't always match, and he's not afraid to let a pause float out there for a while between lyrics.

I really enjoyed sitting down and getting to know him. He grew up in Arlington, Texas and got his first guitar when he was in high school. Once, on a family canoe trip, the only music they had was a Johnny Cash cassette tape, and he became enthralled with the simplicity of Cash's music. Subsequently he became obsessed with any and all music that came from Sun Records in Memphis, including Elvis and other rockabilly sounds. While at the University of North Texas he studied geography but lived in the music dorm and started writing songs in his free time. He graduated in 1997 and married his college sweetheart in 2000. He found a job that utilized his degree, making maps for a large commercial real estate firm in Dallas. But music remained a passion, and he served as DJ for a Dallas rockabilly radio show for seven years.

In 2006 Tex and his wife moved to the hill country outside of Austin where he slowly got the bug, and confidence, to start singing his songs at coffee shops and open mics. It wasn't long before he found his way to the revered Cheatham Street open mic in San Marcos. He built up a body of work and a network of musical friends who encouraged him to record his first album in 2009. It was roughly 85% complete when he played it for his wife, who had never even seen him sing in public before. Her response was favorable and immediate, "I can't believe this!"

In Tex's own words, "she was an instant fan."

That was the one and only time she heard Tex's music. After managing severe depression off and on for years, she took her own life that summer.

Suddenly music was all he had left. He poured himself into songwriting and recording but not without self-doubt. "Who's gonna want to hear all this sad crap? I don't want to be this guy."

Music and songwriting became his therapy. He got it all out. Slowly he was able to talk about his grief more publicly as he emerged out of the "depressed, dark mode." He experienced moments of spiritual clarity that began to put life in perspective. His music began to reflect this phase of mourning and a return to life and light.

Tex talked freely with me about having a spiritual point of view and shared what a profound role Johnny Cash's music and biography had played in his emotional journey. Turns out I'm not the only one who reveres Johnny Cash as inspiration for his less than picture perfect faith walk.

Tex shared, "Did you know Johnny Cash often called himself a C+ Christian?"

I couldn't believe how much tragedy lived inside a guy who maintained such a gentle, laid back demeanor. I was happy to hear that he had started dating again, seeing a girl he knew in college who was also a singer. They started to perform a few duets together, which seemed incredibly poignant, and ultimately got engaged.

I would have rooted for Tex to succeed as a musician solely based on his poetic songs, but I was even more inspired to cheer him on knowing what a sad, triumphant soul he stored within. He exudes kindness and light, and is clearly dedicated to making good music.

I treasure my friendships with Tiffany and Tex – not to mention Ashley, the ultimate connector. And what a life lesson I learned in that simple moment lying on the bed having my eyelashes vamped up. I could have succumbed to the never-ending burden of my hectic to do list and brushed past Ashley's suggestion to meet up with Tiffany, or the same with Tex. But such incredible honky-tonk stories poured out of both! Out of Betty Lash. The irony was almost too delicious…a beautifully packaged day spa juxtaposed against the musical substance within the souls of these two new friends. It just goes to show that sometimes you simply have to extend yourself in order to truly know the people in your midst.

CHAPTER 24 SOUNDTRACK:

Tiffany Anastasia Lowe – June Carter Cash

(JUNE CARTER CASH)

I Still Miss Someone – Johnny Cash

(JOHNNY CASH, ROY CASH JR.)

Loose Talk – Carl Smith

(FREDDIE HART, ANN LUCAS)

Cry, Cry Darling – Goldie Hill

(JIMMY C. NEWMAN)

Goodbye Songs – Tex Smith

(TEX SMITH)

Honky Con Carne

When I drift back to my Boston days, I sometimes wonder what the woman on my right and the woman on my left were thinking about on their respective treadmills while we were all exercising at the gym. Of course I was daydreaming about the Austin live music scene, picturing myself singing on stage with Willie Nelson. (For the record, we killed it, the Red Headed Stranger and I.)

I'm not the only one who made the odyssey to Austin, Texas with dreams of singing at one of its eminent venues. I am, perhaps, the only one without a lick of real talent to fantasize about it with such zeal. The reality is I couldn't land a non-paying Sunday morning gig in the lobby of a Holiday Inn Express in this town. There's just too much talent. It's not a fluke that Austin is called "The Live Music Capital of the World". Granted, the moniker sprung up out of the vibrant scene in the '70s, but I'm here to tell you we are still rightfully claiming the title. I always feel a little guilty, like I'm gloating or rubbing it in, but the cold hard truth remains…whatever you're imagining, it's better than that. We are spoiled filthy rotten in Austin when it comes to good live music.

Over the years I have watched our two juggernaut music festivals, South by Southwest and ACL, mushroom into titanic events that draw music fans from Portland to Australia and all places in between.

Celebrities descend upon the city, TV shows broadcast remotely from Austin for the week, and music industry executives are here to make deals and host parties. It's insane, over-the-top fun, but I always feel a bit sorry for the tourists who come and go and never experience the real Austin music scene. I wish they could know the easier pace of a Sunday night coffee shop gig, the Wednesday happy hour that draws the regular swing dancers, or the breezy biergarten with string lights in the trees and a no-name blues act that sounds like the next Stevie Ray Vaughn. But what do I know? Year after year throngs of people pour in for these music festivals, and year after year they flood social media talking about how much they love them.

I've lived in the same neighborhood over thirteen years, just a block from South Congress Avenue, which runs straight up the gut of old South Austin, north across the river, and right into the middle of downtown. My little south-of-the-river stretch of South Congress was a dicey bet back in the '80s and '90s, mostly a rundown hangout for outcasts and the occasional prostitute. By the time I arrived in 2000, it was just *barely* starting to break out as a trendy hotspot for the cool kids. These days there are weekly busloads of Junior Leaguers showing up with plastic go-cups of white wine ready to stroll among the hipster shops and restaurants. Despite all the permutations (some good, some less good) to the hood, there is still nothing that beats the view looking up South Congress at dusk. The state Capitol is framed in the middle of the city skyline, the air is tinted with a light navy blue hue that won't last long, and all the multi-color neon signs along the avenue are glowing bright, ready for the evening. It's a suspended moment when possibilities for adventure are endless and everything is ahead of you.

Roughly ten years ago one of my best friends from high school, Eleanor, came from California to visit for the weekend. As we walked up South Congress at dusk, she noticed a band playing in a parking lot. They were rocking away in front of a dilapidated little façade that housed a sewing machine repair business.

"Are you kidding me? You even have a band at the sewing machine repair shop?"

"Oh, yeah, I suppose we do. Damn, they sound pretty good, too."

Sadly the sewing machine repair shop didn't survive rising rent and the area's hipster evolution. Currently in its place is the ever-popular and mighty delicious Home Slice Pizza, which has been a terrific anchor of activity for the neighborhood. As a little tot, my daughter Sophie used to like to dine there after an afternoon at the pool, while its by-the-slice operation also nourishes all the lost and sweaty souls pouring out of the nearby Continental Club after a late night show. Family life, daily life, and live music all blend together in Austin – there are very few borders. We like to let both the musicians and the fans run wild here in their native habitat.

The city hardly caters to just one style of music. There are active scenes for hard rock, songwriter rock, funk, punk, Americana, jazz, and other genre-bending bands and fans. But my personal tastes lean toward the Texas rock, blues, alt-country, Red Dirt, and honky-tonk. I pretty much always go for the 2/4 rhythm set to a steel guitar and fiddle. In Austin, Texas you can hear a steel guitar being played live any given weekend...even in the *afternoon*. At a matinée gig! You don't even have to wait until the bigger acts at night. How cool is that?

Now that we're married and Tom has moved to Austin, I feel as if I am falling in love with the music scene all over again as we experience it together – which is hardly to say we are out carousing several nights a week, shutting down the honky-tonks. We are in a different phase of life, working harder than ever before, juggling crazy travel schedules, overseeing middle school math homework, signing field trip permission slips, chaperoning slumber parties, grilling out a dinner that is meant to make us all healthier, and then collapsing into bed before we start it all over again the next day. All of which makes me appreciate my town even more. Because if I *can* find a sliver of time and a modicum of energy to venture out, I know there is almost always going to be some good music somewhere. And most likely there will be a diverse group of people there to enjoy it. Despite having a university with nearly 40,000 undergraduates, the college students and 20-something's don't overrun the town. Because there are just as many 30, 40, 50, 60, 70-year olds (and plus!) out to hear good music. Austin will keep you young if you let it.

One of the easiest ways to hear music is to go out to eat. We like to walk up to a Tex-Mex restaurant called Guero's, which boasts a large outdoor biergarten with live music that makes a 45-minute wait the highlight of the meal. One time we were lounging out there clutching our chips, salsa, and table buzzer, enjoying a teenage act called The Peterson Brothers. They were two young kids rocking the blues with a very old school sound. Turns out they are the hot new thing, having opened for B.B. King and shared the stage with Buddy Guy and Pinetop Perkins. They've caught the attention of Bootsy Collins (bass guitar player for James Brown), who has become a mentor to these young teens in their quest to "Keep the Blues Alive".

If you drive just outside the city limits to enjoy smoke pit barbecue at the Salt Lick, you will likely stumble on some live music, maybe even local honky-tonk outlaw Bo Porter. Aesthetically he has a touch of the David Allan Coe look, although in reality he seems infinitely less daunting. His gravely baritone style delivers classic Texas bluesy honky-tonk outlaw rockabilly country music. But like many outlaws he stores a tender heart under that biker veneer. Bo Porter is known for his sense of honor as much as he is known for his music. One time he was barreling down the road to a wedding gig when he hit a deer and wrecked his motorcycle. He hobbled to Fredericksburg and performed the wedding before tending to his injuries. His response was plain spoken, "I couldn't let the lady down. I was playing her wedding and she was so excited. Besides, if I quit there are three other guys out of work."

Many of the old music joints from the legendary '70s scene are still around in some iteration or another. The Saxon Pub has maintained a dark, dated neighborhood feel and continues to book the musicians that other musicians seem to revere. One time Tom and I wandered in to discover beloved local Guy Forsyth was playing. Guy Forsyth is a dedicated student of the blues as well as a unique roots musician. His delivery ranges from raw to sultry and all spiritual places in-between. He's a pretty regular show around town, and yet the crowd was packed-in like sardines, mesmerized by every morsel of sound he had to give. We were bewildered when he pulled out a saw, stood it on end, and proceeded to play it with a fiddle bow. Infinitely more than a party trick, he lured hauntingly beautiful music out of the most pedestrian

Home Depot tool. I get the feeling Guy Forsyth is a fairly erudite guy when he's not busy melting the crowd into musical submission.

The Scoot Inn is the not-as-dicey-as-it-used-to-be joint over on the East side of town that prides itself on being one of the oldest continuously running beer joints in central Texas. Long gone are the outlaws, ranch hands, rough-necks, and bandits who would stop in this railroad saloon to barter and imbibe. Today it draws an eclectic crowd to listen, drink, and dance. To be honest, I don't recognize ninety percent of the bands on their schedule, but every so often the Scoot Inn books a country singer or a honky-tonk rockabilly group. And it's a cool venue. Recently Tom and I went to hear The Derailers, a Bakersfield-esque rockabilly band that has been wowing Austin audiences and beyond since the 1990s. I used to wear out their *Here Come the Derailers* CD, which had the unlucky fate to be released on September 11, 2001 and thus never had a real shot to achieve the national acclaim it deserved. Lord knows I did my part, venturing out to see them as often as I could, sometimes at locations as far flung as Smith's Olde Bar in Atlanta. Tony Villanueva was the original lead singer, but I heard he left the group to be with his family and ended up an evangelical television preacher somewhere in Minnesota. Sure it may seem like an abrupt left turn, but honky-tonk and gospel are just two horns on the same goat. Country singers often swing on the extremes of Saturday night revelry and Sunday morning redemption.

Brian Hofeldt, who co-founded the band with Villanueva, stepped in as the group's frontman and has kept the music both traditional and relevant for more than a decade. They were sharper than ever when we saw them at the Scoot Inn. It was fun to see the hardcore two-stepping crowd out swinging on the dance floor as The Derailers rocked the legacies of Buck Owens, Roy Orbison, George Jones, and…well, The Derailers.

When it comes to timeless American honky-tonk, just step inside the Broken Spoke on South Lamar and know that you are breathing rarified air. Decade after decade this classic western dancehall continues to showcase live country bands much to the delight of the two-steppers who swirl around the hardwoods night after night. While this venue used to be considered way down south of town, it's currently surrounded by high-dollar condo development projects, holding steadfast as the hole in the donut of Austin's urban sprawl. Despite the ever-changing view from the parking lot, once inside, it's as if time has stood still. Dusty photographs on the walls memorialize the celebrities that have graced The Spoke, including Bob Wills, Willie Nelson, Ernest Tubb, and Dolly Parton. Proprietor James White is usually at the register, clad in full western regalia and greeting guests as they pay their cover and hold out their hand to receive the beloved wagon wheel stamp. (I won't reveal how many nights I have stumbled into bed without washing it off only to awaken with a smudged wagon wheel replica on my face the next morning.) I can't speak for the men's restroom, but the ladies' room still has red bandana fabric covering each stall in lieu of doors. However, the unisex one-person bathroom in the front bar area is perhaps my favorite. It is decoupaged on all four walls with magazine cutouts of George Strait. Sit on down and relax my friend, you have just reached the inner-sanctum, the Sistine Chapel of honky-tonk.

That being said, the real hero of The Broken Spoke is the dance floor. Whether a weeknight or weekend, headliner band or up-and-comer, early hour or late night, I have never seen this dance floor barren and begging for company. It welcomes expert swing dancers, regular two-steppers, tourists, and beginners alike as long as you follow the unwritten etiquette. Maintain the counterclockwise flow, never bring your beer out there with you, and clear the dance floor between each song *even* if you plan on dancing the next one. That's just how it's done.

While the interior of the Spoke may be timeless, the bands are anything but relics. Owner James White has a keen eye for talent and regularly refreshes his lineup with new, albeit traditional country bands. Recently, before a Broken Spoke show, I had the opportunity to sit down with Mike Harmeier, frontman for Mike and The Moonpies, the newest honky-tonk sensation to sweep Austin. With their plaid, pearl-snap western shirts, scruffy beards, and long hair you'd think they stepped straight out of the 1970s outlaw scene. But Mike Harmeier is only twenty-nine and his band mates appear to be around the same age. Harmeier grew up in Tomball, Texas, close to Houston, where he learned to play blues guitar at a young age. His father was a Stevie Ray Vaughn devotee. He explained how at just thirteen he had his own country cover act singing George Strait and Clint Black classics. After high school he made his way to Austin to be a part of the music scene and found himself in an indie rock band. But it wasn't long before he drifted back to his country roots, writing and performing honky-tonk tunes with a new ensemble.

The first time Harmeier played the Broken Spoke he had been hired to perform at a friend's wedding, so it was a private gig. But Mr. White heard the group during their sound check and immediately booked them for a dancehall show. When Mike and I sat down to chat, the Moonpie gig at the Spoke was still a fairly fresh deal, and I had the sense Mike knew what a special opportunity he had on his hands. Don't let the slacker apparel fool you for one second – Mike Harmeier is an eager student and a hungry musician. Hardly satisfied playing just the guitar, he has managed to teach himself piano as well as lap steel guitar. And yet he is keenly aware that his highest and best purpose is reading a live crowd and leading the band. He thrives on the vibe of the Texas music community and hopes to stay connected to it while achieving success on a grander scale. I was utterly charmed by his laidback, friendly demeanor as well as his strategic thinking and careful game plan for the band's future.

"So, Mike," I pressed further. "What do you really want to come from all of this? If you had to pick…do you want to be a Texas dancehall hero, land the big Nashville recording contract, or walk to your mailbox a few times a year to get your songwriting check?"

In a breezy, lighthearted, and almost sweet tone that could not have matched his answer any less, he laughed. "I want it all!"

I loved knowing there were still un-jaded young guns making the trek to Austin to be a part of this music scene, bringing with them talent, big dreams, and energy to burn. And The Moonpie show did not disappoint. The band was tight and the dance floor packed. One woman after the next draped an arm over her dance partner's shoulder, resting her wagon wheel stamped hand on the back of his neck, and off they went, round and round. People were laughing, singing along, catching a buzz, learning to two-step, falling in love, falling out of love, and hopefully back in again. Just another Wednesday night under the spell of the Broken Spoke and its neon glow.

Cruise north of downtown and you'll find the small dive bar, Ginny's Little Longhorn. To date, I have never purchased a winning ticket that matched the number the bird pooped on, but the scene at Ginny's always has a way of inspiring hope, like it *could* happen. Nevertheless I always cheer for the Chicken Shit Bingo winner and dance to Dale Watson with a Lone Star in one hand and a chili dog in the other.

With his black biker apparel, dramatic pompadour, and weathered appeal, Dale Watson still seems to enjoy rocking the Texas honky-tonk scene, having done it now for quite some time. He smacks a bit of Bakersfield, and actually spent some time in California during his early career. But Austin claims him proudly as he continues to pick, croon, and revolt against lost love, bad luck, and trashcan country. Recently Dale found himself in the middle of a very public brush-up between country traditionalists and Nashville newcomers. It all started when Nashville country star Blake Shelton made some rather shocking comments in an interview on GAC's television show *Backcountry*. Shelton posed:

> "If I am 'Male Vocalist of the Year' that must mean that I'm one of those people now that gets to decide if it moves forward and if it moves on. Country music has to evolve in order to survive. Nobody wants to listen to their grandpa's music. And I don't care how many of these old farts around Nashville [sic] going, 'My God, that ain't country!' Well that's because you don't buy records anymore, jackass. The kids do, and they don't want to buy the music you were buying."

Needless to say this did not sit well with fans of traditional country music. Esteemed singer Ray Price took to his Facebook page denouncing Blake and his dimwitted, disrespectful comments. Price responded:

> "It's a shame that I have spend [sic] 63 years in this business trying to introduce music to a larger audience and to make it easier for the younger artists who are coming behind me. Every now and then some young artist will record a rock and

roll type song, have a hit first time out with kids only. This is why you see stars come with a few hits only and then just fade away believing they are God's answer to the world. This guy sounds like in his own mind that his head is so large no hat ever made will fit him. Stupidity Reigns Supreme!!!!!!! Ray Price (CHIEF "OLD FART" & JACKASS") P.S. YOU SHOULD BE SO LUCKY AS US OLD-TIMERS. CHECK BACK IN 63 YEARS (THE YEAR 2075) AND LET US KNOW HOW YOUR NAME AND YOUR MUSIC WILL BE REMEMBERED."

So many people flocked to Price's post in fervent support that Facebook suspected he must have been spamming and shut down his page, locking him out for thirty days. This draconian action fanned the flames even further with outraged TEAM RAY PRICE fans, myself included. Dale Watson jumped into the online mêlée, defending Ray Price as well as all traditional country music artists, and became a de-facto ambassador for the anti-Shelton movement. Seemingly within hours, while on tour in Europe, Dale Watson had written, recorded, and posted a song on YouTube called "A Song for Blake Shelton: I'd Rather Be an Old Fart than a New Country Turd".

For the life of me, I cannot understand how Blake Shelton is still a member of the *Grand Ole Opry*. The only tenuous glue that holds the current country music industry together is the thinly veiled attempt by new Nashville pop stars to at least *feign* respect for the *Opry* greats that came before them. At least I can find solace and vindication in Dale's song, which not only boasts brilliantly hilarious response lyrics but also a pretty catchy honky-tonk melody. Well played Dale, well played.

Not every hotspot in Austin is out of the past. The Rattle Inn is a relative newcomer to the honky-tonk scene, though its founders are Texas nightlife veterans. Restaurateur Kevin Williamson of Ranch 616 teamed up with another investor plus Ray Benson, lead singer of the western swing band Asleep at the Wheel. Together they launched The Rattle Inn, a sort of designer honky-tonk. Located off hip West 6th Street, just a stone's throw from Sandra Bullock's restaurant and other trendy joints, the Rattle Inn is somehow both swanky and legitimate.

Its long, glossy wood bars and stuffed leather booths make it feel like an old-school drinking establishment for West Texas ranchers and wildcatters from a by-gone era. In the room called "Ray's Backstage" they book quality live music in an intimate setting. You might stumble in to hear the ass-shaking, rootsy funk of Shinyribs Russell, better known as the frontman for The Gourds. Or you could hear the lovely and talented songbird, Brennen Leigh. Her music has the soul and twang of honky-tonk with just a hint of bluegrass to keep things interesting. With its old-school feel and eclectic lineup, The Rattle Inn has become an immediate classic in the Austin nightlife scene.

Of course if you feel the need to escape the city limits of Austin, Luckenbach is never far away, spiritually or geographically. This slow-paced scene hosts a picker's circle every weekday and outdoor shows and dances on the weekends. The first time I took Tom to Luckenbach he felt the magic instantly. "There's really not much here," he marveled. "It's really pretty simple." Which is part of its beauty. There's just the General Store and original bar, the dancehall, a small outdoor stage, and a beautiful meadow where they set up the larger outdoor concerts.

Last year I was struggling to conjure up a way to celebrate Tom's 50th birthday. Nearly defeated, I had one more light bulb moment. When I suggested we spend his 50th birthday as a family out at Luckenbach he didn't balk. That was progress. Before he could change his mind, I bought three tickets to a music festival at Luckenbach and booked a room at a nearby inn.

Tom, Sophie and I spent a wonderful July day and evening lounging in the grass at Luckenbach, drinking Lone Stars (lemonade for Sophie), eating ice cream and hearing incredible Texas music. Reckless Kelly opened and then Robert Earl Keen stole the show, playing around dusk. We snacked on barbecue sandwiches for dinner and caught a few tunes by Blacktop Gypsy, a female act who played on the small stage to cap off the night. It's hard to believe I ever brainstormed anything other than Robert Earl Keen and Luckenbach for Tom's half a century birthday bash. It was perfection.

Another valuable music scene that lies just outside of Austin's immediate grasp is in San Marcos, a city just south on I-35. The life force of San Marcos' music community is a venue called Cheatham

Street Warehouse, which opened in 1974 and to this day continues to host its popular Wednesday night Songwriters Circle. People pour in asking the same old question, "Is the list out yet?" The list is a basic sign-up sheet for writers to step up and share their work. Sounds simple enough, but the result is a complex and regenerating coterie of singer-songwriters who band together, develop friendships, collaborate on songs, and become the next generation from "down at Cheatham". While the current batch may not be household names, if they have even a modicum of talent, they seem almost anointed to succeed based on the forerunners who once graced the same stage. Stevie Ray Vaughn was a Tuesday night gig. Guy Clark once took the stage with Townes Van Zandt. And brothers Charlie Sexton and Will Sexton played there when they were just twelve and ten years old, respectively. In 1975 George Strait was a newcomer to the Ace in the Hole Band at Cheatham Street. They played their first fifty or sixty gigs at the San Marcos venue before Strait and his starched Wranglers hit the road and reformed the entire 1980s country music industry with his neoclassical country sound.

Just this past spring, the city of San Marcos played host to The 5th Annual Lone Star Music Awards. I was merely watching from afar (i.e., from my couch in Austin via social media) but it seemed the performances, the crowd, and the speeches combined to make it a vibrant success. Robert Earl Keen won Live Act of The Year and was also inducted into the Lone Star Music Hall of Fame. The Departed won Album of the Year in the Americana/Roots category for their album *Adventus*. And frontman Cody Canada won Musician of the Year.

I promise I didn't rig the ballots.

Everyone knows I am a big Cody Canada fan. Cross Canadian Ragweed was a palpable part of my single mom era as I spent free weekends traveling to see them play in Georgia, Louisiana, Alabama, and California. Oh, and plenty of places in Texas, too. I was *crushed* when they disbanded. But the news coincided with my engagement to Tom, and wedding plans distracted me from mourning. I was barely a new newlywed when word came that Cody Canada had formed a second band called The Departed.

Out of loyalty I played along, but admittedly, I lagged at first in my passion for The Departed, still nostalgic for the old Ragweed days.

That is, until I listened to their first album, *This Is Indian Land*, which was their tribute album to the Oklahoma songwriters who inspired the Red Dirt scene. I didn't know most of the songs so they were fresh to me, and their interpretations were innovative, complex and downright fun. Great driving music. Great summertime music.

The world and I were on board; The Departed had gelled in our minds and in our hearts. We all eagerly awaited album number two, their first original. When *Adventus* came out, one thing was abundantly clear: The Departed had evolved from fraternity-pleasing, rabble rousing, redneck rock and had fine-tuned their musical chops. It felt like straight up rock and roll, it felt like rootsy blues, it felt robust. I loved it.

After hearing *Adventus* I became a dog with a bone trying to get an interview with Cody Canada. It was no easy task as he tours constantly and spends his scant free time with his wife and two young boys in New Braunfels. Ultimately we settled on a phone interview, relinquishing the goal of trying to meet in person. Which was fine, I just wanted a few insights into life with The Departed. And I wanted to hear a little bit about his time back at The Farm in Stillwater, Oklahoma, birthplace of the whole Red Dirt music movement.

On the day of our phone interview I was in Kerrville, Texas delivering the key note speech at a conference, after which I had a book signing. Not unlike Cinderella, I panicked when I realized the time and had to run away from the signing so I could get situated in my car for the interview with Cody. For some reason I drove down the road a bit before realizing I wouldn't get much farther before he called, and I needed to pull over so I would have a free hand to take notes. I wheeled into a Dairy Queen parking lot. My car's air conditioning suddenly seemed deafening so I cut the air to avoid ambient noise. I was sweating, anxious, and excited.

Good heavens, it is hot in this car. Geez that guy's DQ soft serve cone looks good. I wonder why he didn't get the chocolate topping.

As you can see I am not a seasoned journalist. I could learn many things from the ever-poised Christiane Amanpour.

I tried to find composure as I answered Cody's call, although I am pretty sure I was very breathy and nervous while sweat was pooling up between my iPhone and my ear, making it difficult to hear. My nerves aside, Cody Canada could not have been sweeter or more generous with his time. He and the band were on the bus rolling toward Kentucky, yet he acted like he had nothing better to do but talk to me about *Adventus* and how The Departed was jiving as a group and how the Red Dirt scene shaped him as a musician – and as a man. It was riveting.

I asked him about those early days on The Farm in Stillwater. All these years and two bands later I wondered if the synergic scene from The Farm had trickled down into this latest album.

"Definitely," he replied. "It's in the camaraderie, the love this band has for one another. That passion for writing and playing…nobody will ever take that away from you."

Oh man, he is a poet in real life too.

He also described how and why he ultimately made the move from Oklahoma to Texas. The Red Dirt scene started winding down for him in Stillwater. He had the opportunity to perform in New Braunfels, Texas where he ran into talented musicians like Ryan Bingham and felt a refreshed sense of energy and collaboration. Something was drawing him down. It felt like the early days at The Farm in Stillwater, so he and his wife, Shannon, decided to pick up camp and move to New Braunfels. As Canada explained, "I just wanted to be a part of something, be near that music scene."

The conversation was going so well that I knew I needed to end it before I embarrassed myself. I thanked him profusely, angling toward a polite close when suddenly I felt compelled to tell him what a big fan I was. I rambled on about how as a single PTA mom I traveled to so many Cross Canadian Ragweed shows, but these days I am having so much fun getting to know The Departed.

In one final, sophomoric burst I felt the absurd need to share, "Cross Canadian Ragweed was my single band, The Departed is my married band."

Much to my relief, he laughed a fresh hearty laugh. "Yeah, we kinda feel the same way!"

This and other heady conversations with talented people started making me dream above my station. Talking with musicians, learning the backstory of classic honky-tonk songs, immersing myself in country music's history…it all began to churn up some latent fantasies I had long since tucked away. Suddenly I began to wonder if Austin could stand another live music act. Maybe someone needed to be wholly dedicated to singing covers of old classic tunes, keeping them alive for the legions of young music fans that keep flooding into this town. Hell, it would practically be a public service. I could win an award from a cultural arts council or the state's music heritage office. Could I really start a band after all? One day I got going a little fast on the elliptical machine at the gym and suddenly the answer was a resounding *YES! Yes, I should start a band! I should be singing too, just like the rest of them. Life is short, why not me?*

First things first, I needed validation from an expert to see if I could sing decently enough so as not to humiliate myself. I needed a voice coach to magically transform my scratchy, range-less power voice into something more pleasing. I took to social media and made a very bold post. I imagined it would be the kind of swift move that people write about later in their biographies, a shoehorn moment that would unlock doors and break down obstacles. I set aside my fear and asked all of my friends on Facebook if anyone could recommend a vocal coach to help me with my singing.

No one offered suggestions. One person replied, "How about Marcel Marceau?"

Not exactly the resounding wave of support I was anticipating. I nursed my wounded ego privately, but before long, the idea and desire to sing came back, even stronger than before. I found myself thinking about it day and night, designing a flyer in my mind to try and recruit fellow band members. I made a list of venues we could play, bought domain names, and analyzed which platform would be best for the band's website.

I decided once again to go public with my idea. Social media was of no use on the last go round, so this time I decided to share the news with the two people nearest and dearest to me, the two people who love me more than anything in the world and care about my dreams as much as their own. I announced it to Tom and Sophie one night over dinner.

"I have news. I am starting a band."

It's hard to imagine, but their reaction was even less positive than the Marcel Marceau comment.

Tom shot out of the gate with pragmatic obstacles, "You are a wife and a mother. What about us? You're going to be out every night playing in bars?"

"I am flattered you think my band is going to be that big, but that's not really what I'm thinking. I am picturing more of a cover band, afternoon gigs, private parties, free shows that are early."

Being a teenager, Sophie was mainly fearful I would embarrass her. "Mom, this is not a good idea."

"Y'all, come on. Where is the support? Where's the love?"

"We love you plenty, we support you in everything. Not this one."

This comedic exchange went round and round with neither side budging until the idea of band names entered the conversation. Everyone loves to brainstorm band names, so this loosened them up a little.

Tom asked the question as if it was nothing more than far-fetched banter, "What would you have called your band anyway?"

"Oh, I already have a name for my band."

Sophie looked up, wary but curious. "You do?"

"Oh yeah, I've had it for about seven years."

"You've had the name for this band that long?"

"Yeah. I already own the URL and everything."

At this point they set down their forks, looked at each other, and then back at me. Tom couldn't resist, "So what's the name?"

I'd been carrying this one around in my own mind for nearly a decade, so I was eager to share it with the outside world. I knew they would be blown away so I prepared myself for the fanfare as I announced the band name, "Honky Con Carne!"

Sophie tripped over it. "Honky con what?"

"Honky Con Carne."

Tom responded flatly, "Is that Spanish or English?"

"It's like, I don't know. It's a *name*. A band name."

"But what does it mean?"

Sophie piled on, "Yeah, what does it mean?"

"What do you all mean what does it mean? Where is your sense of poetry? Where is your lyricism?"

What was *wrong* with them? It isn't supposed to *mean* anything precisely. You can't pick apart a band name like a scientist plucking the wings off a bug under a microscope. Besides, it's so obvious and clear what it means.

HONKY CON CARNE...it is spice and heat and passion and bravado. It means you should dream big and have soul and sing to the rafters. It's a comedy and a drama all rolled up together. It means you should storm the stage and always give an encore. It's an attitude, a feeling, a way of being. It's the ultimate Tex-Mex superhero, a champion of the underdog spirit. Honky Con Carne isn't just a band name, it's a battle cry.

We didn't get any further at the table that night. A few weeks later Sophie and I were at a dinner with extended family, celebrating Mother's Day Weekend in Santa Fe, New Mexico. Cousins from various branches of the family tree were catching up on life's activities, so I decided to throw my news in the ring.

"I'm starting a band."

My mother half rolled her eyes while Sophie seemed in shock. "I thought this idea was dead!"

"Oh no, it's alive, very much alive."

She pressed further with the entire dinner party watching our exchange, "So this is happening?"

"Oh, it's happening."

I was excited to share the name with this fresh audience, sensing they would be more imaginative and romantic. "The name of the band is going to be Honky Con Carne."

Blank faces stared back at me until my Aunt Cita inquired, "Doesn't that just mean honky with meat?"

I suppose, in its most literal translation, if you absolutely must boil it down...then yes. *It just means honky with meat.*

After a few more months of pushing water uphill, ultimately I conceded and took my plans for a band off the table. Austin will hardly miss the would-be-sensation Honky Con Carne. I suppose there is more than enough meaty music to sink your teeth into here in Austin.

Much of it can be found at one of my all-time favorite music venues, The Continental Club. The Continental Club opened its doors in 1957 and continues to serve as the heartbeat for my South Congress neighborhood. As my husband is keen to point out, "Every trendy graphic designer who strives for a retro look these days, whether they know it or not, is really just trying to achieve the look of The Continental Club." This dark, small, and often sweaty venue offers a more hotrod, rockabilly feel than the country and western tone of the Broken Spoke. But that doesn't mean you won't see a straight up honky-tonk band on the marquee mixed-in with the Americana, rock, blues, soul, and funk acts. Just recently *Rolling Stone* published a piece titled "The Best Clubs in America" and ranked The Continental Club number nine on their list.

And I can walk there from my house.

Not long ago Tom and I went to the Continental Club to see local husband-and-wife artists Bruce Robison and Kelly Willis perform. It was the CD Release Party for their *Cheater's Game* album and at the risk of sounding a bit haughty, I must brag because we were "on the list". That's right, guests of Dame Kelly Willis, herself.

Somewhat incredulously, I had wheedled my way into Kelly's email inbox and managed to secure an interview with her shortly before their album was released. After much exchange about school drop off times and our respective kiddo schedules we set a date and met mid-morning at a coffee shop. We talked about the Austin music community versus the Nashville scene. She shared how much she respects the studio musicians in Nashville, who are really the keepers of the culture and music history. She also shared how the Austin industry manages to keep the fun in making music. We talked about how hard it was as a working mom, touring and juggling four kids. I heard about how much better the *Opry* dressing rooms are now that they have been redone since Nashville's devastating 2010 flood. They have infused a sense of history that better fits the gravitas of being backstage at the *Grand Ole Opry*. We talked about the spirit of honky-tonk and how it transcends a physical place or venue. She described the homesick and displaced Texans in New York City who come out to her shows and dance until the wee hours as they are transported with a musical taste of home. Kelly herself marveled, "No one dances in a club like that in New York. But for that one night, people are reveling in the spirit. The place will be a honky-tonk for one night."

I found Kelly Willis to be utterly graceful, cool, funny, confident, and humble. The humble part is perhaps the most impressive given her multi-decade career that has garnered respect and loyalty from legions of fans and fellow musicians alike. She and her musician husband, Bruce Robison, have been married since 1996, have four kids, and are considered royalty on the Texas musical landscape. But she is quick to point out they have consciously avoided making an album together all these years. They wanted to keep their artistic identities separate. Bruce grew up on Texas outlaw songwriters like Willie and Waylon and Guy Clark and Jerry Jeff Walker. He veered toward rock and away from the "kicker" scene for a spell before cycling back to Texas country himself. Kelly came at music from an aggressive rockabilly point of view. Her influences were Wanda Jackson and Janis Martin, who was once positioned to be "the female Elvis Presley". Despite keeping their careers on separate tracks, seventeen years of marriage and co-parenting has molded both of their sounds, bringing them toward each other in a unique way.

And just this year, in 2013, they decided the time was finally right to release an album together. On *Cheater's Game* Bruce takes the lead on some songs, Kelly does on others, but all of the tracks hang really well together and represent their respective strengths. "I knew we were creating something really special with this one."

The interview was so enjoyable it wasn't until the very end that it hit me. *Her voice.* Kelly Willis was sitting across the table from me talking breezily with the very same voice I had been listening to since I was a sophomore in college. The same voice that had been singing to me via cassette tape, CD, and iPod all these twenty-plus years.

And that voice was as powerful as ever at The Continental Club for the CD Release Party. The crowd devoured every new song from the album and went crazy for the old favorites. The night showcased Bruce's genius as a songwriter and Kelly's God-given talent as a singer. And the two together...sheer magic.

Kelly and Bruce are long time buddies with singer-songwriter Monte Warden as well as the hardest working drummer in the music business, Tom Lewis. I swear I think Tom Lewis keeps the beat for every honky-band in town. You can find him regularly at both The Spoke and the Continental Club. He's hard to miss as he is a towering figure. I don't know how tall he is, but he is tall. He has a dark, mysterious quality to his face, which is immediately undercut once you meet him as he is about the most affable guy on the planet. At any rate, Monte Warden and Tom Lewis have secured a residency at The Continental Club. "Residency" is a music business term that I first learned via The Continental Club. It's not to be confused with a doctor's residency, despite the fact that it, too, means you spend a great deal of time there, working late into the night with little sleep. But a residency at The Continental Club simply means you have booked a coveted weekly gig. Junior Brown used to be the Sunday night residency years ago before he rose to national fame. Dale Watson currently holds the Monday night slot. Tom Lewis is drummer for a band called Heybale, which has held the Sunday night billing for several years now. The swing dancers and the two-steppers come out in full force to sweat and twirl to Heybale, which is fronted by Redd Volkaert, arguably the best Telecaster player in the world. (A Telecaster is a style of electric guitar made by Fender.) This burly Canadian journeyed from British Columbia to Austin via California and Nashville, and has played guitar for just about everyone who is anyone, including Charley Pride, Wanda Jackson, Dolly Parton, Asleep at the Wheel, Ray Price, Johnny Paycheck, Jim Lauderdale, and Rose Maddox. But he is probably best known for touring with Merle Haggard and blowing people's minds on a weekly basis at The Continental Club with his virtuoso skills on the Telecaster. Redd Volkaert *is* The Telecaster Master.

But Red Volkaert isn't Tom Lewis' only band mate because Heybale isn't Tom Lewis' only band. In the 1980s Lewis put together a four-person honky-tonk band called The Wagoneers with Monte Warden as lead singer. The Wags, as they are affectionately called, built a passionate base with music lovers, musicians and industry insiders. Esteemed music journalist Chet Flippo once proclaimed that The Wagoneers were "the Greatest Honky-Tonk band that ever was." Austin music writer Margaret Moser defined them as "The Fathers of Alt-Country and Americana."

The Wagoneers burned bright and faded fast. They played the very first South by Southwest music festival in 1987. They released two critically acclaimed albums in just two years and produced music videos that were considered innovative in their quality. But for reasons that remain a mystery to me, they disbanded in 1989 after just three years.

Austin native Monte Warden supported himself and his two boys by focusing on his solo and songwriting career, and he did well. He wrote songs for power performers such as Kelly Willis, Bruce Robison, Patty Loveless, George Jones, and George Strait, including Strait's runaway hit song, "Desperately". But just when one might relegate this rockabilly cowboy poet to a lone career as a solo artist and behind-the-scenes bard, fate stepped in with a different plan.

While working on a different story, writer Margaret Moser began to notice how many established musicians still cited The Wagoneers as a significant influence…two decades after the band's mere three-year run. Jeff Tweedy of Wilco, Raúl Malo of The Mavericks, and Ryan Adams of Whiskeytown all point to Monte Warden and The Wags for music inspiration and paving a way for their respective Americana success. Moser was inspired as well and became a catalyst for a Wagoneer Reunion at the 2011 South by Southwest music festival.

The guys reconvened in Monte's living room, the first time they were all together in one place since they had broken up twenty-two years earlier. Some had stayed in music. One guy had been driving an Austin city bus. Monte knew it would require a few months of practice to perform at the reunion show. "We couldn't just be as good as we were, we had to be as good as they remembered us."

They knocked it out of the park, the reunion show was dynamite, and by the end of the evening there was talk of cutting a new album. Before long, The Wagoneers landed their Sunday evening residency at the Continental Club, which is where I first saw them perform. I can honestly say I have never seen anything quite like it. It is full tilt, high-octane showmanship set to poetic lyrics and solid rockin' retro style honky-tonk. Monte Warden does not stop shucking and jiving and wiggling and shaking *the entire time*! It's the only band I know that can be considered Cardio Honky Tonk.

The first time I met Monte Warden it was abundantly clear right out of the gate that he is the most cerebral singer-songwriter around. Shortly after the-nice-to-meet-you, he grabbed my notebook and started sketching out code for the human genome. I think? I nodded and pretended to recognize what he was writing while he pointed out how it was the exact same pattern as the seven musical notes in a major scale, A B C D E F G.

"See? Music is hardwired in you, in everyone."

I didn't fully grasp the human code, or the musical scale, or chord, or whatever he was sketching in plain detail, but I had a pretty firm handle on what a fascinating conversation this was shaping up to be. We talked fast and furiously about honky-tonk, life, marriage, and exercise. He runs seven miles a day, which is no doubt how he stays in such great condition to perform the physical shows that he does. He pokes a little fun at Nashville, "For the last twenty-eight years they keep saying 'Oh man, Nashville is starting to get cool.' Well they sure aren't rushing into it!" That said, he is quick to denounce Texans' second favorite sport behind football: Nash-bashing. Monte defends Music City, "I love Nashville. People pick on it, but nine out of ten of everyone's favorite honky-tonk albums were all recorded in Nashville." He admits there is a dearth of creativity in the current country industry and jokes, "Everyone is waiting for the next George Strait to save it like he did in the '80s. They sure are taking their sweet time."

Monte Warden is not a fan of the game show mentality, generating the next country star from reality television competitions. "You have to be a grown-up to do honky-tonk well. These people aren't *growing* into being stars."

Monte Warden definitely grew up in this business organically. As an Austin teen he won his earliest songwriting award with his band called Whoa Trigger! At Austin High he was the "weird kid who was really into Buddy Holly." In his early twenties he was balancing his music career with his first marriage and becoming a father to two young sons. The Wagoneers came and went in the '80s, and then he tackled both the Nashville and the Texas music scenes with a solo career. As much as he is a rare and passionate defender of Nashville, he is just as zealous about Texas and its legacy in music.

"Ernest Tubb, Hank Thompson, Buddy Holly, Waylon Jennings, Janis Joplin, Stevie Ray Vaughn, Willie Nelson…they are all very different. The fact that they are unique is the only thing they have in common. Why does Texas produce so many unique artists?"

Okay, I'll bite. "Why?" I asked.

"That big open sky makes you think you can do anything! How else do you explain Buddy Holly with his bad teeth becoming the next Elvis but with better songs? That sky makes you say, '*Well…I can do that!*'"

I asked him about his one-of-a-kind showmanship, and his reply was as insightful as the rest of his comments. "When you play honky-tonks, your audience is always doing something else. Drinking, dancing, flirting. You have to use vocal tricks and energy to keep their ears interested. You can't talk too much between songs. It's like the Chitlin' Blues circuit of the 1960s, you have to play, play, play. Very similar. Besides, country music is just white man blues."

He shared some other behind the scenes anecdotes, like the two times he teared up upon meeting music idols. He choked up on George Jones' bus when he met The Possum. And again when he met Phil Everly of The Everly Brothers. Mr. Everly politely comforted Monte and said, "It's okay, John Lennon did the same thing."

Monte met his second wife, Brandi, in Nashville at a birthday party for songwriter Harlan Howard. Brandi worked for Decca Records, while Monte, a newly divorced father of two, was in town for meetings. Their romance lit fire in a flash.

Brandi's father wrote songs for the likes of Johnny Paycheck, which is just a narrow sample of how immersed her family has been in the music industry in Tennessee. When she met Monte in 1997, she had not heard of the then-defunct Wagoneers, but her father had. He knew them for their reputation of having top quality music videos. Brandi read all the back press about the Wags and couldn't believe it. "Lord, Monte, you boys have done everything but happen."

Given Brandi's job, family, and ties to the Nashville music industry, when I first met her I had to ask, "Why did y'all settle in Austin instead of Nashville?"

"Monte's boys. Their life was here in Austin."

I almost felt silly for asking since I could relate, "My husband, Tom, was in the same boat. He moved here because of my daughter, Sophie."

Brandi talked about their blended family lovingly. "Suddenly I was surrounded by boys. And then Monte and I had another son."

Something told me if anyone could handle all those guys it was Brandi Warden. Brandi runs her own music publishing business, manages The Wagoneers, and even co-wrote some of the songs for their upcoming album.

She is a girl's girlfriend and makes me laugh at every turn. Brandi is a live wire, has a hilarious sense of humor, and is one of the cleverest people I have ever come across. Somehow amidst all the talking we managed to uncover yet another gem. She knew about the secret society in Austin that hands out raccoon penises to its members. The group that Willie Nelson is in? The group I had daydreamed of visiting? Well, she knew all about it because *Monte is a member*! You could have knocked me over with a feather. I shared my friend Jeff's Willie-Waylon raccoon penis story and told her how Jeff had given me my very Abraham that lived safely in my jewelry box.

Next thing you know, Monte and Brandi invited me to the annual Coon Dick party on some ranch land just outside of Austin. Sophie and I arrived with a salad to contribute to the "side dish potluck" and enjoyed Salt Lick barbecue and good live Texas music. It was easy to spot members – they were the ones walking around with raccoon penises hanging around their necks on leather lanyards. And while famed member Willie Nelson did not show up, I was highly entertained to see Gary P. Nunn, James Hand, and Kevin Fowler all play in such a breezy, intimate setting.

Unreal. I had been to a Coon Dick party. Sometimes life orbits around and completes a full circle…just as my friend Jeff's raccoon penis bone did.

A Wagoneer reunion wasn't the only 2011 development that would alter the Austin music landscape for the better. In December 2011, The White Horse Honky Tonk opened on the east side of town. New bars pop up in this town in the blink of an eye, but every so often things come together in a way that creates more than just another music venue, more than a new neighborhood watering hole. The White Horse has become the next scene. It represents an era for a group of musicians and bartenders and music fans and revelers. Someday they will reminisce about "back in the day" before progress and change and overcrowding. And they will belly laugh about the good times and roll their eyes at the near misses and bond with total strangers who were all there at that magical point in time. At The White Horse.

When I met with its young proprietor, Denis O'Donnell, I likened it to the magic of the Armadillo World Headquarters. Graciously and deferentially he wouldn't accept comparison to such lore. But I'm not the only one who has made the connection. A musician who plays there regularly said the exact same thing. "The White Horse is mixing up the crowds just like the Armadillo did. Except instead of hippies and rednecks it's hipsters and the BMX crowd."

Denis O'Donnell, a musician himself, dreamt of opening a music venue at this location for quite some time. It was a dicey Norteño bar before O'Donnell got his hands on it – which took some doing. Over the course of four years, he gained and lost funding multiple times, including one angel investor who expected O'Donnell to walk the funding across the border taped to his body in the form of cash. Ultimately a longtime friend and mentor decided to jump in and partner with Denis to make it happen. And The White Horse Honky Tonk was born. The musical lineup is as varied as the patrons. Old school honky-tonk, conjunto, rockabilly, Americana, outlaw style country, and rock and roll. Denis offers music every night of the week without a cover, strives to have the friendliest, fastest barkeeps in town, and wants everybody drinking and dancing. He can't offer bands a cut of the door since he doesn't charge cover, so he books a number of up-and-coming bands that are hungry for gigs and can keep the late night audiences entertained. Thus, O'Donnell is indirectly nurturing and shaping a whole new batch of musicians that are starting to gel as a part of this White Horse scene. Mike and The Moonpies, the Austin Steamers, and a western swing style jazz trio called The Biscuit Grabbers are just a few examples.

But honestly, people are flocking to the east side joint without checking the marquee because just as the Armadillo World Headquarters once did, The White Horse just has *it*.

A lot has changed since the days when Willie was rocking the Armadillo, but that doesn't mean Willie doesn't still rock in Austin. We went to see him recently on New Year's Eve at the Moody Theater, a new 2700-seat state-of-the-art production facility and full-time live music venue. Every seat is a good seat and the acoustics are off the charts. The *Austin City Limits* television show has even moved its set to this new auditorium. The Moody is downtown, right on Willie Nelson Boulevard. In front of the building is a relatively new statue of The Red Headed Stranger. Willie himself was there when the statue was dedicated on April 20th, 2012 at 4:20pm.

We recruited two other couples, our dear friends Lezlie and John Glade and Shelley Schmoker and Mike Ditson, to join us at the December 31st, 2012 Willie concert at The Moody. In order to make show time we scheduled dinner at our house so early that we were going to be beating all the blue hairs of the world to their buffet suppers. At some point during the day John learned that there were at least half a dozen opening acts and Willie wouldn't be taking the stage until midnight.

"Midnight!" Tom balked. "Are you kidding me?"

"I don't want to hear it. The man is seventy-nine years old and he is going on at midnight. You can do this."

"Yeah, but he's kicked back sleeping all day at his ranch, he's probably not getting on his bus to come into Austin until nine. I'm working all day!"

"Willie goes on at midnight. We're pushing dinner back. Suck it up, you'll live!"

Our group of six feasted and imbibed and laughed like our dining room table *was* the party for the night. But then suddenly we remembered the concert, tore away from the table with a vengeance and raced to The Moody, grateful we lived so close to downtown. We landed in our seats at 11:40 among a sea of eager Willie fans who had clearly been drinking their way through the six or so opening acts. The vibe was a cross between familial and borderline insane, but definitely electric. At nearly midnight, a bearded guy wearing a toga and Birkenstocks eased down from the ceiling. Apparently he was Father Time? A local radio announcer donned in a tuxedo welcomed Baby New Year onto the stage. Baby New Year was an adult African American little person, tattooed all over, and wearing nothing but a diaper and white tube socks. He danced to rap music as decorative smoke filled the room, strobe lights swirled around, and the crowd began to countdown — albeit slightly off rhythm from the large digital clock showing the official time.

Keep Austin weird...check.

As 2013 drew its first, or maybe second breath based on how you were counting, balloons dropped from above and Willie Nelson took the stage. Someone rolled out a birthday cake and Willie led off by having us sing "Happy Birthday" to his sister Bobbie before he kicked off the concert with "Whiskey River". The crowd went nuts.

And everyone stayed nuts throughout the entire two-hour show. Shelley, Tom, and I marveled at how wild things felt. It was like we'd been transported back to the '70s and the Armadillo World Headquarters with Willie and friends throwing a party on stage, jamming for hours. Ray Benson from Asleep at the Wheel was playing guitar with The Family band all night. Billy Gibbons from ZZ Top joined in at one point, and he and Willie picked the blues feverishly. They worked the crowd into a pitch with a guitar call-and-response style performance of "Milk Cow Blues". Willie himself revved up the tone, kicking balloons and whooping to the crowd and singing as powerfully as I have ever heard him. At one point I felt like we might all just combust in sheer excitement and energy. I think it was the greatest show I have ever seen.

As it was time to wrap things up, Willie shouted out to us, "How 'bout we do some for old Hank?" Willie and The Family played three or four Hank Williams songs, encouraging the audience to sing along. And did we ever. We sang with Willie, we sang with Hank. Some drunks near us were escorted out for fighting, but we all kept going with the Red Headed Stranger. By the last song the crowd was on their feet, hands in the air, singing Hank's "I Saw the Light" from the heart. Willie had taken the place from honky-tonk to revival in the blink of an eye.

Once home, I couldn't stop thinking about the show. What a way to start a new year! I dwelled on the Hank Williams set that closed the concert and smiled at Willie's generosity, his willingness to end the evening with someone else's music. Although technically speaking, it wasn't evening at all, but closer to two in the morning when it wrapped up. And that's when it hit me. It was January 1, 2013. Sixty years to the day since Hank Williams died. And I had marked it by singing with Willie Nelson.

Singing with Willie Nelson. I sang with Willie Nelson...in Austin.

It had actually happened. I sang with Willie. Not quite like I'd fantasized during all those hours on the treadmill since we didn't exactly share a stage, and technically I was just part of the audience. But we were part of one voice at The Moody at a wild show that rivaled my unabashed dreams of the Armadillo days. Maybe in a sense this was my Honky Con Carne moment. Maybe Honky Con Carne was never supposed to be the name of a band. Maybe it's less of a battle cry and more of a whisper. Maybe Honky Con Carne is that little tap on your shoulder, subtly reminding you to open your eyes and realize that your dreams *did* come true. They might be in a different package, and maybe they don't look precisely the way you'd pictured them. Maybe they arrived on a different timeline and in a different way. But is it possible they came true? Maybe Honky Con Carne is the quiet voice reminding you to show gratitude for the versions of your dreams that have already come to life.

Honky Con Carne, Austin. Honky Con Carne.

CHAPTER 25 SOUNDTRACK:

Putting It Down – Mike and the Moonpies

(MIKE HARMEIER)

Backsliding Blues – Brennen Leigh
(BRENNEN LEIGH)

Prayer for the Lonely – The Departed

(SETH JAMES)

Waterfall – Kelly Willis and Bruce Robison

(BRUCE ROBISON)

Tell Me Somethin' I Don't Know – The Wagoneers

(MONTE WARDEN, BRANDI WARDEN)

The Broken Spoke on South Lamar Boulevard, Austin TX

Dale Watson and Christine at The Broken
Spoke, Austin TX, January 2011

Junior Brown rockin' the guit–steel at the Continental Club on South Congress, Austin TX
Photo credit and courtesy: Paul Schuster, www.schusterphoto.com

Behind the bar at the Continental Club on South Congress, Austin TX

The White Horse Honky Tonk, on the East Side, Austin TX

The stage at the The White Horse Honky Tonk, on the East Side, Austin TX

It's Called a Backbeat Bitches!

A thousand years ago I was in college whiling away the hours doing a heap of nothing, as my friends and I were quite often known to do. These are undoubtedly some of my fondest memories from my four years at Chapel Hill. Music was typically rolling in the background, serving as the unofficial soundtrack for these aimless afternoons. Some of my pledge sisters and I were rocking out to a song that escapes my memory when one of my best friends shocked me. Right in the middle of it she turned to me and said, "You know, for someone who's kinda musical you are always clapping at the wrong time. Why are you clapping on the opposite beat?"

Peals of laughter erupted.

I was gobsmacked. Off and on throughout the years I've pondered her benign jab. I wished I had lashed back with a razor sharp wit, with a retort that would have swayed public opinion back my way and reclaimed the laughter. But she won that round of banter. No matter how many times I replay the comment in my mind, the end result is the same. I was rendered mute. I didn't know enough about music to craft a substantive, technical response.

Was I really clapping at the wrong time? Is there a right time and a wrong time? Do people secretly think I am a musical mutant? Do I still embarrass myself with such clapping displays?

Recently the term "backbeat" floated across my computer and onto my radar screen. Having zero knowledge of music theory, I wasn't precisely sure what the term meant, although I had a vague notion. The only thing I knew about beats in music I had learned in dancehalls. When dancing a two-step I could mentally count, "One-and-two, one-and-two." When dancing a waltz, I had it down, "One-two-three, one-two-three." Mine was poor man's music theory.

So I let it simmer. And then one lazy day when my house was quiet, I was inexplicably compelled to search for a more exact definition of the musical term. I didn't have to dig much farther than Wikipedia to uncover more than I'd bargained for about beats and measures and rhythm and syncopation.

For example, in a song with a four-count rhythm the measures have a 1-2-3-4 pulse pattern that repeats itself throughout the song. However, this does not apply to a waltz which employs a 3/4 rhythm and the beats go ONE-two-three, ONE-two-three.

But back to the four-count rhythm, which is the foundation for many honky-tonk songs. Within the four-beat measures, the downbeat is the very first beat and receives the most emphasis. It's called a downbeat because a conductor pushes his baton down on the downbeat. ONE-two-three-four, ONE-two-three-four. The "on" beats are the first and third beats. The first beat (i.e., the downbeat) receives the most punch while the third beat receives the second most punch. The second and fourth beats are the "off" beats.

In music, as in life, it is what happens with the offbeat that interests me most.

As it turns out, when you infuse an offbeat with unexpected syncopation, pulse, or energy, it is then called a backbeat. In a 4/4 rhythm the backbeats are the two and the four. One-*TWO*-Three-*FOUR*.

Now we are cooking with gas.

Early gospel music had a firm grip on the backbeat concept with its hand clapping and tambourines accentuating the backbeat rhythm. Dixieland jazz and the big band sounds of Benny Goodman and Glenn

Miller began to play with a pronounced backbeat. In the 1940s The Delmore Brothers, the *Opry* stars from Alabama, introduced a boogie backbeat to hillbilly music. The snare drum became the keeper of the 2/4 backbeat rhythm. Chuck Berry and The Beatles are often credited with defining a backbeat sound in rock and roll. And Hank Williams incorporated a very prominent backbeat which became a defining characteristic in traditional honky-tonk music.

Shortly after I acquired this academic knowledge of beats and rhythms I realized I had some experts in my own backyard who could shed more light on the topic. Literally, they were out in my yard. Matt Thomas and Huck Johnson are musicians who comprise two-thirds of a western jazz swing trio called The Biscuit Grabbers. But they are also trained arborists and had been working feverishly all day to try to resuscitate our scrappy yard. Toward the end of the day, as they were chucking piles of dead limbs and leaves into the back of their truck, I decided to turn them into my own personal focus group. "Hey, so how do y'all define the term 'backbeat'?"

Matt was quick and literal, "It's on the two and the four."

Huck was slightly more descriptive, "Man, I hate it when people start clapping along at our shows. We don't have a drummer to hold the backbeat and people always start on the downbeat. Then they speed up. But people who are in-the-know always clap on the backbeat."

Hell yeah! I wish I could have transported myself back to that day in college with Matt and Huck as my third-party experts. Because as it turns out, I always clap on the two and the four. Aside from the fact that I was standing barefoot on the curb in front of my house, well into my mid-forties, with no one around but a confused Matt and Huck to witness my joy, the vindication tasted just as sweet as I'd hoped. After more than two decades I finally had my witty retort.

It's called a backbeat bitches!

It is never too late for a comeback.

Suddenly behaving as if I belonged, I began reading musicians' online discussion boards and devouring any and all threads that talked about backbeats. My newfound musical prowess was bolstered by cheeky comments I found from musicians, such as, "Only squares clap on the one and the three beats. Clapping on the one-three beat is really only acceptable at an umpa-umpa polka dance." Or, "Go into any African American church that is rocking gospel music and they are all clapping on the backbeat." And then of course there was my personal favorite, "The backbeat is where the soul lives."

It's called a backbeat bitches!

It was my new mantra. My call to arms. My answer to any obstacle, challenge, or naysayer. I announced to Tom one evening over a cold Lone Star beer, "I think I am going to make t-shirts that say, 'IT'S CALLED A BACKBEAT BITCHES!' and sell them. I think they could be big."

"Yeah...I don't really get it."

"It's attitude. It's cool. It's not about pride or being vengeful or anything like that. It's about having a sense of humor and having soul and embracing the unpredictable gems life has to offer if you only look for them."

"I'm not sure all of that is going to come across."

I wasn't the least bit deterred. In the vein of this newly charged spirit (nay, bravado) I allowed an old idea to creep back in. I earnestly thought the dream was long dead, but as it turns out, it was only playing possum. Tom was right, t-shirts weren't the end game. And neither was Honky Con Carne. I wasn't meant to sing in a band. But what about one song? What about singing one good honky-tonk song? Into a microphone in front of a live audience at a real Austin dive bar.

It's called a backbeat bitches!

Gusto without logistics is simply not enough. My first challenge was to determine where and how I was going to perform said honky-tonk song. I started scouring open mic nights all around Austin and Central Texas. As it turns out, my favorite South Austin dive, The Horseshoe Lounge, just started hosting open mic night on Thursdays. It seemed I had my venue until I presented my idea to Tom.

"Christine, you don't play guitar. There's no music at these open mic nights, everyone plays an instrument while they sing."

Damn. He was right. I began to follow the Horseshoe Lounge open mic night feed on social media, and all of the Friday morning posts supported Tom's point. Every entrant could play guitar.

I was lamenting my limited options one day at the spa while Ashley was working on my eyelash extensions.

"You have to do this!" she cheered. "I love to sing and it is so much fun to sing in public. Why not try karaoke? I do it all the time."

"You do? Where?"

"At Ego's."

Ego's is a divine dive bar located in the bottom of a parking deck tucked behind a Chevron station. The chairs are all beat up Herman Miller office chairs on wheels. I once heard it described as Austin's answer to The Regal Beagle. (Only friends of a certain age who watched *Three's Company* as much as I did will get that reference. Others will have to refer to Google.) I love Ego's.

"Yeah, but how do I know the karaoke machine will have my song on it? I don't think they will have my old honky-tonk music available to sing."

I had no idea Ashley was such a karaoke expert. "Oh, you'd be surprised. It's all digital now, they have everything. Go online and search the karaoke system they use at Ego's. They have tens of thousands of songs. Just show up early enough to get your place in line so you make sure you get to go that night. It fills up pretty fast."

Fantastic! The dream was alive. Karaoke at Ego's...who would have guessed? I raced home and peered through my beautiful long lashes at the computer screen for hours. Ashley was right, there was an endless list of songs covering limitless genres. I found several traditional honky-tonk tunes that I like to sing in the shower. I was honing in. Just as Ashley had counseled me, I went to Spotify and YouTube to find the karaoke versions of my songs so I could practice with the same background music they would have at the bar.

I practiced all afternoon. Over dinner I announced my exciting news to Tom and Sophie, "Ashley at Betty Lash suggested I sing a song on karaoke night at Ego's."

Tom's reaction was immediate and brutally honest, "That is lame."

"Huh?" was about all I could choke out. "But—"

"It's too lame. I mean I can do karaoke. Anybody can do karaoke. That's not what you're trying to accomplish here."

Sophie shot Tom a look which indicated that once again, she was siding with him.

I was crushed. This dream was getting whittled down to little more than a vapor. I started at forming my own band, then singing one song at an open mic. And then, after I had dropped my standards as low as karaoke – even that plebian scheme was being snuffed out.

A few days later I was still pouting. Tom sensed my sense of defeat and clarified his position. "I just think you are trying to do one good song and karaoke isn't the right format for this dream of yours. You deserve better, you can do better. You are about live music. That's where your heart and soul is."

"Okay, okay. You're right. So, well…" I was thinking on my feet. My sense of perseverance returned. "Maybe I could put an ad on Craigslist to see if someone could play guitar for me at an open mic night? That's what I could do!"

Sophie rolled her eyes. Tom almost swerved the car off the road, "Are you out of your mind? You're not soliciting a guitar player on Craigslist!"

And with that, it seemed I was back at square one.

A month passed without any new options, and I found myself back at Betty Lash fretting to Ashley. As usual, her upbeat outlook was undeterred. "Why don't you ask Tex Smith to do it? Tex would *totally* play guitar for you. For one song? He would do it!"

I hemmed and hawed for days on end. Why would Tex, a real singer-songwriter, care to do this? This was so beneath him.

But what the hell, it was worth a try. I mustered the nerve to draft and tweak and then re-tweak a carefully worded email that sounded totally laidback and loosely thrown together. I made my pitch to Tex and proposed he play guitar for me for just one honky-tonk song at The Horseshoe Lounge open mic night.

I was surprised at how quickly he replied. "Sure, why not. But why don't we do it at a more legit honky-tonk than the Horseshoe?"

More legit? Than the Horseshoe? I felt like such a yuppie but was thrilled to know I had found the right guy.

Tex suggested we do it at Sam's Town Point. Fine with me. I emailed a few pre-edited honky-tonk songs that I felt I could sing and asked if he knew how to play any of them. From my list he picked Kitty

Wells' "It Wasn't God Who Made Honky Tonk Angels" since it was pretty straightforward on the guitar, and it was the first hit for a female country solo star. I loved that he knew the song's history.

This was really happening. I felt like Tex was helping me fulfill a "Make a Wish" dream, except I was a perfectly healthy adult, not a child with a terminal illness. But I was riding this train all the way to the microphone.

Unfortunately, our logistics dialog went cold. Tex was no doubt juggling his full time real estate job, music career, and life. But I was desperate to hammer out the details. What I lack in musical talent I make up for in event promotion. But I couldn't promote this if I didn't know when we were doing it. And I knew precisely when I *wanted* to do it.

Tuesday April 28th was fast approaching on the calendar, the very date of Willie Nelson's 80th birthday. First and foremost I believed it should be a national holiday within the state of Texas, but I also felt it would be the most poetic night for me to sing my one and only honky-tonk song. I was nostalgic for the epic Willie Nelson Fourth of July Picnic Annex parties my parents used to host when I was a little girl and wanted to bring the spirit of the tradition full circle.

I tried to play it cool with Tex, but the PTA mom in me wanted it on my calendar in ink. I buddied up with the bartender at Sam's Town Point, Mary, and she was all over my idea to host a party on Willie's 80th. But it really hinged on Tex, so I floated back around to him with a feigned breezy demeanor, desperate not to scare him off.

Finally I was able to nail him down on the date. We would do my song on Willie's big birthday. Tex was going to recruit some other friends to come play, and I was in charge of making a flyer and spreading the word. This was happening. Just one more serious hurdle remained: I had a terrible case of nerves and was crippled by stage fright.

I spent three weeks telling everyone I encountered just how panicked I was, but much to my frustration, people didn't believe me. The dismissals came from different voices and different points of view. "You don't get nervous! You are a great public speaker. You have spoken in front of hundreds of people. You'll do great. You sing all the time."

But I really *was* nervous, like really, really nervous. I don't know exactly when fear gained the upper hand. Maybe it was all these years living in Austin around so much real talent. Maybe it was subconsciously intimidating. Maybe it was the fact that no one has ever really encouraged my singing. My voice lessons in Boston were hardly a rousing endorsement. Every so often Tom smiles and shakes his head, "Baby, I love when you sing in the shower. God forbid anything ever happened to you, I would really miss the sound of you singing in the shower. It's just you." But singing in the shower in the privacy of my own home is a far cry from being on stage with a microphone in front of a room full of faces staring back at you.

I finally convinced two of my closest friends, Shelley Schmoker and Hillary Summers, how scared I was about doing this.

Shelley started to hear me. "What are you really worried about?"

"I am worried I won't hit the notes right. I'm worried I won't sound good. When I sing in front of other people I choke up and my neck gets blotchy and I start to get all breathy."

Hillary had a solution. "I've got it. Propofol. We are going to drug you up on Propofol. It helps regulate your blood pressure so you won't get all nervous and blotchy and breathy."

Shelley was quick to intervene. "Isn't that what killed Michael Jackson?"

I looked back at Hillary in terror.

"Well, maybe it's not called Propofol, but it's something that sounds like that. We'll find the right drug and shoot you up before the show…just like a real star!"

"Okay, alright." I was taking back control. "Thank you all for offering to drug me, but I am going to do this clean. The whole point is to overcome a fear, not zombie my way through it."

Not only was I not dipping into the medicine cabinet, I gave up cheese and red wine. I know. But I had read on the Internet that dairy and alcohol are bad for the singing voice. As is whispering, so I started using sign language around the house with Tom and Sophie. This caused them to shake their heads and leave the room because not only do they not know how to read sign language, I don't actually know how to sign it.

In addition to protecting my moneymaker – I mean, my voice – I threw myself into promoting Willie's birthday. I created a flyer inviting friends and friends of friends to come celebrate "Willie Nelson's Potluck 80th Birthday Party". No one believed me that the *pot*luck idea was accidental, so I finally stopped protesting and let them enjoy the comedy of it. On the day of the party I spent hours making pasta and baking cakes. I ordered an extra cake from our favorite local bakeshop just in case mine were a flop. Then I decorated one cake with Willie braids and another with a detailed icing tribute to Willie's beloved guitar, Trigger. I invested hours in the most minute details and even donated my best eyebrow tweezers to this butter cream masterpiece.

Before I could back out, I found myself walking into Sam's Town Point with a Crock-Pot of pasta, three birthday cakes, and a sheet of typing paper with the lyrics to "It Wasn't God Who Made Honky Tonk Angels" printed on it. I kept telling Tex I had the words licked, but he urged me to have them written down. Everyone agreed that once on stage it's amazing how quickly you forget songs you've known your entire life. So I was prepared.

After hauling food and music equipment into Sam's, Tex and I convened over by a pool table to do our one and only rehearsal.

"I don't even know what key I sing in." I was so nervous to sing in front of Tex I felt my face go flush.

"Don't worry, just sing and we'll figure it out."

I sang the first verse and part of the chorus.

"Okay, good. That's G."

"G? I'm G?" I felt like someone had just told me my blood type.

We tried it one more time and had to slow it down a little. My nerves were in fact making me breathy and I did better slower. At the end of the full song I instinctively sang the final line twice.

Tex was surprised, "Oh, you want to tag the ending?"

"Tag the what?"

"Yeah, that's fine. That sounds good. We'll tag the end."

Did I just learn another actual musician term? Tag the ending. I was on fuego.

Other musicians started to arrive as did regular Sam's Town Point patrons. Slowly but surely a crew of my close friends started to pour in. Everyone assembled food on a long table to the side of the stage. Julia and Deb, who make up the sister act Gladys & Maybelle, took the award for most creative fare on the potluck buffet. They made "Willie Chili" and braided bread sticks. Everyone loved my cakes, which was pleasing, but on this particular night I needed some oohs and aahs about my singing skills, not my icing skills.

The eclectic posse was starting to gel as everyone toasted Willie and sank into the celebration. The music kicked off with Gladys & Maybelle. These beautiful blond sisters are just as genuine as they seem and wowed the crowd in their matching red bandana dresses that they had sewn themselves especially for this very occasion. These Fort Worth girls scoured every craft store in North Texas to get enough red bandanas to make their dresses in honor of Willie. And they did him proud. Typically these girls are playing private parties or busking the streets of the Stockyards in downtown Fort Worth. But on this particular night they held friends and fellow musicians captive as they sang sweet harmonies so vintage they were downright fresh. Tex had asked each musical act to play at least one Willie song, and Gladys & Maybelle did "Good Hearted Woman", which sounded delightful coming from these two lyrical sisters.

Tex had lent his own band, The Haymakers, to the cause, so they backed each act that took the stage. These guys are incredibly talented. They were literally playing along to a set list they were hearing real time. Some songs were country covers they knew, or at least had heard before, but other tunes were originals, and you would never have known they were listening to them for the first time. They stepped in and brought each song to life with guitar, standup bass, drums, and steel guitar.

And I thought I could settle for open mic night. This was a full band. A real show. Butterflies.

Next on the lineup was Josh Buckley, who joined The Haymakers on stage. Typically he fronts his own band, The Gilded Splinters, which leans much more rock. Josh came to Austin from Boston, which is his home town. But he is as much of a Willie-phile as the rest of us, so he was excited to be a part of the show and the party. Josh is thin with dark, full mutton chops. He was sporting a tightly shaped cowboy hat and a t-shirt with the arms cut off, showcasing his tattoos. But I was too busy listening to his dramatic singing voice to decipher his ink. Josh Buckley blew everyone away. My friend, Shelley, was inventing reasons to have a party and hire him to perform. He was *good*. For his Willie song he did "Hello Walls", a nice nod to Willie's songwriting prowess.

When Tex took the stage my stomach did a back flip and my face once again went red hot. I was having so much fun with old friends and new friends and good music that I almost forgot about my crippling fear. Maybe I should have taken Hillary up on the Propofol. She was across the room at the bar. Maybe she had some in her purse? Was it too late to bow out?

In honor of the ultimate Texas troubadour Tex wore a great looking black western shirt with yellow roses embroidered on it. Once again he drew people in with his meandering, lyrical songs that deliver a punch with their poignant ache. I don't remember much about his set because I went into some sort of mental fog (even without the Michael Jackson drug) and I felt as though I was walking under water. Is this what people with chronic fear and panic attacks deal with? Before I could find my way out to the parking lot to hide behind the dumpster, Tex was inviting me up on stage. He asked if I wanted to make a little small talk or tell some jokes while he re-tuned his guitar, but I awkwardly just said, "No." I didn't mean to sound as grumpy as I did, I just didn't have an ounce of banter in me. I was on a mission to sing one damn song.

The intro was familiar. I had the lyrics printed as insurance, but I remembered each and every word. I didn't dare be so bold as to channel Kitty Wells herself. Instead I modestly just tried to channel the version of myself that confidently bellows this song in the shower. She didn't come as quickly as I'd hoped. I missed a few notes in the first verse and in the first chorus. Objectively I would grade myself as a C, maybe C+ with a favorable curve. But the instrumental interlude came just when I needed it. I thought this section of the song would be incredibly awkward while I smiled at the audience dumbly and waited for my turn to sing again. But instead it was unexpectedly calming. I looked around at the musicians on stage with me as they carried the melody of a song I had loved so much for so long. I scanned around to Nick on guitar, Lynette on standup bass, and of course my friend, Tex, nearby on acoustic guitar. I didn't dare crane all the way around in a complete circle and risk missing my next verse, but I could hear Russ on the drums behind me and could see Peter on lap steel guitar out of the corner of my eye. They all sounded *great*, the song was alive. And I was on stage with them. With the band. Confidence seeped in despite my best intentions to remain a basket case.

I came out much stronger on the second verse. I hit every note and was starting to find my stride by the time I arrived at the final chorus. I even found a little room to put some personality into it. My friends were exceedingly generous with their applause and whooping, and I fed off it shamelessly. I mustered the strongest crescendo I could and tagged the ending with gusto.

One good honky-tonk song.

I hugged Tex and thanked all the band members as I sheepishly stepped down from the stage into the waiting arms of my friends. I smiled and deflected their congratulations, but in my heart I was shouting as loud as possible.

It's called a backbeat bitches!

I did it. I made my stage debut in Austin, Texas, Live Music Capital of the World. And I did it with a full band.

Tex continued his set, entertaining everyone with a cover of Willie's "On the Road Again" while I made a beeline to Mary, the bartender. The Voice Protection Program was defunct, no longer required. It was time for a cold Lone Star and Willie birthday cake.

Jason James was the final act of the night, and I was free to kick back and enjoy his set with abundant joy and not a care in the world. Jason James is a young guy making big waves with his traditional honky-tonk. This kid has a voice straight out of 1949. He cites Lefty Frizzell as one of his musical inspirations which is evident in his sound. When I first met Jason he kept calling me ma'am. I urged him to dispel with such aging pleasantries and was delighted when he began referring to me as mama. "Hey, mama, how does this outfit look on me? I dressed myself kinda quick tonight before I came here."

"Looks great, Jason, knock 'em dead."

And did he ever. He sang original songs as well as covers of Hank and George Jones. He surprised me with a Willie song I hadn't heard in ages, "I Gotta Get Drunk".

Tex decided to get everyone who had performed back on stage at the very end of the night to sing together, family style, just like

Willie does. And just as Willie closes his shows with Hank's "I Saw the Light", Tex decided that should be the final song of our birthday show. I couldn't believe it when he asked me to join everyone for the big group encore.

"Are you serious?"

"Of course!"

The bar crowd was thin at this late point in the night, and the diehards that remained didn't seem to care that we flubbed a few of the lyrics. But there I was, squeezing in around a microphone with Gladys & Maybelle, while the guys shared the other mic. The band jammed on while we all belted out "I Saw the Light" and laughed along between verses. As finales go, it was pure magic.

There have been no record deals, no invitations to join a band. But everyone raved about the party, and consensus is we should make Willie's birthday an annual show. People were very kind about my singing, but the truth is I think my real talent shined with the party planning and promotion of the event itself. I may or may not sing again, but I am happy to serve as The Don King of all subsequent Willie birthday bashes. And I will always smile knowing that on his 80th I sang him one good honky-tonk song. For three minutes I chose love over fear – love, and a simple four count rhythm with a prominent backbeat.

It was a night filled with sweet rhymes and high times. A night to pause, a night to be grateful and to take stock. So far I think it's safe to say my life has been an adventure in good music, bad love, true love, and finding Jesus in the jukebox. There have been unexpected trials and blessings at every turn. I imagine that never ends. But the late nights, poor judgment, and smoke-filled barrooms claim less and less real estate when one is trying to navigate midlife with a heart of faith. I aim to live in this honky-tonk world, not of it. And yet the fact remains I am forever tied to the offbeat, the underdog, and the disenfranchised – they are my brethren. And as long as I have a heartbeat I will always look for soul in the backbeat, because in order to see the light sometimes you have to look into the shadows.

CHAPTER 26 SOUNDTRACK:

A Wayfarer's Lament – Tex Smith

(TEX SMITH)

Hot Mouth Momma – Jason James

(JASON JAMES)

Unlucky You – Gladys & Maybelle

(JULIA ROSE, DEB CRAWFORD)

Cut-n-Run – The Gilded Splinters

(JOSH BUCKLEY)

I Saw the Light – Hank Williams

(HANK WILLIAMS)

ACKNOWLEDGMENTS

First and foremost, this book would never have become a reality without the strategic, financial, mental, and editorial support of Bottle Shock Publishing, so thank you, thank you. Just like Willie does with his band, I like keeping it family.

I am indebted to those who carved out precious time and allowed me to interview them. All of these people are an inspiration to me, some have become good friends. Humbly I would like to thank: Bob Wilson, Gretsch Lyles, Kelly Willis, Tiffany Lowe, Robert K. Oermann, Monte Warden, Brandi Warden, Denis O'Donnell, Cody Canada, Tex Smith, Mike Harmeier, and Eddie Wilson.

I would like to express my deep personal gratitude to the music venues, radio DJs, bloggers, and fans who support traditional country. It's a special brand of American music that sometimes feels as if it is slipping through our hands. While I was working on this manuscript, five key figures who impacted this genre and its legacy passed away. God bless: George Jones, Chet Flippo, Charles Carr, Tompall Glaser, and Jody Payne. I do *not* know who is going to fill your shoes. But it makes me even more appreciative for musicians and those in the music community who are stalwart champions of honky-tonk.

To the readers of my blog, *Fly Fish Chick*, thank you for sticking with me on yet another adventure. I've taken you from rivers to jukeboxes and am lucky you hang in there for all the stories in between.

Ashley Pickell. How can I ever thank you? You are a dear, dear soul for connecting me with new friends on this journey and cheering me along every step of the way.

To "The Chicks" who are always ready to hit the road, this time to Georgiana, Alabama. Ashley Jones, Ginna Inge, Robin Minton, Amy Thompson, and Anna Luce, thank you for all the laughter on our Hank Pilgrimage. Where are we going next?

I am always grateful for old friends, especially the ones who journeyed down to Lower Broadway with me so I could finally visit the Ryman Auditorium. It was a day to remember with Carter Dawson, Anne Trainer, Harkness Brown, Margaret Ikard, and Jennifer Frist – only to be topped by our honky-tonk evening at Robert's. All in the name of research...

Big thanks to everyone who made the Willie Nelson Potluck 80th Birthday a red-hot success! Sugar Mama's Bakeshop for the Red Headed Stranger cake; Mary Taskey for letting us have it at Sam's Town Point; Tex Smith for coordinating all the musicians and letting me share the stage with him; Julia Rose, Deb Crawford, Josh Buckley, Jason James, Lynette Wolfe, Nick Young, and The Haymakers for all the good music. I love that friends Blanche and Kin Gill, Lainey and Jeff Fisher, and Mandy Breckbill came without questioning what they were getting themselves into. Thanks to Hillary Summers for wearing her grandmother's gorgeous yellow cowboy boots for the occasion. And Shelley Schmoker...where do I start? You have been my partner in crime for so much good music for so many years, I hope that never ends. We missed Lezlie & John Glade that night, but luckily we were able to ring in the New Year with them at the Willie show. I am grateful to all of you for stepping out, stepping up, and throwing down where good music is concerned.

I asked some close friends to read and critique the first draft of this manuscript. Since these girls truly know where the bones are buried, I am eternally grateful they didn't turn on me considering how many typos I threw in their path. Eternally beholden to Mary Benton, Jocelyn Mangan, Margaret Ikard, Meredith Thomas, Shelley Schmoker, and Amy Thompson.

Not to mention my parents, Nancy and Duck Johnston, who had to read it more than once. Seriously, thank you both for being so damn cool. I love you, and your stellar taste in music is one of the greatest gifts you have passed on to me.

I am blessed to have the most fantastic husband in the world who loves to see live music as much as I do. We have covered some ground, baby! Thanks, Tom, for taking me to see Willie, Loretta, Robert Earl Keen, Guy Clark, and so many others. And thanks for venturing out to the Continental Club with me on so many Sunday nights. I know it's a school night. I'd love you if you didn't go, but I love you even more because you do.

To my daughter Sophie, thank you for wanting me to sing Loretta Lynn to you when you were a baby instead of anything about sheep or curds and whey. I love you *so much* and already see a beautiful fire in you. I can't wait to see the stage where your dreams unfold.

Peace, love, and honky-tonk…xxoo, Christine.

SOURCES

Website sources were accessed during a research period of July 2012 through October 2013.

Chapter 1 Sources:

Nelson, Willie. *Roll Me Up and Smoke Me When I Die*. New York: William Morrow, 2012. Print.

Nelson, Willie and Turk Pipkin. *The Tao of Willie: A Guide to the Happiness in Your Heart*. New York: Gotham Books, 2006. Print.

"Willie Nelson." PBS American Roots Music Oral Histories. *pbs.org*. n.d. Web.

Chapter 2 Sources:

"Badge & Patch History." *fortworthpd.com*. 2013. Web.

Bob Wills Heritage Foundation, Inc. Authorized by the estate of Bob Wills, Inc. *bobwills.com*. 2013. Web.

Editorial. *Daily Gazette* 24 Jan. 1889, Fort Worth, Texas. From the Library of Congress, *Chronicling America*: Historic American Newspapers site. *chroniclingamerica.loc.gov*. n.d. Web.

Texas State Historical Association: The Handbook of Texas Online. *tshaonline.org*. n.d. Web.

"The Panther Story." *pantherfountain.com*. n.d. Web.

Chapter 3 Sources:

Anderson, Jahue E. "SKYLINER BALLROOM," Handbook of Texas Online. *tshaonline.org*. Published by the Texas State Historical Association. n.d. Web.

Arnold, Ann. Ann Arnold speaks to the The River Oaks Area Historical Society about her book *Gamblers & Gangsters: Fort Worth's Jacksboro Highway in the 1940s & 1950s*. *riveroakshistory.com*. 12 Jul. 1999. Web.

Beckham, Wayne. *Tubb, Ernest*. n.d. Photograph. The Panther Hall Photograph Collection, The Wittliff Collections, Texas State University, San Marcos, TX.

Bradford, David K. "The Early History of Guitar in America." The Unstrung History of the American Guitar: The Guitar and 19th Century American Music. *19thcenturyguitar.com*. 2009. Web.

Bradford, David K. "Rural Music: Early Blues and Hillbilly Guitarists." The Unstrung History of the American Guitar: The Guitar and 19th Century American Music. *19thcenturyguitar.com*. 2009. Web.

Collier, Caroline. "The Blues Got The Blues." Fort Worth Weekly Online. *fwweekly.com*. 3 Mar. 2010. Web.

Govenar, Alan. "BLUES," Handbook of Texas Online. *tshaonline.org*. Published by the Texas State Historical Association. n.d. Web.

Govenar, Alan B. *Texas Blues: The Rise of a Contemporary Sound*. College Station: Texas A&M University Press, 2008. Print.

Hendrickson, Matt. "T. Bone Talks." Smoke Music Archive. *smokemusic.tv*. n.d. Web.

Moseley, Willie G. "Stephen Bruton: In the Spirit of Fort Worth Tradition." Vintage Guitar Magazine. *vintageguitar.com*. n.d. Web.

Nelson, Willie. *Roll Me Up and Smoke Me When I Die*. New York: William Morrow, 2012. Print.

Patoski, Joe Nick. Willie Nelson: *An Epic Life*. New York: Little, Brown and Company, 2008. Print.

"Stephen Bruton." *newwestrecords.com*. n.d. Web.

"T-Bone Burnett Remembers Stephen Bruton." *npr.org*. 17 May 2009. Web.

"Tanya Tucker." Wikipedia, the Free Encyclopedia. 9 Sep. 2013. Web. Specific reference in article to Dickerson, James L. "Good Friends Make the Best Records." Nine-O-One Network Magazine, pp. 32-35. Apr. 1988.

Chapter 4 Sources:
Adams, Cecil. "What's the Origin of 'Honky'?" *straightdope.com*. 21 Oct. 1988. Web.
Daniel, Bert. "Native Americans." California Bluegrass Association. *cbaontheweb.org*. 11 Oct. 2009. Web.
Editorial. *The Daily News* 10 Sep. 1894. Tacoma, Washington. From the Library of Congress, *Chronicling America*: Historic American Newspapers site. *chroniclingamerica.loc. gov*. n.d. Web.
Editorial. "THE HONKATONK. Decadence of Oklahoma's Favorite Style of Dramatic Entertainment." *The Sun* 10 Dec. 1899. New York, New York. From the Library of Congress, *Chronicling America*: Historic American Newspapers site. *chroniclingamerica.loc.gov*. n.d. Web.
Editorial. *The Iola Register* 23 Jun. 1893. Iola, Kansas. From the Library of Congress, *Chronicling America*: Historic American Newspapers site. *chroniclingamerica.loc.gov*. n.d. Web.
Edwards, William G. "Ragtime and Honky-Tonk of the 1950s." *perfessorbill.com*. 2004. Web.
Gray, Sally M. *Territory Town: The Ardmore Story*. Oklahoma: n.p., 2006. Print.
"honky." *Dictionary.com Unabridged*. Random House, Inc. 12 Oct. 2013. Web.
"honky." *Online Etymology Dictionary*. Douglas Harper, Historian. 08 Feb. 2013. Web.
Murrah, M. Lee. "The First Honky Tonks." *murrah.com*. 2005. Web.
Quinion, Michael. "Honky-tonk." *worldwidewords.org*. 20 Mar. 2010. Web.
"Wanda Jackson." *history-of-rock.com/wanda_jackson.htm*. n.d. Web.

Chapter 5 Sources:
"Bob Childers." Wikipedia, the Free Encyclopedia. 15 Apr. 2013. Web.
"Down on the Farm in Stillwater." *visitstillwater.org*. n.d. Web.
Erlewine, Stephen Thomas. Online review of "One for the Road." *allmusic.com*. n.d. Web.
Garrity, John. "Slightly Wacky, Totally Waco." *sportsillustrated.cnn.com*. 17 Apr. 2000. Web.
Gray, Sally M. *Territory Town: The Ardmore Story*. Oklahoma: n.p., 2006. Print.
"History." The Red Dirt Relief Fund. *reddirtrelieffund.org*. n.d. Web.
Jurek, Thom. Online review of "Hank Wilson's Back!" *allmusic.com*. n.d. Web.
"Mazola McKerson 1997 Inductee." Oklahoma State University. Library Oklahoma Women's Hall of Fame. *library.okstate.edu*. 2008. Web.
Red Dirt Daughters, LLC. "History of Red Dirt!" *reddirtdaughters.com*. n.d.Web.
"Red Dirt (music)." Wikipedia, the Free Encyclopedia. 21 Aug. 2013. Web.
Red Dirt Rangers Website. *reddirtrangers.com*. 2007-2013. Web.
Rheam, Chase. "Red Dirt Musicians Go Back to the Farm." *Stillwater News Press*. *stwnewspress.com*. 15 Apr. 2011. Web.
"Woody Guthrie." Wikipedia, the Free Encyclopedia. 4 Sep. 2013. Web. Specific reference in article to Dylan, Chronicles, Volume One, p. 244.
Wooley, John. "Jimmy LaFave, Red Dirt's Austin Ambassador." *tulsaworld.com*. 4 Jan. 2002. Web.

Chapter 6 Sources:
The American Heritage® Dictionary of the English Language, Fourth Edition. Houghton Mifflin Company, 2004. Web.
Bob Wills Heritage Foundation, Inc. Authorized by the estate of Bob Wills, Inc. *bobwills.com*. 2013. Web.
"Boogie-woogie." Wikipedia, the Free Encyclopedia. 15 Sep. 2013. Web.

Bradford, David K. "Yodeling Mountaineers: The Alpine Roots of the American Guitar." The Unstrung History of the American Guitar: The Guitar and 19th Century American Music. *19thcenturyguitar.com*. 2009. Web.

Cellania, Miss. "A Brief and Incomplete History of Yodeling." *neatorama.com*. 21 May 2010. Web.

Dodson, Howard. "America's Cultural Roots Traced to Enslaved African Ancestors." *Jubilee: the Emergence of African-American Culture by the Schomburg Center for Research in Black Culture, Excerpt 4*. National Geographic. *news.nationalgeographic.com*. 5 Feb. 2003. Web.

Edwards, William G. "Ragtime and Honky-Tonk of the 1950s." *perfessorbill.com*. 2004. Web.

Evans, Rush. "Bob Wills and His Texas Playboys." *Discoveries* Sep. 1988. *texasplayboys. net*. Web.

Fry, Phillip L. "TUBB, ERNEST DALE." Handbook of Texas Online. *tshaonline.org*. Published by the Texas State Historical Association. n.d. Web.

"Grand Ole Opry & WSM Timeline." *opry.com/pressroom*. n.d. Web.

Lilly, John. "History of Jimmy [sic] Rodgers, Blue Yodeler." *nativeground.com*. n.d. Web.

Mannix, Jeff. "Asleep at the Wheel to Roll Back to Durango." *The Durango Herald* 13 Aug. 2012. *durangoherald.com*. Web.

Neal, Jocelyn R. *The Songs of Jimmie Rodgers: A Legacy in Country Music*. Bloomington, Indiana: Indiana University Press, 2009. Print.

Owen, Blanton. "Alexander 'Eck' Robertson." Old-Time Fiddlers Hall of Fame. *oldtimemusic.com*. n.d. Web.

Patoski, Joe Nick. Willie Nelson: *An Epic Life*. New York: Little, Brown and Company, 2008. Print.

Plantenga, Bart. *Yodel-Ay-Ee-Oooo: The Secret History of Yodeling Around the World*. New York: Routledge, 2004. Web.

Pugh, Ronnie. *Ernest Tubb: The Texas Troubadour*. Durham: Duke University Press, 1996. Print.

"Rhett Miller Honors Johnny Cash with 'Wreck of the Old 97'." *rollingstone.com*. 3 Aug. 2012. Web.

Ruymar, Lorene. "History of Hawaiian Steel Guitar." Hawaiian Steel guitar Association. *hsga.org*. n.d. Web.

"There's a Contest Coming and a Ticket to Nashville: Hillbillies on the Radio." *xroads. virginia.edu*. n.d. Web.

Townsend, Charles R. *San Antonio Rose: The Life and Music of Bob Wills*. The Board of Trustees of the University of Illinois, 1976. Print.

Wolfe, Charles K. and Ted Olson. *The Bristol Sessions: Writings About the Big Bang of Country Music*. Jefferson, North Carolina: McFarland & Company, Inc., Publishers, 2005. Print.

Yates, Michael. "Cecil Sharp in America, Collecting in the Appalachians." Musical Traditions Web Services. *mustrad.org.uk/articles/sharp*. 23 Dec. 1999. Web.

Chapter 7 Sources:

"Dewey Groom & The Longhorn Ballroom." Miscellaneous Accumulation. *paularubia. wordpress.com*. 13 Nov. 2008. Web.

Dickerson, Deke. "Lefty Frizzell 'He Died from Heartbreak'." *muleskinner.blogpost.com*. 11 May 2011. Web.

Liles, Jeff. "Echoes and Reverberations: The Ghosts of the Longhorn Ballroom." *blogs. dallasobserver.com*. 6 Nov. 2008. Web.

Malone, Bill C. *Don't Get Above Your Raisin': Country Music and the Southern Working Class*. Urbana and Chicago: University of Illinois Press, 2002. Print.

Neal, Jocelyn R. *The Songs of Jimmie Rodgers: A Legacy in Country Music*. Bloomington, Indiana: Indiana University Press, 2009. Print.

"Ruby the Nightclub Owner." *mcadams.posc.mu.edu*. n.d. Web.

Texas State Historical Association: The Handbook of Texas Online. *tshaonline.org*. n.d. Web.

"This Week in Texas Music History: Sex Pistols at the Longhorn Ballroom." *kut.org*. 7 Jan. 2013. Web.

Thomas, Dave. "40 Years Ago, Dripping Springs Reunion Helped Create Austin's Musical Identity." *Austin American Statesman* 16 Mar. 2012. *austin360.com*. Web.

Thomas, Dave. "Billy Joe Shaver: Marked for Greatness at the Dripping Springs Reunion." *Austin American Statesman* 16 Mar. 2012. *austin360.com*. Web.

Chapter 8 Sources:
Durenberger, Mark. "Behind the Clear-Channel Matter." *oldradio.com*. 2000. Web.
Erlewine, Stephen Thomas. "Webb Pierce." *allmusic.com*. n.d. Web.
Logan, Horace with Bill Sloan. *Louisiana Hayride Years: Making Music in Country's Golden Age*. New York: St. Martin's Press, 1998. Print.
Louisiana Hayride. n.d. Photograph. LSU-Shreveport Archives and Special Collections, Shreveport, LA.
Morris, Edward. "Kitty Wells and Johnny Wright Sing Their Farewell." *mtv.com*. 1 Jan. 2001. Web.

Chapter 9 Sources:
N/A

Chapter 10 Sources:
Andy-O. "White Animals - Interview on Tomorrow's Television Tonight – NY." Online video clip. *YouTube.com*. YouTube, 7 Jan. 2010. Web.
Duke, Jan. "History of the Ryman Auditorium: Tales & History of the Historic Ryman Auditorium." *about.com*. n.d. Web.
The Grand Ole Opry Site. *opry.com*. n.d. Web.
Moore, Tracy. "Never in Nashville." *nashvillescene.com*. 10 Aug. 2006. Web.
Oermann, Robert K. Personal interview. 1 Feb. 2013.

Chapter 11 Sources:
Robert's Western World. "About." *robertswesternworld.com*. n.d. Web.
Roland, Tom. *rolandnote.com*. 1994-2013. Web.

Chapter 12 Sources:
Fay, Byron. "July Opry Highlights." Fayfare's Opry Blog. *fayfareblogspot.com*. 1 Jul. 2012. Web.
Fay, Byron. "Opry Drops 12 Top Stars—December 6, 1964." Fayfare's Opry Blog. *fayfareblogspot.com*. 5 Dec. 2011. Web.
Jones, Margaret. *Patsy: The Life and Times of Patsy Cline*. New York: HarperCollins, 1994. Print.
Roland, Tom. *rolandnote.com*. 1994-2013. Web.
Ryman Hospitality Properties, Inc. "Backstage Tour." Ryman Auditorium, Nashville, Tennessee. 2 Feb. 2013.
Ryman Hospitality Properties, Inc. "Lula C. Naff." *ryman.com*. n.d. Web.
Wyland, Sarah. "Loretta Lynn Celebrates 50th Anniversary as a Grand Ole Opry Member." *Great American Country. blog.gactv.com*. 26 Sep. 2012. Web.

Chapter 13 Sources:
Allan, Harry. "Tammy Wynette's Wail of Woe." Media Assassin. *harryallan.info*. 19 Mar. 2010. Web.
Bugg, Anita. "Stand By Your Man." The NPR 100 Special Series, NPR Music. *npr.com*. 28 Oct. 2000. Web.
"Censorship & Scandals: Lucy's Pregnancy." *tvacres.com*. n.d. Web.

Cooper, Daniel. "Jean Shepard." Adapted from the Country Music Hall of Fame® Museum's Encyclopedia of Country Music, published by Oxford University Press. *countrymusichalloffame.org*. n.d. Web.

"Dolly Parton." *Biography.* The Biography Channel, Jan. 2013. Originally released with A&E Television Networks, 28 Apr. 2006. Television.

Eby, Margaret. "A Feminist Guide to Country Music" *flavorwire.com*. 19 Jan. 2012. Web.

Fay, Byron. "Kitty Wells." Fayfare's Opry Blog. *fayfareblogspot.com*. 16 Jul. 2012. Web.

Fay, Byron. "Johnnie Wright Passes Away." Fayfare's Opry Blog. *fayfareblogspot.com*. 27 Sep. 2011. Web.

Lynn, Loretta. "Loretta Remembers Kitty Wells." *lorettalynn.com*. n.d. Web.

Moore, Dr. Russell D. "The Cross and The Jukebox: You Ain't Woman Enough (To Take My Man)." Moore to The Point: The Cross and The Jukebox, Russell Moore on Roots, Music, & Religion. *russellmoore.com*. 11 Feb. 2011. Web.

Myers, Marc. "The Love Song of Virginia Pugh." *The Wall Street Journal* 31 Jan. 2013. *online.wsj.com*. Web.

Oermann, Robert K. Personal interview. 1 Feb. 2013.

"Patsy Cline." Wikipedia, the Free Encyclopedia. 13 Sep. 2013. Web.

Wallace, Kelsey. "Adventures in Feministory: Loretta Lynn." *bitchmagazine.org*. 22 Mar. 2010. Web.

Weeks, Tresi. "ARTHUR, CHARLINE," Handbook of Texas Online. *tshaonline.org*. Published by the Texas State Historical Association. n.d. Web.

Wolfe, Allison. "Many Happy Hangovers to You: An Interview with Jean Shepard at The Grand Ole Opry." Ladyfest 2000. *ladyfest.org*. 20 Nov. 1998. Web.

Woodstra, Chris. Online review of "Your Squaw Is on the Warpath." *allmusic.com*. n.d. Web.

Chapter 14 Sources:

Madren, James P. "George Jones Story." *doughbowlmaker.com*. n.d. Web.

Madren, James P. Personal interview. 17 Mar. 2013.

Chapter 15 Sources:

"Down With the CMA (Part2-Corruption in Performances)." *savingcountrymusic.com*. 11 Nov. 2008. Web.

Veith, Gene Edward and Thomas L. Wilmeth. *Honky-Tonk Gospel: The Story of Sin and Salvation in Country Music*. Grand Rapids, Michigan: Baker Books, 2001. Print.

Chapter 16 Sources:

"Cindy Walker." Adapted from the Country Music Hall of Fame® and Museum's Encyclopedia of Country Music, published by Oxford University Press. *countrymusichalloffame.org*. n.d. Web.

Chapter 17 Sources:

Austin City Limits, a production of KLRU-TV, Austin PBS. "History of ACL." *acltv.com*. n.d. Web.

Dalton, Kyle. "Pedernales Country Club: Golf, Willie Nelson-Style." *golftexas.com*. n.d. Web.

Davis, Tom. "August Scholz." *scholzgarten.net*. 1996. Web.

Evans, Rush. "Separate Truth from Fiction in Country Icon Hank Williams' Final Days." *goldminemag.com*. 21 Apr. 2010. Web.

Luckenbach Texas, Inc. "History: A Texas State of Mind." *luckenbachtexas.com*. n.d. Web.

McKinnon, Mark. "Quick Qs." 6 Apr. 2013. E-mail.

Moore, Scotty. "Dessau Hall." *scottymoore.net*. 15 Dec. 2010. Web.

Moore, Scotty. "Skyline Club." *scottymoore.net*. 15 Dec. 2010. Web.

Moser, Margaret. "Groover's Paradise, The Ballad of Soap Creek Saloon." *austinchronicle.com.* 12 Oct. 2001. Web.

Patoski, Joe Nick. Willie Nelson: *An Epic Life.* New York: Little, Brown and Company, 2008. Print.

Reid, Jan. *The Improbable Rise of Redneck Rock.* Austin: The University of Texas Press, 2004. Print.

Threadgill's, Inc. *threadgills.com/history.* n.d. Web.

Wilson, Eddie. Personal interview. 19 Sep. 2013.

Wilson, Eddie. Personal interview. 22 Sep. 2013.

Wilson, Eddie. Personal interview. 4 Oct. 2013.

Chapter 18 Sources:

2 Corinthians 11:25. New International Version. *biblehub.com.* n.d. Web.

Cash, Johnny with Patrick Carr. *CASH: The Autobiography.* New York: HarperSanFrancisco, a Division of HarperCollins Publishers, 1997. Print.

"Dive Bar." *urbandictionary.com.* n.d. Web.

Graham, Billy. *How To Be Born Again.* Waco, TX: Word Publishing, 1977. Print.

Stratton, Christopher. "Johnny Cash Walked the Line." *explorefaith.org.* 2005. Web.

VSPrasad. "What Is the Origin of the Term 'Dive Bar'?" *answerbag.com/q_view/332366.* Answerbag. Web.

Webber, Roxanne. "What's the Origin of the Phrase 'Dive Bar'?" *chow.com.* 14 Oct. 2008. Web.

Willis, Kelly. Personal interview. 22 Jan. 2013.

Chapter 19 Sources:

The Grand Ole Opry Site. "History of the Opry, Will the Circle Be Unbroken?" *opry.com.* n.d. Web.

Jeremiah 12:9. King James Bible "Authorized Version", Cambridge Edition. *kingjamesbibleonline.org.* n.d. Web.

Kingsbury, Paul, *The Grand Ole Opry History of Country Music: 70 Years of the Songs, the Stars and the Stories.* Opryland USA: Villard Books. New York: Random House, 1995. Print.

Luke 23:23. New Living Translation. *biblehub.com.* n.d. Web.

Luke 23: 42–43. New International Version. *biblehub.com.* n.d. Web.

Manheim, James. "About T. Texas Tyler." *cmt.com.* n.d. Web.

Moore, Dr. Russell D. "The Cross and The Jukebox: The Great Speckled Bird." Moore to The Point: The Cross and The Jukebox, Russell Moore on Roots, Music, & Religion. *russellmoore.com.* 25 Feb. 2011. Web.

The Music Barn. "Have I Told You Lately That I Love You – Scott Wiseman." *countrymusictreasures.com/storybehindthesong.* n.d. Web.

Pepper, Johanna. "I'm Thinking Tonight of My Blue Eyes/And Finding the Great Speckled bird/I Didn't Know God Made Honky-Tonk Angels/And Went Back to the Wild Side of Life." World of Music…History, Culture, Life. *johannapepper.blogspot.com.* 7 Feb. 2012. Web.

Chapter 20 Sources:

N/A

Chapter 21 Sources:

Ankeny, Jason. "Don Helms." *allmusic.com.* n.d. Web.

Bull, Debby. *Hillbilly Hollywood: The Origins of Country & Western Style.* New York: Rizzoli International Publications, Inc., 2000. Print.

charlielouvin.net. n.d. Web.

Cooper, Dan. "The Maddox Brother & Rose." *allmusic.com.* n.d. Web.

Dak Alley. "Charlie Louvin, Last Interview." Online video clip. *YouTube.com.* YouTube, 23 Aug. 2012. Web.

Dak Alley. "I see a Bridge Charlie Louvin.mpg." Online video clip. *YouTube.com*. You-Tube, 28 Feb. 2011. Web.

Duke, Jan. "Meet Nashville's Couture Cowboy: Manual." *about.com*. n.d. Web.

Grendel9. "OBIT: Bobbi Nudie [Behind the Stars in Hollywood]." *freerepublic.com*. Free Republic. Web.

Grimes, William. "Don Helms, 81, Who Put the Twang in the Hank Williams Songbook, Is Dead." *nytimes.com*. 16 Aug. 2008. Web.

Louvin, Charlie with Benjamin Whitmer. *Satan Is Real: The Ballad of the Louvin Brothers*. New York: HarperCollins Publishers, 2012. Print.

Marling, Karal Ann. *Graceland: Going Home with Elvis*. Cambridge, MA: Harvard UP, 1996. Print.

Miller, Nikki. "Are You Ready for the Country: Top 10 Sibling Acts in Country Music History." Minneapolis City Pages. *citypages.com*. 14 Jul. 2011. Web.

Rhapsody International. "Brother Acts/Close Harmony." *rhapsody.com*. n.d. Web.

"Steel Guitar Hall of Fame." Steel Guitar Hall of Fame. *squidoo.com*. n.d. Web.

Chapter 22 Sources:

"Alabama Dry Dock and Shipbuilding Company (ADDSCO)." *encyclopediaofalabama. org*. Encyclopedia of Alabama. 19 Feb. 2008. Web.

Chadbourne, Eugene. "Jack Cardwell." *allmusic.com*. n.d. Web.

Davidson, Lisa Enoch. "Jack Cardwell." *findagrave.com*. 2 Jul. 2011. Web.

Drye, Willie. "El Dorado Legend Snared Sir Walter Raleigh." *science.nationalgeographic.com*. n.d. Web.

"Jack Cardwell." *hillbilly-music.com*. n.d. Web.

Johnson, Rheta Grimsley. "Catching a Rare Glimpse of Hank Williams." *The Tuscaloosa News* 18 Oct. 1995. Print.

Light, Alan. "Stars Add New Tunes to Country King's Lyrics." *nytimes.com*. 23 Sep. 2011. Web.

Lyles, Gretsch. Personal interview. 16 Jan. 2013.

Moore, Scotty. "Ladd Stadium." *scottymoore.net*. 5 Dec. 2008. Web.

Poe, Edgar Allan. "Eldorado." *poetryfoundation.org*. n.d. Web.

Travis, Dave. "Curtis Gordon." *rockabillyhall.com*. Rockabilly Hall of Fame. Jan. 1995. Web.

Wilson Jr., Robert W. "On Meeting Bob Dylan (a Brief History and Memoir.)" *rightwingbob.com*. Sean Curnyn's website Right Wing Bob. 29 Jan. 2009. Web.

Wilson Jr., Robert W. Personal interview. 15 Jan. 2013.

Chapter 23 Sources:

1 Corinthians 9:19-23. New International Version (NIV). "Paul's Use of His Freedom." *biblegateway.com*. n.d. Web.

Acts 13:9. King James Bible. *biblehub.com*. n.d. Web.

Catholic Answers Staff. "Why Did God Change Saul's Name to Paul?" *catholic.com*. Catholic Answers Site. n.d. Web.

Curious7777777. "It is unclear." *askville.com*. In reference to question "In the bible, how did Saul get his name changed to Paul?" on the website Askville. n.d. Web.

Escott, Colin, with George Merritt and William MacEwen. *Hank Williams: The Biography*. New York: Little Brown and Company, 2004. Print.

Evans, Rush. "Separate Truth from Fiction in Country Icon Hank Williams' Final Days." *goldminemag.com*. 21 Apr. 2010. Web.

Logan, Horace with Bill Sloan. *Louisiana Hayride Years: Making Music in Country's Golden Age*. New York: St. Martin's Press, 1998. Print.

Luginbill, Robert Dean, Ph.D. "What is the Significance of Biblical Name Changes?" *ichthys.com*. Ichthys Ministry: Bible Study for Spiritual Growth. n.d. Web.

Mathews, Burgin. "Help Me Understand: Hank Williams as Luke the Drifter." *ladymuleskinnerpress.com*. 15 Nov. 2008. Web.

Simmons, Leona. Personal conversation at The Hank Williams Boyhood Home & Museum in Georgiana, Alabama. 5 Dec. 2012.

Turpen, Brian. *Hank Williams "Revealed: The Unreleased Recordings" Disc Three-Luke the Drifter. facebook.com*. 1 Dec. 2009. Web.

Veith, Gene Edward and Thomas L. Wilmeth. *Honky-Tonk Gospel: The Story of Sin and Salvation in Country Music*. Grand Rapids, Michigan: Baker Books, 2001. Print.

Williams, Roger M. *Sing a Sad Song*. Urbana: The University of Illinois Press, 1981. Print.

Chapter 24 Sources:

Lowe, Tiffany. Personal interview. 25 Jan. 2013.

Smith, Tex. Personal interview. 26 Mar. 2013.

Chapter 25 Sources:

Bush, John. "Monte Warden." *allmusic.com*. n.d. Web.

Canada, Cody. Personal interview. 5 Mar. 2013.

Fay, Byron. "The Grand Ole Opry Needs To Fire Blake Shelton." Fayfare's Opry Blog. *fayfareblogspot.com*. 24 Jan. 2013. Web.

GAC Staff. "Blake Shelton Explains His Controversial Comments." *blog.gactv.com*. Great American Country Blog. 24 Jan. 2013. Web.

Harmeier, Mike. Personal interview. 29 May. 2013.

"History." *cheathamstreet.com*. Cheatham Street Warehouse Website. n.d. Web.

Knopper, Steve. "The Best Clubs in America." *rollingstone.com*. n.d. Web.

O'Donnell, Denis. Personal interview. 3 Apr. 2013.

Smith, Tex. Personal interview. 26 Mar. 2013.

Volkaert, Redd. "Bio." *reddvolkaert.net*. n.d. Web.

Warden, Brandi. Personal interview. 26 Feb. 2013.

Warden, Monte. Personal interview. 21 Feb. 2013.

Willis, Kelly. Personal interview. 22 Jan. 2013.

Chapter 26 Sources:

"Beat (music)." Wikipedia, the Free Encyclopedia. 15 Sep. 2013. Web.

INDEX